A Small Price to Pay

Studies in Canadian Military History
Series editor: Dean F. Oliver, Canadian War Museum

The Canadian War Museum, Canada's national museum of military history, has a threefold mandate: to remember, to preserve, and to educate. Studies in Canadian Military History, published by UBC Press in association with the Museum, extends this mandate by presenting the best of contemporary scholarship to provide new insights into all aspects of Canadian military history, from earliest times to recent events. The work of a new generation of scholars is especially encouraged, and the books employ a variety of approaches – cultural, social, intellectual, economic, political, and comparative – to investigate gaps in the existing historiography. The books in the series feed immediately into future exhibitions, programs, and outreach efforts by the Canadian War Museum. A list of the titles in the series appears at the end of the book.

A Small Price to Pay
Consumer Culture
on the Canadian Home Front, 1939-45

Graham Broad

UBCPress · Vancouver · Toronto

© UBC Press 2013

All rights reserved. No part of this publication may be reproduced, stored in a retrieval system, or transmitted, in any form or by any means, without prior written permission of the publisher, or, in Canada, in the case of photocopying or other reprographic copying, a licence from Access Copyright, www.accesscopyright.ca.

21 20 19 18 17 16 15 14 13   5 4 3 2 1

Printed in Canada on FSC-certified ancient-forest-free paper (100% post-consumer recycled) that is processed chlorine- and acid-free.

Library and Archives Canada Cataloguing in Publication

Broad, Graham, author
  A small price to pay : consumer culture on the Canadian home front, 1939-45 / Graham Broad.

(Studies in Canadian military history series, 1499-6251)
Includes bibliographical references and index.
Issued in print and electronic formats.
ISBN 978-0-7748-2363-0 (bound). – ISBN 978-0-7748-2364-7 (pbk.)
ISBN 978-0-7748-2365-4 (pdf). – ISBN 978-0-7748-2366-1 (epub)

  1. Consumption (Economics) – Social aspects – Canada – History – 20th century. 2. Marketing – Social aspects – Canada – History – 20th century. 3. World War, 1939-1945 – Canada. 4. Canada – Social conditions – 1939-1945. 5. Canada – Economic conditions – 1918-1945. I. Title. II. Series: Studies in Canadian military history

HC115.B693 2013   306.30971'09044   C2013-904435-3
                                                C2013-904436-1

Canadä

UBC Press gratefully acknowledges the financial support for our publishing program of the Government of Canada (through the Canada Book Fund), the Canada Council for the Arts, and the British Columbia Arts Council.

This book has been published with the help of a grant from the Canadian Federation for the Humanities and Social Sciences, through the Awards to Scholarly Publications Program, using funds provided by the Social Sciences and Humanities Research Council of Canada.

Publication of this book has been financially supported by the Canadian War Museum.

UBC Press
The University of British Columbia
2029 West Mall
Vancouver, BC V6T 1Z2
www.ubcpress.ca

Contents

Illustrations / vii

Acknowledgments / xi

Introduction / 1

1. Mrs. Consumer, Patriotic Consumerism, and the Wartime Prices and Trade Board / 16

2. Business as Usual: Adworkers and the Coming of War / 50

3. Finding a Place for Wartime Advertising / 71

4. Advertising to Win the War and Secure the Future / 88

5. Buying and Selling Big Ticket Items / 125

6. "The Grim Realities of War, as Pictured by Hollywood": Consuming Leisure / 156

Conclusion / 182

Appendix
Guns and Butter: Consumer Spending, Inflation, and Price Controls / 196

Notes / 211

Selected Bibliography / 247

Index / 255

Illustrations

Figures

1.1 "Purchasing Agent (Just Appointed)," *Marketing*, 16 September 1939 / 18
2.1 "Enjoy Life!" *Maclean's*, 1 March 1940 / 65
2.2 "Get Them to Write Often," *Maclean's*, 15 September 1940 / 67
3.1 "Go On, Spend It ... What's the Difference?" *Maclean's*, 1 July 1942 / 75
3.2 "To Market! To Market!" *Marketing*, 8 January 1944 / 86
4.1 "Saboteur!" *Maclean's*, 1 May 1943 / 92
4.2 "A Long Time Learning," *Canadian Homes and Gardens*, January-February 1943 / 94
4.3 "Strange Things Go into Tanks!" *Canadian Forum*, May 1943 / 95
4.4 "Tonight I Leaned across 10,000 Miles and Kissed You!" *Maclean's*, 15 December 1942 / 97
4.5 "More Than Ever *This* Year," *Canadian Home Journal*, 2 January 1943 / 98
4.6 "Your Hands Now Need Campana's Balm Protection *More Than Ever*," *Maclean's*, 15 January 1944 / 98
4.7 "Five Happy, Smiling Maids Are We," *Maclean's*, 1 January 1942 / 102
4.8 "I Man the Home Front," *Maclean's*, 1 September 1942 / 102
4.9 "We Are Still the Weaker Sex," *Chatelaine*, August 1944 / 104
4.10 "Me – Enter a Beauty Contest?" *National Home Monthly*, February 1943 / 104
4.11 "My Dad Is *So* a Soldier," *Canadian Homes and Gardens*, March-April 1943 / 107
4.12 "Watch the '43 Fords Go By!" *National Home Monthly*, April 1943 / 109
4.13 "Swat This Mosquito," *Canadian Homes and Gardens*, August-September 1944 / 111

4.14 "And We Have Some Thrilling Ideas for That New Kitchen of Yours," *National Home Monthly*, October 1943 / 116

4.15 "Tomorrow's Tube ... Today," *Maclean's*, 1 December 1944 / 117

4.16 "A Better Day Is Coming," *Canadian Homes and Gardens*, December 1942 / 118

4.17 "It's Coming ... the Rocket Express!" *Maclean's*, 15 July 1944 / 120

4.18 "What's Coming Is ... PLENTY!" *Maclean's*, 1 June 1943 / 121

4.19 "Buy Victory Bonds and Bring Back the Pleasures of 'Freedom,'" *Marketing*, 8 May 1943 / 123

5.1 "Horse Laugh," *Sudbury Star*, reprinted in *Hardware and Metal*, 14 February 1942 / 145

5.2 "August at Eaton's College Street," *Toronto Daily Star*, 10 August 1943 / 153

6.1 Montreal's Orpheum Theatre, May 1944 / 172

C.1 "Social Security? ... Why We've Had It for Years at Dominion Oilcloth!" *National Home Monthly*, September 1944 / 189

Tables

3.1 Advertising linage in *Maclean's*, 1939-45 / 83

3.2 National advertising linage by category, in *Maclean's*, 1939-45 / 84

5.1 Retail automobile sales (units) and per capita ownership by province, 1940 / 128

5.2 Retail sales of new motor vehicles in Canada (units), 1938-45 / 129

5.3 Percentage household ownership of selected durable commodities, 1941 / 148

5.4 Production of electrical domestic appliances (units), 1939-45 / 149

5.5 Production of coal, wood, and gas stoves in Canada (units), 1939-45 / 150

5.6 Gross production value of selected household furnishings at current market values ($), 1939-45 / 151

6.1 Apparent consumption of beer, wine, and spirits (imperial gallons), 1939-45 / 161

6.2 Motion picture theatres, admissions, and value of receipts, 1939-45 / 169

6.3 Per capita spending on movie entertainment by year and province / 171

A.1 Consumer spending by category at current market values, 1939-45 / 197
A.2 Retail sales by category at current market values, 1939-45 / 198
A.3 Department store sales by selected departments, 1941-45 / 200
A.4 Per capita personal expenditure and retail sales at 1939 prices, 1939-45 / 201
A.5 Personal expenditure on goods and services in 1939 prices, as a percentage of disposable income, 1939-45 / 202
A.6 Monthly cost-of-living index, 1939-45 / 206

Plates *(following page 124)*

1 Donald Gordon, chairman of the WPTB from 1941 to 1947
2 Wartime coupon rationing
3 Eaton's store window display during "Mrs. Consumer Week," 1944
4 Directors of the Consumer Branch of the WPTB
5 WPTB propaganda discouraging needless spending
6 A 1942 Chevy, the last civilian passenger car manufactured in Canada
7 Dining out at the Capitol Theatre in Ottawa, Christmas 1942
8 The well-stocked interior of Bryson's Drug Store in Montreal

Acknowledgments

I FEAR THAT THIS MODEST achievement is unworthy of the many people who have assisted me in its completion. I am fortunate to have had the likes of Dorothea Gucciardo, Wes Gustavson, Renée Soulodre-LaFrance, Jonathan Vance, and Robert Ventresca as friends, allies, and intellectual tutors. Earlier versions of this book benefitted from the insight offered by Edward Comor, Keith Fleming, Benjamin Forster, Jeffrey Keshen, Douglas Leighton, and Alice Taylor. More recently, the anonymous peer reviewers chosen by UBC Press provided commentary that was both serious and reassuring. I trust they will recognize some of what they recommended in what follows.

All writers should be so lucky to have an editor like UBC Press's Emily Andrew, whose reputation for professionalism and patient counsel is well deserved, as is that of the book's production editor, Lesley Erickson. Deborah Kerr and Cheryl Lemmens served as precisely the kind of meticulous and unforgiving copy editors and proofreaders that the book needed in its final stages.

Luck, too, played some part in securing the assistance of several excellent research assistants, especially Lisa Koverko, Caitlin McCuaig, Kelly McKinney, Dave Poisson, and Nicole Sedgwick. Their enthusiasm for this project helped to restore mine during occasional, and occasionally lengthy, periods of ennui.

A particular thanks is owed to Dean Oliver of the Canadian War Museum, who selected the book for inclusion in the excellent Studies in Canadian Military History series, of which he is general editor. I hope it does not suffer by comparison in such august company.

I have forgotten others, no doubt: teachers, students, colleagues, friends, librarians, and archivists aplenty. But I cannot forget that my foremost thanks is reserved for Amanda Green, who over the course of several years both financed the struggle and maintained morale on the home front. This book is for her.

A Small Price to Pay

Introduction

The great tragedy of our time is that no democracy has been able to understand or to accept the demands of total war until their homes were under actual bombing attack.

– Donald Gordon, Consumer's News, *May 1942*

Man lives by certain civilizing influences. These include the luxuries of the daily newspaper, art galleries, and fine pictures; music and theatrical entertainment; movie shows; and rapid transit, motor cars, airplanes, time saving appliances, even a knife, a spoon, a few serving plates, an ornament or two for various parts of the house ... To have a good heart for war work, people must have something extremely desirable to fight for.

– Editorial, Trader and Canadian Jeweller, *April 1942*

IN JULY 1942, THE National War Finance Committee placed a remarkable advertisement in *Maclean's,* one of the most popular magazines in Canada. The ad (see Figure 3.1) depicts Adolf Hitler leaning over the shoulder of a woman as she opens her purse. "Go on," Hitler whispers into her ear, "spend it. What's the difference?" The copy goes on, "*Canadians* ... the time has come when every nickel, dime and quarter you spend *needlessly* is money spent in the cause of our enemies! NOW, more than any time since this war began, national THRIFT is essential ... From now on, resolve that *needless* spending is out!"[1]

The following year, under the tagline "When you ride alone, you ride with Hitler," a US propaganda poster portrayed Hitler in the passenger seat of a car. Ottawa's parallel message was that when you went shopping, you went shopping with Hitler – or perhaps *for* him. Until late 1941, the government had urged mere restraint on the part of consumers, asking at most that they "serve by saving." But in 1942, it adopted this far tougher line in response to retail sales that continued to rise, threatening calamitous inflation in an economy where many goods were in short supply.

Appearing on the same page as this rather severe admonishment against unnecessary spending, however, were two other ads. One was for Woolrich-brand wool skirts, imported from England, and the other was for made-to-order vacation cottages; that issue of *Maclean's*, like most others during the war, featured dozens of ads for all manner of non-essential products: luxury clothing, cosmetics, soft drinks, and even jewellery. Modern readers might be puzzled by the appearance of ads for imported clothes and getaway cottages alongside propaganda equating such things with treason, but by the mid-point in the war, Canadians had learned to take these contradictions in stride. As one retailer put it the following year, "My inventories are shrinking. Shelves are showing bare spots. Many lines of merchandise are in short supply, and business is booming."[2]

A Small Price to Pay is a contribution to the ongoing effort to produce a history of Canadians' domestic experience in the Second World War. Some decades ago, the eminent military historian C.P. Stacey mused that "the fog of war has a way of drifting into the historian's study and getting into his eyes; and when to the grey fog of war is added the golden haze of romance, visibility tends to fall to close to zero."[3] No doubt, but many historians of Canada have had more clear-eyed vision than that. In the past decade alone, works such as Jeffrey Keshen's *Saints, Sinners, and Soldiers,* Jennifer Stephen's *Pick One Intelligent Girl,* Serge Durflinger's *Fighting from Home,* and Stephanie Bangarth's *Voices Raised in Protest: Defending North American Citizens of Japanese Ancestry* have presented a more discerning view of what Keshen calls "the not-so-good-war."[4] Beneath the fog of patriotic enthusiasm encouraged by wartime propagandists – and sometimes carried on by misty-eyed sentimentalists of the kind that Stacey warned of – we find that our own "greatest generation" consisted of human beings after all. Petty politics, regional tensions, self-interest and greed, skepticism, and outright cynicism existed side by side with genuine patriotic self-sacrifice in wartime Canada. These very human virtues and vices were also notable features of the subject of this book – wartime consumer culture.

"Consumer culture" refers to the economic, social, and cultural practices associated with the manufacture, marketing, sale, and purchase of commodities. As a generation of cultural theorists and historians of consumerism has argued, personal consumption became one of the most powerful social and economic forces in the industrial world during the late nineteenth and early twentieth centuries.[5] Far more than a mere exchange of goods and services, consumerism became an activity around which governments shaped policies and that transformed the cultural, material, and even spiritual lives of millions of people.[6] Increasingly, consumers bought things not just to fulfill their material needs but also to satisfy an array of non-material desires.[7] People craved fun, comfort, sensual pleasure, improved social status, friendship, affection, and love. As historians and theorists of consumerism have long observed, the emergent consumer culture promised to animate the world of material objects, vesting them with the power to deliver all this and more. As I will argue, wartime consumer culture promised nothing less than to satisfy Canadians' yearning for victory and a prosperous peace.

The pervasiveness of the belief that it is virtuous to want more and better things is a hallmark of modern mass consumer society.[8] One of the recurring subjects of this study is how social tensions arose when the government and patriotic organizations urged savvy and often newly prosperous wartime consumers to buy less and to make do with the things that they already had. Admittedly, "wartime consumers" may seem like an oxymoron. In the hallowed spaces of patriotic memory, non-essential consumption is usually described as having been suspended for the duration of the conflict. Textbooks, television documentaries, and popular histories recount how Canadians "pulled together" to scrimp and save, buying little apart from their meagre rations and Victory Bonds, which they nestled alongside their growing savings, awaiting a triumphant day when their pent-up consumerist desires could be unleashed. Oral histories of the war often dwell on what was new and novel: rationing, shortages, scrap metal drives, and "make-do" reviews, where old clothes were made over into new fashions. Even academic historians have sometimes followed a narrative of home front sacrifice whose origins are found as much in wartime propaganda and subsequent mythologizing as in the actuality of lived experience. Michael Bliss writes that "elaborate controls limited civilian purchasing power, which did not rise above Depression levels" in wartime Canada; J.L. Granatstein contends that Canadians' personal savings rose because "consumer goods were unavailable" on the home front; and Joy Parr, in her important study *Domestic Goods*, concludes that there were merely "few" goods available for consumers to purchase.[9] Readily available statistics on per capita incomes, retail sales, and the production of consumer goods suggest otherwise, but the myth of widespread material deprivation on the home front persists nonetheless. Writing for *Maclean*'s after the September 11th, 2001, attacks on the United States, journalist Ken MacQueen reflected on changing social mores since the early 1940s and especially in the consumer habits of civilians on the "home front." During the Second World War, he stated,

> The role of the home front was one of scrimp, salvage, and sacrifice. Victory gardens were planted. Victory Bonds were bought. Hoarded cans, used foil, and scrap iron were made into battleships. Food and fuel were rationed, nylon stockings vanished, even new tires for the family car were a squandering of war resources. It was a penurious kind of patriotism, ill-suited to these modern times.

By contrast, "the war on terrorism ... is a shop-til-you drop proposition," in which politicians and their corporate allies forge symbolic links between consumption and patriotism while manufacturers devise new consumer products whose purchase promises to deliver, as MacQueen put it, "a body blow to psychopathic terrorists everywhere."[10]

As this work will demonstrate, however, there is nothing novel about mobilizing consumer impulses on behalf of a military effort, and social memories of "penurious patriotism" reflect only part of Canadians' wartime experience. When war erupted in September 1939, hardly anyone called on Canadians to make material sacrifices, because hardly anyone believed that such sacrifices would be necessary. In fact, the editors of *Maclean*'s expressed the very sentiment that MacQueen, writing for the same magazine, would find so alarming six decades later. They advised readers to "carry on" with their consumer lifestyles, because, they wrote, "the best service that can be rendered is to keep our national economic structure functioning as normally as possible."[11] Throughout the business press, the most fervently expressed hope was that mobilization for war would result in a renewed surge of consumer confidence and spending after the long, lifeless years of the Great Depression. Such views were echoed throughout the corridors of power in Ottawa. Eager to avoid a repetition of the political and economic turmoil that had engulfed the country during the First World War, Prime Minister William Lyon Mackenzie King promised Canadians a war of "limited liability" whose domestic impact would be minimized. This time, he promised, there would be no mass slaughter of Canadians in the mud and blood of the western front, no conscription crisis to imperil national unity, no runaway inflation that would threaten the ability of Canadian women to feed their families.[12] Throughout the press, the rallying cry was "business as usual" (only better), and millions of Canadians, wary of war but weary of Depression, rallied to it.

Of course, all this was before the succession of catastrophes that the Allies suffered in May and June of 1940. During the so-called phony war that preceded Nazi Germany's spring 1940 offensives, Canadian mobilization proceeded steadily but without any sense of urgency. For their part, the British treated Canada, in the words of their own official history, as a "purely marginal source of supply."[13] Following France's capitulation in June 1940, however, a torrent of munitions orders poured forth from panicked British ministries, and the Canadian government's own fiscal restraint was, as historian Robert Bothwell put it, "jettisoned virtually overnight."[14] But if this was a turning point in Canada's military and industrial effort, many months elapsed before Canadian consumers felt its full impact. For another year, manufacturers, many of whom had laboured, half-idle, throughout the Depression, either added new productive capacity or were able to mobilize partially idle plants to meet military orders without seriously disrupting the flow of consumer goods. From some quarters of the government, calls for greater consumer sacrifice began to emerge in late 1940, but if anything, the "business as usual" rhetoric simply intensified elsewhere. In September 1940, even while the Battle of Britain raged across the skies of southern England, *Chatelaine,* Canada's most popular women's magazine, published a special issue whose theme was "shopping to win the war." Women's organizations such as the Imperial Order Daughters of the Empire (IODE) and the Federated Women's Institutes, whose members had often expressed grave misgivings about what they perceived as the excessive materialism and dissolute self-indulgence of modern times, urged Canadians to "buy victory now," not with War Savings Certificates or through participation in the War Loan, but through the purchase of British-made goods.[15] When G.F. Towers, the governor of the Bank of Canada, called for reduced consumer spending and greater war savings in an address to the Canadian Club during the summer of 1940, he was widely denounced for being premature and alarmist.[16]

So the Canadian consumers' phony war went on. Although British consumers felt the pinch of war from its earliest days, and Americans did even before Pearl Harbor, Canadians enjoyed two years in which they seemed neither at peace nor fully at war. Granted, throughout 1941 a growing number of anxious officials began to argue that more severe restrictions on civilian consumption were inevitable.[17] The year was nonetheless the best to date for the production of washing machines, stoves, refrigerators, toasters, and other appliances; furniture store sales were three times higher than they had been just prior to the war; and as late as June 1941, even as the armoured spearheads of the German war machine pierced the Red Army's skin and plunged deep into the belly of the Soviet Union, the editors of *Canadian Automotive Trade* wrote reassuringly that Canada's car business could go on as usual, there being no evidence that immediate changes were required.[18]

Sooner or later, however, the demands of the entire Commonwealth's rapidly expanding war effort, coupled with the American rearmament program's enormous requirements for raw materials, were bound to result in the large-scale rededication of the Canadian consumer economy for military purposes. In the last quarter of 1941, King's government finally ordered drastic cuts in the production of most consumer durables, placed restrictions on consumer credit to curtail installment buying, and imposed sweeping wage and price controls to combat inflation. "We must face the fact," King said over the CBC in mid-October, "that there are not enough men; there are not enough machines; there are not enough materials to meet both the demands of consumers and the demands of war ... We have no choice but to reduce our consumption of consumer goods. To us, too, has come the choice between guns and butter."[19]

The consequences of the large-scale mobilization of the economy for military production are well known, but some of the figures are so striking that they bear emphasis. Between 1941 and 1944, civilian tire production plummeted 96 percent, the output of electric toasters dropped 97 percent, while electric refrigerator manufacturing fell from a high of 64,000 to just 237 – a decline of over 99 percent.[20] For millions of Canadian motorists, the most conspicuous, and subsequently the most memorable imposition, was the government's decision to suspend passenger car production in early 1942.[21] In the preceding two decades, automobiles had become a hallmark of the consumer society. Canadians bought a quarter of a million cars and trucks in the first two and a half years of the Second World War alone. In 1943, by contrast, fewer than a thousand cars were sold to civilians, and the Wartime Industries Control Board's motor vehicle administrator reserved those meagre few for drivers whose jobs he deemed essential to the war effort.[22]

Nineteen forty-two was also the year that coupon rationing, which had never been adopted in the First World War, began. The board imposed rationing for gasoline, sugar, tea, and coffee in the spring and summer of 1942, butter later that year, and meat beginning in May 1943. Provincial governments also legislated a variety of measures, including coupon rationing in some cases, to reduce the consumption of alcoholic beverages – the latter initiative being met with the approval of the nation's still very vocal supporters of temperance and prohibition, including the leaders of most of the major women's groups. All this coincided with a doubling of direct personal taxes, which had already increased a bruising sixfold since the beginning of the war, and an immense propaganda effort aimed at discouraging consumer spending.[23] For the remainder of the war, consumers were forced to choose from a narrower range of sometimes inferior goods. Local and temporary shortages, brought on by panic buying or delayed deliveries that occurred for a number of war-related reasons, became an everyday fact of life. Service clubs and patriotic women's groups that had hitherto supported the "buy British" campaign now worked hand-in-hand with half a dozen government agencies to issue an unremitting deluge of propaganda in the form of public speeches, posters, billboards, advertisements, radio addresses, and documentary films to underscore the importance of combating inflation and preventing any diversion of resources to satiate needless consumer demand. Some of this propaganda, such as the 1942 Hitler ad that appeared in *Maclean's*, went so far as to equate spendthrift consumerism with treason.

Was this, the union of nationalistic moralizing with apparent consumer deprivation, the "penurious patriotism" to which MacQueen and others have alluded? In part, it certainly was. Against this, however, must be measured the fact that retail sales continued to rise, and that Canadians were bombarded with competing and even contradictory messages. Even after Ottawa suspended the production of many consumer durables and coupon rationing began, private manufacturers and retailers devised ingenious new ways to sell their remaining goods by converting a myriad of wartime anxieties into rationales for continued consumption. For every ad urging conservation and thrift, there were many more that encouraged patriotic shoppers to part with their paycheques – ads whose essential message was that buying, under the correct circumstances, was neither wasteful nor unpatriotic but a meaningful contribution to the war effort, at times even a sacrifice that consumers made for freedom. In so doing, manufacturers, advertisers, and retailers offered Canadians an additional justification for war. It was not merely for Britain and empire, nor only for nationhood and liberty, but also for free enterprise, for a "selling way of life," and for access to a future of limitless consumer abundance, where the expectation was not of further sacrifice, but of a hard-earned share in a world of plenty.[24]

Still, it is altogether too obvious to say that the wartime consumer society was, as the overused phrase goes, "contested terrain," as if there is something exceptional about the discovery that a historical period contains ambiguities, contradictions, and paradoxes. Consumerism has always been attended by disagreements about its propriety, and apart from the contemporary environmentalist critique of consumerism, very little about these arguments has changed over time. In the 1940s, consumer capitalism's defenders in the business community asserted that it generated prosperity, was democratizing, socially levelling, and even civilizing. Moreover, they suggested, not without a degree of plausibility, that the rise of Nazism, and hence the cataclysm of the war itself, stemmed in part from the Weimar government's failure to provide for the material wants and needs of Germans. By contrast, many middle-class moralists feared that the excessive pursuit of consumer pleasure led to vice and moral decay, undermining the time-honoured Christian virtues of plain and pious living centred on hard work, thrift, and sobriety. Meanwhile, a body of intellectual critics – which the business press referred to, with an air of contempt, as "university professors" – condemned mass culture and mass consumerism as homogenizing and stupefying. Many of them were Marxists or socialists who held that consumerism was predicated on the exploitation of labour, even as it eroded working-class solidarity with its seductive but ultimately counterfeit vision of human emancipation. What makes the war years of particular interest in the ongoing debate over consumerism is the extremity that these arguments reached. In part, the dispute was about the extent of material sacrifice that people were expected to make in a nation at war. It also fit into a broader debate over the place of consumer capitalism in Canadian society – including whether or not it would have a place, which we sometimes forget was very much a live question at the time.

The study of the wartime consumer economy is also of interest because it highlights the immense economic and cultural influence that the United States already had in Canada by the late 1930s. Historians have tended to emphasize the British character of wartime Canada, with most taking it for granted, as Granatstein has maintained, that Canada went to war in 1939 because Britain did and for no other reason.[25] Although there is no denying the Britishness of much of English Canada during the Second World War, it is equally true that by the late 1920s, Canadians were awash in a sea of American consumer goods and cultural products. They drove cars, listened to radios, read magazines, cooked with stoves, wore clothing, and applied cosmetics manufactured in the United States or in Canada by American subsidiaries. Hundreds of thousands of Canadians tuned in to American radio stations every night, and the most popular programs on Canadian radio were American ones. As for the movies, the relative dominance of the allegedly crass and degraded products of Hollywood that so alarms Canadian cultural nationalists in the early twenty-first century was as great, if not greater, during the 1940s than in the present day (on this, see Chapter 6).

Still, given the extremity of what was at stake in the Second World War, a reader could be excused for thinking that the study of wartime consumerism is a trivial or even frivolous diversion from weightier matters. It is tempting to observe (and literally true) that ration coupons and consumer response surveys did not defeat the U-boat menace or breach the Atlantic Wall. But it is also important to understand that the politics of personal consumption and their relationship to the war effort were vital aspects of national economic planning and quite central to civilian life on the home front. Politicians, civil servants, businesspeople, heads of voluntary associations, academics, journalists, novelists, poets, advertisers, and indeed everyday consumers added their voices to the throng in a sustained and evolving discussion about the place of consumerism in wartime, and for reasons that are eminently comprehensible. Apart from the immense social and cultural significance of consumerism, personal consumer spending, it is too readily forgotten, continued to account for the majority of economic activity in Canada throughout the war. In *Arms, Men and Governments*, his official history of the King administration's war policies, C.P. Stacey estimated that Ottawa's total war-related expenditure from 1939 to 1945 was $19 billion.[26] By comparison, retail sales – which are just one facet of consumer spending – totalled just under $25 billion in the same period. In no fiscal year of the war, not even in 1944, did the Department of National Defence's expenditure surpass retail sales for the corresponding calendar year. In fact, the latter were exceeded by total war expenditure of all government departments, by the narrowest of margins, only in the fiscal years ending 31 March 1944 and 31 March 1945.[27]

Having said that, there should be no mistaking this work for an economic history of the Canadian home front, although a healthy measure of "hard" economic considerations will be found throughout. Nor is it primarily a study of government regulation of the consumer economy, although inevitably the presence of the Wartime Prices and Trade Board, the agency most directly involved in consumer affairs, looms large over some chapters, much as it did over the transactions made by consumers and retailers. Administrative histories of the WPTB and related agencies such as the Department of Munitions and Supply (DMS), which oversaw military conversion and armaments procurement, have already been written.[28] Rather than an economic history or an examination of policy and administration, then, *A Small Price to Pay* is a study of a consumer culture in time of war. It emphasizes how the buyers, sellers, and advertisers of commodities attempted to negotiate the tensions between satiating consumer desires and meeting the increasing demands for greater sacrifice that emanated from the government and scores of voluntary associations.

Needless to say, any work that attempted to investigate the full scope of regional, class, and ethnic responses to such matters in a country as large and diverse as Canada would require several volumes. Instead, I have attempted something more modest, a sketch of the consumer culture in wartime Canada. Whenever possible, I have used data gathered by the Dominion Bureau of Statistics (DBS), WPTB, and other agencies to account for regional and class differences, but I concede that a great deal remains to be said. I have written nothing at all, for instance, about the Far North, the First Nations, or the Métis, and not very much about farmers. In fairness, this work is concerned mostly with those who manufactured, marketed, regulated, bought, and sold consumer goods. In respect to these matters, there is much less to write about the many Canadians who, even at the peak of wartime prosperity, lived without electricity on farms or in small communities in remote regions, far from the shops, restaurants, and theatres that were the mainstays of the rather idealized world of urban middle-class consumerism that is the focus of this work. I hope that some time soon more specialized studies will add perspective to the somewhat two-dimensional landscape that I unveil here.

In addition, my emphasis is on civilians rather than soldiers. As contemporary writers employed it, the term "home front" referred not just to a geographic location but to all civilian activity undertaken in Canada on behalf of the war effort. Accordingly, Canadians tended not to think of soldiers stationed in Canada as part of the home front. We lack good social histories of Canadian soldiers in the Second World War and especially of the half of the armed forces that never left the country, but it is sometimes forgotten that, even at the height of mobilization in 1944, when nearly three-quarters of a million Canadians were in uniform, over 90 percent of Canadians, including the majority of males of military age, were civilians. Undeniably, soldiers stationed in Canada, including thousands of sailors and airmen from Allied nations, could be enthusiastic consumers, especially of movies, restaurant meals, and certain illegal recreational services that are beyond the scope of this study, but statisticians in Canada did not distinguish between a dollar spent by a soldier and one spent by a civilian.

This illustrates a chief difficulty in undertaking any examination of consumerism: the most elusive aspect of consumer history is frequently the consumer him- or herself. Almost invariably, the people who manufactured, marketed, sold, and regulated goods were more systematic in their record keeping than the people who bought them. Corporate records and trade journals offer insight into the inner workings of the business world; advertisements provide perspectives on the worldview of marketers; newspaper editorials and magazine articles dealing with every aspect of the nation's economy are easily found; and government agencies laid low whole forests to document their doings. But consumers themselves steadfastly refused to anticipate the needs of future historians. Even wartime adworkers and retailers, for all their pseudoscientific pretenses about their ability to activate consumer desires with the ease of throwing a switch, often found themselves powerless to sway customers whose manifold motivations were at times frustratingly inscrutable. As Keith Walden writes in his innovative examination of early-twentieth-century grocery store window displays, "Customers did not confide to diaries or share with correspondents the pleasures of buying a pound of cheese or a jar of pickles. Surviving account ledgers reveal little about human activities in and perceptions of the stores."[29] So it was with wartime consumers. Throughout this work, I have attempted to buttress my arguments with voices of ordinary consumers drawn from letters, diaries, and published oral histories. Admittedly, these are a strictly hit-or-miss affair, for all the reasons cited above. They can provide qualitative evidence and anecdotes concerning wartime consumerism, but quantitative historians might, and perhaps with some justification, challenge the statistical significance of such remarks.

This is not to suggest that this work will have little to say about "ordinary" consumers – far from it. Indeed, I hope to reveal a good deal about them. It is possible to deduce much about consumer behaviour from a careful study of the reports produced or commissioned by government agencies, including the 1941 census. And though market research and polling might have been in their infancy (or perhaps early adolescence) during the war, a significant number of attempts to elicit the opinion of consumers were made on the home front. These included polls by the new Canadian Institute of Public Opinion as well as numerous efforts undertaken by the WPTB's Consumer Branch, which served as a liaison between the public and board officials.[30] The results of these quantitative surveys are admittedly rather arid at times, but they are indispensable sources of consumer opinion nonetheless. Finally, it must be remembered that those who worked on the "supply side" were themselves consumers. Adworkers, for example, believed that they knew what made the typical consumer tick in part because they knew what they themselves found appealing. They may have overestimated the extent of their insight into the motivations of the general public (incurable self-importance seemed to be a hallmark of their trade), but the ads they produced may yield what consumer history pioneer Roland Marchand calls "plausible inference" into certain aspects of consumer behaviour.[31] Much the same can be said about the strategies to maintain and even expand consumer spending, despite wartime pressures, that retailers and service providers devised, wrote about in their trade journals, and spoke about in countless conferences.

Most of all, our understanding of wartime consumer behaviour must be anchored to one fact that belies all notions about penurious patriotism: consumer spending in Canada increased by leaps and bounds during the war. France fell to the Nazis, and consumer spending went up. Britain reached out in desperation for Canadian aid, and spending went up. Ottawa and the provinces mandated new taxes, and spending went up. They placed restrictions on the manufacturing of dozens of goods, and spending went up. They imposed rationing, and spending went up. They likened consumerism to treason in their propaganda. And spending went up. Historians have often referred to the post-war consumer boom. I contend that there was instead a *post-Depression* boom that began with the outbreak of war in 1939. Between 1939 and 1945, retail sales grew by 49 percent, even after accounting for inflation. By comparison, during the corresponding years a decade later, 1949 to 1955, retail sales grew by just 32 percent after inflation.[32] These figures do not tell the whole story, of course, but they do raise serious queries about why the myth of penurious patriotism was adopted in the first place. Over the course of the war, jewellery, women's clothing, and shoe and drugstore sales doubled, restaurant business tripled, and paid admissions to movie theatres leapt from 138 million in 1939 to 208 million in 1944.[33] At Toronto's annual gift show, where wholesalers displayed their wares to the nation's retailers, the number of attendees increased more than sevenfold during the war.[34]

The shortages, too, were not in all cases as sweeping or severe as they are often remembered to be. An examination of magazines and newspapers from the last two years of the war reveals page after page of retail advertising, incorporating all the obligatory watchwords about savings and thrift but featuring such decidedly non-essential items as china, silverware, dinette sets, ice refrigerators, children's toys and games, fur coats, and even diamond rings. Coupon rationing, which did not begin until the war was nearly three years old, applied to only a handful of goods and did little to curtail spending. Polls revealed that the majority of consumers approved of rationing, even in Quebec, and some even hoped that it would continue in some form after the war ended (on this, see the discussion in Chapter 1 and the Appendix). In theory at least, rationing was social levelling in a way that the free market was not. Moreover, Canadians were often exhilarated by the opportunity to serve their country in a risk-free fashion. Having accomplished that, having "done their bit" by buying their rations of sugar and meat and taking their change in War Savings Stamps, many Canadians felt entitled to do some shopping, eat out, and go to the movies, as the retail spending figures clearly reveal. Certainly, most advertising attempted to furnish them with every rationale for doing so.

As for the nation's retailers, the war presented them with many challenges, not the least of which was the requirement to observe a byzantine array of evolving and sometimes conflicting government regulations. Still, for most retailers, sales went up as did profits (though only as far as the ceiling on excess profits permitted), and though they grumbled about regulations, many retailers found that they benefitted from at least a few regulations that they hoped would continue when the conflict ended.

During its final year, as victory approached, many Canadians looked longingly toward a future where their social security would include a share in a world of material abundance, where the world "fit for heroes" that had failed to emerge after the Great War would finally materialize. As one advertisement put it in 1943, the war was "a small price to pay" for the opulent future of limitless, guilt-free consumption that would follow victory.[35]

A Small Price to Pay is divided into seven chapters that examine functionally related aspects of the wartime consumer society. Chapter 1 studies the interaction between the female consumer and the regulatory state. Histories of Canadian women at war have tended to emphasize the importance of women's participation in paid labour and the armed forces. I contend that, from the perspective of the WPTB at least, a woman's most important contribution to the war effort would be made not in the workforce but in her traditional role as wife, mother, homemaker, and principal buyer for the family: on the checkout line rather than the assembly line. Moreover, I argue that the leadership of some of Canada's largest and most influential women's organizations enthusiastically endorsed this view, perceiving varying approaches to consumerism as a means by which women could simultaneously aid the war effort and stake out a greater claim for political and economic equality.

Chapters 2, 3, and 4 deal with the crucial topic of marketing and advertising. As the propaganda arm of the system of consumer capitalism, advertising plays an important role in communicating rationales for mass consumption to the buying public. Adworkers, advertisers, and indeed, their social critics believed that it influenced consumers' buying behaviours, and it may even have done so. It is in advertising's symbolic tableau that we find the most visible representations of the tensions inherent in the wartime consumer culture. By 1942, it was not uncommon for the readers of magazines and newspapers to find appeals for conservation juxtaposed with ads urging them to spend as a contribution to the war effort. Sometimes they existed within the same ad.

From late 1941, department stores, clothiers, booksellers and stationers, grocers, and other retailers were forced to contend with shortages of varying severity and many new regulations – it would be both tedious and trivial to itemize them all – but they usually profited from the seller's market. Many consumer durables, however, were simply unavailable after 1941. The production of automobiles, stoves, electric refrigerators, radios, and other big ticket items fell victim to the large-scale diversion of raw materials and productive capacity for military purposes on both sides of the Canada-US border. Such items may have accounted for a minority of overall consumer spending, but they had had an enormous transformative impact on the lives of millions of Canadians in the years leading up to the war and were important symbols of the modern mass consumer society. Chapter 5 concerns the uniquely difficult circumstances faced by retailers and consumers of durable commodities, and especially automobiles, when their production suddenly came to an end in early 1942.

Chapter 6 concerns the consumption of leisure in the form of public amusements, with a particular emphasis on the most popular form of public entertainment: movie-going. Canadians also went to dances, concerts, live theatre, and spectator sports, but they spent comparatively little on these sorts of pleasures. Ninety percent of their wartime entertainment budget was spent on attending the cinema. It therefore seemed fitting to dwell at some length on movie-going. The concluding chapter considers the relationship between the emerging welfare state and a competing vision of the future – one where economic prosperity would be secured through private enterprise built upon a foundation of personal consumerism. Finally, the book includes a statistical appendix to lend some heft in support of my arguments concerning the wartime consumer boom. Readers interested in a detailed analysis of spending and varying estimates of inflation rates should look there.

Some readers might question the decision to confine my analysis to the war years. A case could be made for beginning earlier, in order to better observe the consumer culture in the late years of the Depression, or for extending the book's focus to 1947 on the grounds that the WPTB's consumer controls did not entirely end until then. But as Graham Greene wrote in *The End of the Affair* – a novel set amid wartime austerity in Britain – a story has neither a beginning nor an end; the writer must pick a point from which to look forward and back.[36] For that purpose, the years 1939 and 1945 are as good as any and better than most.

1
Mrs. Consumer, Patriotic Consumerism, and the Wartime Prices and Trade Board

The women of Canada have been recognized as a most important ally in the price ceiling plan ... We have a chance to build our organization, to regiment ourselves, voluntarily, and show that, because of our years of efficiency in our own organizations we can take our place in Canada's national life – and make history by the way we conduct ourselves.

– Byrne Hope Sanders, director of the Consumer Branch
of the Wartime Prices and Trade Board, March 1942

They may cut down on my bacon, they may take away my ham;
they may ship all my beef to Britain, and leave me fowl and lamb;
they may send across the ocean all the quantities they wish of our
*   famous, our delectable, our most delicious fish;*
and I wouldn't care a penny if, quite lawfully, they seize, for the
*   gallant folks in Britain, all our fine Canadian cheese.*
They may weaken up my cream, and I shall manage very well,
*   though I'm partial to this wholesome food, yes, more than I can tell.*
They may take away my sugar bowl – small sacrifice, say I, and
*   certainly not worth a thought, much less a sob or sigh.*
But I wonder, yes, I wonder, what mad ravings I should utter if they'd
*   lay their desecrating hands upon my precious butter!*

– *Anonymous*, Toronto Globe and Mail, *February 1942*

IN SEPTEMBER 1940, the editor of *Chatelaine,* Byrne Hope Sanders, who was soon to become the director of the Wartime Prices and Trade Board's (WPTB) consumer-relations efforts, took a moment in her monthly column to advise the women of Canada not to "take on too much work."

Remember, she wrote, "that your first loyalty and duty must be to your family."[1] According to the popular and pervasive "Rosie the Riveter" mythology – which began during the war itself – the war's insatiable demands for industrial labour eroded traditional gender mores such as these, if only temporarily. But it is also true that the more traditional conception of women as wives, mothers, homemakers, and caregivers expressed by Sanders not only persisted throughout the war but at times assumed an even greater tone of urgency. Domesticity, the argument went, had long been society's bulwark against moral decrepitude. Now it would be pressed into service as the foundation of the country's moral and economic defence against Nazi fascism.

Personal consumption, in turn, was one of the pillars upon which modern domesticity had been built. In the late nineteenth century, historian Cynthia Comacchio writes, "middle-class women gradually became the managers of household consumption."[2] By the 1930s, the claim that women were responsible for eighty-five cents of every consumer dollar spent in Canada ("and had a pretty good idea of what happened to the other 15," Sanders liked to say) was taken as granted in women's magazines and in speeches by businesspeople and the leaders of women's service clubs.[3] A typical housewife, said a presenter to the Toronto Advertising and Sales Club in 1940, "decides what money is going for this and that, not her husband," because, she concluded pointedly, "men are saps when it comes to buying."[4] A succinct and visually striking expression of this idea can be found in a September 1939 advertisement for *Chatelaine*, which depicts a young woman, beaming in her bridal gown (see Figure 1.1). Under the tag line "Purchasing Agent (just appointed)," the accompanying blurb reads, "Joyous shouts of 'Here comes the bride!' have a wealth of meaning. The radiant girl you see is not only a bride. She is also a woman embarking on a lifetime career in the business of home making. Among other duties which she will now assume are those of purchasing agent for her new household."[5]

Household science experts, consumer magazine columnists, retailers, marketers, and advertisers all agreed that discretion over the family's shopping budget was a momentous responsibility, especially in hard times such as depression and war. Innumerable advice books as well as articles and ads in consumer magazines argued that a woman's failure to be an informed and judicious consumer was tantamount to failure as a wife and mother. Providing food, clothing, comforts, and appropriate gifts for one's

FIGURE 1.1 It was an article of faith in the popular and trade press that purchases made by women accounted for 85 percent of all consumer dollars spent. This ad draws a remarkably explicit parallel between housewife and consumer. | "Purchasing Agent (Just Appointed)," *Marketing*, 16 September 1939, 7.

family was a duty upon which both the health and happiness of the whole family depended. Shopping was a serious business, not a leisure activity, even if major department stores did everything they could to make it as leisurely as possible with amenities such as beauty salons and dining rooms.[6]

Historian Jennifer Scanlon has argued that scholars of consumerism have often taken it for granted that, historically speaking, consumer culture has reinforced a highly sexist domesticity that subordinated women within the confines of the home.[7] On one level, Byrne Hope Sanders's admonishment that Canadian women should avoid taking on "too much work" – by which she meant paid labour outside the home – can be understood in this way. Many prominent women of the time, including Sanders herself, however, would have resented and rejected any suggestion that women's domestic duties were less important than any other, even if they might have agreed that women remained in many respects subordinate to their husbands both at home and in the male-dominated public sphere. During the Second World War, this already complex relationship between the Canadian homemaker and consumer culture adapted to rapidly changing circumstances as the circumstances themselves unfolded. When the war began, Canadian women's organizations such as the National Council of Women, the Federated Women's Institutes, the Catholic Women's League, and the Imperial Order Daughters of the Empire promoted what I have ventured to call "patriotic consumerism" as a guiding principle for their members. Patriotic consumerism was a means by which women could fulfill their duties as wife and mother while simultaneously asserting themselves in the public sphere, lending support to the war effort and to their own claim to a fuller and more active public citizenship. Throughout the war, the Canadian homemaker, often referred to generically as Mrs. Consumer by women's organizations and the WPTB, was repeatedly entreated to consider her homemaking duties, and especially those related to consumerism, as enormously important contributions to the struggle against the Axis. "We women have been called in to wage a battle which is one of the most important ones in history," said Sanders in March 1942, having just assumed the directorship of the WPTB's Consumer Branch. "Every one of us," she went on,

> has our own patrol – the beat we tread on our shopping routes. Our weapons are our pencils and a list of prices ... Our great and mobile defense line is

the Wartime Prices and Trade Board. Our allies are our merchants; we know full well the horror of our foe – inflation. The success of any battle lies in knowing all about the defense. So for the army on this home front, your country has picked soldiers who for years have been drilling for this work ... May we be worthy of this great hour in our history.[8]

With its Churchillian cadences and overtones, this speech and others like it may sound hyperbolic (and perhaps slightly ridiculous) to modern ears, but it must be understood in terms of the clichés of wartime propaganda, which always used military metaphors in an effort to valorize patriotic volunteerism. Moreover, to Sanders's intended audience, the speech might not have sounded extravagant in at least one regard. For those Canadians old enough to remember the runaway prices that had attended the last half of the First World War and the first two years of the peace, the fear of inflation ran very deep.[9] Nothing threatened a woman's ability to provide necessities for her family so much as inflation. The need to combat it was one of the few things about which nearly everyone on the home front agreed.

It is difficult to overstate the extent to which patriotic messages from the government and service organizations were designed to appeal to Canadian women in their capacity as consumers. Here was a ready-made "war job" for millions of women, one that did not ignite anxieties about gender roles in the way that participation in the industrial workforce or the armed forces was wont to do.[10] In thousands of newspaper editorials, radio addresses, public speeches, and propaganda posters, Canadian women were told that their foremost contributions to the country's war effort would be made as wives, mothers, homemakers, and consumers. This core argument never wavered, not even as Canada's war effort reached proportions far greater than anyone had predicted in 1939. When he spoke to the National Council of Women in June 1943, Finance Minister J.L. Ilsley praised the women of Canada for undertaking munitions work and serving in the armed forces but also for performing "the most important job of all – the vital job of maintaining Canadian homes and raising Canadian families" by being informed and thrifty consumers.[11]

The definition of what constituted patriotic consumerism, however, changed over time in response to the changing circumstances of the war. Rather than engaging in the scrimping and sacrifice of penurious patriotism, consumers, in tandem with advertisers, retailers, and service providers, devised elaborate and evolving discourses of patriotic consumption. Until late 1941, patriotic consumerism entailed no particular demands for a reduction in spending. On the contrary, calls for *increased* consumer spending were the norm in the first two years of the war. During the years of rationing and shortages that followed, the meaning of patriotic consumption became more hotly contested. The government and most women's organizations urged consumers to buy only essentials, but advertisers and retailers threw all their ingenuity into expanding the boundaries of what consumers were entreated to think of as "essential." Some marketing efforts, as the advertisements in the coming chapters will show, tested the boundaries of credulity, but growing retail sales throughout the latter half of the war provide very strong evidence that most consumers continued to buy far more than just the necessities of life, even in the years when so many lives were on the line.

CANADA'S DECLARATION OF WAR in September 1939 touched off the biggest proportional consumer spending boom in the country's history (for a discussion, see the Appendix). The last vestiges of the Depression evaporated as war put unemployed Canadians to work and as work put money into their pockets. Years later, one First World War veteran would recall to the writer Barry Broadfoot that he and his family had scraped by on a meagre seven hundred dollars per year during the Depression. During the Second World War, by contrast, he found full-time employment at good wages as a truck driver, his wife took a job in a Toronto-area war plant, and their son, in the Royal Canadian Navy, sent half his pay home every month: "We bought some house furniture and a big second-hand radio this high and this wide down on Spadina, and we went to Prescott for a summer holiday and by the living Jesus, we were living. She working and me working and overtime, and the money just rolled in ... In the war we lived good. Real good."[12] Richard Needham, associate editor of the *Calgary Herald*, recounted a similar story told to him by a woman who, having nearly starved to death during the Depression, remarked, "It's a terrible thing to say, but I hope the war goes on for a long time. This is the first security I've known for a long, long time."[13] This was an oft-repeated sentiment. Undeniably, poverty remained an enduring facet of life for many Canadians, but the war also elevated tens of thousands of families into the ranks of the middle class. During its first two years alone, unemployment dropped from over 500,000 to just 135,000.[14] In the same period, per capita retail sales grew by 20 percent, even after adjusting for inflation, a rate of growth more than twice as great as in the post-war boom of 1946 and 1947.[15] Retailers exalted in the rebounding economy. In a typical editorial, the editors of *Bookseller and Stationer* exclaimed in February 1941, "We're so darned busy we don't know which way to turn – and to think we owe it to the war!"[16]

Both the objective circumstances of the war and the policies of King's government aided in the prolongation of Canada's phony war.[17] Desperate to avoid a repetition of the previous conflict's conscription crisis, which had imperilled national unity and torn the Liberal Party apart, King's administration promised Canadians a war of "limited liability" in the first week of September 1939. Only volunteers would be sent overseas, King pledged, and Canada's major contributions to the war effort would be economic and materiel rather than manpower.[18] Initially at least, the Opposition Conservatives, eager to pick up seats in Quebec, concurred.[19] Their first wartime leader, Robert Manion, actually accused King of hijacking the policy of limited liability from him, and even King's bête noir, the former Conservative prime minister R.B. Bennett, remarked on the eve of war that what the British really wanted was not Canadian troops but Canadian factories to build planes and Canadian schools to train pilots.[20] All this was underscored by a public mood that has been described, both by contemporary commentators and by historians, as dutifully resigned, in sharp contrast to the apparently naive jingoism of August 1914. Germany's startling victories, which culminated in France's capitulation of June 1940, may have even indirectly served King's political interests rather than resulting in the sudden end of limited liability, as is often suggested. In the wake of France's defeat, Canada assumed the position of Britain's ranking ally until the German invasion of the Soviet Union a year later, but the German conquest of western Europe was one of the factors that kept the Canadian Army out of sustained combat until the summer of 1943. Rather than being sent to the meat-grinder of a fighting front, the bulk of Canada's army overseas was deployed to England, where it trained and grew and did not fight, awaiting an invasion that never came. To the end of 1940, the army lost just fifteen men killed in action. As late as December 1941, the number stood at less than a hundred.[21] Casualties in the navy and air force were higher but nowhere near the catastrophic losses that Canadians, recalling the terrible experience of the last war, had braced themselves for in 1939. Until late 1941, there was correspondingly little talk of "sacrifice" at home.

Desperate, too, to avoid a repetition of the annual double-digit inflation of the First World War and the years of recession and strikes that had followed it, King's government took steps in 1939 to ensure the orderly regulation of the consumer economy. By Order-in-Council, the government created the Wartime Prices and Trade Board on the very day that Britain declared war. That this occurred a week before Canada's own declaration of war is indicative not only of the inevitability of the country's entry into the conflict, but also of the government's determination to put a lid on economic upheaval regardless of how circumstances unfolded. Initially composed of just three members, the tiny new board had the ambitious mandate of regulating the supply of food, fuel, and other commodities. For the first two years of hostilities, however, when no large-scale diversion of resources from the consumer economy was required and store stocks were plentiful, the board operated, as historian Christopher Waddell puts it, "on the periphery of the economy."[22] Early regulations, such as a November 1940 order prohibiting the introduction of most new kinds of products and design changes to old ones, were hardly noticed by most consumers and considered only a trifling inconvenience by retailers (on this, see Chapters 3 and 5). Apart from bringing down a handful of regulations concerning maximum prices on certain staple goods to discourage hoarding, the board did not begin to make serious impositions on the consumer economy until late in the summer of 1941.[23] Even then, the various restrictions and regulations did not take effect for some time. Consumers had only just begun to feel the pinch when Christmas 1941 rolled around. Writing to a friend that December from Saint John, Archie Thompson of the Canadian Grenadier Guards mentioned that "everybody here is out doing there [sic] Christmas shopping. I went out on a pass last night in the city and it was nice to see all the windows all dressed up with all kinds of nice presents and toys. The streets were full of boys and girls looking at them."[24]

Visitors noticed it, too. In 1940 and 1941, American tourists, lured by a massive advertising campaign mounted in US newspapers, were surprised to discover that many Canadians carried on their day-to-day affairs as though war had never been declared at all. In a lengthy travelogue written for the *Atlantic Monthly* in late 1941 and early 1942, the American journalist William Henry Chamberlin recounted the notable contributions Canada was making to Britain's war effort. On the other hand, he detected no small measure of reticence and reservation, which he ascribed to something more than the taciturn nature of the Canadian character. "There has been," he wrote, "less flag waving, less hysteria, less enthusiasm, perhaps more grimness than in the First World War."[25] Above all, he was struck by how little the war effort had impinged upon the everyday lives of Canadian consumers: "A day of stern sacrifice and deprivation is being predicted. But up to the spring of 1942 the majority of Canadians were probably living a little better than they were before the war began. Shops were well stocked; restaurants were crowded; there was plenty of money in circulation."[26] It was in this somewhat surreal environment, in a country nominally at war but displaying many signs of one prosperously at peace, that Canada's homemakers carried out their duties as consumers for the first two years of the conflict. From the beginning, the country's biggest voluntary women's associations had adopted a policy, not of consumer restraint, but of "buying British" in order to shore up the mother country's economy. As early as September 1939, representatives of the National Council of Women, which purported to speak on behalf of eighteen women's organizations and their 1.5 million members, had met with officials in Ottawa and declared their readiness to serve the war effort as the moral heart of the family and as the economic heart that pumped the national economy. At its annual congress in the summer of 1940, the council officially endorsed the "buy British" policy – with "buy Canadian" enumerated as a secondary priority.[27] Other organizations, including some that had previously expressed misgivings about the excessive materialism of modern life, adopted the policy as well. "The clothes you wear, the beverages you drink, the presents you give this Christmas could help win the war," wrote a columnist for *Echoes*, the official magazine of the Imperial Order Daughters of the Empire, in December 1940. "Do you realize that the expenditure of only 50 cents a day on British goods by each Canadian could make a profound difference to Britain's financial position?"[28]

"Buy British" and "buy Canadian" were common refrains throughout the popular press as well. J.L. Rutledge, editor of the Canadian edition of *Liberty* (which claimed the highest newsstand sales of any magazine in the country), called the "buy British" platform "the fourth arm of defense" in an unqualified endorsement in November 1940.[29] *Chatelaine*, the country's most popular consumer magazine, also embraced the idea with enthusiasm. With more than 200,000 subscribers and probably twice as many readers, *Chatelaine* was the sacred temple of mass consumption for hundreds of thousands of Canadian women.[30] In September 1940, even as the Battle of Britain raged over southern England, the magazine published a special issue whose theme was "shopping to win the war," featuring tips on "what's smart to wear and patriotic to buy." Columnist Alice

Sharples reflected that "we women of Canada have burned with a desire to 'do something' toward waging and winning the war." But what to do? Her answer: shop to win the war by buying British- and Canadian-made goods. Far from endorsing any ethos of sacrifice or constraint, Sharples wrote that "it is our *duty* not to wear our old tweeds but to buy new ones ... not to make last year's frocks 'do' but to launch out in famous English prints; not to do without tea but to serve more tea than ever."[31] She proposed the slogan "Every woman a mannequin," urging her readers to model British fashions and goods, especially for American tourists. In the following issue, editor Byrne Hope Sanders promised that "shopping for victory" was a slogan that *Chatelaine* would "hammer away at" for the duration of the war.[32] As matters would have it, Sanders would be preaching a different gospel less than eighteen months later, one in which savings and thrift were the central tenets, and *Chatelaine* would be publishing articles about how to make last year's frocks "do" after all, but the notion that a woman's patriotic duties were functionally and intimately related to her responsibilities as consumer never subsided.

As CANADA'S WAR EFFORT grew, and as Britain suffered further defeats in the Balkans, Crete, and North Africa, demands for greater sacrifice began to emanate from Canadian political speeches, war propaganda, and magazine and newspaper editorials. One widely read and frequently quoted pamphlet, *Come On, Canada!*, co-written by the economic historian Stanley Saunders, mounted a seething indictment of what Saunders believed to be Canadians' free spending and carefree living while Britons suffered and the Red Army endured the bulk of the fighting:

> The blame cannot be shifted: the responsibility rests squarely on the shoulders of the Canadian people. Are they still to be content with halfway measures when nothing but a total effort can save the situation? A total war is not now being made, and will not be made so long as men and women who are free and able to work are not at work, so long as the civilian population is being supplied with goods and services that are not essential, and so long as more people are engaged in any industry than are needed for maintaining the necessary output.[33]

Increasingly, observers began to contrast the circumstances faced by Britons living under a veritable siege with the lack of hardship in Canada as a means of reminding Canadians that comparatively few sacrifices had been required of them. In a Christmas 1941 radio address broadcast on the CBC, Vincent Massey remarked that, "in England,"

> the civilian consumer has cheerfully learnt to curb his needs. Ships to Britain must carry bombs and shells – not silk stockings and oranges. Clothing coupons are the subject of brisk competition in even the best-regulated families. British workshops now make only bare necessities. A great boot and shoe factory today turns out torpedoes; anti-gas preparations are now made by beauty cream specialists; aero-engines come from a firm which produced hairpins; and aircraft frames from works which used to manufacture toys.[34]

Subsequent chapters will consider how the buyers and sellers of products attempted to reconcile growing consumer purchasing power with the increasingly strident demands for consumer sacrifice that began to be voiced in late 1941 and early 1942. Obviously, the chasm between the two positions sometimes led to unintentionally humorous and even embarrassing juxtapositions. In late September 1941, J.L. Rutledge, who only a year earlier had endorsed the buy British policy, now deployed his monthly column in *Liberty* to lament Canadians' "tendency ... to think of this as the government's war." Only 20 percent of Canada's manufacturing potential was committed to war production, he wrote. The remainder generated "commodities that we all use to assure our comfort and convenience." Canadians, he went on, "have almost duplicated the fabulous spending jag of 1929" and "have not yet felt the cost of war," having made "little, if any, sacrifice of our accustomed comforts." What was wanting was thrifty and sober living. "We can have either more consumer goods," Rutledge warned, "or we can have more shells and more guns and more ships. The inescapable fact is that we can't have both."[35] The contrast with an article published later in that same issue could not have been more striking. The regular "Girl Meets Girl" column offered readers a lengthy piece titled "September Shopping Spree," in which the author (the improbably named Bubbles Schanasi) exclaimed, "If you love nice things, you can't just wish for them, you *must* shop for them." She recommended "an early start, comfortable shoes, a carefully thought out list, and plenty of time to mull over the merits of each item," and she proceeded to describe a fanciful shopping whirlwind, with nary a mention of the war.[36]

Although the retail economy would continue to be far more vibrant than is usually remembered in the patriotic narrative of home front sacrifice, guiltless shopping sprees of this kind were coming to an end by late 1941. By mid-year, it had become obvious to officials in Ottawa that the trajectory of civilian consumption was bound to collide with the rapidly escalating scale of the war effort. Canada's war expenditure for the fiscal year ending in March 1940 was $118 million. It increased an incredible six times over the following twelve months, to $752 million, and would double yet again the year after that.[37] Canadian resources were strained not only by the demands of Canada's own armed forces but by the rapid growth in British and American war orders as well. British orders alone increased more than sevenfold in the year following the fall of France and then doubled the next year. Meanwhile, the American Lend-Lease and rearmament programs greatly reduced the quantity of American goods available for export to Canada for civilian consumption. Following the Hyde Park Declaration of April 1941, Canadian and American planners developed a complex system of financial and economic cooperation between their respective countries. Subsequently, American manufacturers were granted parity in terms of right of access to Canadian raw materials to meet US military needs. The reverse was true, as well, but the net effect was to further reduce the quantity of materials available for non-essential needs in Canada.[38]

Between rising consumer purchasing power and diminishing supplies – circumstances one nervous WPTB official described as being like "loose cannon on a shipboard in a storm" – the only possible outcome was inflation.[39] In 1940 and the first three months of 1941, the cost-of-living index had increased 4.2 percent – an average of 0.3 percent per month. Officials in the Department of Finance considered such increases high but acceptable, especially given that commodity prices at the outbreak of war had been lower than normal due to the deflationary effect of the Depression.[40] Further inflation, however, threatened labour unrest and a discontented electorate, both of which greatly alarmed the government. Already by February 1941, the National Council of Women and other groups had begun to agitate for price controls on a broad range of "necessities of life," including milk, on the grounds that food prices were increasing faster than the general cost-of-living index.[41] Then, between March and August 1941, the cost-of-living index rose by a truly alarming 6.7 percent – three times the rate of the previous fifteen months.[42] More decisive action was required.

Early in the summer of 1941, officials from the Department of Finance, the WPTB, and other related departments and agencies began to consider price controls in various forms, having arrived at a broad consensus that an inflationary spiral would do far more than impinge upon consumer purchasing power. Severe increases in costs could threaten to destabilize the entire war effort since the government itself had become the country's single largest purchaser of goods.[43] After protracted discussions, officials decided on the radical proposal of freezing both wages and prices altogether.[44] The price ceiling would be administered by the WPTB, now operating under the auspices of the Department of Finance. With the advent of the price ceiling, the board became a critically important part of the government's domestic social and economic planning agenda. Over the next two years, its staffing exploded from 150 to over 5,000 paid employees and volunteers.[45] It also burst into the public consciousness. In October 1941, having already secured the support of the nation's foremost labour leaders, Prime Minister King explained the wage and price ceiling and the board's role in enforcing it to the Canadian public in a typically dour and overlong radio address.[46] But the real public face of the price ceiling was to be Donald Gordon, the former deputy governor of the Bank of Canada, selected by King to become the board's new chairman commencing November 1941.[47] Dubbed King's "no man" by *Saturday Night*, Gordon became the most visible of all the "Ottawa men," the nickname given to the civil service elite, many of them drawn from the ranks of private industry, who steered the ship of state from behind the scenes throughout the war years.[48]

Gordon had a well-deserved reputation for being a hard-drinking workaholic, and it is perhaps revealing of his pugnacious character that for most of the war, he persisted in clinging to his little postage stamp of a moustache, nearly identical to Hitler's, unfashionable though it must have been at the time. Under his leadership, the board became a ubiquitous presence in the life of Canadian consumers. In a succession of addresses to representatives of business, industry, labour, and women's organizations, and to the Canadian public at large, he repeatedly beat the same drum: modern war required sacrifices, including the subordination of non-essential consumer desires to the war effort. Every cent not spent on War Savings Certificates, every yard of fabric that made dresses rather than uniforms, every gallon of gasoline pumped into a passenger car rather than a military vehicle, materially aided the Axis. All societal resources that could be spared had to be directed to the great cause of Victory, and Gordon and his subordinates in the WPTB would be relentless in imposing economies on manufacturers and retailers. A joke going the rounds at the time went like this: the local strongman, showing off in a tavern, crushed all the juice from a lemon in his immense fist. He defied anyone to squeeze one drop more, at which point Donald Gordon stepped up and squeezed out two.[49]

As subsequent chapters will demonstrate, hardly any aspect of the consumer economy escaped WPTB attention. New consumer credit regulations required heftier down payments and shorter terms for installment plans.[50] Regulations reduced deliveries to save labour and gas, cut store hours and store lighting, "froze" women's hat styles, and banned cuffs on men's trousers. Hugh Mackenzie, the board's deputy administrator for retail sales, even stipulated the precise number of pins a haberdasher could use to secure the folds in men's shirts – twelve, reduced from the usual eighteen. So, when a board order concerning regulations governing conversation in retail stores appeared in 1942, it might not have seemed surprising. Why not regulate conversation? Shortly thereafter, a correction appeared: the order had meant to say regulations concerning *conservation:* there were, as yet, no rules requiring a reduction in workplace chit-chat.[51]

Above all, Gordon relentlessly extolled the necessity of combating inflation. "The present danger cannot be overstated," he said in an April 1943 speech. Arguing that Hitler would never have seized power in Germany had the Weimar state kept its economic house in order, he warned that Canadian democracy, too, could be imperilled if the cost of living exceeded the ability of ordinary citizens to keep up with it. "Uncontrolled inflation results in the demoralization and gradual disintegration of our democratic system ... it strikes at the very roots of any system of social security and creates conditions in which freedom of opportunity can have no place."[52] On the face of it, the price ceiling he governed seemed simple enough: retailers and service providers were required to fix their prices at a level no higher than the highest they had been during the "basic period" from 15 September to 11 October 1941. Then, in December, the price of nearly everything, from foodstuffs to funerals, would be frozen. No increases would be permitted without WPTB permission. To ensure that retailers were not saddled with rising costs but frozen prices, prices were fixed along the entire chain of production and distribution, from the primary resource extractors, to the manufacturer, to the wholesaler, to the retailer. Even private sales of used goods were, theoretically, governed by the price ceiling. Where the board could not control prices, as in the case of imported goods, it would pay a subsidy to retailers to help offset any increase. Further unanticipated increases that impinged on the ability of wage earners to buy staple goods would be offset with a cost-of-living bonus, initially amounting to twenty cents for every point of inflation, but this varied over time. In December 1943, under pressure from organized labour, it was abandoned altogether in favour of rolling the existing bonus into standard negotiated wages.[53] The initial wage freeze, Desmond Morton has suggested, could only have been "imposed on a divided labour movement, conscious of its weakness and eager, as it had not been in a previous war, to prove its patriotism."[54] It is also true that the price freeze made the wage freeze at least palatable, and despite many complaints from labour leaders, polls taken later in the war showed that most working people thought that the price ceiling worked (see the discussion in the Appendix). It also helped that they had more money than ever. Wages may have been frozen, but more and better work was available for nearly everyone. By the end of the third year of the war, real disposable incomes had increased by almost 40 percent, and unemployment had virtually disappeared (see Appendix, Table A.5).

The American government's equivalent of the WPTB, the Office of Price Administration, had its roots in New Deal era government intervention in the consumer economy.[55] In Canada, by contrast, the wage and price ceiling constituted an economic experiment of unprecedented complexity. K.W. Taylor, secretary to the chairman of the board, reflected shortly after the war that the price freeze had been "a novel experiment" exceeding in its ambition comparable measures undertaken in the United States, the United Kingdom, and even Nazi Germany.[56] Commanding, threatening, cajoling, and pleading, thousands of orders, edicts, and memorandums poured forth from board offices every month. New restrictions were announced; old ones were clarified, amended, replaced, or rescinded. It was, as historian Christopher Waddell later called it, "a bottomless pit of regulation," so complex that board officials could barely keep it straight themselves.[57] Enforcement was the key to maintaining all this, but the board had at its disposal nothing like the tens of thousands of personnel that would have been necessary to police the countless commercial transactions that occurred daily across the country. Gordon grasped at once that the nation's housewives and the organizations that represented them were the logical choice to police the ceiling. In one of his first radio addresses to the nation, delivered the Friday before the imposition of the price ceiling, he struck this ominous note from the outset:

You, who are listening to these words, will be going into the fight next Monday ... and make no mistake, you will be on one side or on the other. In this fight against inflation you cannot be a neutral. You will either be helping to save yourself, your family, and your country from a terrible calamity – or you will be working for the enemy.

The "terrible calamity" was runaway inflation, and he singled out "Mrs. Consumer" for special duty in the struggle against it. In words that might have been written by Byrne Hope Sanders herself, he remarked that "the housewife must be the real guardian of the law. Her job, for her country, will be to watch prices every day. She is the soldier in the battle line. She must battle against dishonesty, greed, stupidity – all the human weaknesses which are the allies of inflation and destruction."[58] The war against inflation, then, would involve both governmental intrusion into private commercial relations on a vast scale and also the mobilization of Canadian housewife-consumers at the grassroots level. The price ceiling, administered from Ottawa, would be enforced locally in the countless daily transactions between housewives and retailers. Moreover, Gordon urged Canada's housewives to reduce family expenditure and to eliminate nonessential purchases altogether, a point the prime minister had made in his own address a month earlier: buy only what you need and invest the remainder in Victory Bonds.

The price ceiling came into effect on 1 December, a Monday. Sunday, 7 December, was Pearl Harbor. Canada's long phony war was over.

ORGANIZED LABOUR MAY sometimes have wavered in its support for the board, but the leaders of the major women's organizations never did. In that fateful first week of December 1941, women's groups that had formerly endorsed the buy British and buy Canadian policies dropped them in favour of slogans such as "use it up and wear it out," "make-over, mend, and make-do," and calls for conservation and thrift to combat inflation and unpatriotic wastefulness. Over time, these calls became increasingly strident. In his summer 1943 address to the National Council of Women, J.L. Ilsley asked the assembled members to "establish a social code that frowns upon ostentation, waste, and unnecessary spending, bearing in mind that at this time a blatant spender should be considered a social outcast," to which the members responded with an enthusiastic endorsement.[59] Heads of women's groups and columnists in women's magazines underscored that Canadian housewives had for many years cultivated the skill of economical homemaking, and now they called on them to turn that skill to public account and help to win the war. As Byrne Hope Sanders put it,

> These are characteristics women have always shown in their private life in relation to problems affecting their homes. Some of the greatest unsung pages of history have to do with the way women have held their homes through depression, under the strain of war losses through strain and stress. Now your country asks us to demonstrate these virtues for the protection of our nation.[60]

One crucial development in the board's efforts to mobilize Canadian women's groups was the creation, in early 1942, of the Consumer Branch, whose mandate was to act as a liaison between the board and the nation's housewives.[61] The Consumer Branch itself had its genesis in a series of meetings between representatives of some eighteen Canadian women's organizations and Donald Gordon in December 1941. The outcome of these meetings was the establishment of a Women's Regional Advisory Committee (WRAC) in each of the board's thirteen administrative districts. These regional committees were subdivided into local volunteer subcommittees, of which there were more than four hundred by mid-1943. The Consumer Branch, in turn, was created to oversee the WRACs, liaise with women's associations, and report their views back to the board.[62] Gordon personally chose Byrne Hope Sanders, with her high profile among Canadian women – and useful lack of public political affiliation – as its director.[63] As Sanders remembered their first meeting, Gordon told her, "I don't know just what your job is, Miss Sanders, nor how you're going to do it. But it's there to be done."[64] Indeed it was. Sanders and her staff carved out an even more ambitious role for the Consumer Branch than had originally been intended. It was responsible for price watching; it communicated rules and regulations to the public; it "channeled" consumer opinion, principally through the WRACs; it provided volunteers for ration offices; it established housing registries to help place the thousands of Canadians in need of temporary accommodation; and it worked alongside other government agencies and voluntary groups to promote a nationwide conservation campaign.[65]

By mid-1943, the Consumer Branch had become a very large voluntary organization in its own right, with an Ottawa head office of fifty paid members, including Sanders herself, and nearly eleven thousand volunteers across the country. By the end of the war, the number of volunteers had grown to sixteen thousand.[66] Approximately a third of them were liaisons to local women's organizations, including the WRACs. Price control was their most urgent task, and they formed the backbone of an effort in which every Canadian housewife was encouraged to participate. To aid them in this task, the Consumer Branch printed hundreds of thousands of booklets in which housewives were encouraged to record daily prices, keeping an eye out for unexplained increases. Contact information for the local WPTB offices was included at the back of each booklet. There is every indication that these "blue books" (so called because their covers were printed on blue card stock) were widely used and that their appearance in the hands of shoppers may have had a significant disciplinary effect on retailers. In a report to the Consumer Branch, the board's enforcement officer described his office as being completely overwhelmed with "a deluge of complaints" regarding price infractions.[67] Investigating them all was impossible, but an important aspect of the board's public relations efforts was the appearance of taking every complaint, regardless how small, very seriously. In southwestern Ontario, board investigators looked into a discrepancy of two cents in the cost of a half-pound bag of processed cheese.[68] The board fined a northern Ontario grocer a hefty fifty dollars for slicing a loaf of bread, which was prohibited under rules designed to save labour. In North Battleford, Saskatchewan, a farmer's wife complained that the price of dairy pails had risen by ten cents: the merchant received a warning and lowered his prices. In Winnipeg, the board scrutinized a three-cent difference in the price of pork kidney.[69] Frivolous though these individual cases may seem, they underscored the seriousness with which the board and the Department of Finance took the issue of price control.

Enforcement officers found, however, that many reports of price infractions resulted from misunderstandings about the price ceiling and rationing rules. The WPTB frequently permitted modest price increases on certain scarce commodities. Not knowing any better, people often reported these as infractions. The Consumer Branch also had to remind consumers that the price ceiling did not equal price levelling or price fixing – retailers were free to compete, provided they did so under the ceiling. In fairness, there were so many rules and regulations that even the board's own personnel had difficulty keeping up with them all. To help consumers cope with the staggering array of rules, the Consumer Branch issued a steady stream of information updates, and it coordinated efforts with the CBC to launch two radio programs, *As a Matter of Fact* and *The Household Counsellor*, that were intended to update homemakers on WPTB policies. The branch also began to produce a regular bulletin, *Consumer's News*. Distributed by WRAC volunteers, it kept homemakers abreast of the rules and explained changes when they occurred. Circulation eventually reached 318,000 (a third of them in French), making it the most widely distributed periodical in the country.[70] There is no way of knowing how well *Consumer's News* and the CBC Radio programs were liked, or how far their message penetrated into the minds of readers. No doubt many readers found them useful but also tiresome in their constant cajoling. Years later, one Canadian complained,

> The newspapers, they were just propaganda sheets ... how to cook cabbage, make cabbage rolls, and then drink the cabbage juice. Or carrots. Swiss chard. Spinach. Did they think we didn't know that stuff, like how to make a dollar do the price of ten? You'd think the idiots in their big offices in Toronto and Ottawa didn't know about the Depression we just went through.[71]

To be sure, amid practical advice for navigating the labyrinthine world of regulations, the board's stream of missives also pestered and nagged consumers unrelentingly, and the essential message conveyed was a contradictory one. The Consumer Branch repeatedly emphasized that the sacrifices asked of consumers were comparatively small, especially compared to those made by servicemen on fighting fronts and civilians in Britain, but it also argued that these sacrifices were of monumental importance in winning the war. Although polls taken late in the war reassured board officials that most Canadians, even in Quebec, approved of the WPTB and its regulations, they nonetheless recognized a "constant need to interpret the Board as a beneficent organization for the housekeeper," as their unpublished official history put it. "As regulations impinged more and more on the home, the Board had to be sold over and over again," the history concluded.[72]

Other duties undertaken by Consumer Branch volunteers proved to be of unexpected urgency, such as the laborious task, in the summer of 1942, of enumerating nearly 12 million Canadians for their ration cards and helping to staff the nearly six hundred ration offices established throughout the country.[73] Coupon rationing of selected foodstuffs – sugar was the first – began in July 1942, the thirty-fourth month of war. It began in the United States during the same month, the eighth month of the war for Americans. Britons, of course, had been coping with a very strict rationing regime since 1939.[74] Once again, we are reminded of the surprising fact that food rationing, which comes so readily to the fore in so many accounts of life on the home front, did not even begin in Canada until the country had been at war for nearly three years. Admittedly, board officials had recognized the likelihood of having to impose coupon rationing ever since they had brought in the price ceiling. Price controls were untenable if shortages of certain staple foods led to panic buying, hoarding, speculation, and black markets. The seven-month gap between the imposition of the price ceiling and the beginning of food rationing reflected the time required to get the administrative machinery for rationing up and running, rather than any uncertainty regarding its necessity.[75] Coupon rationing of sugar was followed by coffee and tea rations in August, butter in December, and meat rationing in May 1943. A complex scheme for the rationing of preserves and sweeteners such as honey, molasses, and maple syrup followed in September.[76] Rationing regulations varied over time, and some, such as those for the sale of beer, wine, and spirits, were administered provincially by liquor control boards.

The WPTB introduced coupon rationing of selected foodstuffs for two related reasons. The first was to reduce consumption of scarce goods. Coffee, tea, and sugar were imported: the naval war and the desperate need for shipping resulted in a drastic decline in the quantity of available supplies. The other was to create equitable distribution. There was no general shortage of meat or butter in Canada – indeed, the production of both increased dramatically. However, export requirements sometimes created temporary and regional shortages that, prior to rationing, often led to panic buying and hoarding. Only reluctantly did the board impose rationing in such cases, usually only after acquiescing to public pressure. This in turn underscores an important fact. Although rationing is often described as one of the hardships that consumers endured in Canada, it was not always or uniformly unpopular. Minutes of WRAC meetings provide an important source for assessing public perceptions of rationing. Participants in the WRACs complained about the size of rations (including, according to the board's labour representative, Christine White, that they were sometimes *too big* and therefore too expensive for single people or small working families); they complained about the inflexibility of rules that did not permit the purchase of half rations; they complained about abusers of the system, as all evidence suggests that large numbers of people broke the rules when it served their interests to do so; and they complained about the inconvenience of handling ration books and coupons, but they hardly ever complained about rationing in principle.[77] Polls indicated that most Canadians accepted the necessity of rationing (for some goods more than others), and requests for the extension of rationing to other goods that had periodic or local shortages, such as canned fruit, vegetables, and even clothes, were sometimes voiced in the WRACs.[78]

Butter rationing, for example, had followed an enormous number of demands for its adoption. In October and November 1942, severe shortages of butter hit a number of cities in central and eastern Canada. Dispatched to report on the butter situation in the Toronto, Hamilton, and Niagara region, Christine White met hostile and resentful WRACs and agitated grocers, one of whom mentioned daily "rows" over butter in his store. She also arrived just in time for a near-riot, when a mob of three hundred women beset a succession of Toronto stores, demanding butter, and had to be turned away by police.[79] A week earlier, the board's food administrator, J.G. Taggart, had emphatically denied that there was any general butter shortage. The problem, he said, was localized panic buying and hoarding. Taggart estimated that some 8 or 9 *million* pounds of butter was being squirrelled away and insisted that there was not "the remotest possibility of rationing of butter in any future time I can foresee." Nevertheless, between continued shortages and public pressure – reported back to the board by WRAC liaisons – Taggart and his superiors assented to a rationing scheme and brought it into effect just before Christmas.[80] "Store officials, from the largest down to smallest are agreed that rationing came in the nick of time to save their sanity," the editors of the *Toronto Telegram* wrote.[81] The butter ration, a remarkable example of the pressure that consumers could exert, provided an ample half-pound per person per week – which entailed no reduction in consumption at all. What it did entail, at least in theory, was an equality of distribution that the free market could not provide under those circumstances. Polls showed that it was a popular measure. "There has just been an announcement over the radio that butter rationing begins tomorrow," wrote Toronto's Marie Williamson in a letter to the mother of two English boys whom she took in during 1940. She went on,

> I am awful glad. There has been a shortage for a month now – I only had 2lbs for 3 weeks. The govt. kept issuing statements that there was enough butter

if *only* people would not be selfish and everyone would cut down consumption by one ounce a week. And every statement just sent the selfish ones out combing the shops for *more* butter to store in their cellars ... I'm so glad it's to be rationed so I'll know where we are.[82]

Meat rationing, too, was discussed for several months and requested by countless participants in the WRACs before it was imposed in May 1943. Beef and pork production had increased since the beginning of the war but could not keep pace with the demands of both the domestic market (including the armed forces stationed at home) and soaring export requirements to Britain. In many major cities in central Canada and the Maritimes, temporary though occasionally severe meat shortages became commonplace in 1942.[83] Many grocers and butchers began to complain of difficulty getting enough beef to sell. There was a broad consensus in the press that the black market was diverting meat from legal sellers. At one point, board officials intervened to secure 20 million pounds of beef from wholesalers and slaughterhouses in order to guarantee supplies for the armed forces, but they believed that safely meeting export quotas and ensuring equitable distribution to civilians would require rationing.[84] When meat rationing came into effect in May 1943, its aim was to reduce individual consumption by just 15 to 20 percent. Rations still permitted a substantial portion of about two pounds of beef or pork per person per week, depending on the cut purchased, whereas poultry, game bird, venison, rabbit, and fish were not rationed at all, although the war severely hampered the Atlantic fishing industry.[85] Some buzz made the rounds in the press concerning the alleged epicurean delights of domestically raised muskrat as a substitute for beef and pork, but there is no evidence that demand took off.[86]

For the sake of administrative ease, meat rationing rules permitted the same quantity for every member of the household – including infants and young children, who presumably could not consume their weekly allotment of up to two pounds.[87] This meant that families with young children probably saw an increase in their consumption of beef and pork, and for most others the substitution of a meatless meal or an additional night of chicken would have sufficed to make up the difference. According to the Combined Food Board, the total calories of meat available per person per day dropped from 450 in 1943 to just 430 in 1944 (and subsequently to 400 in 1945), but these numbers still remained well above the 340 calories available per person in 1940.[88] Estimates from the Department of Agriculture arrived at a similar conclusion, finding that apparent per capita consumption of beef was just over fifty-four pounds in 1940, rose dramatically to just over sixty-nine pounds in 1943, and fell only to sixty-seven pounds in 1944.[89] This is perhaps unsurprising. There was supply enough for the armed forces, Allied nations, and civilians at home – by legal means or otherwise. Between 1939 and 1945, Canadian beef production doubled.[90] All the while, meat market sales continued to grow, albeit at a reduced pace.[91] The board suspended meat rationing in late February 1944 (but recommenced/resumed it for a year in September 1945), believing that it had served its purpose in helping the country make its export requirements, easing distribution problems, and reducing instances of panic buying. A subsequent survey of grocers and meat markets conducted by the board's Research and Statistics Administration concluded that sales of rationed meat had declined by just 5 percent during the ration period and were more than offset by a nearly 20 percent increase in fish and a 14 percent increase in poultry and game birds.[92]

In response to griping about various aspects of rationing, women's organizations and the Consumer Branch pointed out – correctly – that Canada's ration regime was far less severe than the one suffered by Britons. Certainly, returned servicemen, Britons stationed in Canada, and war brides noticed the difference. Having just returned from the United Kingdom, Group Captain Denton Massey, MP for Toronto-Greenwood, told the House of Commons in 1944 that "to a man coming back from overseas Canada seemed more like a country enjoying its greatest carnival of prosperity in history, than one in which everyone should be making an all out war effort."[93] One Welsh war bride, arriving in Canada in 1944, could scarcely believe the cornucopia of food enjoyed by Canadians, even under the strictest wartime conditions. On her trip west, she later recalled, "The first meal on the train was breakfast, and they served me six slices of bacon and two eggs. Imagine, two eggs and all that bacon! I ate everything put in front of me."[94]

In Canada, the initial coffee and tea rations permitted everyone aged twelve and over enough for about a dozen cups of each per week, and there was nothing to stop anyone from getting an extra cup (though no more than one per sitting, under the rules) at one of the country's proliferating diners and restaurants.[95] The size of coffee and tea rations was increased in September 1943 and again in May 1944, but in September 1944, barely two years after it had begun, rationing of these products was eliminated altogether. On the other hand, the half-pound per week sugar ration, which required a significant reduction in personal consumption, frequently engendered genuine hostility and resistance, despite the annual release of additional sugar rations for the purpose of canning for the remarkable 97 percent of housewives who did so.[96] A stream of complaints about the size of the sugar ration flowed steadily from the WRACs, especially in rural areas, where, according to the board's research, housewives used an average of 25 percent more sugar per year than their counterparts in the city.[97] But people did their best to make do, saving up their regular sugar rations (even though, technically, this constituted hoarding) and bartering when necessary. One member of the Mansfield, Ontario, Women's Institute recalled, "My grandfather had a sweet tooth and could have used up the family ration by himself. Rather than skimp on his cereal, he would eat his porridge without sugar for several days, so he could have it to his liking on occasion."[98] For once, restaurants were not much help. Exacting rules governed their dissemination of sugar: it could be served only on request; no loose or wrapped sugar was to be left on the table; perforated shakers were prohibited; and customers were limited to no more than three lumps or two teaspoons of sugar for any coffee, tea, cereal, or dessert. Curiously, there were no rules about buying soft drinks, either in restaurants or stores, though there were slight shortages in supply.[99] The same was true of candy. Many participants in the WRACs protested that soft drink and candy companies seemed to have no limit on their sugar supply (in fact, they did) when ordinary housewives did not have enough to make all the preserves they wanted to. "You can't spread Coca-Cola on bread," one WRAC liaison fumed.[100]

Complaints of this kind highlight the fact that rationing posed innumerable and often unforeseen administrative and public relations challenges. Lost, stolen, or accidentally destroyed ration books had to be replaced. Zoos asked about additional meat rations for carnivorous animals. Vegetarians – rare at the time – inquired about trading theirs for different kinds. Families asked if a recently departed loved one's rationing coupons could be used for the wake rather than being surrendered.[101] Other administrative problems were less trivial. In order to stave off criticism and the emergence of black markets in communities along the Canada-US border, where a disparity in supplies or ration regulations was most visible, the board established a small Washington office in early 1942. It was intended to harmonize rationing and other consumer-related policies with its American equivalents, but in practice both sides soon discovered that the differences between the two countries' circumstances were so great that coordination proved impossible. Moreover, the Washington office staff thought that the American government "tended to cut back civilian produce to a greater extent than seemed desirable," but on the whole, relations between them and their American colleagues seem to have been harmonious.[102]

Unexpectedly, ration administration officials found themselves working in conjunction with the new Division of Nutrition Services of the Department of Pensions and National Health to develop criteria for granting extra rations on medical grounds. Headed by Lionel Pett, a biochemist and medical doctor at the University of Alberta, Nutrition Services had been created to "aid in the war effort by helping to maintain and improve the nutrition of the Canadian people."[103] Pett produced an extensive list of medical conditions that did and did not warrant extra rations. For examples, diabetes, eczema, and tuberculosis were grounds for additional butter; senility, rheumatism, and obesity were not. Expectant mothers were dealt with on a case-by-case basis. With a doctor's note, people whose conditions were on the approved list could receive additional ration coupons from the local ration office. Others could appeal to Pensions and National Health, and they did.[104] The Committee on Special Rations received hundreds of appeals from Canadians for additional meat, butter, and especially sugar, often on the most dubious medical grounds and with the complicity of their physicians. A woman in Montreal asked for six times the normal sugar ration per week, claiming myocarditis; a gastritis sufferer in Langley Prairie, British Columbia, asked for the same; another Montrealer requested four times the standard butter and sugar ration on the grounds that he was capable of eating nothing else except bread and milk; a man in Listowel, Ontario, asked for an eightfold increase because of "an inability to eat sufficient food."[105]

From 1942 on, despite rationing, few weeks went by without at least one important item being in short supply in any given town or city. Minutes of the WRAC meetings reveal consumers' frequent frustrations regarding certain staples that, without apparent rhyme or reason, suddenly became hard to find. One week it was preserves in Moncton, the next milk in Winnipeg or canned fruit in Saskatoon. London, Ontario, actually ran out of potatoes for a brief period in the summer of 1945.[106] Though seldom severe or long-lived, these flash shortages imposed greater burdens on homemakers' grocery shopping and meal planning. For those who could afford it – and more and more families could – dining out relieved some of the pressure. For home cooks, consumer magazines, ladies' columns in newspapers, and dozens of cookbooks offered countless "Victory recipes," with tips on how to stretch food further. Another way of coping was to break the rules. The biggest administrative challenge facing the board was enforcing the rules, as people found any number of ways to bend or break them in accordance with their own sense of fairness. As the Consumer Branch repeatedly explained, ration coupons and goods were not to be bartered, bought, sold, or raffled, although they could be given as gifts to servicemen on active duty. On the other hand, rationed foods, once bought, could be shared during the course of a meal, and many consumers failed to see the difference.[107] There was simply no reliable means of policing what went on within families or between friends and neighbours, and there is abundant anecdotal evidence that a steady interpersonal trafficking of ration coupons went on. "Of course you could always trade with your neighbours," Effie Donnell from Ontario later remembered. "My shortage was always tea ... I drank tea by the gallon. Which meant I was always on the lookout for someone who wasn't quite so addicted."[108] Likewise, Bob Bolster remembered that "there were ration stamps for sugar, tea, and meat and people in our community used to trade them around like baseball cards."[109] Eventually, the board gave up trying to police rationing within families, but some people pushed enforcement agents to their limit. In one such case, a man in Toronto was brought up on charges because he managed to secure a ration card for his dog. Unmoved by his argument that loyal "Andy" *was* a member of the family, the judge, evidently a cat person, fined him a hundred dollars.[110]

Meat and butter rationing posed the greatest administrative and enforcement headaches. Coffee, tea, and sugar were imported and could be regulated at the point of entry, but meat and butter were produced by thousands of individual farmers whose activities were much harder to oversee. Farmers who slaughtered livestock or made butter for their own use were supposed to surrender coupons to the nearest ration office, but enforcement depended almost entirely on the honour system.[111] A significant black market for meat existed throughout the country, with board officials believing that some Quebecers possessed especially "indulgent attitudes" toward it.[112] Nearly as troubling to the board was the so-called grey market in which a friendly grocer might put aside good cuts for favoured customers – or for any customer who was willing to buy at the back door for higher prices. As a warning to the public, *Consumer's News* included a monthly sampling of punishments meted out to rule-breakers, and most newspapers and magazines carried similar stories on a daily basis. Criminal prosecutions for infractions of rationing rules grew steadily. There were 1,201 in 1942, 3,663 in 1943, and 4,166 in 1944, and these figures do not include the thousands of prosecutions, usually for gasoline and tire-related infractions, made on behalf of the controllers of the Department of Munitions and Supply.[113] We cannot know how many actual infractions occurred – presumably, successful prosecutions represented only a small percentage of the total. Despite their frustrations, board officials believed that most people were obeying the rules and even came to regard trading within families and between neighbours as a kind of safety valve against public discontent.

What the board could not abide was hoarding, which it likened to sabotage even if it amounted to no more than adding this week's allotment of coffee, tea, sugar, butter, or meat to any unused portion from the previous. Hoarding undermined the whole basis of the rationing program – in the case of butter, it had led to it in the first place – and threatened inflation if it resulted in further shortages. Ella Monkcton, a Consumer Branch volunteer and an aspiring writer, wrote a rather wan but widely performed one-act propaganda play, *Waiting for Mary*, on this very theme. The play concerns a group of women who have gathered on a porch to gossip about the neighbourhood food hoarder, old Miss Powell. They are joined by Carl Bauer, an elderly Austrian immigrant, now a patriotic Canadian with two sons in the fight. Bauer lectures all assembled about how hoarding could lead to price inflation, having witnessed first-hand the catastrophe that befell his homeland after the First World War. "I came back to Vienna when the fighting was over," he says in his broken English,

> My mother and my two little sisters were still alive and at first I thanked God for that. But soon I find that there is not much to be thankful for. I could not get work. My mother she spend half her time scrubbing office floors for which she was paid in paper money, oh, quite a thick pile of it – only it was not worth anything. The rest of her time she stand in the food queues waiting in the rain in the hopes of getting a little bread. Think of it, hundreds and hundreds of paper bills, and they would not buy enough food to keep us from starving or fuel enough to keep us from freezing. That is inflation. It kill my mother and my two sisters. I pray that here in Canada you may never know the full meaning that word.

The message was clear enough: even a countryman of Adolf Hitler could see the dangers of inflation.[114] This was a drum that the Consumer Branch was still beating a year after the war ended.

RATIONS PROVIDED FOR generous portions and in some cases were even welcomed by the public, though clearly some people broke the rules when they wanted or needed to. Despite temporary and regional shortages that were at times quite sharp and that occasionally encouraged rule breaking, no general food shortages occurred in Canada during the war, in part because food production soared throughout the entire period. Although the total number of acres under cultivation remained about the same, and good farm hands became harder and harder to find, excellent weather and guaranteed markets contributed to a dramatic increase in yields from 1939 to 1945.[115] The gross value of Canadian agricultural production increased from just under $1.2 billion nationwide in 1939 to $2.5 billion by 1944. In Saskatchewan, the war boom brought about an almost complete reversal of the province's Depression-era misfortunes. In 1937, the value of Saskatchewan's farm output was a mere $92 million. By 1944, it had bounded sevenfold to $624 million.[116] National wheat stocks increased from 23.5 million bushels in 1938 to 579 million bushels in 1943; during the same period, oat stocks increased from 9 million to nearly 29 million.[117] Similar increases occurred in livestock production. Beef production increased from 645,000 pounds in 1939 to 1.1 million pounds in 1945; pork production nearly tripled, from 625,000 pounds in 1939 to 1.5 million in 1944; and poultry production rose from 152,000 pounds in 1940 to 200,000 in 1944.[118]

Granted, growing demand from the United Kingdom, whose continental food supplies had been cut off, absorbed a significant portion of these increases – in 1943, the value of Canadian food exports to Britain actually exceeded that of munitions and weapons stores.[119] Nonetheless, reports of the Combined Food Board indicate that the quantity of food available for civilian consumption continued to increase as well, from an estimated per capita average of about 3,000 calories per day in 1940 to just under 3,300 in 1944.[120] Grocery store sales rose $584 million in 1939 to $1.04 billion in 1944.[121] Of course, these figures indicate only the quantity of food available per person and do not reveal how much food people were buying or actually eating; nor do they account for regional and income-based inequities in distribution. However, the combination of increasing agricultural production and the wartime boom in grocery store and meat market sales gives us reason to believe that most Canadians were receiving, if not precisely a fair share, at least a bigger share than ever before. Admittedly, the board permitted greater-than-average inflation in food prices, but even accounting for such increases, these figures suggest that Canadians on average were buying, and presumably eating, more food than ever.

What about the nutritional quality of that diet? Perhaps no issue other than maintaining the price ceiling so galvanized voluntary women's organizations as nutrition. In 1940, the National Council of Women adopted the improvement of public health, with a particular emphasis on "the importance of a correct diet," as second only in importance to the promotion of national unity on its program of activities.[122] Over the course of the war, the council helped to sponsor thousands of lectures on proper nutrition. Here again was a cause ready-made for women's groups. The rural Women's Institutes had been founded for the express purpose of disseminating knowledge of "domestic science," and nutrition was never far from the agenda of the IODE, the YWCA, and a host of other associations.[123] Nutrition was also a cause inextricably bound up with consumerism. Women had long been responsible for buying and preparing food for their families. With the advent of nutritional science, they assumed the additional duty of assuring the nutritional quality of the food they served. Once again, the war added a patriotic urgency to an already existing social cause. In a CBC Radio address announcing a nationwide nutritional education program, Edna Guest, the convener of the National Council of Women's Health and Nutrition Committee, called the "scientific understanding of the food necessary to retain good health and good morale" the "second line of defense."[124]

Countless articles in consumer magazines and on the women's pages in newspapers stressed the same point. The popular consumer magazine *National Home Monthly*, for example, ran a monthly column called "On the Kitchen Front," and many companies, as part of institutional goodwill campaigns, offered free booklets of Victory recipes. The war years also saw unprecedented government activity in the realm of nutritional education and study, much of it in coordination with women's groups. The National Council of Women's request that a nutritionist be appointed to the Department of Pensions and National Health was one of the factors that led to the creation of Lionel Pett's Nutrition Services Division.[125] Throughout the war, Pett and his colleagues undertook numerous studies to assess its impact on nutrition. These surveys measured diets against two nutritional standards. Prior to 1942, they used the Canadian Dietary Standard, adopted in 1938 by the Canadian Council on Nutrition, an advisory body created within the Department of Pensions and National Health that same year.[126] In 1942, in the interests of standardization on a North American basis, the council replaced this initial measure with a slightly modified version of the Recommended Daily Allowances (RDAs) used in the United States, which was employed as the basis for study until 1945.[127]

National nutrition surveys gave empirical support to what nutritionists had already suspected. The earliest studies, conducted in 1939, concluded that Canadian families were not so much undernourished as poorly nourished. There was, they claimed, an urgent need for nutrition education. Although the diets of most surveyed families were adequate in terms of caloric intake, protein, and fat (though less so for women than for men), researchers found that most Canadians had significant vitamin and mineral deficiencies, of which a shortage of Vitamin C was usually the most severe.[128] Four large surveys conducted in late 1942 and early 1943 underscored the same conclusion: people were eating enough but not the right kinds of food – at least not as Nutrition Services defined it.[129] Significantly, the researchers also concluded that these dietary deficiencies were unrelated to the war. Lending support to this conclusion was the only wartime study to employ the same methodology in the same sample group over time – one conducted among students at a high school in East York Township, near Toronto – which revealed a marked improvement in the students' diets between 1942 and 1944. The researchers concluded that rationing, which had come into effect since the original survey, had "not caused any deleterious effect upon the food supplies of the group."[130] Granted, some serious deficiencies remained: nearly half of all students had a poor Vitamin C intake – a reflection of the fruit shortage so often alluded to in the WRAC panels. In addition, two-thirds of boys reported fair or poor intake of thiamin (Vitamin B1), a sure sign that they were not eating their vegetables. But these were problems that had existed before the war and would persist afterward – there is no particular evidence that war exacerbated them. In fact, the overall picture derived from the survey is remarkable: diets had improved in almost every instance, apart from a very small but not detrimental decrease in protein for girls, though with 90 percent of girls and 100 percent of boys reporting good or excellent protein intake, the study's authors stated that meat rationing, too, had not had a negative impact on the nutritional quality of their diets.[131] Unfortunately, as this was the only instance of a wartime nutritional study attempting to measure changes over time, no definitive conclusion about the impact of the war on the nutritional quality of Canadian diets is possible. Certainly, there is no evidence that diets worsened and some to suggest that people were eating better than before. Nationwide, the number of reported deaths directly related to nutritional deficiencies, though low in any case, declined still further, from eighty-one in 1940 to forty-two in 1944.[132]

WHILE BYRNE HOPE SANDERS and her executive directors progressively expanded the scope of the Consumer Branch's activities into realms such as nutrition awareness, the branch also continued to perform its original function as a conduit between the WPTB and the Women's Regional Advisory Committees. Members of local WRACs met at their own convenience, and their activities were remarkably spontaneous and decentralized. They reported to the Consumer Branch through their chairpersons but did not answer to it. Inevitably, some jurisdictional confusion resulted, and tension occasionally flared between the WRACs and local women's groups who preferred to report directly to the Consumer Branch. Nor was all harmonious within the committees. Board liaisons reported that, despite their best efforts, many women were poorly informed and had come out with an "axe to grind."[133] This, they said, was especially the case in small towns and farm areas, where accusations that the board was a "racket" and the Consumer Branch no more than a sop for discontent sometimes emerged. WRAC liaisons appointed by local unions or from working-class towns and neighbourhoods often complained that the board favoured big business over the general public.[134] Liaisons in Quebec reported that they faced the additional difficulty of dealing with intruding men who were "generally less willing to accept a woman as head of a government organization."[135]

Nevertheless, WRAC meetings served as an important grassroots forum for asking questions and raising concerns, many of these regarding rationing rules, alleged infractions of the price ceiling, and various shortages. Equally, they served as an opportunity for Consumer Branch volunteers or visiting WPTB officials to clarify board policies. The local WRACs also acted as a catch-all for concerns that were, in some cases, more properly the domain of other government agencies and sometimes not for any government agency at all. One WRAC chair in Saskatchewan reported that her group was assisting members with problems ranging from marital difficulties to community planning to personal finance.[136] Above all, the

WRACs were a forum for the airing of grievances. One frequent complaint in rural areas was that farmers seldom obeyed the price ceiling, professing ignorance of board policies. Other members protested that many merchants flaunted regulations: selling from the back door, openly displaying prices above the ceiling, and threatening to blacklist whistleblowers brandishing their blue books. If so, this was no small threat to the many consumers who depended almost exclusively on local stores for their needs, especially after the imposition of gasoline rationing made longer shopping trips impracticable. It is not clear how often this actually occurred. Any merchants who made such a threat risked very serious punishments, but the fear of earning their displeasure seems to have been real nonetheless, as evidenced by the most frequent complaint voiced by members of the board's enforcement branch: that the majority of grievances it received from consumers were submitted anonymously, which made thorough investigations very difficult.[137] It bears repeating, however, that board investigators believed that many complaints were the result of poor communication. The board permitted thousands of incremental price increases every year, resulting in huge numbers of mistaken objections, while protests regarding the quality of goods were often unrelated to wartime circumstances.

Byrne Hope Sanders personally attended innumerable conferences of WRAC liaisons across the country. In her addresses to them, she praised the women of Canada for their tireless efforts in maintaining the price ceiling and obeying rationing rules. But it is clear that "Mrs. Consumer" often asserted her right to feed and care for her family in whatever manner she felt was appropriate, even if it sometimes involved bending or breaking the rules. Moreover, in recruiting Canada's housewife-consumers to monitor the price ceiling, the Consumer Branch had unknowingly provided them with a means of asserting themselves as consumer activists in what was otherwise a seller's market. As the chair of the Central Ontario WRAC committee noted in 1944, she had received many complaints from retailers about "snooping women."[138] The snoops supported the WPTB and its rules when they seemed to work to their advantage but could be strident critics when they felt that they did not.

IF THE WPTB'S EFFORTS to promote fealty to rationing rules were only a mixed success, Donald Gordon could at least report a resounding victory over prices when the war ended. Throughout the war, the board assured Canadians that the ceiling was holding, but it continued to urge further vigilance lest the system break down. If anything, these efforts intensified as victory in Europe and the Pacific approached. At the Consumer Branch's national conference in March 1945, Gordon warned members that "more and more as the war appears to be ending, there is a breakdown in the belief that wartime controls are necessary [and] we cannot possibly provide the enforcement staff to prevent it."[139] He reminded the members that the defeat of Japan might yet take years and urged Consumer Branch liaisons to carry this message back to the WRACs. Sanders herself repeated the warning at the annual meeting of the Ontario IODE the following month. "There is no reason to assume that the danger of rising prices will cease in Canada with the defeat of Germany," she said, and she advised the members not to "relax and toss their caps in the air on the home front with the approach of V-E day."[140] A year later, she was still urging Canadian women to maintain their vigilance, but as ceiling prices were gradually eased in the two years following the war, prices did, in fact, jump up significantly.[141] Inflation in the year after Japan's surrender was nearly 9 percent. But until then, officials could boast that Canada had the lowest inflation rate of any major combatant. According to the Dominion Bureau of Statistics, the growth in the overall cost of living was just 3.5 percent between December 1941 and the end of the war.[142] Skepticism about the official cost-of-living figures, especially where food prices were concerned, was often expressed in the WRACs and by writers in left-wing and labour publications, but polls and surveys conducted in the last two years of the war did not reveal a general disapproval of the wage and price ceiling; nor did they indicate a particularly widespread belief that the ceiling had failed. One 1944 survey conducted on behalf of the board indicated a remarkable 92 percent approval for the price ceiling as a general policy, with just 7 percent of respondents claiming that it had failed altogether.[143]

In one of many such tributes made late in the war, Gordon, speaking to the Women's Canadian Club in March 1945, praised the women of Canada for their "splendid response" through "habits of orderly buying and support of price controls."[144] Of course, Canadian women also responded splendidly to appeals to take up jobs in such non-traditional vocations as war industries and the armed forces. The story of how civilian women were mobilized into a vast labour army that filled the factories, and were then cast back into the doldrums of an oppressive suburbia after victory, is central to nearly every account of the Canadian home front. Hundreds of thousands of women did join the paid labour force, especially in the last half of the war, and approximately forty thousand joined the armed forces. According to the Department of Labour's estimates, in 1939, there were 575,000 women in Canada's paid labour force. By mid-1944, there were 935,000, and this does not include the hundreds of thousands who worked without wages for family businesses and on family farms.[145] As indispensable as these efforts were, it is also true that for thousands of Canadian women, voluntary participation in organizations such as the National Council of Women, the IODE, the Federated Women's Institutes, and the WRACs formed the core of their war work. In their speeches and pamphlets and radio broadcasts, representatives of women's organizations often dwelled upon the contributions made by the millions of housewife-consumers rather than the tens of thousands who were in the armed forces or in munitions factories. Their contributions to winning the war were buying British, shopping for victory, defending the price ceiling, obeying rationing rules, and sharing information about nutrition.

It is perhaps natural that officials such as Gordon and Byrne Hope Sanders sometimes over-idealized the female consumer's contributions to victory, and overlooked, in public at least, the extent to which many women were also willing to break the rules. They also knew that, despite all the board's efforts to discourage it, consumer spending increased throughout the war. Everyone agreed that the duties of wife, mother, and consumer were critical to victory, but consensus about how those duties ought to be undertaken was often elusive. If a unanimous view on what constituted patriotic consumption existed anywhere, it was probably in the advertising industry. That industry's efforts to advance a rationale for consumerism in wartime will be the subject of the next chapter.

2
Business as Usual
Adworkers and the Coming of War

During the last war many well-meaning but misguided bodies believed the way to win was to start a self-denial campaign. A man was almost ashamed to be seen in a new suit of clothes ... Now, all this has been changed.

– Canadian Printer and Publisher, *January 1940*

Now is the time to live abundantly ... The soldiers away from home want to feel that at home life is pursuing its normal course so that they will come back to a world they know rather than one that is changed.

– Lillian Foster of the Toronto Telegram *to the Women's Advertising Club, Toronto, February 1940*

BY 1939, ADVERTISING had long since colonized – its many detractors might have said "vandalized" – the whole expanse of Canada's cultural landscape, a conspicuous reminder of conspicuous consumption. Canadians encountered advertising in newspapers and magazines, along highways and in theatres, on the radio and on streetcars. "Almost daily the encroachment of the advertiser into the common round becomes more marked," Robert Legget lamented in *Queen's Quarterly*. "The blue sky is befouled with calligraphic smoke; even the pleasant sounds of the street are apt to be drowned by the blatant cacophony of an itinerant loud speaker."[1] But where Legget saw "one of western civilization's wasting sores," most Canadian businesspeople saw incontestable proof of national progress, and few saw it more clearly than the stakeholders in newspapers, magazines, and radio stations.[2] They competed ferociously in the trade papers for the advertising dollars that were their bread and butter. Some of them even confessed that, from a strictly economic point of view, their publications existed for the sole purpose of drawing an audience for advertisers. "I am," *Saturday Night*'s editor B.K. Sandwell confessed, "one of the best-known parasites on the advertising body."[3]

Self-effacing though the joke might have been – Sandwell was speaking to a conference of adworkers – it was essentially correct. *Saturday Night*, like most magazines, relied on advertising for roughly half its revenue. For most newspapers, the figure was closer to 75 percent.[4] In 1939, *Maclean's*, whose 260,000 subscribers made it the country's most widely read magazine, typically ran to eighty pages, thirty or forty of them devoted to advertising.[5] The first wartime issue of *Chatelaine* had over fifty pages of advertising alone. Moreover, these figures emerge from a year when advertising linage, like the economy generally, had not yet fully recovered from the Depression.[6] In addition, modern consumer magazines such as *Chatelaine*, *Mayfair*, and *Canadian Homes and Gardens* had nearly erased the distinction between editorial and advertising content. With feature articles focusing on fashion, automobiles, the latest domestic appliances, and the appropriate decor for the modern home, such magazines existed in large measure to assist readers in making correct choices when buying – as the continuation of shopping by other means. Whenever possible, layout editors complemented feature articles with related advertising, and they had long since mastered the practice of dismembering an article and strewing it throughout a magazine, forcing readers to pick their way through a commercial wilderness to finish it. Writers in the advertising trade press even admonished newspaper editors for failing to fully exploit this technique. "Why are stories always played on page one?" Carrol Lake asked in *Canadian Printer and Publisher*. "The big revenue ads are always inside. Unless the readers are drawn inside the paper, those ads will not be read." In Lake's opinion, the problem with newspapers and magazines was that they featured too much editorial content, even in wartime. "I do not care what the occasion," he wrote in February 1940, "there is no news story that is worth more than a column of reading space today."[7]

Still, Canadians seem to have had an immense appetite for news. In 1940, over 110 English and French daily newspapers, 750 weeklies, and 275 magazines were publishing in Canada. A 1944 poll conducted by the Research and Statistics Administration of the Wartime Prices and Trade Board found that 85 percent of Canadians read the newspaper daily and another 10 percent occasionally.[8] Throughout the Depression, newspaper readership had remained very high, and readership of Canadian magazines had nearly doubled. In part, this was because of a hefty tariff that R.B. Bennett's Conservatives had levied on American magazines, cutting their Canadian circulation by more than two-thirds. When the resurgent Liberals killed the tariff in 1935, the circulation of American magazines bounced back but not at the expense of Canadian publications.[9] In an effort to balance the trade deficit, and also to strike a blow against publications that politicians deemed morally unworthy, Ottawa banned a variety of American comic books and pulp magazines in 1940. More wholesome American mass-market magazines, however, remained a major presence in Canada, rivalling the subscription sales of the most popular homegrown magazines, including *Maclean's* and *National Home Monthly*.[10] In 1940, the *Saturday Evening Post, McCall's,* and *Ladies' Home Journal* boasted very respectable circulations of approximately 150,000 each (these figures would only increase over the course of the war), and the Canadian edition of one American magazine, *Liberty,* had the highest newsstand sales of any magazine in the country.[11] These American magazines tended to be even more advertising-intensive than Canadian ones. A typical issue of *Ladies' Home Journal* would carry over a hundred pages of ads.

Advertising on both sides of the border was attuned to an idealized, modern, middle-class, urban consumer. In 1931, the census had reported for the first time that the majority of Canadians lived in urban areas, and the Depression merely increased the imbalance by accelerating rural flight. By 1941, the urban population outnumbered the rural by more than a million people.[12] This was a historic change. "An incalculable thing has happened to Canada," Bruce Hutchison reflected in *Maclean's*. "The whole historic balance of the country is shifting."[13] And though Canada may have been transforming into a nation of cities, many Canadians retained a romantic attachment to its small towns, farms, and wilderness, and the nation's writers, poets, and painters jumped at every opportunity to get misty-eyed about the waning of the pastoral life. "I am *cheated* of life to please," the poet Lyon Sharman reflected,

> The upholstered god of ease ...
> Who will turn me outdoors into life?
> I envy the lumberman in the wood,
> The cowboy galloping over the widening plain,
> The farmer cutting his grain:
> I covet their hardihood.[14]

Here was a vision of Canada that no adworker could abide: anti-modern, rustic, contemptuous of luxury, atavistic even. It was, of course, a hopelessly sentimental view of rural life, one that discounted the many hardships that often attended life in the nation's small towns and countryside. It did, however, contain a kernel of truth. In 1939, the gospel of "the upholstered god of ease" was only just beginning to reach beyond the cities. Adworkers on the eve of war were confronted with the steadfast fact that most of Canada's debt-laden farmers were not "consumers" in the sense that they used the word. Rural electrification, an enormous and expensive venture, especially in the vast, sparsely populated ranges of the prairies, proceeded at a glacial pace, and most farmers relied on generators for electricity, if they had electricity at all.[15] Consequently, with the exception of automobiles and, to a lesser extent, radios, most farm families owned few of the modern conveniences such as electric stoves, fridges, washing machines, and vacuum cleaners, or even such basic amenities as bathtubs and showers that were already commonplace among urbanites.

But it was for precisely these reasons that farmers became an attractive target to advertisers once farm incomes began to grow by leaps and bounds after the war began: they represented an untapped market. Ronald McEachern, editor of the *Financial Post*, predicted that the whole Canadian market could become "more citified" as national magazines and radio broadcasts penetrated into rural areas and the mobility of modern life increased because of widespread car ownership. What farmers needed, McEachern insisted, was exposure to more advertising. It could persuade them that "mod cons" were indispensable, just as Canadians in the nineteenth century had had to be persuaded that they needed toothpaste.[16]

From the point of view of the advertiser, at least, the differences between urban and rural consumers were soluble. Such was the thinking behind a series of wartime ads placed by the Agricultural Press Association (APA) in the trade papers. Representing such popular farm papers as the *Farmer's Advocate* and the *Canadian Countryman*, the APA assured potential advertisers that the modern farmer (or at least his son) was "no longer a country bumpkin": he was "alert," "well-informed," and "keenly aware," and he wanted the same products as his city cousins.[17] Along similar lines, the venerable *Family Herald and Weekly Star*, whose readership was surpassed in size only by the biggest daily newspapers, predicted that war would bring "a radical improvement in the economic position of Canadian farmers," which it most certainly did.[18] Wartime advertisements in the trade papers depicted farmers receiving salesmen with open arms, or even meeting with bankers on friendly terms.

Of course, print was not the only means by which advertisers appealed to Canadian consumers. Despite the Depression, the number of Canadian homes with radios tripled in the 1930s. By 1941, three-quarters of Canadian households had radios, and in most big cities the figure approached 100 percent.[19] Radios had started to appear in cars, and manufacturers had begun to market portable radios for the cottage or beach. Historian Mary Vipond has revealed that advertising was so integral to the fiscal viability of Canadian broadcasting that even advocates of a public system conceded it to be necessary. Advertising "spots" and sponsored radio programs underwrote the operating costs of private and public stations, and gave local and national advertisers the opportunity to be heard over the din of commercial American broadcasts that the Canadian public found appealing, at least in part, precisely because of the advertising.[20]

In broad strokes, then, Robert Legget was correct: advertising had become a ubiquitous part of Canadian life. A small but highly professional industry sold it, sustained it, and, through innumerable conferences, meetings, and luncheons, continually sought new and better ways to create it.[21] In 1941, some forty-nine advertising agencies operated in Canada, almost all of them in Toronto and Montreal. Some were very small – just a handful of adworkers in a cramped office, clustered around some drawing boards and perhaps a telephone – but collectively they employed nearly twelve hundred people. On average, seven-eighths of advertising in Canadian magazines originated in Canada, as even Canadian subsidiaries of American firms tended to recruit local talent for their advertising needs.[22] In 1938, advertisers in Canada spent over $55 million in magazines and newspapers alone – an enormous sum of money, greater than the nation's military expenditure that year.[23] For their services in 1939, agencies billed their clients $30 million. Advertising was big business. It only got bigger during the war. Billings more than doubled, and by 1945, fifty-six agencies were operating in Canada.[24] In the opinion of critics, the ad industry was too big, generating needless expenses that businesses passed on to the hapless consumer.[25]

Adworkers saw themselves as much more than creative middlemen in a commercial enterprise. In this modern, urban, industrial Canada of the twentieth century, they claimed a special place for themselves – a claim they would renew all the more forcefully when war erupted. As Roland

Marchand, the pioneering historian of American advertising, observes, adworkers in the interwar years saw themselves as the modern world's apostles and more: they were its champions, guardians, and counsellors, too, since they claimed to have unique insight into consumers' anxieties and the cure for them. Above all, they possessed a boundless faith in progress and the capacity of free enterprise, with advertising as its herald, to solve social problems, charting a course to the future without jettisoning the desirable aspects of the past.[26] In Canada, adworkers on the eve of the Second World War breathlessly hailed the country's modernization, with its ever-expanding industrial economy and increasingly bumpkin-free farms. In their view, modern mass society required an informed and highly sophisticated consuming public, much as constitutional government required a highly literate, judicious, and reflective electorate. Advertising was the educational arm of consumer capitalism, and adworkers took up this didactic mission with an almost messianic zeal. Educating consumers was not a job – it was a calling.[27]

Of course, exaggerating the extent of the country's modernity as well as the wants and needs of its consuming public served the business interests of Canadian adworkers. Undoubtedly, many Canadians in 1939 had little to spare after the necessities of food and rent were attended to.[28] As war loomed, millions of Canadians could still be described as poor, and unemployment remained in the double digits.[29] Nonetheless, the advertising industry's preoccupation with the pace of change was not mere puffery. Even apart from the rural-to-urban shift, Canadians in the years after the Great War really had witnessed an extraordinary, bewildering, and often worrying transformation of the country they had known. They could find evidence of industrial and technological progress nearly everywhere they looked. For the poet Verna Loveday Harden, modernity had endowed Canadians with a godlike command of the natural world:

> We have chained the very elements
> to do the bidding of our lofty will;
> the sea is ours; we fly among the clouds;
> the pantings of our mighty engines fill
> the quiet valleys with their brazen voice;
> the heavens and the earth our servants are;
> we owe no servitude to other gods
> who walk as gods ourselves.[30]

The 1930s, it is often forgotten, had been a decade of both depression and modernization. Poor though many Canadians remained, many others were considerably better off in 1939 than they had been ten years earlier. Certainly, many more of them owned cars, radios, electric refrigerators, stoves, telephones, and toasters at the end of the Depression than at its beginning.[31] More than mod cons, these and countless other technological wonders were hard evidence of progress, of the belief that life could be made better through material acquisition. Adworkers credited themselves with having played a central role in bringing about these extraordinary changes. Late in the war, such views were exemplified in a series of trade press advertisements, illustrated by Walter Yarwood, for the *Star Weekly* newspaper. They depicted Canadians enduring a bleak and impoverished life before the advent of modern advertising. In the most Dickensian of them, a grim-faced woman slaves over a wash-basin, her life little more than "a dawn-to-dark battle with the scrub board and the mop, the hand wringer and the old-fashioned kitchen range." But then, the ad declares, "came a great change": *advertising*, "to educate Canadian women in a brand-new school of freedom from back-breaking hard labor."[32] Another ad in the series, illustrating the "clutter of bins and barrels" of nineteenth-century stores, makes the connection more explicit: "And then came advertising" the tag line reads, a "partnership of progress" between manufacturers, retailers, and adworkers that gave all Canadians "a higher standard of healthy living."[33]

Perhaps the most zealous expression of this view appears in *The Story of Advertising in Canada*, a gushingly uncritical account of the Canadian industry's history, written by H.E. Stephenson and Carlton McNaught, employees of Canada's biggest agency, the Montreal-based McKim Limited. Stephenson and McNaught outlined an argument already commonplace in the editorials of the trade press: that advertising had been the prime mover in the dominion's transformation from a colonial-minded, parochial, and agrarian society to an independent, forward-thinking, urban, and commercial nation ready to assume a leading role on the world stage. Canada's economic development since the late nineteenth century, they suggested, had been encouraged, underwritten, and otherwise facilitated by advertising. Advertising had made the availability of goods known to consumers, educated them about the precise nature of a host of modern maladies, and then offered them a range of appealing solutions. In helping consumers to make informed buying decisions, it had generated greater sales for business, provided incentives for technical innovation, expanded production, encouraged economies of scale, rationalized mass production, and resulted in an explosion in the number, type, and quality of consumer goods available. Almost the entire expansion of the Canadian economy and the nation's standard of living in the prior fifty years owed itself to advertising, they claimed. When the economy had suffered, advertising prevented its further deterioration. More recovery was prevented only by the interference of misguided politicians whose social welfare policies had increased tax burdens and reduced consumer purchasing power.[34]

Such views were not unique to adworkers, of course. With only slightly less conviction, they were widely held throughout the business community. Writing in the University of Toronto's *Commerce Journal*, political economist Samuel Stocking claimed that Canada's standard of living owed more to advertising than to anything else, with the possible exception of "steam, gasoline, and electric power" and that "advertising is as basic to freedom of enterprise ... as freedom of speech is to democracy."[35] Even Harold Innis, who harboured grave concerns about the influence that profit-driven media would have on the free exchange of information, suggested that in securing the financial well-being of newspapers, advertising had played an essential role in the expansion of the free press in North America. He worried that fascism loomed if advertisers abandoned newspapers for the more ephemeral medium of radio.[36]

In article after article in the trade press, adworkers and marketing experts returned to these themes. Advertising, they insisted, was far more than an informational service that businesses offered to consumers. In preserving the independence of the press and in playing a key role in securing the material prosperity of the nation, it was, as one adworker boasted, "the spark plug of democracy."[37] It actually extended the freedoms customarily associated with political democracy by granting the consumer sovereignty in the marketplace: the economy itself functioned democratically – consumers "voted" with their pocketbooks. Advertising performed the vital function of providing Canadians with the knowledge they needed to make educated decisions in their selection of goods, just as newspapers gave them the information they needed to be effective citizens.[38] Speaking to the Advertising and Sales Club of Toronto in early 1940, ad executive E.W. Reynolds put it this way: "When Mrs. Jones is shopping, she is not buying in a wilderness of products ... She shops with standards in mind. Mrs. Jones is an educated buyer and the cost of that education has been paid by advertising as an integral part of modern business."[39] *Marketing*'s John Kirkwood went further, arguing that if any business was to be viewed with suspicion, it was the one that did *not* advertise. Those that did were putting their wares on display for all to see, in the imaginary shop window of advertising. What, Kirkwood wondered, did non-advertisers have to hide?[40]

Of course, hyperbole of this sort engendered negative responses. Although Canadian adworkers in the late 1930s and early 1940s were certainly not reading the critical Marxism produced by the Frankfurt School, they did sometimes refer contemptuously and condescendingly to "university professors," identifying them as the source of a body of intellectual opinion that was critical of the mass consumer society.[41] Moreover, they saw fit to defend themselves on many occasions from the related although less theoretically sophisticated argument that advertisers were the modern equivalent of travelling hucksters and snake-oil salesmen, foisting worthless goods on a hapless and gullible public. Philip Spencer articulated this view in a 1940 article for the *Canadian Forum:* "In only a few years whole nations have taken to smelling their armpits and underwear suspiciously – they're B.O. conscious. We decry this. We laugh at it. Yet this advertising-created incubus drives millions of people to the soap counter and the deodorant counter."[42]

On the contrary, adworkers insisted, no chicanery was at work, only honest persuasion in the consumer's best interests. They pointed with pride to their own efforts to "clean up" the industry in the form of self-regulation and support for "truth in advertising" legislation that had made it illegal knowingly to publish false claims in ad copy.[43] Indeed, the House of Commons had broadened portions of the Criminal Code pertaining to fraudulent advertising in 1939 and had done so with the support of the industry, although *Canadian Printer and Publisher* noted with some amusement that the regulations applied only to commercial advertising – false promises made in political advertising were exempt from prosecution. "Nobody believes them anyway," was the editors' wry observation.[44]

Canadian adworkers had viewed the ascendancy of the New Deal in the United States with great concern, noting that the American advertising industry had been assailed through the 1930s by New Dealers who demanded accountability for the sometimes extravagant claims made by the industry.[45] "Business in the United States has been very much on the defensive," a *Canadian Advertising* writer observed in 1939. "It has been under attack by the government."[46] He cautioned Canadian adworkers that they should promote the virtues of free enterprise at every opportunity in their own self-defence. Fortunately, the consumer movement, another observer stated, had thus far "cut little ice" in Canada.[47] Apart from regulations concerning alcohol advertising, which varied from province to province, and federal legislation regarding "truth in advertising," Canadian adworkers operated under fewer constraints than their American counterparts.[48] What troubled adworkers in late 1939 and early 1940 was that the outbreak of war would vastly expand the government's regulatory powers – in the wrong hands (the CCF, for instance), these powers could spell doom for the industry.

Another worry was a body of opinion *within* the business community, which held that most advertising was a needless expense passed on to the consumer. Lively debate about the efficacy of advertising and whether it was a positive investment for business appeared in such journals of opinion as *Queen's Quarterly, Dalhousie Review,* and *Canadian Forum*.[49] "Many higher executives ... still regard advertising as a necessary evil, if not a plain out-and-out evil," the editors of *Canadian Advertising* had noted in July 1939.[50] Indeed, a figure no less august than Henry Ford himself had for many years harboured immense suspicions about the utility of advertising.[51] For many in the old generation of business leaders, a man's personal success had always depended on sobriety and hard work, industriousness and thrift, and above all a willingness to delay gratification. In 1937, Alfred P. Sloan, the outgoing president of General Motors, described the profit motivation not as a means to material comfort, but as an incentive for greater accomplishment. "The anxieties, responsibilities, the necessity of living the life of the cause rather than one's own life could not possibly be compensated for in any material way," he said.[52] But what would become of such values if the new consumer ethos emphasized the soft pleasures in life, the dreaded "upholstered god of ease" that Sharman sought to escape, with its gospel of leisure and immediate self-gratification underwritten by credit buying at the expense of long-term security? More to the point, how could a society dispossessed of its vigour and self-reliance – made indolent even – by the comforts of mass consumerism confront an enemy as cruel and determined as Nazi Germany?

Reflecting on the occasion of the first Christmas of the Second World War, *Marketing* columnist John Kirkwood wrote of humanity's "natural tendency to be slothful – to settle down in ignoble content." Modern life and its conveniences could free people from toil and drudgery, but he feared that, freed from strife, struggle, and competition altogether, Canadians might "indulge their gross nature" like the "illiterate peoples of the world." For Kirkwood, sustained advertising was the solution to this problem. It would ensure that people would never be content with "satisfying existing wants." Rather, it would appeal to Canadians' "higher nature" – the aspiration for a better life that was possessed only by literate people – uncovering "their unperceived and unfelt wants" for "finer things of social life."[53] Kirkwood believed that this aspiration for "finer things" would most often be expressed in material terms: a desire for better homes, better cars, better clothes, and the like. But only through the acquisition of material comfort would it be possible to actualize non-material desires for "the highest culture" and "spiritualism in the highest degree." All this, of course, was attainable only if business were free to elevate the standard of living without the encumbrance of government regulation. Since the aspirations of civilized people are infinite, Kirkwood reasoned, they could never be exhausted, provided that advertisers continued to incite desire "to the point where possession becomes one's purpose." Hence, there was no danger that people would slip into the complacency and frivolity that others so feared. Rather, advertising would help people achieve material, moral, and spiritual self-actualization; it would build national prosperity; it would continue to ensure that the press could perform its vital role of safeguarding the free exchange of information – and it would help to win the war.[54] In the world of advertising, all things were possible.

Such high-minded idealism, however, sat uneasily next to the more mundane preoccupations of the ads themselves. In April 1940, *Marketing* carried a cautionary story about a Spanish woman who had toured Canada and the United States shortly before the war. On the crossing from Europe, she confessed certain worries to another passenger. What would North Americans be like? Having read the advertising in their magazines, she had concluded that they would be unendurable – malodorous, foul-breathed, constipated, and physically infirm.[55] If advertising were to be believed – and of course adworkers insisted that it was – the Spanish woman had made a reasonable supposition. Colgate, for instance, warned that "76 percent of all people over the age of 17 have bad breath."[56] Lifebuoy Soap ads included "scientific facts about 'b.o.,'" such as the "fact" that the human body's 2 to 3 million sweat glands, working overtime in the fast-paced modern world, generated "1 to 3 pints of perspiration *daily.*"[57] Lysol warned that overburdened housewives often neglected feminine hygiene to the detriment of their marriages. In advertising, modern life seemed fraught with such stresses and was utterly unforgiving toward those who failed to attend to them. But it also offered the educated consumer solutions to such anxieties, including, as we shall see, those brought on by the war itself.

By 1939, national advertisers had long since abandoned the purely "informational" format of nineteenth- and early-twentieth-century ads that had straightforwardly described the physical properties of goods and told readers where they could buy them, an approach sometimes referred to as "salesmanship in print."[58] As has often been observed, a very different kind of advertising had emerged by the 1920s, one that aimed to exploit non-material motivations for consumption. Adworkers sought to bring consumer goods alive by vesting them with social significance not directly or necessarily related to the actual properties of the commodities themselves.[59] In advertising, commodities became a passport into a world where modern consumers' anxieties about personal health (and the health of their families), social status, household and workplace responsibilities, and even love and romance could be resolved through consumption.[60] Oftentimes, the commodity itself played a minor role in advertising, compared to what it promised. Automobiles provided not just efficient transportation but fun, freedom, and social recognition; appliances did not just relieve the drudgery of housework but promised actual female emancipation; personal hygiene products – the particular obsession of 1930s advertising, as the Spanish traveller noticed – were essential ingredients in courtship, romance, marriage, successful friendships, business relations, and so on.

Roland Marchand has described how advertising helped acculturate early-twentieth-century Americans to the urban, industrial, and technological society in which they suddenly found themselves and sought to assuage their apprehension about the rapidly emerging mass society.[61] What advertising promised Canadians, wherever they lived, was a better future through consumption, but it almost never came across as encouraging frivolity, much less hedonism, as some of its critics contended. Indeed, what strikes the modern reader most forcefully about the period's advertising is its gravity. It occasionally featured comical characters, but the intentionally funny or self-mocking ads so familiar to audiences in the early twenty-first century were unheard of in the 1930s and '40s. Advertising was a serious business. Advertised products addressed social matters of real importance – or at least adworkers would have people believe that they were. It heralded a more efficient, less burdensome, and in short, a more modern way of living. As Marchand observes, we may glibly dismiss the solutions proposed by advertising for modern problems, but we should not be so dismissive of the problems themselves or the desire to solve them.

Overwhelmingly, women were the intended audience for advertising. As women took on a greater range of responsibilities in the coming war, an even greater percentage of ads would be targeted toward them. Perhaps this was why they were somewhat better represented in the advertising profession than in most others. It was hoped that they could offer some insight into the most unpredictable aspect of the market, the female shopper herself, whose nature often remained elusive. Many male adworkers conceived of women as fundamentally irrational and emotionally impulsive, capable of making sensible choices only if properly persuaded to do so. In the world of advertising, marital breakdown, unruly children, and disorganized homes were almost invariably the fault of a woman's poor or uninformed buying decisions.

Broadly speaking, such was the nature of national advertising in Canada and the philosophy of Canadian adworkers when war began in September 1939. But a further comment must be made about the relationship between the Canadian and American advertising industry, a relationship that preoccupied writers in the trade press. Canadian adworkers had always had an attenuated relationship with their American counterparts, viewing them as unwelcome competitors when American agencies expanded operations into Canada but also as a source of creative inspiration.[62] In the interwar years, Canadian agencies had followed in the wake of American innovation, borrowing ("plagiarizing" was the indelicate word used by advertising executive Thornton Purkis) concepts Americans had adapted, often rather haphazardly, from applied psychology and the new "science" of market research.[63] At a 1940 industry conference in Atlantic City, B.W. Keightly, an ad manager of Canadian Industries Limited, told the American audience that Canadian adworkers were indebted "beyond all words" to them for their "inspiration and example, precept and practice."[64] It was this creative debt that led Harold Innis to complain about the comparative "immaturity" of Canadian adworkers. But adworkers responded that their creative genius was in transposing American innovations to the vagaries of the Canadian market and its buying public. Canadian and American markets, a writer in *Canadian Advertising* mused, are like ham and eggs: "generally and advantageously associated ... But they are hardly the same thing."[65]

In some respects, Canadian adworkers had a tendency to exaggerate the differences between the two markets. In reality, most Canadian consumers who could afford it wanted the same things that Americans did.

After all, they read many of the same magazines, drove the same cars, drank the same sodas, and even listened to many of the same radio programs. But the war, when it came, gave greater credibility to adworkers' claims about the uniqueness of the Canadian market. War really did effect changes in the Canadian marketplace, and Canadian consumers felt its influence, both good and bad, to a greater extent than Americans did until they too were at war. In addition, the war forced Canadian adworkers to adapt and innovate for themselves. The United States was not yet involved, so there were no American models of war-related advertising to follow, and advertising from the Great War was of another age, offering adworkers little in the way of inspiration or direction.[66] Canadian adworkers would have to apply their own talents to the unique circumstances of this strange new war, where amid growing patriotic clamour, very little actual sacrifice was made during its first two years.

Throughout late 1939 and 1940, "business as usual" and "carry on" were the rallying cries of the business community – though many retailers noted with satisfaction that running in the black for a change was quite unusual indeed. What the terms really meant was that the health of the nation depended on continuing business practices without fear. *Marketing* reminded its readers that panic had engulfed retailers and the buying public in August 1914.[67] In those uncertain times, the editors pointed out, many firms had cancelled their advertising, and long-term plans were shelved. Consequently, the public forgot about businesses that failed to advertise during the Great War, the editor of *Canadian Advertising* warned, and those firms never regained lost buyers.[68] When national advertising linage experienced a slump in September 1939, with fewer ads placed and many pulled at the last minute, industry leaders were galvanized with renewed purpose. Speaking to the Montreal Advertising and Sales Club in October, Spalding Black, of Canadian Industries Limited, proposed a wartime agenda for the industry. Advertising would be the home front equivalent of the leaflet raids the RAF was now conducting over Germany, only with the goal of bolstering home front morale. Its most immediate task was to allay fears, to avert panic buying of the kind being reported in the press, and to promote economic stability by assuring consumers that there was no imminent danger of shortages.[69] Furthermore, the editors of *Canadian Advertising* hoped, Canada's role in the war would, in keeping with the King government's promises, favour materiel over manpower. With the techniques of scientific mass persuasion at their disposal, adworkers could assuage the consuming public's anxieties, bolster retail sales, and strengthen the whole economy for the coming struggle. Advertising could therefore assume the vital role of "maintaining the regular business life of the country."[70] Moreover, if life on the home front were attended by uncertainty and the potential for widespread economic disruption, it was also rife with opportunities for forward-looking adworkers to seize and exploit – and they saw no contradiction between their own economic interests and those of the nation as a whole. Over the next year, a succession of articles in the trade press reiterated the same argument. In peacetime, advertising had brought prosperity. In wartime, it would defend it.

Adworkers predicted that once the initial shock of war had worn off, the demand for advertising would greatly intensify, because war meant higher employment, increased wages, and growing consumer demand. But in the early months of the war, they also shared a virtual consensus that ads should not refer directly to it. *Marketing* quoted one senior ad executive who said, "In not one single case are any of our clients planning any copy theme that ties us with the war or war activities." Another remarked, inaccurately, that even British advertisers had rejected war themes as unduly pessimistic.[71] Byrne Hope Sanders, while still editor of *Chatelaine*, made the same observation to the Women's Advertising Club of Toronto. "Advertisers," she said, "are not going to employ patriotic appeals of war to sell their products."[72] Within a year, they would be doing precisely that, but during the interregnum between the fall of Poland and the Battle of Britain, the most striking fact about advertising in *Maclean's* and other national magazines in Canada is the almost total absence of any reference to the war (see Figure 2.1). On occasion, an oblique or mild metaphorical reference did appear. Nabob Coffee promised buyers "no war profiteering" in its prices; Steeplechase Cigarettes assured customers that its product would retain its "pre-war quality," which is to say, the same quality of three weeks earlier; but direct, thoroughgoing "war copy" was not to be found.[73] In this, national advertisers reflected the "business-as-usual" consensus, although the appearance of an ad for Italian vacations in the 15 September 1939 issue of *Maclean's* was probably a reflection of press deadlines rather than the tourism industry's determination to "carry on" as if the war had never begun.

A combination of circumstances made the business-as-usual ethos more tenable than it might otherwise have been: The King administration's initial commitment to a war of limited liability, the eight-month period

FIGURE 2.1   The urge to avoid "war copy" in the first year of the war was so great that it sometimes led to embarrassing juxtapositions between advertising and world events. This DeSoto ad was published in March 1940, the month before Germany launched its spring offensives that overran much of northern and western Europe. | "Enjoy Life!" *Maclean's*, 1 March 1940, 25.

of virtual non-aggression that the British press dubbed "the sitzkrieg" and the public called the phony war, and the general growth in economic prosperity that coincided with the beginning of the war. Unemployment fell, retail sales went up, and a year-end poll conducted by *Marketing* found that nearly 40 percent of advertisers planned increased ad budgets, citing consumers' greater purchasing power; only 5 percent of advertisers intended to spend less in 1940 (and those were mainly exporters whose foreign markets had been cut off by the war).[74]

The shattering defeat of Allied arms in the summer of 1940 marked the beginning of a transformation in advertising copy and artwork. Although another year or more would pass before the majority of ads referred to the war directly, some began to display the bellicose language of the era. "Enlist for the war on germs" (no accidental pun, to be sure) was Lysol's new message.[75] Life Savers gave its rather cloying comic-strip ads of the pre-war period, which depicted young lovers brought together by their mutual affection for the mints, a more contemporary feel by dressing the young man in uniform. So many ads followed suit that regulations emerged banning the use of Canadian military uniforms for commercial advertising purposes. Artists stayed within the limits of the law by drawing uniforms inexactly.[76] Other advertisers focused on the material needs of soldiers, urging consumers to do their patriotic duty by buying practical gifts for their loved ones in uniform. The first explicitly war-themed ad to debut in *Maclean's*, a very small appeal for a balm called "Mentholatum," appeared on 15 August 1940, nearly a year after the war began. It promised relief in some unspecified fashion for "dozens of minor ailments," including "head-colds, sunburn, bruises, sprains and cuts, burns and scalds, tired and aching feet and other conditions."[77] A decidedly more sophisticated full-page ad for Parker Pens appeared a month later, promoting the Parker Active Service Set Pen and Pencil, designed to meet uniform regulations, and encouraging the boys overseas to write more often to their families and sweethearts (see Figure 2.2).[78] Ronson simultaneously marketed pocket lighters for soldiers and sailors as well as table lighters for household use.[79]

As we have seen, over the course of 1941, growing purchasing power and retail sales, coupled with the accelerating war effort and a diminishing availability of many goods, led King's government to adopt increasingly intrusive regulatory measures to stave off inflation. It was therefore a year in which the business-as-usual ethic was subjected to serious pressure. Free-market evangelists such as John Kirkwood continued to preach the

FIGURE 2.2   The earliest war-themed ads recognized that soldiers were a potential market for useful items and encouraged patriotic civilians to buy for them. Such ads display, in embryo form, one of the most enduring themes of wartime advertising: that carefully considered buying was a patriotic contribution to the war effort. | "Get Them to Write Often," *Maclean's*, 15 September 1940, 4.

"carry on" gospel, but throughout most of the advertising industry, this was a period of coping and adjustment as the government demanded progressively greater sacrifices and planned the mobilization of the economy for a protracted military struggle. Before the House of Commons in late February, C.D. Howe, the all-powerful minister of the Department of Munitions and Supply, actually accused the *Financial Post* of being "the number one saboteur of Canada" for its consistent criticism of the government's industrial mobilization plans. Without mentioning their names, Howe implied that many other business publications were guilty of the same.[80] The *Financial Post* was owned by John Bayne Maclean's Maclean Publishing Company, as were the majority of the nation's trade papers and *Maclean's* itself. These organs of opinion greeted Howe's comments with widespread derision (nowhere more strenuously than in the pages of *Maclean's*, whose editors, without naming Howe, stated that if anyone were guilty of sabotage it was "the type of official who fawns, alibis, wangles, and wheedles to hold a job he's not competent to fill"), but they were nonetheless a clear sign that the King administration was losing patience with the business-as-usual approach.[81]

Even as full employment returned and retail sales grew, then, the advertising industry began seriously to discuss whether the war might actually imperil the existence of national advertising for commercial purposes.[82] Already the government had closed certain advertising-related tax loopholes. Confronted with excess profit taxes, many businesses had planned to expand their advertising budgets, incurring an additional tax-deductible business expense. In January, however, the Dominion Income Tax Department had announced that no deductions would be permitted for "unwarranted" advertising increases.[83] Were other regulations coming? Certainly, the trade press paid a great deal of attention to the enormous constraints under which the British advertising industry operated and wondered what the future might bring for Canadian firms.[84]

There were other troubling questions as well. Should firms that had converted to military production continue to advertise? Could the purchase of luxury goods be justified when the boys overseas were risking their lives and all Europe endured the agony of the Nazi jackboot? Was commercial advertising patriotic when the government was increasingly urging Canadians to plough their earnings into Victory Bonds? Ironically, in the industry's view, the most immediate peril was the fact that the war had put many retailers in such a favourable position. In a seller's market, where the biggest problem was not failing to sell but failing to have enough to sell, would they conclude that advertising was unnecessary? At conferences, seminars, meetings, luncheons, and in countless articles published in the industry's trade journals, the question of continuing to advertise was discussed – at least rhetorically. Of course, the only possible answer was "yes" – the industry was not about to suspend operations voluntarily. But these discussions also betrayed a realization on the part of adworkers that the consumer economy, however strong it might seem at the moment, was about to undergo radical changes to which advertising would have to adapt creatively.[85] The key to survival would be to adapt pre-war justifications for advertising to wartime circumstances. Surely in this time of crisis, industry leaders argued, consumers needed more guidance than ever in making appropriate buying decisions.

One example was John Kirkwood's interpretation of the government's Victory Bond slogan "serve by saving." The slogan was, Kirkwood claimed, a rallying call for consumers to spend *more*. Since saving more necessarily meant earning more, logic suggested that the sources of employment for so many Canadians – manufacturing, advertising, distributing, selling, or servicing merchandise – would have to operate on a progressively more profitable basis. To induce the public to buy, retailers to stay in business, and manufacturers to keep producing consumer goods, advertising budgets and expenditures would need to be increased. "More pressure," he wrote in March 1941, "must be applied to consumers to buy foods and clothing, furniture and furnishings ... luxury and indulgence products."[86] Although this reasoning certainly fell into the category of creative adaptation, it soon became less tenable. Over the course of the year, as the demands of the war effort expanded, the conversion of industrial capacity to military production, and more critically, the strategic allocation of raw materials for military needs, resulted in progressively deeper cuts into the production of consumer durables and shortages of many other goods as well (on this, see Chapter 5).

The industry's realization that it could no longer afford to be blasé about the war was reflected in further changes to advertising design. For example, in the autumn of 1941, automotive ads began to allude to the "timeless" styling and "guaranteed durability" of the 1942 models, a clear reference to the possibility that one's new car might have to last for a long time indeed.[87] War-themed ads became more frequent and patriotic appeals more explicit. Ads for useful gifts for soldiers on active duty became commonplace. Others began to allude to the war-related needs of civilians on the home front. Owning a Sparton brand radio-phonograph, for instance, would keep you informed and "help you 'do your bit' entertaining the service boys."[88] Frigidaire ads emphasized the savings to families who owned an electric refrigerator: $10.70 monthly, according to "a survey of 58,590 women." Although appealing to economy was an old technique, the suggestion that the savings could be ploughed into Victory Bonds was not – the bottom corner of the ad featured the new slogan "Serve by Saving: Buy War Savings Certificates." Clearly, the purchase of a Frigidaire would serve the interests of the consumer and the war effort simultaneously.[89]

Increasingly, ads for Victory Bonds and other kinds of war savings (which were often produced by the same agencies that generated commercial ads) began to demand not mere thriftiness from Canadians but outright sacrifice. Probably the most strident example to date appeared late in November 1941. It quoted Kipling's 1914 poem "For All We Have and Are," written after the catastrophic Battle of Mons: "No easy hope ... shall bring us to our goal / but iron sacrifice / of body, will, and soul." In case anyone missed the point, the ad stated, "All the dollars Canadians can spare are not yet in the fight. Some are spending less, but many are not. Many have not yet faced the need for sacrifice – for self-denial ... Ours is the softest job of all, and yet we are slacking in it."[90] Such ads, issued by a range of government agencies, were to become routine in 1942, but this explicit demand to end frivolous consumer spending was novel. "Serve by saving" had been a mild exhortation compared to the new one: "*Sacrifice* to buy more War Savings Certificates."

In the face of such pressures, could commercial advertising carry on? What some critics had seen as a wasteful business expenditure, a needless cost passed on to the consumer, and a source of sloth and indolence in peacetime became, in their eyes, a threat to national survival in wartime. Even Samuel Stocking of the University of Toronto, a pro-advertising evangelist in the mould of John Kirkwood, proposed that advertising ought to be placed at the government's disposal for the duration of the war.[91] Speaking in May at the conference of the National Association of Industrial Advertisers, B.K. Sandwell said that, in wartime, advertising could justify its continued existence only if it somehow advanced the war effort.[92]

It was about to get its chance. On Monday, 1 December 1941, the price ceiling was introduced. That Sunday, 7 December, was Pearl Harbor. "Business as usual" was over.

3
Finding a Place for Wartime Advertising

Our readers will require no argument to convince them of the unpardonable waste that continued advertising is causing, waste that compares so strikingly with the sacrifices being made by most of the citizens of this land.

– "Advertising and the War," Canadian Forum, October 1942

They, more than any others tell us how to live, how to get from life its supreme possibilities, how to attain the altitudes of our dreaming. Our national advertisers are not just profit-chasers and fortune hunters; they are, in all truth, civilizers.

– John Kirkwood, Marketing, December 1942

BUSINESS AS USUAL was over. Or was it? In August 1941, Samuel Stocking noted in the *Canadian Journal of Economics and Political Science* that some observers of the Canadian wartime economy were arguing, not without justification, that "Canadian consumers are tending to defeat the war effort by their insistence on buying more and more of these luxury items instead of putting their money in war savings. Others, seeing somewhat the same result, place the blame on businessmen, and say that their pleas for 'business as usual' really mean 'twice as much business as usual.'"[1] The following month, Paul Garrett, director of marketing for General Motors, proposed that the business community, faced with rising criticism and growing pressure of civilian production, needed "something better and more vigorous" than its customary "business as usual" rhetoric. "We need business as *un*usual," he said.[2]

By January 1942, it was obvious that business was going to be unusual regardless of what businesspeople wanted. Not only had the price ceiling descended – accompanied by dread warnings from the Wartime Prices and Trade Board (WPTB) about the calamity that would follow if it failed – but rationing, it seemed, could not be far off.[3] From the perspective of many Canadian consumers, the most significant change was the suspension of the production of durables such as radios, toasters, vacuum cleaners, stoves, refrigerators, and above all passenger cars. Since the Great War, these things had become an indispensable part of life for millions of Canadians. Suddenly, the appliance-department shelves in Eaton's, Simpson's, and the Hudson's Bay Company were empty, and strict regulations governed the sale of the few remaining passenger cars. In the wake of these changes, the quantity of commercial advertising linage in national magazines began to drop. In March 1940, automotive ads alone had accounted for a third of the advertising linage in *Maclean's*. In March 1942, there were no automotive ads at all.

A sense of crisis seized the nation's adworkers. In September 1939, they had taken up the mantle of "business as usual" with evangelical zeal, believing that the key to victory lay in economic prosperity, just as they believed that free enterprise, with advertising as its herald, had been the key to the nation's economic and cultural development since Confederation. But grandiose posturing of this kind had a tendency to obscure the more humdrum fact that advertising's real job was to move merchandise, and now adworkers were faced with the possibility that there would be far less merchandise to move. What place for advertising then? By 1942, the industry's leaders could no longer answer this question with the steady confidence that they had exhibited at the beginning of the war. In January of that year, *Marketing* published the results of a survey finding that only one advertiser in nine planned to increase advertising budgets in 1942, whereas a quarter planned to reduce them. "Our agency goes into 1942 with its automobile advertising, silk stocking advertising, [and] partial payment advertising down to the irreducible minimum," was one anonymous agency owner's response.[4] "I for one would hesitate even to hazard a guess as to what is going to happen to advertising in 1942," another remarked. "Frankly, I am very much afraid."[5] Such fears were only compounded by rumours that the government intended to restrict or even order a stop to commercial advertising.[6] *Saturday Night*'s P.M. Richards put the matter bluntly: "The government thinks there is too much advertising being done, and it intends to curtail it."[7]

A number of the industry's free-market ideologues remained unflappable, however, believing that if the Depression had demonstrated anything, it was that opportunity attended upheaval for professionals savvy enough to seize it. *Marketing*'s John Kirkwood, as might be expected, quoted approvingly from an advertisement that took umbrage with pessimists who pitied the 1942 New Year's babies: "Why should you feel sorry for that kid? Because he was born into a world that seems to be tumbling about his head? That's a lot of nonsense ... That kid is born into the greatest opportunity a fresh crop of humans ever faced!"[8] Later that year, Maurice Brown of the Cockfield, Brown Agency echoed Kirkwood's optimistic appraisal of the situation. Speaking at a conference of the Canadian Association of Advertisers, he said,

> It is among the mass of people where a great morale-building job needs to be done, and every day makes this urgently more necessary. Thousands upon thousands of Canadians are now drawing, what by comparison with past earnings is "big money," and inasmuch as the tax burden does not yet rest heavily upon them, the temptation is to spend freely.[9]

Likewise, the editors of *Canadian Advertising* sought to assure their readers that "our Dominion Government had recognized advertising as a war weapon ... Legitimate business need have no fear."[10] Nevertheless, the industry seems to have grappled with unease and uncertainty throughout the year.

The optimists were undeniably right about at least one thing. Most Canadians had more money than ever, even if they had less to spend it on – the very fact that had compelled the government to introduce the price ceiling. By 1942, per capita disposable incomes had grown more than 40 percent in real terms since the beginning of the war. For advertisers, it was simply a question of getting Canadians to spend it on something.[11] Here, the experience of radio advertisers proved instructive. Consumer durables had seldom been advertised on the radio, the assumption being that listeners would not buy big ticket items that they could not actually see. Consequently, radio broadcasters barely perceived the loss of ads for consumer durables and carried on with the ads that had always been their mainstay: for food, pharmaceuticals, tobacco, soap, and cleaning products. By early 1942, radio advertising revenues were at an all-time high.[12] Moreover, as Glen Bannerman, president of the Canadian Association of Broadcasters, observed in February 1942, radio advertisers had a new and wealthy client: the Canadian government, which had at last "recognized [radio] as an advertising medium worthy of being paid for its services along with other media." Indeed, Bannerman observed, "prior to 1941 practically no Government advertising campaign took broadcasting into consideration, now practically no Government advertising campaign is planned *without* taking broadcasting into consideration."[13] Print adworkers, too, found that the government had become an important client. By mid-year, newspapers and magazines had begun to explode with recruiting, fundraising, and informational ads placed by a dozen federal government agencies. If the apostles of small government and free markets objected, they kept their own counsel.

The circumstances facing the advertising industry in early 1942 were therefore not nearly as bad as many adworkers feared. Still, most of them realized that their stock answers from 1939 to questions about advertising's place in wartime were no longer tenable – at least not in their original form. The whole country was mobilizing for war on a gigantic scale, and Ottawa was insisting in the most emphatic ways that consumer spending must be curtailed in favour of war savings. Already, the cost of the war had exceeded almost everyone's expectations. In 1941, military expenditure totalled $1.3 billion, nearly forty times what it had been in 1938. In 1942, it would be twice that – more money than had been spent on the armed forces in all the years since Confederation put together. In 1943, it doubled again.[14] Modern war was staggeringly expensive, and no one could predict what further sacrifices the government might compel from Canadians to pay for it.

Ottawa's increasingly strident and even accusatory propaganda underscored the unease felt by many adworkers. In 1940 and for most of 1941, the WPTB and other agencies had been content with such comparatively placid slogans as "serve by saving." Suddenly in 1942, they began accusing spendthrift consumers of outright treason, a hard line adopted in the face of retail sales that continued to grow (see Figure 3.1). In May 1942, sales were nearly 35 percent higher than they had been in the corresponding month two years earlier.[15]

Propaganda such as this often appeared in consumer magazines alongside earnest editorials about the necessity for thrift, and amid acres of commercial advertising, too. We do not know what magazine readers thought about the juxtaposition of ads for non-essential commodities with propaganda accusing frivolous consumers of aiding Hitler, but the community of adworkers was certainly aware that contradictions such as these were potentially very embarrassing. The fear of accusations of unpatriotic

Figure 3.1 Government propaganda urged Canadians to plough their earnings into Victory Bonds, and they did. But retail spending continued to increase in spite of shortages and rationing. With the return of full employment, most Canadians had enough money to spend and save at the same time. | "Go On, Spend It ... What's the Difference?" *Maclean's*, 1 July 1942, 28.

wastefulness was palpable throughout the trade press. "After the war," a typical warning in *Canadian Advertising* read, "when pent-up emotions are released, the cry 'profiteering' will again be raised, and business will be called upon to defend itself against unjustified accusations."[16] Facing a government whose position was that "business as usual" was over and that needless consumerism was the equivalent of sabotage, adworkers were pressured to find new ways to justify the continued existence of commercial advertising. Negotiating the narrow channel between legitimate non-military consumption and what their critics called unpatriotic selfishness would preoccupy adworkers for the remainder of the war.

Commercial and corporate advertising had offered little comment on the war in its first year and had only just started to in its second, but war-themed advertising was routine by mid-1942. In the last half of the war, hardly any national advertisement failed to refer to it in some way. Some commentators noted that a perceptible change in ad copy had begun almost immediately after the price ceiling was established in December 1941. "Ad writers live in a topsy-turvy world," *Business Week* mused in January 1942. "So much has the world played havoc with the laws of time and space that copywriters now turn out such eye-arresters as '10 Ways to Avoid Buying New Tires' or 'If Your Electric Washer Will Do, Don't Buy Our New Model.'"[17] The editors of *Marketing* envisioned "thirty ways" that adworkers might rescue their industry. Some of these, such as "improve and maintain morale," were familiar from the early years of the war. Others were new, reflecting the rapidly changing circumstances. Advertising could, for instance, "explain shortages in stores" and, as *Business Week* observed, sometimes even "ask consumers not to buy," or at least postpone, nonessential purchases for later.[18] For the remainder of the war, the task before Canada's adworkers was to convert a myriad of wartime anxieties into essential rationales for consumption. Although they often lacked the artful elegance of their American colleagues, for whom the tradition of producing visually arresting ads was deeply rooted in the leading agencies, their ads, starkly utilitarian though they tended to be, were ingeniously conceived in their own right.[19] Enthusiastically, whole-heartedly, and at times no doubt cynically, they went about their task. They readily co-opted the new patriotic watchwords of conservation, thrift, and self-denial, even though their underlying message often flatly contradicted the official line. Beneath the patriotic veneer, the real agenda was what it had always been: to move merchandise. Recruiting posters, Victory Bond ads, and all manner of patriotic propaganda increasingly employed the discourses of sacrifice that Canadians were familiar with from the Great War and the long period of national mourning that had followed it. Commercial advertisers often had very different ideas about what constituted "sacrifice," but they did not deny its centrality to winning the struggle against the Axis. On the contrary, with innumerable variations, hundreds of ads claimed that, under the correct circumstances, buying a product was neither wastefulness nor extravagance: it was a contribution – perhaps even a sacrifice – made by consumers on behalf of the war effort. Since curtailing consumer spending was one plank in the WPTB's anti-inflation program, and given the chorus of critics alleging that Canadians did not know the meaning of sacrifice and were not really "in the fight," arguing that their particular product was an exception to the general rule of conservation, thrift, and self-denial was the only strategy open to advertisers hoping to evade accusations of unpatriotic wastefulness. If the WPTB urged Canadians to buy only necessities, advertisers sought to transform virtually every commodity into one. Some ad executives recoiled at the thought of this tactic ("In the Garbage Pail Lies the Future of the Nation," was one agency president's derisive summation of such ads), but it became the backbone of wartime commercial advertising techniques.[20]

By contrast, institutional advertising aimed to generate public goodwill and to promote brand-name recognition in order to secure future markets. This form of advertising was not new when the war erupted in September 1939, but it remained something of a novelty, and institutional campaigns mounted by a given firm usually generated comment and analysis in the trade papers.[21] Canadian adworkers readily apprehended the significance of institutional advertising in wartime, especially for firms wholly converted to war production. An immense number of articles lauding its virtues appeared in the trade papers beginning in 1941. "One could measure the after-the-war standing of brands by their advertising practice now," the editor of *Canadian Advertising* wrote in late 1942.[22] In the eyes of the industry, advertising was already a form of friendly persuasion, a kind of benevolent propaganda, and adworkers prided themselves on possessing unique insight into the motivations of a typical Canadian. Institutional advertising, they argued, could rescue the reputations of firms still suffering from the pent-up ill will toward capitalism felt by many Canadians during the Great Depression. Well-placed institutional campaigns could pre-empt accusations of war profiteering that were sure to arise from certain quarters, just as they had during the Great War.[23] As the following chapter will demonstrate, institutional advertising offered

Canadians a sustained argument about why and for what the war was being fought. It was, moreover, an argument that differed in emphasis from the one advanced by government propaganda. Where the government depicted a war fought for the democratic institutions of the British way of life, institutional advertising stressed the virtues of free enterprise and the boundless progress made possible when the entrepreneurial spirit was given unhindered reign. Many institutional ads reinforced the necessity of supporting the government in its two sacred causes – maintaining the price ceiling and buying Victory Bonds – but they also stressed that such sacrifices were only temporary delays in consumerist gratification (institutional advertising during the last three years of the war will be further discussed in Chapter 4).

But if the themes, motifs, visual iconography, and justification of peacetime advertising proved relatively easy to transpose into wartime, so too did the arguments of advertising's critics. Shopworn complaints about the excessive materialism of modern life and the advertising culture that promoted extravagance and wastefulness were readily grafted onto the circumstances of "total war." After the annihilation of two Canadian battalions at Hong Kong in December 1941 and the succession of disasters for British arms in the first half of 1942, the commercial exploitation of the war by advertisers seemed unpardonably crass to many commentators. C.D. Watt complained in *Canadian Forum* that, on the one hand, advertisers were "urging John Canuck to support the war effort, while with the other they are still trying to encourage him to go on a buying spree," and he urged Ottawa to "crack down on this continued pseudo-patriotic advertising."[24] Less than two months after the catastrophe at Dieppe, the editors of the same journal lamented the "unpardonable waste that continued advertising is causing, waste that compares so strikingly with the sacrifices being made by most of the citizens of this land."[25] By maintaining consumer demand, they claimed, advertising diverted labour and resources to non-essential production, undermined Ottawa's efforts to combat inflation, and generated competition for Victory Bond sales. In November, an editorial in one major daily remarked that Canadians had thus far "been spectators of this war ... spectators to Britain's agony," a fault the author laid at the feet of those "cursed by the spirit of advertising" into wanting to preserve "our way of life" – the consumer way of life – when survival required material sacrifice.[26] Dorothy Thompson, an American writer whose column "On the Record" was carried by the *Toronto Globe and Mail*, fired frequent broadsides at what she derided as a lackadaisical Allied war effort. Dubbed by *Time* "the second most influential woman in America" (Eleanor Roosevelt was first), Thompson was a frequent visitor to Canada and often took aim at King's government for its unwillingness to enact conscription for overseas service. In October 1942, a particularly vitriolic screed by Thompson against the consumer culture was excerpted with aggravated astonishment throughout the business press. The United Nations, she wrote, were losing the global struggle because a generation of hedonistic mass consumerism had produced citizens incapable of enduring the sacrifices necessary to wage total war. Decades of "super-salesmanship" had instilled false needs in the buying public by creating fears and social anxieties, and then offering solutions to them. A weak-willed citizenry not merely unaccustomed to sacrifice, but unwilling to actually make it, was the entirely predictable outcome, she argued. By contrast, the Germans and Japanese suffered no such afflictions: they were accustomed to deprivation. "The world," Thompson wrote, "is being given a shellacking by Japs who live on a handful of rice and a little fish; by exactly that generation of Germans who were undernourished in their childhood," and only the Russians, "who for twenty years have sacrificed consumer goods in order to build a great industry," were making strenuous efforts to defend it. What was wanting, in Thompson's view, was sacrifice – sacrifice on the part of pampered consumers – and governments with the courage to impose it.[27]

NO DOUBT, MANY OFFICIALS in the government were nearly as exasperated by this sort of thing as were leading businessmen across the country. Since late 1941, the WPTB and other government agencies had done all they could do – or indeed, needed to do – to mobilize the economy for a protracted struggle. Donald Gordon had himself said publicly on more than one occasion that "the system of free enterprise is at an end," a fact already evident given the huge number of economic regulations that his and other related agencies had passed.[28] On the other hand, as of mid-1942, officials had given the advertising industry little sense of how to proceed. In February 1942, an official statement from the WPTB called for "the elimination of extravagant marketing practices," without defining what, precisely, such practices were.[29] That summer, Byrne Hope Sanders contributed an article to *Canadian Advertising* in which she defended the virtues of continued advertising, provided that it served the purposes of both the advertiser and the war effort. Perhaps, as the former editor of *Chatelaine*, she could hardly have been expected to do otherwise, but the piece was nonetheless reassuring to adworkers.[30] In September, John Atkins, the WPTB's administrator for printing and publishing, assured the industry that "normal advertising, when it serves to sell goods or services in reasonable quantities and in a manner consistent with wartime regulations," was permissible and would not be restricted. Moreover, Atkins defended the continued use of institutional advertising: "In a period when war needs have withdrawn so many goods and services from civilian use, advertising may be used by many manufacturers and retailers to maintain the reputation, trade marks, and their assets of goodwill."[31] If this quelled the fears of adworkers, the effect was only temporary. In November, Joseph Bradette, a senior Liberal MP from the riding of Cochrane (and later deputy speaker of the House), expressed his "shock" over such newspaper "extravagances" as double-page ads. He suggested that newspapers should be reduced in size to save newsprint, a process that publishers could initiate by cutting out advertising.[32] Shortly thereafter, Prime Minister King himself declared to the House of Commons, "Advertising is clearly not necessary to promote sales, nor is it justifiable if sales and consumption are to be curtailed." Board officials assured the advertising industry that King had been referring only to ads for alcoholic beverages (the banning of which was the sole serious wartime concession that Ottawa would make to lingering prohibitionist sentiment), but this had not been explicit in the original speech.[33] It was impossible for adworkers to dismiss such talk as mere hyperbole, especially when the government had just enacted a slate of new and restrictive tax regulations concerning advertising. Before that point, businesses had sought to minimize or even circumvent the impact of excess profit taxes with increased advertising expenditures, since this resulted in higher operating expenses and lower profits. The Revenue Department had anticipated the use of such a loophole and disallowed "abnormal" advertising budgets for tax purposes.[34] Advertisers protested that the circumstances virtually mandated higher expenditures, noting that, for example, gasoline rationing had nearly eliminated the travelling salesman, forcing his replacement with print advertising. In addition, they noted that American advertising continued to flow, without hindrance, into Canada, giving unfavourable advantages to certain brands, but departmental officials were unmoved.[35]

Where might such regulations end? Morgan Eastman, a Toronto ad executive, wondered if the new regulations were "inspired by the breath of the big bad wolf – personified by the C.C.F. – hot on the neck of our government."[36] Throughout 1942 and 1943, the trade papers carried frequent articles dealing with the plight of advertisers overseas, looking, perhaps, for a hint of dread things to come if the government decided to reverse the board's promises and enact severe restrictions on the publication of advertising. In the United Kingdom and most other Commonwealth nations, advertisers operated under very strict constraints. In Britain, serious shortages had the twofold effect of reducing consumer expenditure while simultaneously creating a seller's market, where surviving retailers felt little need to advertise since they sold everything they had. Paper shortages resulted in further regulations on the size of advertising. A writer in the British trade journal *Advertiser's Weekly* noted that British advertisers were compelled to make do with a half-column, where they "used to spread over whole triple or double columns."[37] Only half of British ad agencies survived the war.[38] In Australia, ad linage declined 50 percent in 1941.[39] Shortfalls in American newspaper pulp imports resulted in severe cuts in the size of Australian publications. Only small and simple ads were permitted, and the printing of show-cards was banned outright. Further regulations barred copywriters from employing words such as "glamorous," "exciting," "stimulating," and phrases such as "a must"; illustrators were forbidden to depict consumers enjoying a product, and all ads were required to advise consumers on how to prolong the life of their product. Commercial poster advertising could not be illustrated at all.[40]

Much to the relief and surprise of adworkers, regulations of this kind never materialized in Canada. The closing of tax loopholes in 1942 marked the most intrusive government regulations imposed on the Canadian industry as a whole. Early in the summer of 1942, Donald Gordon instructed the board's Division of Simplified Practice, whose mandate was to seek out and implement economies in the manufacturing, marketing, and selling of commodities, to formulate a policy on the role of wartime advertising. In the event, its policy might easily have appeared in any midwar issue of *Canadian Advertising* or *Marketing*. It began by acknowledging that all the nation's resources must be directed to the military struggle but observed that advertising could be "harmonized with the war effort." "Government and industry," the policy said,

> are pressing advertising into service as an effective method of informing and convincing the public that in a democracy greater efforts and sacrifices must be volunteered than totalitarian states can impose by dictatorship. In normal

times the persuasive influence of advertising reflects the freedom of choice of a free people, and even in the present crisis war objectives and much war financing have been made possible by appeals to the patriotism and thrift of the people of Canada. Modern advertising accomplishes the task performed in earlier centuries by royal proclamations. It explains the meaning of the necessity of new laws, taxes, loans, rationing plans, and other governmental measures. Canadians are showing themselves willing to accept and obey all such demands on their loyalty, but frequent reminders and admonitions are often necessary to overcome unawareness of urgent needs.[41]

Although the concerns of the industry were by no means unjustified – in numerous instances, Ottawa reversed earlier policies and imposed draconian measures in response to unforeseen events – it is nonetheless the case that the records of the WPTB, the sole agency that might have regulated or even banned advertising, do not indicate that this was ever seriously discussed. It must be recalled that many WPTB directors and administrators were drawn from the very industries over which they now had authority. They endured accusations from the likes of *Marketing's* John Kirkwood and the editors of the relentlessly critical *Toronto Telegram* that their intent was to stifle free enterprise, but in fact the mirror-image allegations of the Co-operative Commonwealth Federation – that board directors were generally pro-business in their decision making – were much closer to the truth. WPTB printing and publishing administrator John Atkins, for example, acknowledged in an internal memo that any mandatory reduction in advertising would result in lost revenue for magazines and newspapers, and would threaten the public service performed by the free press.[42] Whenever possible, he and his colleagues attempted to minimize the impact of necessary regulations on the industries that had employed them in the past and, they hoped, would do so again after the war was over.

It is very likely that more severe restrictions on advertising, such as the kind that suddenly and unexpectedly suspended passenger car manufacturing at the beginning of 1942, were never more than another Allied defeat away. But the gloom that had gripped so many adworkers in early 1942 gradually gave way to cautious optimism and then something like jubilation as Allied victories mounted in the year that followed. Midway, El Alamein, Stalingrad, Sicily – these victories marked such an extraordinary reversal in the fortunes of war that many overzealous optimists began to predict that it would end in 1944.[43] Discussion about the role of advertising in wartime had disappeared from the trade papers by late 1943, and its critics turned their attention to other matters. Perhaps arguing about the role of advertising seemed pointless in a war that might soon be over. Adworkers began to preoccupy themselves with the question of what role they would play in reconstruction and peacetime. Their fears had not been unjustified, but they were not realized, either. Despite shortages and rationing and the best efforts of anti-consumer propaganda, retail sales continued to grow. The advertising industry's own business was busy and getting busier by the year. The decline in linage that so alarmed adworkers at the beginning of 1942 had proven to be nothing more than a temporary downturn, a period of adjustment following the end of consumer durable production. New kinds of ads, new customers, and institutional ad campaigns revived linage by the end of 1942. In *Maclean's*, for instance, it not only recovered in 1943, it significantly exceeded the levels of the first two years of the war.

As Table 3.1 demonstrates, apart from the temporary decline in 1942, total national advertising linage in *Maclean's* steadily increased until 1945. Not surprisingly, advertising as a percentage of total magazine linage followed a similar pattern. Throughout the war, *Maclean's* sold a progressively greater volume of advertising space and did so despite the loss of most

Table 3.1

Advertising linage in *Maclean's*, 1939-45 (column inches)

Year	Total magazine linage	Private advertising	Government ads	Ads as % of total linage	Ratio of private to government ads
1939	71,766	27,935	162	39	172:1
1940	74,746	31,005	135	41	230:1
1941	74,736	31,775	432	43	74:1
1942	68,796	26,034	1,458	39	18:1
1943	76,248	32,548	1,565	43	21:1
1944	78,540	35,159	2,067	44	17:1
1945	81,648	37,344	1,474	46	25:1

NOTE: Data on advertising linage for *Maclean's* were not readily available. I therefore undertook to measure it for myself. Published bi-weekly, *Maclean's* was the mostly widely circulated national magazine in Canada during the Second World War and seemed a fit subject for this analysis. Advertising was (and is) sold in column inches. A column inch is determined by measuring the depth of the ad in inches and multiplying by the number of columns. A full page in *Maclean's* occupied 54.0 column inches, a half page 27.5 column inches, and so forth.

Table 3.2

National advertising linage by category, in *Maclean's*, 1939-45 (column inches)

	Advertising		
Year	National	Commercial	Institutional
1939	27,935	27,010	837
1940	31,005	29,659	986
1941	31,775	30,695	1,080
1942	26,034	22,793	3,241
1943	32,548	25,507	7,041
1944	35,159	27,030	8,129
1945	37,344	30,521	6,823

NOTE: Sometimes the distinction between an institutional ad and a commercial one was rather subjective, especially late in the war when they began to make specific reference to the future availability of certain goods. For the purposes of this survey, ads were defined as institutional if they did not serve an immediate commercial purpose.

automotive-related ads. Moreover, the results for *Maclean's* are consistent with the general picture of national advertising reported in *Marketing*, *Canadian Advertising*, and other trade publications.[44]

In part, this recovery owed itself to the explosion in the number of institutional ads that began to appear in late 1941 (see Table 3.2). In *Maclean's*, institutional ad linage in 1943 was 700 percent greater than in 1940. However, it is not the case that institutional advertising by itself somehow "saved" the advertising and publishing business in wartime Canada, as Frank Fox claims that it did in the United States.[45] Commercial advertising continued to constitute the overwhelming majority of ads that appeared in *Maclean's* during the war.

At no point did institutional advertising account for more than a quarter of the magazine's total ad linage. Another striking fact is that though Ottawa became one of the country's biggest single advertisers, ads placed by government agencies never constituted more than 5 percent of the total ad linage in *Maclean's*. Readers of *Maclean's* were subjected to as many purely commercial impressions at the peak of the war effort in 1944 as they had been in 1939. Given the surprising persistence of commercial advertising and the enormous increase in goodwill advertising, it is clear that from an advertising standpoint, *Maclean's*, and probably most other national magazines, had never had it so good. This is not to suggest that the same was true for the Canadian consumer, but the persistence of so much national advertising does suggest, at the very least, that the war did little to curtail the willingness of advertisers to market themselves and those goods that were still available. Out of sight of the general reading public, ads in the trade papers were often remarkably forthright about the favourable economic circumstances.

A May 1944 ad for the *Canadian Home Journal* summed up the industry's renewed spirit of optimism and economic opportunity. Under the tag line of "To Market! To Market! With Money to Spend!" the ad noted that "the war has created thousands of new prospects for advertisers. Women have assumed new responsibilities, filled new jobs, and have gained new buying power. Women look for advice and guidance on the biggest, toughest buying job of this or any other generation. Start selling to this powerful woman market now, now while they are more receptive than ever before" (see Figure 3.2).[46]

The development of new tactics and the growth of commercial advertising linage should not be construed as evidence that adworkers did not want to "do their bit," only that, as apostles of free enterprise, they were not fully in accord with the government's position on how Canadians at home could best serve a nation at war. Modern readers may find the commercial exploitation of the war distasteful, as did many contemporary critics, but it would be wrong to think that advertisers and adworkers were the wilful saboteurs imagined by their critics, even if they quite consciously sought to imbue personal consumption with the moral character of the great crusade against Nazism. Adworkers saw no necessary conflict between their self-interest as businesspeople and the interests of Canadians as a whole, or indeed between moderate personal consumption and the war effort. On the contrary, they had always maintained that the national interest and self-interest were functionally connected. The businessman who pursued personal gain elevated his fellow Canadians by the wealth he generated and, perhaps more importantly, through the example of entrepreneurship and industriousness that he provided. When confronted with accusations of "unpardonable waste," the adworker could point to the extraordinary efforts of Canada's businesses on the part of the war effort. Was it not free enterprise, after all, that was producing the implements of war, without which victory was impossible? Were private businesses not also paying vast tax revenues into government coffers and drumming up Victory Bond sales and participating in every conceivable patriotic endeavour proposed to them by the government or community

86   Chapter 3

FIGURE 3.2   Not the message we associate with the home front, but manufacturers, retailers, and advertisers had to negotiate the tension between the official line ("serve by saving") and the reality of consumers spending more money than ever before. | "To Market! To Market!" *Marketing*, 8 January 1944, 2.

organizations? In this sense, the principle on which the "business as usual" ethos had been built – that a free society drew its strength from free enterprise – had not become extinct during the war; it had evolved in order to survive. But just as the peacetime rhetoric of advertising as "the blesser of mankind" was often belied by the mundane concerns of the ads themselves, the claim that advertisers were waging a parallel war on needless consumption was frequently undercut by the ads they produced. The ads themselves, and the way in which the war was refracted through the adworker's creative lens, will be the topic of the next chapter.

4
Advertising to Win the War and Secure the Future

As a free people, we possess a 'secret weapon' forever lost to Hitler; a weapon subtle, yet so powerful it is speeding the day of his destruction. That weapon is advertising.

– Editorial, Marketing, *21 June 1941*

"Buck up, Bill! There's a war to be won!"
"Two wars, Jack. The big one, and my own private little bout with constipation."

– Kellogg's All-Bran advertisement, *February 1943*

Advertising was a big business in wartime Canada, but the community of adworkers that produced it was small. Most of them plied their trade for minor firms in Toronto and Montreal, imitating their American brethren and imitating one another. Notices in the trade papers and frequent conferences, luncheons, and awards banquets kept them acquainted with one another. They had observed the outbreak of war and the unrelenting expansion of government authority over all aspects of the domestic economy with trepidation. Despite their fear that the wartime security state might evolve into an anti-business social security state, they sensed that the moment was alive with opportunities. Predictably, they boasted that they could make decisive contributions to the war effort while simultaneously boosting sales or securing future markets for their clients. "Advertising will still be needed to do its accustomed job of promoting individual goods, services, and institutions," Carlton McNaught wrote in *Canadian Printer and Publisher*, "but over and above this it will, I think, be called upon to fill a vitally important role in shaping the ideas of people on all sorts of issues."[1]

Did it actually accomplish that, as it encroached further and further, as Robert Legget put it, into the public round? Certainly, adworkers and advertisers believed that it did. Hundreds of thousands of Canadians absorbed huge numbers of commercial impressions every day from the pages of newspapers and magazines, posters on streetcars, and ads on the radio. The continued growth of retail sales throughout the war suggests at the very least a rough harmony of interests between advertisers and consumers. More importantly, as adworkers themselves acknowledged with pride, wartime advertising did more than merely hawk goods: it carried and transmitted a cultural ideal. It situated consumers in the discourses of patriotic consumerism and the national myth of total war. It advanced an unambiguously modern and secular worldview in which the "good life" of health, happiness, social status, prosperity, and political freedom could be secured through personal consumption and material progress. In enthralling and often brazen ways, it aimed to excite the imagination of readers, awaken patriotic fervour, and arouse fantasies of a world "fit for heroes" that would materialize from the crucible of war. If people sometimes saw through the nationalistic gleam and objected to goods being foisted on them at a time when authorities demanded thrift, advertisers could reply that it was the Wartime Prices and Trade Board and its allies in the leading women's groups who had politicized consumption and issued a stream of propaganda persuading women that their consumer choices were decisive in the struggle against the Axis. Advertisers, they said, were simply walking the path of patriotic consumption blazed by government agencies and voluntary associations during the first two years of hostilities.

In his pioneering work of consumer history, *Advertising the American Dream*, Roland Marchand describes in meticulous and painstaking detail how national advertising in the 1920s and early 1930s offered readers an assortment of "parables," "social tableaus," and "visual clichés" that served to acculturate the American middle class to the fast pace, changing social mores, and economic opportunities of modernity.[2] Likewise, wartime advertising deployed a small number of marketing strategies organized around a handful of stock phrases and illustrations that, over time and through continual repetition, became clichés. Some of these had been transposed from peacetime; others were responses to the particular circumstances of the war itself. A few had even been employed during the First World War. In the deeply symbolic shorthand of advertising methodology, manufacturers, sellers, and consumers navigated their own course between the government's campaign against needless spending and the realities of an economy where Canadians had more spending money than ever. At its most fully elaborated, wartime advertising offered consumers much more than reasons to keep spending; embedded in its clichés were clear and no doubt highly palatable arguments concocted to satisfy Canadians' hunger for clarity about what the war meant, how it would be won, and what the rewards of victory would be.

PERHAPS THE MOST PROMINENT of these clichés, the "misguided friend," had been a key character in advertising since the 1920s. Hundreds of interwar ads presented vignettes about a well-meaning but naive person set straight by a friend, colleague, or family member already in the know. Oftentimes, the misguided friend's problem was one of those that had so scandalized the Spanish tourist we encountered in Chapter 2: constipation, body odour, halitosis, a spouse whose affections had suddenly flagged, or any number of potentially embarrassing modern tribulations. Firmly but tactfully offered solutions were advanced from many quarters. Mothers imparted time-tested wisdom to modern daughters; daughters demonstrated modern *savoir faire* to old-fashioned mothers; wives upbraided their husbands (husbands being the most hapless creatures of all); and doctors gave reassuring and expert counsel about a host of contemporary maladies. There were innumerable variations, but the solution was always a commodity – a trusted brand of soap, a scientifically engineered tonic, a labour-saving appliance from a dependable manufacturer.[3]

Wartime adworkers made good use of the misguided friend, albeit with an even greater sense of power and self-importance. In advertising, the war thrust misguided friends' personal problems into the public realm, where they became matters of national concern. Body odour, constipation, poor nutrition – these and other everyday complaints could lead to lost jobs and lost loves in peacetime, but in wartime they undermined morale, health, and work ethic, threatening the security of the whole nation. Numerous ads, for example, contrasted the lacklustre job performance of underfed workers with the energetic performance of the well nourished. The misguided friend figured prominently in such ads, always ready to be corrected by some knowing co-worker possessing remarkable gifts of linguistic virtuosity. In one Kellogg's All-Bran ad, Jack, a machine-tool operator, exclaims to a weary and pained co-worker, "Buck up, Bill! There's a war to be won!" "*Two* wars, Jack," Bill replies, "the big one, and my own private little bout with constipation." Long hours and the rigours of war work have caught up to him, Bill explains. "Better do what I did," Jack says, "try getting at the *cause* of your trouble. If you've got the common type of constipation due to the lack of 'bulk'-forming material in the diet, eat Kellogg's All-Bran regularly!"[4] With an eye to the changing demographics of the industrial workforce, Kellogg's offered a version of the same ad, featuring women working on a metal lathe ("Snap out of it, Sue, there's planes to be built!").[5] Advertising depicted female war workers as susceptible to a variety of infirmities, particularly the never fully defined ravages of "trying days." In a Kotex ad, pouting at the reader from her bed, a despondent young woman asks, "I don't want to be an Absentee – but what's a girl to do? We *know* how much our plant – our country – depends on us, when every minute counts! But how *can* we keep going?" In this variation on the cliché, Kotex itself assumed the role of the knowing friend, offering a free booklet entitled *That Day Is Here Again* "to aid these workers, and the war effort." Described as "the answer to an S.O.S. from a war plant nurse" who had noticed the frequent absences of female assembly line workers, the booklet offered advice on everything from how to curb cramps to what to do when "the stork's expected." That the advice most assuredly centred on the use of Kotex-brand products was, seemingly, incidental. The commercial message was submerged beneath an appeal to patriotism, one that concluded – as was typical of so many wartime ads – with a reminder that victory overseas depended upon the exertions made by civilians on the home front: "Each time you stay at home – you keep our boys away from home, longer!"[6]

Wartime ads usually depicted misguided friends as merely uninformed rather than intentionally malicious. Implicitly, however, such ads carried the suggestion that if their problems went undiagnosed or untreated for too long, misguided friends threatened to become, however unwittingly, a drain on the war effort and, in more extreme cases, de facto shirkers and saboteurs. A 1943 ad for Sanforized washable fabrics depicted an elderly woman with her arms full of shopping bags (see Figure 4.1). "Saboteur!" is scrawled in bold letters across the image. The omniscient narrator exposes the misguided friend's failings for all to see: "It was flannellette Grandma was after ... but when the clerk mentioned flannellette was getting scarce, she bought the whole bolt! Grandma didn't *mean* to be a saboteur. But she is ... she's a hoarder." Only belatedly readers might have noticed that the advertiser was also selling something: "It's so terribly important to buy wisely ... In the case of washables, for instance ... it's

FIGURE 4.1 Faced with official demands for austerity, wartime advertising sometimes recommended moderating or delaying purchases. Other ads, such as this one, concealed the sales pitch beneath a cloak of patriotic sentiment. | "Saboteur!" *Maclean's*, 1 May 1943, 21.

important to get them Sanforized if you can, to avoid waste from shrinkage." But this is incidental – the supposed purpose of the ad is to aid in the war against Hitler.[7]

Misguided friends suffered from an even wider range of maladies in wartime than in peace. To such afflictions as irregularity and trying days, the war added hoarding, profligate consumerism, faltering morale, and such foibles as rumour mongering and self-interested labour agitation. Only proper instruction in patriotic behaviour could rally misguided friends to the cause. One institutional advertisement for Anaconda American Brass parachuted the reader into the thick of an argument in a factory canteen about the wage and price ceiling. "So what if there is a ceiling on wages!" exclaims one worker to the others, his right hand clenched in a fist (itself a prominent advertising cliché, as Roland Marchand observes). "Maybe we are working harder, and more hours. Maybe the income tax is tough! But look! My boy's in it. He's fighting! I spent 20 years raising that kid ... Do you think I'd let him down now for a few dollars?"[8] Dozens of similar variations on the cliché of the misguided friend appeared in institutional advertising during the last half of the war. Labatt's, barred from advertising alcoholic beverages since early 1943, deployed misguided friends in a series of ads entitled "Ain't It the Truth," in which shirkers, hoarders, and extravagant spenders were set straight. On the other hand, misguided friends were sometimes cautioned that excessive and unwarranted government regulations could undermine home front morale. Labatt's advanced this argument in a 1943 ad, in which a man getting a shave and haircut expounded on the dangers of resurgent temperance and prohibition forces to his skeptical barber (see Figure 4.2). "It's not prohibition they want this time, but rationing of beer, same as tea and coffee," protests the barber. "Does it make sense to you, when working men have to do with less of two beverages, to force them to have less of a third as well?" the customer replies. "Put that way, it does seem silly," the barber at last concedes, at which point the customer cries, "Worse than silly – dangerous! It's a threat to the morale of the home front."[9]

For their failure to shop wisely and conserve when necessary, for not keeping fit, buying bonds, respecting the price ceiling, and for a host of other offences – including, at times, overzealous enthusiasm for unnecessary regulations – misguided friends were tacitly and sometimes explicitly implicated in undermining the war effort. But knowing friends, and the products and firms they represented, were always ready to instruct or

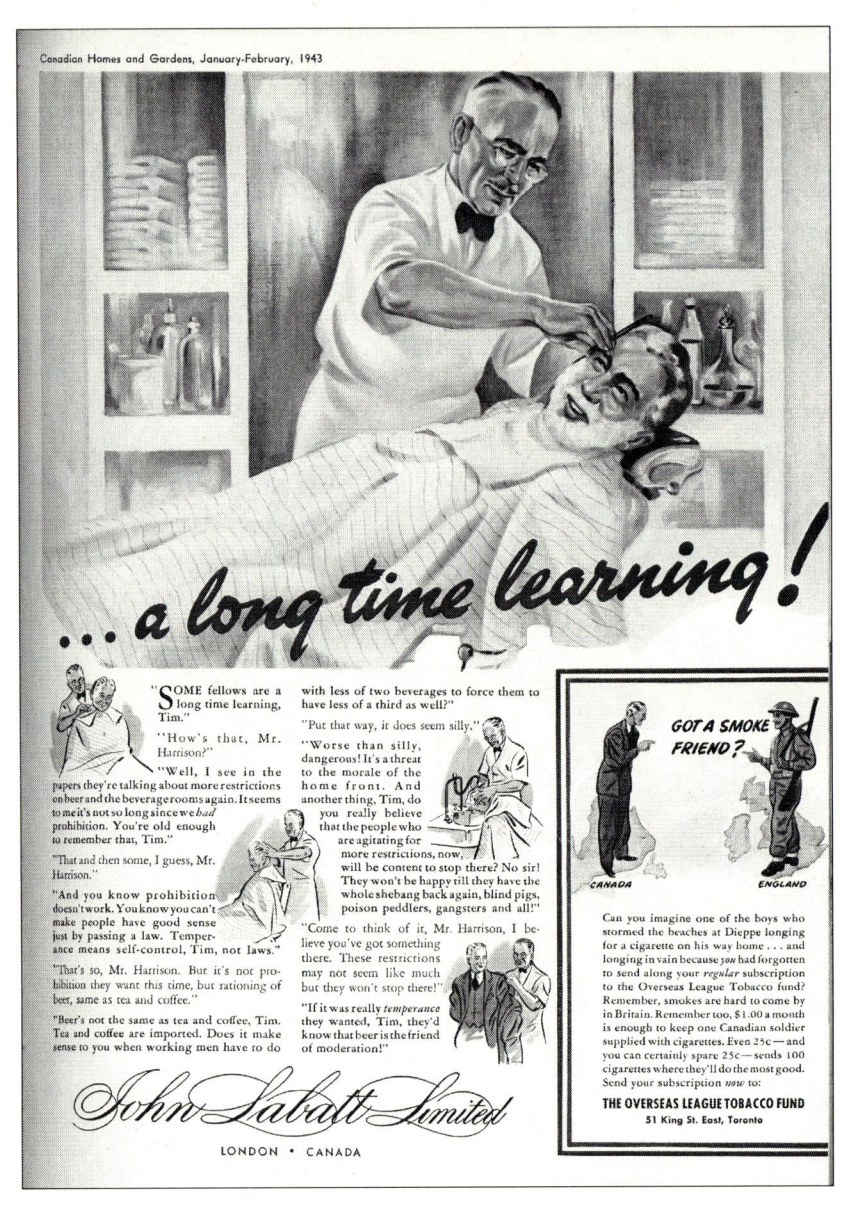

FIGURE 4.2   Misguided friends figured prominently in wartime advertising. Here, a man sets his barber straight about the danger posed to the war effort by temperance and prohibition supporters. | "A Long Time Learning," *Canadian Homes and Gardens,* January-February 1943, 33.

FIGURE 4.3 *(facing page)*   This Victory Bond poster expressly equated the sacrifices made by consumers with increased industrial production. | "Strange Things Go into Tanks!" Victory Bond Poster, *Canadian Forum,* May 1943, 48.

shame them and, by extension, misguided consumers, back onto the path of patriotic righteousness through correct consumption (see Figure 4.3).

A SOLDIER AND HIS GAL lock lips over the world in miniature, the havoc of war forgotten for a blissful moment, the vast distances between them reduced to nothing, their bonds of love restored, all by the simple act of gift giving (see Figure 4.4). "Tonight I leaned across 10,000 miles and kissed you," reads the heading of this sumptuous ad for Gruen watches. "This will be a Christmas," it goes on,

> More than any other Christmas – which will call for the reassurance of human faith and understanding, for the remembrance of the sympathy and affection human hearts can hold for each other. Is there at this time any gift you could make to a loved one – half the world away, or close at home – more meaningful than a truly fine watch?[10]

With the definition of patriotic consumerism changing rapidly toward one that emphasized personal austerity, and with propagandists urging greater sacrifice still, post-1941 ads used the phrase "now more than ever" and variations of it brazenly and repetitiously. Nothing so signified their unwillingness to comply without reservation to the "serve by saving" philosophy. It also stands as a reminder that, as far as most advertisers were concerned, the ethos of shopping for victory never really ended. On the contrary, the countless examples of this cliché were unified by an underlying theme – that the very qualities that had made their products desirable in peacetime were required all the more urgently now that the nation was fighting for its survival.

For Christmas 1942, Pepsi envisioned families entertaining soldiers at Christmastime and struck a chord that resonated throughout many ads that used the "now more than ever" cliché: when it came to bolstering morale, saving money, or keeping fit, buying the right things was more than smart shopping – it was a duty served on behalf of the war effort. The Pepsi ad proclaimed, "More than ever *this* year thoughtful women will entertain with this thrifty, delightful beverage ... *Say – that practically writes an order for 'Pepsi-Cola'*" (see Figure 4.5).[11] Similarly, using the tag line "Snapshots never meant so much as now," Kodak portrayed a soldier on furlough reunited with his family.[12] Campana's Balm informed female readers that "your hands now need Campana's Balm protection *more than ever*," portraying a woman working on a machine tool in one corner and accepting candy from a gentleman caller in the other, her hands protected for war work and lovely for social occasions (see Figure 4.6).[13] In a rather improbable Pratt and Lambert Paint ad, a tank crew reminds readers at home that, "in these times, good paint is more economical than ever."[14] Predictably, dozens of other advertisers appealed to the importance of good nutrition in a nation at war. "Now, more than ever before, steady

FIGURE 4.4   In the world of advertising, even jewellery and luxury watches could serve the war effort, under the correct circumstances. Here, they restore the bonds of affection, even across oceans. | "Tonight I Leaned across 10,000 Miles and Kissed You!" *Maclean's*, 15 December 1942, inside back cover.

nerves and sturdy bodies are needed on the home front. To keep fit is more than a personal ideal – it is a patriotic duty" read one ad for the H.J. Heinz Company.[15] Lysol told readers that in a world at war, babies are "more precious than ever," and so, too, was Lysol in the battle against

FIGURES 4.5 AND 4.6 Far from acquiescing to the government's pleas for conservation, many firms argued that buying their products was a consumer's patriotic duty. | "More Than Ever *This* Year," *Canadian Home Journal*, 2 January 1943, 33; "Your Hands Now Need Campana's Balm Protection *More Than Ever*," *Maclean's*, 15 January 1944, 35.

household germs. Busy housewives, doubling as war-workers, found the "quick-cleaning qualities" of Bon Ami "twice as important" since they were now working "twice as hard."[16]

Many of the commodities described as more necessary than ever were brands of food or useful gifts for soldiers overseas. Even the most ascetic patriot could hardly begrudge anyone a box of cereal or a decent pen for a man in uniform. The more challenging task for adworkers was to justify the continued purchase of luxury goods. In such cases, their recourse was almost always to the sacred cause of building morale – the seldom defined quality that nearly everyone agreed was in some way critical to the war effort. While government propaganda and a whole host of home front critics sought to discourage needless consumerism, wartime commercial advertising attempted to recast Canadians' relationship to commodities in ways that legitimated their continued purchase. Suggesting that the war made the acquisition of a given product, whether breakfast cereal or motor oil or jewelled watches, more rather than less important constituted the clearest possible affirmation that, for some advertisers, the "business as usual" spirit had not become a casualty of war: it had evolved to survive. Given that, to the Wartime Prices and Trade Board's unending frustration, retail sales continued to rise, there is every reason to believe that many Canadians welcomed the message that they could both continue buying and keep their social conscience intact.

WHEN PUBLIC FIGURES IN Canada talked about "sacrifices" after December 1941, it was usually to admonish Canadians for not having made enough. As the war effort grew, officials never tired of reminding Canadians that the sacrifices required of them were trifling in comparison to those imposed on Britons and the millions of people suffering and toiling under Axis occupation. Paradoxically, however, home front propaganda also made continual use of military metaphors and imagery that strongly insinuated an equivalence between the home front and the war being waged overseas. Poster propaganda and ads for Victory Bonds, for example, frequently portrayed civilians serving side by side with soldiers in uniform, and they sometimes even featured soldiers expressing their gratitude to civilians for buying bonds and making similar sacrifices. Commercial and institutional advertising was even more explicit in depicting soldiers and civilians as waging a parallel battle against the Axis (see Figure 4.7). Such characters as the misguided friend, the shirker, and the unwitting saboteur were the subject of many ads, but an even more prominent cliché was the typical civilian – the businessman, factory worker, and especially the housewife – symbolically transformed into a soldier through war work, conservation, and patriotic consumerism. No doubt many gendered assumptions underpinned adworkers' preference for portraying women performing their traditional homemaking and motherly duties, but such ads also acknowledged a demographic reality that persisted even though many women sought out paid work during the war. Moreover, advertising merely underlined the non-stop missives from the Wartime Prices and Trade Board (WPTB) and most women's organizations that stressed the importance of women's work in the home, and most especially their duties as "purchasing agent" (as *Chatelaine* put it) for their families. In emphasizing the special role of the homemaker, the ads reaffirmed the centrality of traditional notions of womanhood and the sanctity of the home, notions that seemed threatened by the social upheaval of war. Using the most reverent words and images, advertising upheld the role of wife, mother, and homemaker as vital to the war effort and the preservation of the values Canadians were fighting for. In late 1941, advertisers began to use the language and iconography of war in their depiction of the homemaker's daily life. One ad after another symbolically transformed the housewife into the woman that *Chatelaine*, in an October 1942 ad, called "the soldier in the apron." "Today's housewife," it read,

> is a soldier in action in her own battle dress, playing a sterling role in the fight for freedom. Other women may serve in overalls or in uniform. She serves by sustaining morale. Hers, too, is the task of feeding the nation to win the war. She is studying the nutritional values of available foods. She is learning to stretch the family dollar further, to scrutinize the values in every purchase.[17]

Copy like this echoed innumerable speeches made by Byrne Hope Sanders and Donald Gordon, and "soldiers in aprons" appeared in hundreds of ads. "What is the most vital war work housewives can do?" asked an ad for Metropolitan Life Insurance Company. "Of all the many types of war work in which Canadian women are engaged – one takes first place. Today, more than ever before, they must help keep their families healthy. Physical fitness and a high level of national health are vital to Canada's war effort."[18] Likewise, "Everybody has a war job," a woman in a Modess Sanitary Napkins ad says. "Mine is in my house ... shopping, mending, cleaning, cooking, and looking after my family. To keep them healthy, well-fed, and happy is my contribution to victory," tasks made easier when certain other worries are eased by the "downy, soft comfort of Modess" (see Figure 4.8).[19] Snapping a crisp salute, a housewife in a Lysol ad calls on other women to "enlist for the war on germs!" (no accidental pun, to be sure). "The housewife plays a vital part in National Defense. It is as important to protect health in the home as to protect the physical well-being of the army."[20] Yet another ad portrayed an army of housewives marching in a long column down a suburban lane alongside women in uniform, an equation of homemaker and soldier made possible by the time-saving properties of Old Dutch cleanser.[21]

AS MANY HISTORIANS HAVE argued, the increasing rate of women's participation in formerly male-dominated professions, including heavy industry and the armed forces, was the source of much social anxiety throughout the war. Ruth Roach Pierson writes that women's war work, even when prompted by patriotic zeal, "sharply challenged conventions in respect to women's nature and place in Canadian society."[22] Female war workers and women in uniform were the subject of genuine patriotic gratitude for their efforts, but they often endured accusations of "loose" morals and of neglecting their traditional duties to the detriment of society. Some historians have felt that Pierson may have overstated the backlash against women who took up non-traditional roles.[23] Nonetheless, in many ads tensions played out between the necessity of recruiting women into the armed forces and war industries and the desire to retain – or at least eventually regain – more traditional demarcations of gender. General Motors may have declared, in an extraordinary three-page ad, that "a woman's place is everywhere," but most ads portrayed women in their customary (albeit symbolically and temporarily transformed) roles.[24] Moreover, to further assuage fears regarding the social upheaval that would result from any break with gender conventions, most ads that illustrated women as soldiers and factory workers reassured readers that they remained conventionally feminine.

Cosmetics ads exemplified these efforts. Historian Kathy Peiss has observed that by the 1930s, the application of makeup became "one of the tangible ways women in their everyday lives confirmed their identities as women."[25] If industrial war work and military service threatened to destabilize this identity, advertising for cosmetics aimed to both valorize patriotic service and traditional conceptions of feminine beauty. "It's a reflection of the free democratic way of life that you have succeeded in

102   Chapter 4

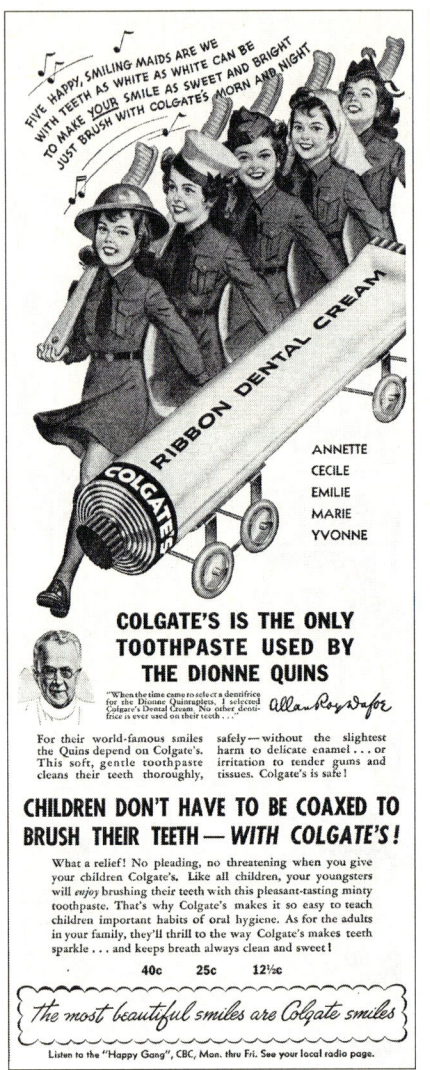

FIGURES 4.7 AND 4.8   *Left:* Canada's most famous girls, the Dionne quintuplets, transformed into soldiers by Colgate. *Right:* The female consumer, "manning" the home front by virtue of patriotic consumerism. | "Five Happy, Smiling Maids Are We," *Maclean's*, 1 January 1942, 23; "I Man the Home Front," *Maclean's*, 1 September 1942, 37.

keeping your freedom – even though you're doing a man's work," read a 1943 Tangee Cosmetics ad that appeared in *Chatelaine*. As always, wording such as "free democratic way of life" is synonymous with consumer choice, a point that the ad confirms. "No lipstick ... will win the war," it read, "but it symbolizes one of the reasons why we are fighting ... the precious right of women to be feminine and lovely under any circumstances."[26] The headline on another Tangee ad, this one featuring women in uniform, made the point even more explicitly (see Figure 4.9). "We are still the weaker sex," it read. "It's still up to us to appear as alluring and lovely as possible."[27] Other manufacturers rebranded their cosmetics to be more reflective of the times: a Louis Philippe lipstick was christened "Patriot Red," and a Cutex nail polish "for women at war" was named "Honor Bright."[28] A Helena Rubinstein cosmetics ad, depicting a smiling young member of the Canadian Women's Army Corps (CWAC), carried the headline "Eager to serve ... yet eager for beauty," reminding women that war work and remaining attractive were not mutually exclusive.[29] Palmolive ads described the beauty routine of Dorothy Linham, the nineteen-year-old winner of a Toronto-area beauty contest that crowned "Miss War-Worker" in 1942 (see Figure 4.10).[30] Similarly, Blachford Shoe ads presented footwear specifically "made to fit the shapely feet of Canada's CWAC's, Airwomen, and Wrens."[31]

In addition, advertising sought to comfort readers with the thought that any changes in women's identities imposed by the war would last only for its duration. A 1944 institutional ad by Standard Sanitary and Dominion Radiator (manufacturers of plumbing and heating fixtures) alluded to the already iconic Rosie-the-Riveter figure but only to cheer her forthcoming return to the home. When "Rosies stop riveting," every woman's real "dreams will come true" – in the form of a new kitchen with "double drain-boards, swinging spout faucet, basket type strainer, and convenient storing cabinets."[32]

MALE SUBJECTS POSED additional challenges for adworkers. Adult women could justifiably be depicted as mothers and homemakers not only because so many actually were, but also because of widely held societal expectations that they should be. By contrast, even though a slight majority of men of military age did not serve in uniform, adworkers had to contend with widely held societal expectations that they should be. Ads usually portrayed male civilians as too old or even too important (as in the case of research scientists) for military service. They, too, could be symbolically transformed into fighting men. A cooperative advertisement for Canada's life insurance companies introduced the "pilot without wings" – the apparently widowed father of two young children. "You may not be required to fly a bomber and risk your life," it reads, "age and health may bar you from service on the fighting fronts, but as a family man, you are

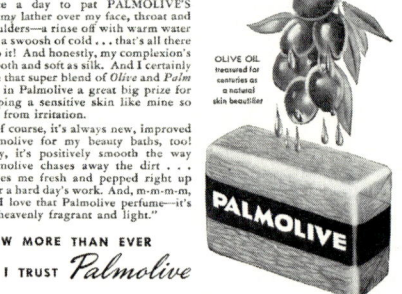

FIGURES 4.9 AND 4.10   Beauty products help to assuage gender anxieties caused by the movement of women into non-traditional occupations such as soldier (left) and factory worker (right). | "We Are Still the Weaker Sex," *Chatelaine*, August 1944, inside back cover; "Me – Enter a Beauty Contest?" *National Home Monthly*, February 1943, 19.

a pilot on the home front. You face unforeseen hazards."[33] In a series of ads, Vitalis, a hair-care product for men, featured "men of action" of a different sort: scientists, engineers, plant managers, and construction foremen, doing their bit for the war effort from home, aided, of course, by the newly found confidence they derive from Vitalis-restored hair.[34]

Male farmers, too, were readily metamorphosed into soldiers. Dozens of ads in which they appeared contained variations of the phrase "food is a weapon of war" – a position the government itself explicitly endorsed, foodstuffs being one of Canada's foremost contributions to the Allied war effort. In its recruiting drives, the Ontario government's Farm Service Force, which oversaw the allocation of labour to farms, used the slogan "join the farm commandos," expressly equating civilian agricultural workers with soldiers – and in this case, the most famous and romanticized soldiers of the war. A striking May 1944 full-colour ad of this kind by Green Giant posed an elderly man and a boy (his grandson, perhaps) on a hilltop, gazing out over a rural vista. "It's pretty here," the old man says, "just sun and wind and soil and us – and the lazy buzz of an early bee." Only a great artist or composer, he muses, could "paint this picture or put these sounds to music." Then, in the second panel, a new image appears: a long column of soldiers, marching off to war:

> But if you'll shut your eyes a minute, Sonny,
> you'll hear another sort of rhythm
> over some other kind o' fields ... it's the
> tramp of marching men over the fields of war.
> They are fighting on those fields, not farming them.
> The seeds they plant are bullets ...
> The crops they harvest are victories ...
> They are fighting on those fields of war
> to save these fields of peace.[35]

International Harvester also cast the farmer as soldier and his tractor as a war machine in a series of ads published in the last three years of the war. The most explicit of these features a farmer on his tractor under the tag line "He drives a weapon." The ad notes, "In the fields at home, and on foreign battlefields – *farmers* are driving the machines of war. Tens of thousands of farm boys are in the Armed Forces ... Here at home, in history's greatest battle for FOOD, every farm machine is mobilized. This year every tractor operator drives a weapon in the war for Victory and Freedom."[36] Similarly, very little effort was required to imagine industrial workers as virtually equivalent to combatants, especially if they were directly involved in the manufacture of war materiel. Such associations arose repeatedly in both propaganda and institutional advertising campaigns. One memorable Anaconda American Brass ad featured two boys in a schoolyard fight (see Figure 4.11). "My dad is *so* a soldier – even if he isn't in uniform!" cries one boy, threatening to punch the other. "He was in the last war, but he's too old for this one. But gee, *that doesn't stop him from fighting!*" His father, the boy goes on, is working to "turn out all the copper for tanks, 'n ships, 'n planes, 'n everything."[37]

"Production soldiers," as one Canadian General Electric ad called them, were defined by their visual clichés.[38] Male factory workers usually looked rugged and determined, serious but not grim. Often they appeared a shade too old for active service. Were they younger, they would surely be in uniform, but nose to the grindstone, each is determined to "do his bit." Beleaguered and fatigued, they look up from their jobs just long enough to deliver the advertisers' message. "Our job isn't done 'til victory is won," says a miner, fixing the reader with a hard stare. "Canada's mining men are fighting a battle of production that is helping to tilt the balance in favour of the United Nations."[39] International Harvester introduced readers to the "Miracle Man on the Truck Front," a service shop mechanic "whose skill and training and equipment" keeps Canada's trucks "delivering the stuff of victory," whereas a young girl in an ad for Perfect Circle Piston Rings exclaims to her mechanic father, "Dad, they ought to give you a medal, too!"[40]

MANUFACTURERS THAT HAD entirely converted to the production of war material still sought brand-name recognition and to foster goodwill through institutional advertising. They endorsed Victory Bond campaigns, rationalized shortages, ruminated on the contributions they were making to the war effort, and praised the self-sacrifice of their workforce. In the last three years of the war, institutional advertising blossomed into a full-blown system of home front propaganda. Whereas government propaganda dealt with the defence of Canada, the British Commonwealth, and their mutual democratic traditions, institutional advertising offered Canadians a further argument about what was at stake in the conflict – the survival of free enterprise. By the 1940s, the contours of this argument were familiar: free enterprise (never "capitalism," as if the word were much too vulgar to use) lay at the root of all democratic freedoms. It had created prosperous ground in which liberty flourished, for political freedom was possible only where citizens had their material needs satisfied. The war added a powerful new corollary to the original reasoning – namely, that the Allies would be victorious *because* of free enterprise. Confronted by the ingenuity of free people who were driven by the desire to defend

FIGURE 4.11 Anxious to avoid accusations of war profiteering, firms mounted institutional advertising campaigns that emphasized their patriotic service – and the contributions to victory made by their workforce. | "My Dad Is *So* a Soldier," *Canadian Homes and Gardens*, March-April 1943, 12.

"the finer things," the fearful teeming millions of the Axis powers and their blundering, hidebound leaders could not possibly hope to prevail. Indeed, they could barely even comprehend the vast resources arrayed against them (see the discussion of these themes in Chapter 2 and the Conclusion).

Advertising conveyed these broad ideas through a variety of clichés. As we have seen, misguided friends and soldiers in aprons sometimes appeared in institutional ads, usually as part of the wage-earning labour force or in the form of a customer who gladly postpones a purchase on behalf of the war effort. In addition, just as ordinary civilians could be transformed into combatants by means of their relationship to commodities or their producers, so, too, could non-military consumer goods be transmuted into implements of war when advertising worked its magic. In one 1944 example, a woman cooking over an old-fashioned stove muses, "Perhaps they're bombing Berlin tonight with the metal that might have gone into my new Findlay range."[41] In 1943, Ford unveiled its new models with an ad that read, "Watch the '43 Fords Go By!" but these are revealed to be a parade of military trucks and armoured fighting vehicles (see Figure 4.12).[42]

On one level, ads such as these served the immediate and very pragmatic purpose of informing the public why certain products were unavailable, often accompanied by promises that they would return, better than ever, once victory was secured. More significantly, they cast the advertiser as a self-sacrificing member of the business community, a public relations move of no small significance given the frequent accusations of profiteering that many firms had endured since the Great War.

No mention was ever made of the financial arrangements that underpinned production, and an uninformed reader could be excused for thinking that firms such as Ford and General Motors had donated their output to the armed forces – but that, too, was part of the public relations agenda of companies seeking to bolster their public image. General Motors of Canada adopted the slogan "Victory Is Our Business" just as passenger car production was suspended for the duration of the war. In four words, the slogan captured the essence of the public image that nearly every firm engaged in the production of materiel wished to convey: that of private enterprise waging its own battle against the Axis through technical ingenuity and industrial prowess. "V used to be just another letter in the alphabet," says one of the company's many institutional ads. "But it has become the foremost symbol in the world ... It is the rallying sign of the free. It is

FIGURE 4.12 Wartime institutional advertising aimed to generate goodwill by emphasizing the important role that the advertiser was playing in securing victory. Jack Bush, later a prominent abstract painter, illustrated a series of ads showcasing the array of military vehicles built by Ford of Canada. | "Watch the '43 Fords Go By!" *National Home Monthly*, April 1943, 21.

the target of our toil, the sole business of the nation ... Our only models are Victory Models." The ad described the "Victory Models" and praised the "pooled ingenuity of engineering brains" that devised them.[43] Similarly, Dominion Rubber showed a bomber crew, forced to ditch at sea but saved by "an inflated rubber raft that will keep them afloat for days or weeks."[44] In another instance, the crew of a stricken merchant vessel, "exposed to days of drenching rains, biting winds, and freezing cold," was saved by the new "seaman's protection suit" designed and manufactured by Dominion. Dominion, the ad concluded, is "a good name to remember" because "when peace comes, all our experience and resources will be devoted to making still better tires, footwear, and other products for civilian needs."[45] Gooderham and Worts, a Toronto-based distillery, described how even the agony of war wounds could be banished through "the miracle of ether," of which pure alcohol was a basic ingredient.[46]

Above all, institutional ads continually praised the ingenuity of unfettered free enterprise. By contrast, they described the Axis powers as utterly waylaid in their efforts to keep pace with the productive capacity and technical genius of their enemies. In a characteristic 1944 ad titled "Swat This Mosquito!" depicting the famous two-engine bomber of the same name, GM taunted the Axis nations directly in words that envisioned the triumph of free enterprise over the Nazi slave state (see Figure 4.13):

> Here, you Axis supermen, is the plane you'd like to stop! Swift, stinging death from the skies above ... striking back again and again until your war plants are flaming ruins and the foundations of your doctrines shattered ... General Motors is proud to be the builder of its intricate, all-wood fuselage ... and so, in one more way General Motors gives evidence that, "Victory is Our Business"![47]

Addressing the enemy was itself a major cliché of wartime institutional advertising. Seagram's goaded the Führer directly, announcing in one ad that it had "a bushel of trouble" for him: "As you well know, Herr Hitler, high-proof alcohol is an essential ingredient in the manufacture of smokeless powder for our shells, bombs, mines, and torpedoes ... Over here, Herr Hitler, we have plenty of grain and ample facilities to make almost unlimited quantities of alcohol for war ... Yes, Herr Hitler, you are really in trouble."[48] Similarly, an American Caterpillar Diesel ad titled "Coming at you, Schicklgruber!," reprinted in *Maclean's* and several other Canadian magazines, presented readers with the spectacle of a bulldozer plowing

Advertising to Win the War and Secure the Future 111

> # Swat this Mosquito . . . if you can!
>
> Here, you Axis supermen, is the plane you'd like to stop! Swift, stinging death from the skies above . . . striking back again and again until your war plants are flaming ruins and the foundations of your doctrines shattered. Versatile and light in weight, this fastest of all bombers answers the sky-fighter's every need. As the Allies are proud of the Mosquito's war achievement, so General Motors is proud to be the builder of its intricate, all-wood fuselage . . . and so, in one more way General Motors gives evidence that, "Victory Is Our Business"!
>
> **GM GENERAL MOTORS**
>
> CHEVROLET · PONTIAC · OLDSMOBILE · BUICK · CADILLAC · CHEVROLET & GMC TRUCKS

FIGURE 4.13   In this striking ad, General Motors of Canada envisioned the victory of free enterprise over the Nazi state in both material and ideological terms. | "Swat This Mosquito," *Canadian Homes and Gardens*, August-September 1944, 52.

under the ruins of the Reich while German planes spiral downward, trailing smoke and flames. "Maybe you overlooked this machine when you planned your world conquest, Adolf," it says. "But soon you'll be seeing it in your nightmares! You said we North Americans couldn't fight. Well, we're learning."[49] Here is yet another hallmark of the "Victory Is Our

Business" cliché: how a reluctant people took up arms in defence of the cause of freedom and, armed with the industrial might and technological resourcefulness of capitalism, were bringing ruin and defeat to the enemy on every front. Studebaker praised those "carefree Canadian boys" who "only yesterday ... were learning in their classrooms the fabled exploits of Alexander the Great, of Julius Caesar, and Genghis Khan" but who were now "making history themselves ... almost next-door to many of the storied battlefields they read about in school" – carried, of course, in the back of Studebaker trucks.[50] In 1943, Jack Bush, an artist with the Cockfield, Brown advertising agency, produced a series of ads for Ford of Canada entitled "Action Pictures," portraying Canadian troops in Ford-built Canadian Military Pattern vehicles engaging the enemy. The copy, some of it attributed to Ford of Canada president Wallace Campbell, praised Canada's "scientific warriors" who, with "modern mobile equipment ... take the impossible in their stride."[51] Another in the series described Canadian soldiers as being among "the best trained" and "best-equipped striking forces in all history."[52] Much of this was fanciful – most of the Action Pictures were printed before the Canadian Army had seen much action – but advertising had always been a door to the realm of fantasy and desire, however grounded in the real world the problems it addressed may have been. What mattered was not merely the depiction of the world as it was, but of the world as it should be and could be.

In *Madison Avenue Goes to War,* Frank Fox finds that such themes were also quite central to American institutional advertising during the war.[53] Given the close cultural and commercial ties between the two countries, it is not surprising that many Canadian institutional ads were often thematically indistinguishable from American ones. Some actually were American, produced by American agencies and printed in Canadian magazines with only minor changes to the text. US adworkers, however, frequently alluded to an ideal that would readily have been comprehended – if not precisely defined – by their countrymen: an "American way of life" that centred on the pursuit of an "American dream." Canadian adworkers made far fewer references to the elusive and amorphous "Canadian identity" that has so preoccupied subsequent generations and so often been described as having emerged during the world wars. Of course, the generation of English Canadians who fought the world wars often felt no particular distinction between their identity as Canadians and as citizens of the larger British Commonwealth, but the absence of historical allusions in Canadian institutional ads remains notable nonetheless. American ads could, and frequently did, appeal to the revolutionary spirit of their founding fathers: Washington, Jefferson, Adams, Franklin (and their heir, Lincoln), but John A. Macdonald, George-Étienne Cartier, and Thomas D'Arcy McGee are almost never found in the patriotic appeals of Canadian wartime advertising. Certainly, William Lyon Mackenzie King rarely made an appearance in a Canadian institutional ad, though Roosevelt and Churchill often did. King had many talents – inspirational leadership was not among them. Even so, some institutional ads did allude to unique aspects of Canada and its history. Some would scarcely be comprehensible to Canadians today, such as a series that trumpeted the glories of that most unglamorous of metals, nickel.[54] One Canadian Pacific Railway ad waxed rhetorical about the luminous, even transcendent, experience of encountering the immense geographical breadth of the country and the pioneering spirit of those who tamed the land:

> We have faith in Canada. We have faith in her past, faith that the courage of the pioneers and the spirit which achieved Confederation and linked a continent with the shining steel of railways have laid strong foundations for national greatness and unity. We have faith in her present, in the part she is playing to save the world from tyranny ... in her young men and women who serve on land and sea and in the air ... in her workers, who labour for more than wages ... in every man and woman and child striving for Victory ... Our faith is a faith in a land we love, whose soul speaks to us from every free acre of Canadian soil ... in the splendour of the Rockies at sunset, the blue mystery of a Laurentian dawn, the quiet of an Ontario woodlot, the far call of prairie horizons, the sound of the surf on the Atlantic shore and the wash of the Pacific tides ... Our faith is a faith in her people ... and by whose united effort, sacrifice and creative vigour the greater Canada of tomorrow will be built.[55]

General Motors of Canada, always eager to distinguish itself from the American parent company, often alluded to patriotic themes. It quoted "O Canada!" in one colour ad, and in another, under the tag line "We've a War That Must Be Won!" it depicted European explorers trading with Aboriginals, farmers plowing fields, cities and factories, children learning the words to the national anthem, and – rarity of rarities – the Fathers of Confederation at Charlottetown. All this was accompanied by the following verse:

These are the shores our fathers found;
To us this country is hallowed ground.
This is the Canada we have known,
The land we love and call our own;
Here we have worked and here we have played;
These are the cities our hands have made;
These are the fields our plows have turned;
This is the wealth our toil has earned.
This is the fruit of our fathers' dreams;
Of forest and plain and mountain streams;
This is the Canada we have known,
The land we love and call our own.[56]

Advertising's real preoccupation, however, was with the future, not the past, and a remarkable transformation in the themes of institutional ads began to occur as what Churchill called "the hinge of fate" swung in the Allies' favour.

BY THE AUTUMN OF 1943, nearly everyone agreed that Allied victory was inevitable. Day by day, German cities were being pounded into rubble by Allied heavy bombers. North Africa had been secured and Italy defeated. The U-boat menace was at long last surmounted, and the German army was reeling from crushing defeats at Stalingrad and Kursk. As hard-earned victories mounted for the Allies in late 1943 and in 1944, ads that concerned themselves with the future became increasingly prevalent, and the image they presented became more coherent. They began to declaim incessantly on the theme of "tomorrow." With its just-around-the-corner connotations, "tomorrow" was almost always preferred to the phrase "the future," which implied something more indistinct and distant. What tomorrow promised was immense, much more than the return of husbands, fathers, sons, and sweethearts. It held forth the promise of a nation fit for these heroes, where uncertainty about gender roles would be resolved by the return to domesticity of any women who had temporarily left it for paid labour, and where concerns about economic and social security would dissolve in a world of material comfort. Oneida silverware envisioned a day when a young woman's sweetheart would "come home for keeps," a reunion that would also mark the return of all the essential accoutrements of middle-class married life. "Crystal will gleam and silver will sparkle on a table set for two," the text gushed. The ad was so popular that Oneida received several thousand requests for copies.[57] Dozens of ads furnished similar scenes from "tomorrow," of reunited families released from the burden of further sacrifice through a new world of lavish homes and sumptuous commodities. Many of them explicitly linked the fighting of "today" with the luxuries of "tomorrow," often through the use of a montage juxtaposing images of the war with those of the consumerist future. "Today his home is on wheels," says a homemaker in an ad for Dominion Oilcloth, thinking of her husband overseas, "but he's fighting for his home of tomorrow." Her thoughts then shift to a gleaming kitchen. "New ideas will make that home more modern, more convenient and more comfortable."[58]

Splendid new commodities were central to the "world of tomorrow." If the world fit for heroes had not only failed to appear in 1919 but had collapsed amid sickness, recession, and civil strife, a much better version would be delivered when the current conflict ended – one of universal luxury and ease, made possible by the rededication of wartime scientific and technical resources to peacetime production (see Figure 4.14). As a 1943 General Steel Wares ad noted, "The metal can on a gas mask ... is one of the many war items being manufactured by General Steel Wares these days and nights. But in between times, General Steel Wares craftsmen make mental notes of bright new ideas ... They just *can't help* dreaming up wonderful improvements for your postwar kitchen."[59]

One hallmark of "tomorrow" was the transformation of the housewife-consumer's dreams into reality. Ad after ad depicted Canadian women fawning over the dream homes, dream kitchens, and dream appliances of tomorrow – remuneration for services well rendered but no longer required. Even "the towels of tomorrow," available in "glorious colours, charming designs, many sizes," and, significantly, "plentiful supply," would be "like a dream come true," according to one ad.[60]

Although articles in the trade magazines sometimes counselled caution, warning that advertisers who made extravagant promises would be held accountable for them if they failed to materialize, few ads were content to make more plausible promises (see Figures 4.15 and 4.16).[61] Much of the promise of tomorrow concerned the continuation of economic prosperity and full employment, a response to the widespread fear that the end of the war would signal not just the resumption of peace but also economic depression as the armed forces and war industries scaled back

FIGURE 4.14 Late in the war, many advertisements heralded a post-war world where swords would be beaten into stoves – and other commodities. | "And We Have Some Thrilling Ideas for That New Kitchen of Yours," *National Home Monthly*, October 1943, 33.

their labour force requirements. Successive advertisements assured readers that consumer demand would fuel the post-war economy. "War savings," said one Canadian General Electric ad, "will be turned to equipping homes for better living – with a host of electrical 'servants' whose manufacture will provide employment for thousands of Canadians."[62] Similarly,

Advertising to Win the War and Secure the Future 117

Tomorrow's **TUBE** ... *Today!*

Many a motorist today drives safe from blowout dangers because he wisely replaced his ordinary inner tubes with Goodyear LifeGuards. In the 9 years since LifeGuards were first introduced, not one has ever failed to function... and many disastrous blowout accidents have been prevented. If you are eligible for new tubes, and fortunate enough to find a set of the few LifeGuards left in dealers' stocks... performance has proven you can't make a finer purchase. Otherwise, insist on LifeGuards when you get your new car!

GOODYEAR *LifeGuards*

FIGURE 4.15 Goodyear envisioned futuristic automobiles of "tomorrow," made possible by the technical ingenuity unleashed by the war. | "Tomorrow's Tube ... Today," *Maclean's*, 1 December 1944, inside back flap.

Northern Electric promised that "tomorrow's living" would be "lighter and brighter" and accompanied by "one solid fact: you can be sure of plenty of labor ... as soon as the war is over."[63] Farmers, too, would reap the benefits of wartime technology. An ad for International Nickel portrayed soldiers driving a jeep in one panel and farmers using the same

FIGURE 4.16 Flying cars hurtle over the city of tomorrow in this ad from White Label Ale. At its most exotic, "tomorrow" resembled the science-fiction dreamscapes of Flash Gordon movie serials, with domed cities, towering skyscrapers, and rocket planes criss-crossing the sky. | "A Better Day Is Coming," *Canadian Homes and Gardens*, December 1942, 10.

jeep to haul a plough in the next. "Today, the army has a new mule," it commented. "*Tomorrow*, the farmer will harness it!"[64]

Seagram's ran a series of ads about the plans being laid by "men who think of tomorrow" (see Figure 4.17). Such plans included rocket ships, closed-circuit television presentations in movie theatres, and even a technological means of reclaiming some of the war's losses. One such ad envisioned a futuristic "salvage submarine of tomorrow," described the "more than 40 million tons of shipping have been sunk in World War II," and exclaimed, "What a treasure trove of valuable metals and non-perishable cargoes may be reclaimed ... But until the day arrives when men and machines are free for such fascinating exploits, we have a lot of salvaging to do on the home front!" "Tomorrow will come," it concluded, "but it will be all the brighter for the sacrifices we make today."[65]

Perhaps no institutional ad made the promise of a brighter future more explicitly than one placed by Sanforized washable clothes in June 1943 (see Figure 4.18). "What's coming is ... PLENTY!" it read:

> Plenty of coffee, tea, bananas, butter, lard. Yes, and plenty of Sanforized washable clothes. All the things we had before it started, and others we never had. Plenty of good cheap housing – thanks to new building methods. Plenty of light practical inexpensive cars, cradles and carriages – thanks to wartime expansion of aluminum production. Plenty of cheap fast air transportation – thanks to the rapid development of the aviation industry. It's going to be a good world – a world of *plenty* – a world worth all the sacrifice that's being made ... It's a small price to pay for what's coming.[66]

The promise of a future enhanced by material abundance appealed to many of those in a generation that had known war, want, and then war again. Here, as in so many other ads, consumer satisfaction was tendered as compensation for everything that Canadians had sacrificed in wartime. Embedded in the Sanforized ad are the customary promises of a return of commodities once easily obtained and the advent of remarkable new ones. But the truly extraordinary claim is that the war's sacrifices constituted no more than "a small price to pay" for a future where boundless satiation of consumer desires would be the norm – the land fit for heroes delivered at long last.

War-themed ads began to disappear from Canadian magazines and newspapers shortly after Germany's surrender and vanished altogether by the end of the summer. Very little discussion of this change appeared

FIGURE 4.17 Almost no promise about the "world of tomorrow" was too extravagant – a world where consumers would be compensated for their wartime sacrifices. Published even as German V-1 rockets were raining down on London, this Seagram's ad envisioned a future where rocket technology would be put to more civilized use. | "It's Coming ... the Rocket Express!" *Maclean's*, 15 July 1944, 23.

Advertising to Win the War and Secure the Future 121

What's coming is . . . PLENTY!

MAYBE not this year. Maybe not next. But *sometime* we're going to win this war — and what's going to happen then is *plenty*.

Plenty of coffee, tea, bananas, butter, lard. Yes, and plenty of Sanforized washable clothes. All the things we had before it started, and others we never had. Plenty of good cheap housing — thanks to new building methods. Plenty of light practical inexpensive cars, cradles and carriages — thanks to wartime expansion of aluminum production. Plenty of cheap fast air transportation — thanks to the rapid development of the aviation industry.

It's going to be a good world — a world of *plenty* — a world worth all the sacrifice that's being made. So if you can't get some of the things you've learned to count on, don't fret about it. It's a small price to pay for what's coming.

•

Right now many Sanforized fabrics are going to the Armed Forces because they more than anyone need the comfort of garments that really fit. Fortunately, however, there are still garments made of Sanforized fabrics available to civilians. When you do buy a shirt or overalls or a dress, try to get one that's Sanforized. It's just as important to avoid waste from shrinkage as to avoid hoarding.

·SANFORIZED·
Reg. trade-mark

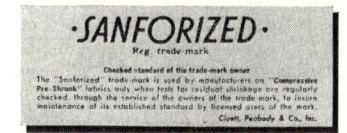

FIGURE 4.18   According to this extraordinary ad, the war's sacrifices were "a small price to pay" for the future of limitless, guiltless mass consumption that would follow victory. | "What's Coming Is ... PLENTY!" *Maclean's*, 1 June 1943, 23.

in the trade journals, as if adworkers had reached a tacit agreement that, though the war might have been waged in advertising, it would not be commemorated by it. Perhaps the urge to avoid gloomy matters that adworkers had felt in 1939 and 1940 reasserted itself when the war was won. Had wartime advertising worked? Had it kept consumers informed, bolstered the reputation of manufacturers, and sped the day of Hitler's destruction? Few adworkers would deny that it had, even if they knew that establishing a causal link between advertising and consumer behaviour remained the Holy Grail of their profession. At the very least, advertising's wartime clichés had furnished manufacturers, sellers, and consumers with rebuttals to those critics who argued that they were undermining the war effort. Particularly during the crucial middle years of the war, when an enormous amount of discussion about home front sacrifice was attended by comparatively little actual deprivation, advertising's clichés reassured consumers that they, too, were "in the fight." Whether or not such a claim could withstand cold, hard scrutiny was beside the point: adworkers passionately believed it, and no doubt, many Canadian consumers wanted to.

At their most grandiloquent, Canada's adworkers claimed that they were agents of civilization rather than mere facilitators of consumer purchases. In editorials and speeches, they declaimed tirelessly on what they believed truly distinguished modern Canada from the Axis tyrannies: the leisure, comfort, and security of the person furnished by the "democracy of goods" – that cornucopia of "finer things" modern consumers could buy. No claim was too grandiose. Advertising, they stated, had done much more than rationalize the complex and chaotic process of consumer choice. It made consumer choice possible in the first place, and in so doing had delivered economic democracy to the free world. It is therefore not surprising that adworkers also believed they could help solve the most urgent problem of their time: to secure victory on terms most favourable to the continuation of the way of life of which they were self-appointed heralds. Unashamedly, they described their craft as propaganda in defence of private enterprise and consumerism. As we shall see, when reconstruction began to dominate the political agenda late in the war, adworkers adopted a new cliché: that an essential "fifth freedom," the freedom of consumer choice, was threatened from within by advocates of a social welfare state. While government propagandists described the war as a struggle for political liberty and free institutions, commercial advertisers added that free

Advertising to Win the War and Secure the Future 123

BUY VICTORY BONDS
AND BRING BACK THE PLEASURES OF 'FREEDOM'

GO AND BUY IT...a new refrigerator, a washing machine, a set of Hagen irons, a built-in bath tub...go and buy it...a tankful of gasoline, a set of tires, a trip to Gaspé...go and buy it! No priorities! No ration books! No red tape! Just go and buy it... whatever you want, whenever you want it! DON'T YOU WISH YOU COULD JUST GO AND BUY IT! Speed back such pleasures of 'freedom' by buying Victory Bonds now! And when Victory comes, use your Bonds to make the pleasures real.

RAPID GRIP *and* **BATTEN LIMITED**
W. HOWARD BATTEN — President

LARGEST PRINTING PLATE MAKERS IN THE DOMINION OF CANADA

FIGURE 4.19   The pleasures of freedom, illustrated here not as political rights in the traditional sense, but as gasoline, tires, sugar, butter, refrigerators, and radios. In the world portrayed by advertising, access to a wide variety of consumer goods was a political right, one for which the war was being fought. | "Buy Victory Bonds and Bring Back the Pleasures of 'Freedom,'" *Marketing*, 8 May 1943, 12.

enterprise and unrestricted consumer choice were the most important freedoms of all. They conceded that times of supreme crisis when consumers might have to curb their spending did occur, but this simply leant greater urgency to the task of speedily defeating the enemy. "Buy Victory Bonds and bring back the pleasures of freedom," one institutional ad declared – and represented the "pleasures of freedom" as an avalanche of consumer goods (see Figure 4.19).[67]

More than thirty years later, the British cultural theorist Raymond Williams coined the phrase "magic system" to characterize how advertising reified inanimate objects, infusing them with greater social significance than their form and function alone dictated.[68] Adworkers themselves thought that their skills were more like those of scientists than of magicians, but certainly they believed themselves vested with powers of transformation. Symbolically, they had recruited virtually every aspect of the consumer economy on behalf of Canada's war effort. In the worldview they so vigorously advanced, all things could be attained through consumerism – even victory itself. But if advertising served as a glimpse into a realm of imagination where misguided friends were enlightened, housewives were transformed into soldiers, and science-fiction fantasies became everyday realities, the actual experience of buying and selling things could not help but be more mundane by comparison. In retail stores, consumers encountered the more troublesome day-to-day reality of purchasing goods that were often difficult to come by and not all that advertising promised.

1 **DONALD GORDON,** chairman of the powerful Wartime Prices and Trade Board from November 1941 to March 1947. Dubbed King's "no man" by the press, Gordon was the tireless defender of the price ceiling both behind the scenes and in public. | Photo by Karsh, Library and Archives Canada, e010944097.

2 **COUPON RATIONING,** which began in 1942 for a handful of staple goods, is sometimes remembered as one of the hardships wartime Canadians had to endure. Polls taken at the time, however, show that most Canadians approved of rationing, even if they occasionally bent the rules. | Library and Archives Canada, e010944098.

3   **THE WAR SAW HUNDREDS** of thousands of Canadian women take up jobs in war industry. From the perspective of the Wartime Prices and Trade Board, however, women's most important task was on the checkout line rather than on the assembly line. This display in an Eaton's store window recognized their efforts during "Mrs. Consumer Week," 1944. | Library and Archives Canada, e010944101.

4 **THE DIRECTORS** of the Consumer Branch of the Wartime Prices and Trade Board. Established in 1942, the Consumer Branch was created to act as a liaison between the board and the nation's housewives. Its director was Byrne Hope Sanders, the former editor of *Chatelaine (top centre)*. | Library and Archives Canada, PA-213462.

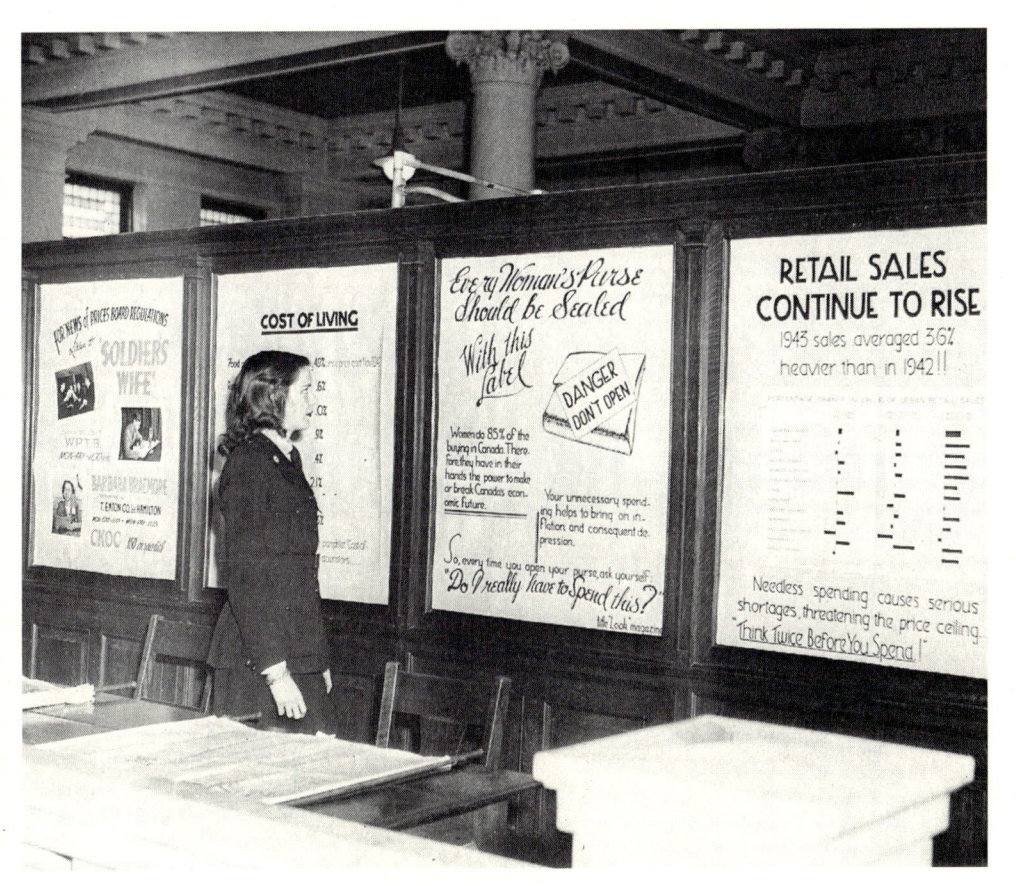

5   **THE WAR TOUCHED OFF** the biggest consumer spending boom in Canadian history. After 1941, the Wartime Prices and Trade Board issued a steady stream of propaganda discouraging needless spending. Retail sales rose anyway. This information display appeared at the Hamilton Public Library in 1943. | Library and Archives Canada, PA-213457.

6 **THE LAST CIVILIAN PASSENGER CAR** manufactured in Canada during the Second World War, a 1942 Chevy, rolled off the assembly line in Oshawa, February 1942. Just hours later, General Andrew McNaughton arrived to inspect the production of military vehicles. | Courtesy of Oshawa Public Library.

7 **DINING OUT** at the Capitol Theatre in Ottawa, Christmas 1942. With 2,500 seats, the Capitol was one of Canada's great "movie palaces" and a perfect venue for patriotic fundraisers. Eating out could ease war worries and relieve some of the pressures of rationing. Restaurant business exploded during the war. | Library and Archives Canada, PA-166790.

8 **THE WELL-STOCKED INTERIOR** of Bryson's Drug Store in Montreal, with the soda fountain shown at right, May 1942. Despite rationing, shortages, and a dearth of reliable help, many retailers said that they had never had it so good as during the war. | Courtesy the *Montreal Gazette,* Library and Archives Canada, PA-108296.

5
Buying and Selling Big Ticket Items

The most powerful secret weapon so far brought to light by the war was found in the possession of the automotive industry. It was not a death ray or a lethal projectile of any kind, but rather a technique – the technique of mass production. It has now been shared, or is being shared, to the fullest extent with every branch of industry building the tools of war. It may well win the war.

– T.R. Elliott, Canadian Geographical Journal, *May 1942*

Canadians should be proud to do without many things which an equal peacetime prosperity would place within their reach. What a minor matter it is, after all, to have the Dominion's supply of electrical refrigerators and electrical-metal-tub washing machines further curtailed, as was announced yesterday, or to have to get along with fewer motor cars and less gasoline. The fact is that in the matter of rationing the Canadian people as yet hardly realize that they are at war.

– Toronto Daily Star, *20 December 1942*

In 1937, the Canadian poet Francis Pollock set pen to paper to consider how the Olympian god of sun and light might have felt about an automotive replacement for his celestial chariot:

Chromium-plated, classical, straining forward,
Homeric, Greek-limbed, aiming the fiery arrow,
Sun-God, Song-God, set in the stress of the streamline,
   Far-darting Apollo!

> Set with the roar of the multiple motors behind you,
> Driving you forward at more than a mile in a minute,
> You clutch your lyre, your bow, in stifled amazement,
> > Angry and breathless.
>
> This is a movement that never was dreamt of in Athens.
> You find yourself in a totally new environment;
> Sing to me now what you think of the new twin-sixes,
> > Phoebus Apollo![1]

Pollock was never more than a minor writer, but the poem serves as a reminder of a time when it was still possible to wax rhetorical about the novelty of the automobile and the "totally new environment" it had created. When the war began, an era when cars did not exist resided easily within the compass of living memory. As late as the beginning of the First World War, there had been only forty thousand cars in all of Canada, and most of those were little more than puttering contraptions in the hands of hobbyists.[2] Then, in the late teens and early twenties, American automakers seeking a back door into the tariff-walled nations of the British Commonwealth subsumed Canada's own small and scattered automobile manufacturers. Within a few years, American subsidiaries propelled Canada into the position of the world's second-leading auto manufacturer.[3] It was a distant second, to be sure: in 1929, at its peak before the Depression, the Canadian industry produced over 260,000 new cars and trucks, more than twice as many as the third-place United Kingdom but barely one-twentieth of American output.[4] This was also a production achievement that would not be surpassed for another twenty years.[5] The result was that by 1929, there were more than twice as many cars in Toronto alone as there had been in the entire country fifteen years earlier.[6] Across Canada, there were more than 1 million registered cars and over 100,000 trucks and buses.[7]

Productive as it was, the Canadian automotive industry was reliant on American-made parts and heavily export-oriented. A third of the parts of Canadian-built cars, measured in terms of value, came from the United States, and four out of every ten vehicles manufactured in Canada were sold overseas. The industry was therefore highly susceptible to fluctuations in the international economy, and the Depression's impact upon it was catastrophic. Exports plummeted 88 percent, from 102,000 to just 12,500, in the same period.[8] Domestically, new car purchases fell from 160,000 in 1929 to fewer than 50,000 in 1932.[9] Thousands lost their jobs as production dropped. By the late 1930s, struggling American manufacturers DeSoto, Packard, and Studebaker had closed down their Canadian operations, leaving only the "big three" – General Motors, Ford, and Chrysler – producing significant numbers of cars in Canada when the war began.[10] By contrast, British and German car production increased during the same period due to the emergence of middle-class motoring in the first case and in large measure because of the Nazi leadership's enthusiasm for automobiles in the second.[11] By 1937, Canada's automotive industry had fallen to fourth on the list of the world's leading car producers, behind the United States, Great Britain, and Germany. Nonetheless, that fourth-place ranking is remarkable, given that Canada was by far the least populous country among the top manufacturers, with just one-quarter the population of the United Kingdom and about one-sixth of Germany's.[12] In terms of per capita automobile ownership rates, Canadians remained second only to Americans, with one Canadian in eight and about one family in three owning a car by the outbreak of war.[13] This rate would increase slightly before passenger car production ended in 1942 and then remain roughly static until after the war. Regional variations in automobile ownership were very large, however. Whereas nearly half of households in St. Catharines, Ontario, owned an automobile, just one in seven did in Montreal.[14] Overall, Quebec's per capita automobile ownership rate, about one car for every fifteen people, was the lowest in Confederation.[15] Montreal teenager Mary Peate recalled her mother reading aloud from a wartime goodwill advertisement that promised a "streamlined" and "powerful" automobile in the driveway of every home. "I went over to the kitchen window," Mary later wrote, "and peered around for sight of the streamlined car, shielding my eyes against the glare of its gleaming chrome. There was none. Streamlined or otherwise."[16] Still, about one Canadian youngster in three looking out the window did see a car, streamlined or otherwise (see Table 5.1).

A slightly earlier study conducted by the Dominion Bureau of Statistics measured automobile ownership based on family income and concluded that just over one-tenth of the poorest Canadian families owned an automobile, compared to more than three-quarters in the highest income bracket.[17] Surprisingly, however, even the lowest ownership rates in Canada – whether measured by income or by region – still exceeded the national averages of Great Britain and Germany by a large measure. In Germany, despite National Socialist efforts to produce an inexpensive "people's

Table 5.1

Retail automobile sales (units) and per capita ownership by province, 1940

Province	Sales	Total registered vehicles	Ratio population to vehicle ownership
Ontario	58,104	703,872	5.4:1
Quebec	23,284	225,152	14.4:1
British Columbia	8,718	128,044	6.1:1
Saskatchewan	11,599	126,970	7.5:1
Alberta	10,191	120,514	6.6:1
Manitoba	7,715	90,932	8.1:1
Nova Scotia		57,873	9.7:1
New Brunswick	10,941	39,000	11.7:1
Prince Edward Island		8,070	11.9:1
Yukon	0	402	9.9:1

SOURCE: (Sales) "Number of New Motor Vehicles Sold at Retail by Provinces, 1940," *Facts and Figures of the Automobile Industry* (Canadian Automobile Chamber of Commerce, 1941), 15; (registrations) "Standing of Provinces in Motor Vehicle Registrations, 1939," *Facts and Figures,* 19; (population figures by province) Urquhart and Buckley, *Historical Statistics of Canada,* Series A2-14. Automobile sales figures for the individual Maritime provinces are not available.

car," automobile ownership remained, as historian Adam Tooze has written, "the preserve of a small minority," affordable to just 5 percent of the working class in 1939.[18] Only Americans had a higher rate of car ownership than Canadians.

By the Second World War, the car had become an indispensable part of life for millions of Canadians, including people who did not own one. Cars and buses carried Canadians to work, and trucks hauled their commerce. The automobile's monumental influence could be perceived in everything from urban architecture – new homes had driveways and garages now – to startling new courtship rituals practised by young couples who now possessed the means to escape parental surveillance. Another effect was the vast expansion in paved roads. A trans-Canada highway was proposed by Conservative prime minister R.B. Bennett as a public works project in the early years of the Depression. The highway may have stumbled due to the usual suspects of Dominion-provincial relationships and the subsequent indifference of the resurgent Liberals, but by October 1942, it really was theoretically possible to drive from coast to coast, though not entirely on paved roads yet.[19] The automobile industry also became a bellwether for the nation's economic health. Provincial governments raked in millions of dollars from vehicle registrations, gasoline taxes, and fines,

Table 5.2

Retail sales of new motor vehicles in Canada (units), 1938-45

Year	Passenger cars	Trucks and buses	Total
1938	95,751	25,414	121,165
1939	90,054	24,693	114,747
1940	101,789	28,763	130,552
1941	83,642	34,431	118,073
1942	17,286	13,070	30,356
1943	984	3,814	4,798
1944	2,156	9,514	11,670
1945	4,526	19,830	24,356

SOURCE: "Retail Sales of New Automotive Vehicles in Canada, 1937-1945," *Facts and Figures of the Automobile Industry* (Canadian Automobile Chamber of Commerce, 1946), 12.

and automobiles employed tens of thousands of Canadians in everything from car and truck factories to dealer showrooms and service stations. In 1940, *Maclean's* estimated that directly or indirectly one Canadian in seven owed his or her employment to the automotive industry.[20] This may have been an exaggeration, but it highlights the car's economic and social significance. Perhaps no other object of desire glittered so brightly in the firmament of the modern consumer society. Small wonder that the cessation of its production and practices such as families putting their cars on blocks "for the duration" and then carpooling or packing onto streetcars are so firmly entrenched in the social memory of the war.[21]

DOMESTIC AUTOMOBILE SALES gradually recovered in the last half of the 1930s, but even as late as 1939, they remained significantly lower than they had been a decade earlier. Export sales, too, had not yet recovered from the Depression and would decline again with the outbreak of war.[22] In 1939, Canada's automotive plants were still operating at only about 50 percent of their productive capacity.[23] This proved to be an unexpected boon for Canadian car buyers, however. By mobilizing idle manufacturing capacity after the war began, the automotive industry was able to meet military orders for two years without significantly disrupting the production of passenger cars. Between 1939 and 1941, truck production, much of it stimulated by military orders, increased 268 percent. In the same period, passenger car production still managed to increase slightly, before falling off by just 12 percent in 1941.[24] Consequently, an ample supply of passenger cars remained for consumers – consumers who, as we have seen, had more money than ever and every incentive to keep buying until late 1941 (see Table 5.2).

Although 1939 as a whole saw a very slight dip in sales over 1938, this was not the result of wartime restrictions, as none were passed during that year.[25] If anything, the declaration of war led to a spate of panic buying: retail sales of automobiles jumped 29 percent in September 1939 over the same month a year earlier, and the remainder of the year saw a substantial increase in sales over the corresponding months in 1938.[26] The following year, 1940, became the second-best year for car sales since 1929, and even 1941's sales figures are greater than those of 1932 and 1933 put together. Granted, new car sales remained well below those of 1929, but the circumstances need to be viewed from the perspective of consumers who had endured a long economic depression and who now faced the prospect of a protracted world war. Seen in that light, the persistence or even growth of car sales during the first two years of the war is remarkable. It forces us once again to adjust our preconceptions about "penurious patriotism" and of a wartime economy where, in the inexplicable estimation of one historian, passenger cars supposedly were "not made" by the automotive industry.[27]

The experience of Canada's automotive retailers and car buyers in the two years following the country's declaration of war was unique. In the United Kingdom, by way of comparison, passenger car production came to an almost immediate halt in late 1939. British consumer spending on personal motoring declined from £113 million in 1939 to £38 million in 1940.[28] During the next year, civilian motoring virtually ceased to exist in Britain.[29] In Germany, the production of cars for civilian buyers started to decline even before the war began, dropping from 211,000 in 1938 to 168,000 in 1939, before plunging to 26,000 in 1940 and then to just 3,000 in 1941 – a falling off of 98.6 percent.[30] American production also began to diminish, even before the country was at war, as industry scrambled in the second half of 1941 to meet Lend-Lease orders and the requirements of the American rearmament program.[31] Orders terminating civilian car production in the United States were issued just three weeks after Pearl Harbor; the last civilian car rolled off the line on 10 February 1942, at which point the country had been at war for about eight weeks.[32] By contrast, Canadian plants continued to produce large numbers of cars for domestic consumption for twenty-eight months following Canada's declaration of war in September 1939. The following June, the very month that France fell, and according to some historians the beginning of the era of total war in Canada, car sales were 46 percent higher than in the previous June.[33] A progressive tax on auto purchases, introduced that summer, did little to quell consumer demand.[34] Moreover, there were, as yet, very few serious calls for reductions in automotive production and spending. In September 1940, a writer for *Saturday Night* responded angrily to any suggestion that there should be. "Canada's automotive industry is too important a factor to treat lightly," he asserted. "Important cities – Windsor, Oshawa, St. Catharines – are almost entirely dependent on the automobile industry. Thousands of workers in other industries and cities also owe their livelihood to it. It is one of the biggest contributors to industrial research and progress. Obviously this is no industry to monkey with."[35] In October, the editors of *Canadian Automotive Trade* urged dealers to make local newspapers aware that curtailing civilian production was neither necessary nor desirable, given the importance of civilian motoring to the economy.[36] In the same month, a *Maclean's* article underscored the point:

> In the circumstances indicated, it is apparent that any arbitrary curtailment of passenger car and commercial vehicle production would be unwise. Some proponents of total war have urged that the entire resources and energy of all industries, the automotive industry included, should be devoted to the production of war materiel. A little vital consideration that these extremists ignore is how a nation at war is to clothe and feed itself, let alone defray the cost of the sinews of war, by the exclusive production of those sinews.[37]

As might be expected, *Chatelaine* published a gushing four-page buying guide to the new 1941 car models that month without mentioning the war at all. "If there's one thing that's more than another calculated to make a girl wish she'd been born rich instead of beautiful," the author wrote,

> it's the new cars of 1941 ... Next year's automobiles vie with each other to give us more streamlining, more colour, more chrome, more glass, as well as softer cushions, roomier seats, sturdier bumpers, and safer door locks for the children ... The cars of 1941 are a lure and a temptation. When you see them, you'll probably contemplate selling the house or nagging your husband to distraction.[38]

Perhaps it was this sort of thing that prompted CCF member A.M. Nicholson to complain to the House of Commons in November about the quantity of automotive advertising in national magazines and to inquire why the government was not demanding more sacrifice from consumers.[39] His was a rare voice crying in the wilderness. There was money to spend and plenty to spend it on: What had events in France to do with that?

As matters would have it, civilian auto manufacturing simply could not continue without disruption. Even in 1940, military demands put a ceiling on it, which, though healthy by comparison to the 1930s, remained well below the production peaks of the late 1920s. In addition, in November 1940, an Order-in-Council issued on behalf of the practically omnipotent Department of Munitions and Supply (DMS) prohibited the introduction of most design changes in consumer durables, excepting cases where the changes resulted in materials savings.[40] In February 1941, the DMS created the office of Motor Vehicle Controller (MVC). Controller John Berry's legal authority over both the automobile industry and the country's civilian motor pool was so far-reaching that the trade papers referred to him as the industry's "dictator" for a time after his appointment.[41] They did not exaggerate. Not only was Berry vested with the authority to regulate automobile production and sales, he could in an emergency appropriate civilian vehicles.[42] Although this power was never exercised, rumours began to circulate in the United States, warning American tourists travelling to Canada that their cars might be seized. Canadian border authorities responded by handing out pamphlets assuring Americans that they could travel freely throughout Canada, and without fear of losing their cars or having the gasoline siphoned from their tanks – at least by any legal authority.[43]

Powerful though it might have been, the office of Motor Vehicle Controller imposed few restrictions on car production and none at all on the retail selling of automobiles in the first few months of its existence. Then, in April, anticipating shortages of parts and materials, Berry issued an order capping new car production for the remainder of 1941, albeit at a healthy 80 percent of what it had been in the equivalent period in 1940.[44] In addition, he banned the importation of American-made automobiles as part of the general effort to create a more favourable balance-of-trade situation with the United States, but this amounted to no more than a few hundred cars and had no significant impact on car sales in Canada.[45] Sales had always increased in the springtime, and 1941 was no exception. New passenger car sales rose from 6,700 in February to 16,000 in April, one of the highest monthly totals since 1929. In spite of the progressive tax, first-quarter car sales in 1941 were nearly identical to those of the same period in 1940 and were up 30 percent from the first quarter of 1939.[46] In June, even as the war escalated to frightening new proportions after the German invasion of the Soviet Union, the editor of *Canadian Automotive Trade* reassured readers that car production in Canada would probably continue without interruption.[47]

This proved to be a hugely optimistic assessment of the situation. Approximately one-third of the parts and materials that went into a Canadian-built automobile were imported from the United States.[48] As indicated in Chapter 1, the economic cooperation agreements forged between Canada and the United States after the Hyde Park Declaration in April 1941 effectively created a single economic block, wherein each country was granted access to the other's resources on the basis of a schedule of priorities that placed non-essential civilian needs below military requirements. The combined effect of the American rearmament program, the escalation of British war orders in both Canada and the United States (especially after the passage of the Lend-Lease bill in March 1941), and the growing demands of Canada's own armed forces left manufacturers struggling to acquire the necessary parts and materials for civilian production.[49] Despite a 100 percent increase in Canadian production, their most urgent need was for steel. In November, the DMS steel controller, F.B. Kilbourn, estimated that Canada would need to import nearly five times as much steel from the United States in 1942 as it had in 1939 to meet all production requirements. With insufficient resources to meet both military and civilian demands, regulators in Ottawa progressively curtailed consumer durable production during 1941.[50] At the end of July, the DMS announced that production of cars would be reduced in 1942 to 44 percent of 1941's output. Berry explained that unanticipated shortages of parts and materials were becoming more frequent, resulting in whole days where production lines and workers sat idle. "Rather than wait for actual material shortages to hinder production of automobiles," he wrote, "a fixed curtailment has been put into effect and this will permit established schedules to be carried through." He estimated that the cuts would result in a savings of more than fifty thousand tons of materials in 1942 alone.[51] In addition, he asked automakers to slash the number of models to 79 in 1942, down from 147 in 1941.[52] These orders were serious impositions, to be sure, but they seem to have been greeted with equanimity by most car and appliance dealers as the best compromise possible under the circumstances. It hardly mattered to manufacturers whether they were building civilian cars or military vehicles, as long as their firms remained profitable and their brand, if not their actual product, continued to be "sold" to Canadian consumers until full civilian production could resume.

As the war entered its third year, the overall outlook for automakers, car dealers, and civilian buyers was not as gloomy as might be expected. Granted, in response to oil tanker losses, the government launched a gasoline conservation campaign that summer, but in practice this involved nothing more than appeals for conservation and the mandatory closing of pumps after 7:00 p.m. and on Sundays.[53] This brought complaints from some farmers – and a spirited denunciation on their behalf in the *Toronto Globe and Mail* from Agnes Macphail – on the grounds that they needed to drive to market on Saturday nights, after the pumps closed.[54] Realistically, however, very few restrictions had been imposed on car sales or on driving. Dealers enjoyed steady sales and, judging from editorials and letters published in the industry's trade journals, actually welcomed at least some of the restrictions, which offered the automobile business opportunities to serve the war effort without making substantial sacrifices. Furthermore, no one in the industry itself seemed to believe that a total suspension of car production was likely. As we have seen, a few automobile ads, published in late 1941, made special reference to the durability of that year's new cars, but no articles in the trade papers forewarned dealers of an imminent order to cease production; nor was there speculation in the general media that such an order was likely. A Canadian Press story, published on 6 December (one can imagine the Japanese carrier planes being readied for takeoff as the story came off the presses), quoted the minister of trade reiterating that car production would only be cut in half in 1942.[55] Perhaps most tellingly, there was no great "run" on sales in November and December 1941, as had happened in other cases of panic buying when the public believed that certain goods would become unavailable. If anything, war jitters may have had the opposite effect, as sales were slightly lower than usual at the end of year despite adequate stocks on car lots. Presumably, buyers believed that a sufficient quantity of passenger cars would continue to be available.

However, the continuation of car production, not to mention of a whole host of domestic appliances and other metal consumer goods, was contingent upon the continued neutrality of the United States. Pearl Harbor and the American declaration of war touched off an avalanche of restrictions from Ottawa in anticipation of gigantic increases in American demands for raw materials. When the dust settled just over three weeks later, the consumer landscape had been transformed beyond recognition. On 8 December, Berry banned the further use of chrome, copper, and nickel in automobile trim. On the eleventh, confronted with the complete collapse of crude rubber imports from the Pacific in the face of the Japanese onslaught, the DMS rubber controller froze tire stocks and prohibited rubber processing except for military and essential industrial purposes.[56] On the twelfth, children bore the brunt of an announcement suspending the production of a host of metal consumer goods, including tricycles, wagons, ice skates, roller skates, and metal toys. Other bans fell on the production of metal goods ranging from sandwich toasters and waffle irons to ashtrays, coat racks, footstools, and lawn swings. On the same day, Minister of Munitions and Supply C.D. Howe informed Canadians that coupon rationing of gasoline – the first rationing that Canadians would experience in the war – would commence in April. On the fourteenth, Berry banned the sale of spare tires with new cars. On the fifteenth, the production of additional metal articles, including a wide range of furniture, was banned, and reductions in the output of commercial refrigerators were announced. On the seventeenth, the DMS ordered a reduction in commercial laundry equipment production and placed a bevy of household metal products on the restricted list. On the nineteenth, new orders forbade the use of brass or bronze in a variety of familiar items, including door knockers, nameplates, and hat and coat hooks. Another order imposed severe restrictions on tin, freezing its use altogether except for essential purposes. Yet another reduction in the output of washing machines and refrigerators came down the same day. By the end of the month, further orders had cut the production of dry cleaning equipment, forbidden the use of galvanized fittings in civilian plumbing, reduced the quantities of metals available for bed frames, and restricted the use of steel in civilian construction.[57] On 1 January 1942, C.D. Howe made the most momentous announcement of all: civilian car production would cease no later than the end of March, or once the existing inventories of prefabricated parts had been assembled – whichever came first. On the same day, a parallel order was issued in the United States.[58] A ban on civilian truck production followed in both countries within a few weeks.[59]

WHAT LED TO THE suspension of passenger car production in Canada for the remainder of the war was not greater demands for wheeled military vehicles, as these actually declined after 1942.[60] It was the post–Hyde Park integration of the Canadian and American war economies coupled with the reliance of Canadian manufacturers on parts and materials that the United States could no longer supply for non-essential needs. In a sense, the Order-in-Council that suspended car production was redundant. With the United States at war, the strategic allocation of resources was bound to bring Canadian production of civilian cars to a halt, regardless of any decision made by Canadian authorities.[61] In fact, this was precisely what happened in the case of electric stove and refrigerator production, which had virtually ended by 1943, even though no order mandated it. Similarly, car production ended a month before the date stipulated by the Order-in-Council. The last civilian car, a 1942 Chevy, missing only its spare tire, rolled off the assembly line on Friday, 27 February 1942.[62] There was a modest ceremony. When General Andrew McNaughton embarked on a tour of automotive facilities in Ontario the following week, it was to inspect military production.[63]

Judging from the response in the trades, the order to cease car production seems to have caught most auto dealers and service station owners unaware. A clever few, however, had seen the writing on the wall and prepared themselves. One garage owner recollected that he had stockpiled parts throughout 1941 in anticipation of the lean years to come: "Things like carburetors, springs, wheels with tires on them, steering wheels and transmission, headlights, just about anything that would come off without a cutting torch." Then, he recalled, "the Americans went into the war and stopped making cars ... and cars and trucks started breaking down and farmers were selling the junk in their yards for scrap for the war effort, and the supply of auto parts just dwindled away. That left me sitting pretty."[64] Despite being the continual bearer of bad news, Motor Vehicle Controller Berry seems to have maintained a genial relationship with most auto dealers and garage owners. He often met with industry representatives and proved amenable to persuasion in more than one instance.[65] If the claims made by some advertisers or retailers about the importance of their particular product in wartime seemed fanciful or slight – as indeed, they often were – the automotive industry, at least, had a plausible claim to indispensability. Recognizing this, the Order-in-Council suspending production made provisions for the manufacture, if necessary, of small numbers of cars to meet essential civilian needs. Ideally, most requirements would be met by means of a reserve pool consisting of some 4,500 cars drawn from existing stocks. The controller would review applications to buy pool cars on a case-by-case basis.[66] Berry permitted dealers to sell their remaining stocks at their own discretion, but panic buying was to be discouraged. To that end, he advised dealers to offer very low trade-in prices on used cars and promised them his office's support in the event of complaints.[67] Dealer stocks did not last long (in 1942, just seventeen thousand new cars were sold in Canada), and Berry was remarkably parsimonious in releasing cars from the reserve pool: he authorized just 984 sales in 1943.[68] Of the original 4,500, nearly 1,500 remained in the pool by the end of 1944.[69] More pressing industrial and agricultural requirements for new trucks were met by diverting a small percentage of newly manufactured military vehicles, stripped of any combat-applicable hardware, to the civilian sector. In 1944 and 1945, Berry diverted 23,000 trucks for these purposes.[70]

Berry also coordinated efforts with the Wartime Prices and Trade Board (WPTB) to regulate the sale and pricing of used cars, which were available only by permit after April 1942. He imposed a rather crude formula for pricing, in which a car that was one year old would be worth 90 percent of its original value, a two-year-old car would be worth 80 percent, and so forth, but it seems improbable that these rules were observed in person-to-person sales. Among the many cynical tales recounted in Barry Broadfoot's oral history of wartime Canadians is one concerning a man who sold his 1934 Pontiac for twice its ceiling price despite having filled out the appropriate paperwork claiming he sold it for its legal value. "Everybody," the seller recalled, was "laughing his head off at all the government regulations."[71] Well, perhaps not *everyone*. Dealers, facing greater scrutiny, had to be more circumspect in their behaviour. In April 1942, *Canadian Automotive Trade* estimated that used car dealers had forty thousand cars and twenty thousand trucks on hand but noted that about 6 percent of these were "junkers" and that fully a quarter had poor tires, making them "hard sells" at a time when new tires were becoming difficult to find.[72] Nonetheless, a healthy trade in used cars continued throughout the war. Although precise figures for their sales are not available, a minimum number sold by dealers can be ascertained from financing figures. In 1941, just over 141,000 used vehicles were financed; in 1942, 57,000; in 1943, 38,500; in 1944, 30,599 – a total of 267,000 vehicles.[73] It is worth repeating that this represents an absolute minimum for the number of used cars sold in the last four years of the war, since not all sales were financed; nor do these numbers take into account a very large number of private sales that must have occurred and that were exceedingly difficult for the WPTB to regulate. A 1945 survey undertaken for Maclean Publishing found that 17 percent of the cars owned by those surveyed had been acquired in the past year alone, and a further 27 percent in the two years before that.[74] Even allowing for used cars bought and re-sold, it seems probable that as much as a third of the nation's motor pool changed hands after the suspension of civilian automotive production.

FROM THE CAR DEALERS' point of view, the contrast between the first and last half of the war could not have been greater. For them, the remainder of the war became a struggle to stay in business. Like all retailers, they were further burdened by a baffling array of new regulations and mountains of paperwork to go with them. One retailer's plaintive cry in verse made the rounds of the trade journals in late 1942 and early 1943:

Forms! Forms! Forms!
Forms that ask for your name in reverse,
Forms that ask for your last name first,
Forms with a lot of useless dope,
That you couldn't read with a microscope,
Forms that plead for defense priorities,
Forms that go to the wrong authorities,
Red forms, yellow forms, pale blue, pink forms
"Please write plainly" and "please use ink" forms,
Single forms, double forms, triplicate forms,
Most of them are out-of-date forms ...
Blanks that you fill in the space marked X
Blanks for your height, weight, age, and sex,
Blanks to swear to and blanks to swear at
Dotted line that you cannot tear at,
Blanks with a space you mustn't write in
Big enough to fly a kite in,
Spaces the size of a pygmy flea
For a resume of your history:
Tax blanks, draft blanks, gas blanks, bank blanks,
And just plain blankety, blank, blank, blanks![75]

Nothing could be done about the paperwork. But auto dealers could try to cope with having nothing to sell by reorienting their business toward automotive service in order to keep the nation's irreplaceable cars and trucks running. Many converted part or all of their showrooms to garage space, anticipating a healthy volume of maintenance work in the years ahead. Service station owners were optimistic from the outset. Articles in the trade journals offered highly technical advice, especially for the benefit of new mechanics, about keeping older vehicles on the road. One station owner in Ottawa wrote, "We will eventually run into a period when we won't be able to buy parts [but] it is wonderful what you can do with an old lathe in your garage ... We make rings, valves, and even pistons on an old lathe."[76] A Vancouver firm profiled in *Canadian Automotive Trade* was forced to reduce its sales staff from ten to two (the lucky pair were retained to look after used car sales) but prospered on account of a 400 percent increase in its service business.[77] It helped that the military often contracted civilian firms to repair military vehicles. The biggest problem faced by service stations was not finding business but finding skilled mechanics – the armed forces drew off hundreds more every month. At their national conference in October 1942, the members of the Federation of Automobile Dealers Associations adopted a resolution calling on the National Selective Service to categorize auto mechanics as an essential profession, protected from conscription and barred from quitting.[78] The Motor Vehicle Controller shared their view. Its studies concluded that 70 percent of passenger cars were performing at least some essential work. John Berry wrote of the urgent need "to prolong the average life of such units and to take every action possible to retard the normal trend of scrapping" old cars. The MVC estimated that nearly nineteen thousand mechanics would be required to keep the nation's automotive fleet operating – a tall order given the huge outflow of trained mechanics into the services.[79] Under the circumstances, surprisingly few dealers were forced to shut their doors: nationwide, only eleven failed in 1942 and just four in 1943. A few more garages folded: twenty-five in 1942 and seven in 1943, but in each case this amounted to a minuscule fraction of the trade, and many of these closures were attributed to an inability to find mechanics rather than customers. In 1941, there were 1,962 dealers and 3,156 garages in Canada. In the twenty-four-month period of 1942 and 1943, their failure rate was less than 1 percent.[80]

No doubt the cessation of production came as a disappointment to the many families who planned to buy a car, and it presaged the possibility of real difficulties for farmers and businesses that actually needed an automobile, especially since no one could foresee when production would resume. Its actual impact, however, was not as great as people might have initially feared, for the simple reason that it did not last long enough to alter automobile ownership rates to any significant degree. Given the healthy auto sales of the first two years of the war, the number of registered cars in 1945 actually stood slightly higher than it had in 1939. The number of commercial vehicles, too, grew slightly over the course of the war, with the largest proportional increases occurring outside of Ontario – yet another example of the modernizing impact of the war. In Prince Edward Island, for instance, the number of commercial vehicle registrations nearly doubled between 1939 and 1945, and a very significant increase in the number of trucks was also seen in the Prairies.[81] The principal impact of the suspension of car production was to frustrate those consumers who had hoped to buy a replacement car in the near future. It did not alter passenger car ownership rates – it only delayed their expansion until after victory.

Of greater significance to those Canadians who already had cars was the shortage of gasoline, spare parts, and especially new tires. In November 1941, C.D. Howe had announced that gasoline rationing would commence as soon as the necessary administrative details were worked out.[82] By February, plans were in place for a comprehensive rationing scheme to commence on 1 April. The plan took account of everyone, from urbanites who used their cars for everyday transportation, to doctors, rural mail carriers, foreign diplomats, American tourists, and even Christian Science healers, apportioning gasoline on the basis of their probable needs. Ration booklets were distributed to drivers in the weeks prior to the beginning of the campaign, with the federal government snapping up a tidy $1 million in "registration fees."[83] Apart from the inconvenience of the ration books themselves – which was borne mainly by gas station attendants, who by law had to detach the coupons for their customers – the initial rations were a comparatively minor imposition. Non-essential "class A" users received a ration of sixty five-gallon "units" per annum, good for about five thousand miles of driving, and no restrictions at all were imposed on most commercial vehicles, including trucks, buses, ambulances, and even taxis, provided that their use was not unreasonably higher than in 1941.[84] Subsequently, tanker losses and soaring consumption (aviation gasoline consumption alone was *twenty-two* times higher in 1942 than in 1939) forced the DMS to announce stricter rations.[85] By September, rations for most non-essential users (now categorized "AA") had been halved, and commercial vehicle operators began to feel the pinch of restrictions, too.[86] As always, government regulators accounted for even the smallest details.

Taxis were allotted up to 150 gallons per month but limited to operating within a fifteen-mile radius of the municipality in which they were stationed to prevent their use for intercity travel.[87] The DMS Transit Control Board assumed authority over rental cars, restricting their use to travellers on essential business in order to prevent people from renting them for pleasure driving or businesses from using them for non-essential deliveries.[88] The effect of these restrictions was dramatic. Legally monitored civilian consumption of gasoline dropped from 746 million gallons in 1941 to 529 million in 1943, an annual savings that the DMS described as being "equivalent to 64 voyages of an average size ocean tanker."[89]

An even greater deterrent to pleasure driving was the critical shortage of new tires. After the war, the official history of the DMS would describe the rubber shortage as the most serious supply crisis Canadians faced during it. Ninety percent of Canadian crude rubber was imported from Indochina, Malaya, Java, Sumatra, and the East Indies. The Asia-Pacific War severed these imports at the source of their supply, and the production of synthetic rubber, which began belatedly and only experimentally in early 1942, could not make good the difference. Consequently, the DMS ordered drastic cuts in the quantity of crude rubber dedicated to the consumer economy. Production of standard tires for civilian cars plummeted from 1.4 million in 1941 to 56,000 in 1942 – a staggering 96 percent nosedive in a single year. Production of heavy-duty tires dropped from 557,000 to 23,000 in the same period, and tube production fell from 1.9 million to 80,000.[90] Overall civilian consumption of crude rubber fell from over 30,000 tons per year to fewer than 3,000 in 1944. Even so, with military requirements soaring, rubber stocks declined from just under 34,000 tons in 1941 to 6,800 tons in 1944.[91] An Order-in-Council even made it a criminal offence to discard or destroy anything made of rubber without a proper permit.[92] Massive campaigns urged manufacturers and consumers to turn over "scrap" rubber. In 1942 and 1943, over 28,000 tons were collected.[93] Housewives complained to the Women's Regional Advisory Committees about children's skirts and pants that fell down – drawstrings being no substitute for elastic waistbands![94]

Although every government agency acknowledged that the maintenance of the civilian automobile fleet was essential to the war effort, the DMS nonetheless estimated in 1942 that fewer than one car in sixteen could be issued a new tire in 1942 and 1943, and that even at that rate the stockpile of tires available for civilians would be exhausted by mid-1944. Conservation therefore became an urgent mission. Tires were rationed by permit rather than by coupon and thus were never apportioned to consumers on a schedule in the way that gasoline was. Stocks of tires, which had been frozen after Pearl Harbor, were made available on a case-by-case basis to essential users, though even then the buyer was required to surrender his old tires when picking up new ones.[95] In July 1942, the rubber controller announced that 375,000 drivers in the "essential" category might be granted permission to buy retreaded tires or to have their existing tires retreaded. For everyone else – some 800,000 car owners – new tires would simply not be available by any legal means until after the war.[96] Provincial governments, hoping to extend the lives of tires, imposed a maximum speed limit of forty miles per hour, an indignity that the poet Raymond Souster bemoaned in verse, longing for the bygone pedal-to-the-metal days of hurtling down the nation's new highways:

To drive the newest, shiniest, longest, most cylindered, most featured of the latest models down the four-lane highway bound for supper club or the weekend summer hotel.

This is to live, this is to meet the moment of each day with the maximum prescribed measure of pleasure.[97]

Although the official history of the DMS reports that gasoline and tire regulations "were observed by the vast majority of Canadians," a great deal of evidence points to a thriving black market for both.[98] An examination of Canadian newspapers from 1942 to 1945 reveals that the theft of tires and gasoline coupons, as well as prosecutions of retailers, consumers, and even corrupt government officials for various other rationing infractions, were a daily occurrence. Probably the most commonly reported type of prosecution was of gas station owners who sold gasoline without receipt of legitimate coupons. In August 1942 alone, the oil controller temporarily closed 225 gas stations in Montreal, Toronto, Winnipeg, and Vancouver for violations of rationing rules. In November, a further 72 stations in southwestern Ontario were closed in a typical inspection sweep.[99] In one sting operation in Windsor, undercover Mounties operating a gas station found that only four out of eighty customers they served during a two-hour period presented them with proper ration booklets.[100] So serious was the situation that the editors of the *Toronto Globe and Mail* – perhaps a little more than half serious – proposed that the black market could be brought under control only by flogging first-time miscreants and executing serial offenders.[101] No such punishments were forthcoming, of course, but prosecutions did increase. There were more than a thousand in 1943, with hefty fines and even an occasional prison sentence handed down.[102] Other forms of punishment sometimes awaited violators, too. In Vancouver, to cite one example, city council voted to suspend the civic trade licences of any retailer who participated in the black market.[103]

The office of the Oil Controller also introduced a number of measures designed to curtail the reuse of old tickets. These included requiring the ration coupon holder to write his or her licence plate number on the back of the ticket and making gas station attendants stamp all coupons in indelible ink.[104] Still, there is every indication that black market activity continued to grow. A large underground traffic in fake, used, and expired gasoline coupons existed. In one instance, new ration booklets worth 74,000 gallons of gasoline mysteriously "disappeared" from the truck delivering them.[105] A Hamilton-based racket managed to steal a total of 500,000 used coupons before being broken up by the RCMP.[106] In Montreal, an even bigger black market syndicate was caught before it could distribute as many as three-quarters of a million fake or stolen coupons.[107] One truck driver later recounted the following incident: While playing cards with strangers in a hotel, he let slip that he was desperately short on gas. Later that night, someone knocked on his hotel room door:

> I let this fellow in, and his friends with him, and they've got a suitcase. He puts it on the bed and opens it and there it is, full, crammed to the top with gasoline ration books ... They *were* gold, as good as gold, and as I live and breathe here right now, I couldn't tell if they were forged or not ... Upshot is, I made a deal, and it was that I'd give those two a quarter of my gross take, every week, every month, and they'd give me the books I wanted, and the harder I worked, the more everybody made. It was sure a lesson in free enterprise.[108]

So it went, on and on. In April 1944, the *Toronto Globe and Mail*'s frustrated editors likened the problem to bootlegging in the prohibition era, claiming that "tens of thousands" of Canadians were partaking in it.[109] A few days earlier, the paper had published an incendiary full-page ad placed by the Joy Oil Company, which operated gas stations in Windsor, Toronto, and Montreal. The ad alleged that an underground distribution of 300 *million* gallons of gasoline was occurring annually. Rationing affected only honest, independent gas station owners, the ad claimed, whereas big oil and gas companies, who had Oil Controller George Cottrelle in their pocket, criminally disregarded rationing rules.[110] Such allegations proved too much for the authorities to endure, and Joy Oil's owners were brought up on the very serious charge of attempting to subvert the war effort. In the subsequent trial, the judge, while disputing the claim that 300 million gallons of gasoline had been illegally distributed the previous year, found *in favour of* the defendant.[111] No doubt, the figure of 300 million gallons alleged by the Joy ad was far too high, but in its annual report for 1944, the WPTB itself admitted to "widespread evasion" of its gasoline regulations. Of 7,706 prosecutions for various consumption-related infractions that year, some 2,558 were connected with gasoline. Although the WPTB report claimed that "the vast majority" of Canadians were obeying the rules, it also noted that the number of prosecutions reflected only a small percentage of all offences being committed. "No one party to such a deal [a black market transaction] has any incentive to make a disclosure or complain," was its blunt assessment of the circumstances.[112]

It is impossible to establish with any certainty how widespread gasoline and tire infractions were, especially since there is evidence to suggest that many Canadians were at least willing to tolerate such impositions and possibly even make further sacrifices if necessary. In May 1942, the *Globe and Mail* reported the results of a survey that found that most motorists would be willing to give up their car altogether, if need be.[113] In July, a Canadian Institution of Public Opinion poll found 84 percent of respondents agreeing that the government should, if necessary, appropriate tires from non-essential vehicles – provided that the owners were properly compensated, of course.[114] Regarding gasoline rationing and the shortages of tires, Toronto's Marie Williamson may have spoken for many when she wrote to a friend in England during the summer of 1942:

> We cannot feel that it will be much of a sacrifice ... It is going to be hard on the people who live on the outskirts of the city, with children to get to school, etc. So many of our habits, customs, and ways of life have been developed and predicated on the practically universal ownership of cars that doing without them creates more problems than in communities where cars are simply luxuries which can be eliminated without altering any of the essentials of life.[115]

Editorial cartoons in newspapers and magazines often made light of gasoline rationing and tire shortages, as if to suggest that they were not

FIGURE 5.1 Editorial cartoons in both Canada and the United States sometimes made light of gasoline and tire restrictions. | "Horse Laugh," *Sudbury Star*, reprinted in *Hardware and Metal*, 14 February 1942, 12.

much of a burden (see Figure 5.1). One example depicted a woman at a formal ball, wearing what an onlooker calls "her family heirloom" – a rubber tire – around her neck.[116] Writing in *Mayfair* in April 1943, Robert Stark cracked wise about the "good old days" of guiltless gasoline consumption: "Yes sir, life was mighty full. I remember how proud my own

Pop was when we had a car that got only fifteen miles to the gallon of gas. He was awful jealous when the man next door showed up with one that only got thirteen."[117] Symbolic acts of patriotism by prominent Canadians made good news copy, too. In spite of his own greater-than-average gasoline allowance, General Motors of Canada president Sam McLaughlin demonstrated both his patriotism and some nostalgia for his family's carriage-making heritage when he started driving a horse-and-buggy to his Oshawa office.[118]

Some farms and a handful of commercial services really did start using horses again, but given the far more generous gasoline rations accorded to farms and most businesses, not to mention the difficulty of procuring wagons, carriages, and harnesses under wartime conditions, this seldom proved necessary or desirable. A service station owner in Nova Scotia who displayed a full-size replica of a horse-drawn carriage under a sign that read "1943 taxi" was only joking.[119]

Undoubtedly, there was a substantial underground economy in gasoline and tires, but it may not have been as great as some critics suggested. Abundant evidence, such as the demonstrably huge increases in the number of passengers on planes, trains, and buses, suggests that people were driving less. For the typical urbanite, public transportation and carpooling proved an important practical means of offsetting gasoline shortages. The number of buses operating in Canadian cities increased from 1,700 in 1941 to 2,600 in 1944 and would have expanded further had American bus manufacturers been able to fill their Canadian orders.[120] In Toronto, bus and streetcar ridership increased by 84 percent during the war.[121] This was actually lower than the national average of 120 percent, the bulk of which occurred after the introduction of gasoline rationing, with ridership exploding from 857 million passengers in 1941 to 1.4 billion in 1944.[122] Rules prohibited buses from operating sightseeing or pleasure tours (unless on behalf of war charities), and intercity buses were restricted to a fifty-mile range where trains duplicated the same service.[123] Intercity bus service took off nonetheless, with expanding routes and a staggering increase in ridership: from 17 million passengers in 1939 to 85 million in 1943.[124] Bicycles afforded yet another way of getting by, at least when the weather was agreeable and while their tires lasted. In response to consumer demand, the DMS increased the quota on adult bicycle output by 150 percent to 150,000 units in 1942, while streamlining the number of bicycle models to just three adult types. Manufacture of children's bicycles, however, was eliminated.[125] Smart hardware dealers got the jump on selling used and refurbished bicycles, for which there was no fixed ceiling price until 1944.[126] Police complained that increasing bicycle traffic was a serious hazard, with cyclists riding three and four abreast, but the number of cyclists killed in 1943 was sixty-eight, about half of what it had been in 1939.[127] Yet another indication that people were driving less, or at least driving more carefully, is the decline in traffic offences. Convictions for such offences dropped by nearly a third from 369,000 in 1941 to 270,000 in 1944. The number began to climb slightly in 1945 and mushroomed to nearly 454,000 in 1946, once gasoline and tires were widely available again.[128] Some skepticism is warranted here, as such statistics are always hostage to rates of reporting. Perhaps it is more telling that the numbers of automobile fatalities, which were not likely to be underreported, dropped by nearly a quarter as well. The accidental death rate per ten thousand automobiles diminished from 11.78 in 1941 to 9.14 in 1944 – a decline from 1,852 deaths in 1941 to 1,372 in 1944 – before beginning to climb back up again in 1945.[129] Black markets or not, people were driving less.

IN MANY RESPECTS, the circumstances surrounding appliances paralleled those of automobiles. During the 1930s, despite the Great Depression, there was a very large increase in the percentage of Canadian households owning electrical appliances.[130] As was the case with automobiles, these rates lagged well behind those of the United States but were far ahead of those in Europe. Regional variations in Canadian electrical appliance ownership varied to an even greater extent than did automobile ownership. The availability of a steady supply of electricity was the major limiting factor. The 1941 census found that 99 percent of households in cities of thirty thousand people or above had electric lighting, compared to just 20 percent in rural farm areas. In Ontario cities, just under half of all households owned electric refrigerators, whereas on Saskatchewan farms, less than half of 1 percent did.[131] The only electrical appliance whose use can be described as widespread regardless of region was the radio, with ownership rates in most major cities exceeding 90 percent and falling below 50 percent only in rural Quebec (see Table 5.3).[132] Only one farm in twenty was electrified on the Prairies, but in British Columbia, central Canada, Nova Scotia, and New Brunswick, the vast and expensive project of rural electrification had made significant headway in the late 1930s despite the Great Depression. By 1941, about a quarter of farms in Nova Scotia, New Brunswick, and Quebec were "on the grid" as were nearly

Table 5.3

Percentage household ownership of selected durable commodities, 1941

Commodity	Farm	Rural	Urban	All Canada
Radio	60.6	70.6	88.6	77.8
Telephone	29.3	27.8	49.7	40.3
Electrical vacuum	4.4	17.7	36.2	24.2
Electrical/Gas stove	7.4	23.0	60.9	39.6
Electrical refrigerator	3.6	15.6	31.2	20.9
Automobile	43.8	36.9	33.1	36.7

SOURCE: Dominion Bureau of Statistics, *Eighth Census of Canada, 1941*, vol. 9, *Housing* (Ottawa: Dominion Bureau of Statistics, 1941), Tables 12, 17, 18.

40 percent of those in Ontario and British Columbia.[133] Farmers saw their properties electrified and their incomes recover just in time for the supply of electrical appliances to dry up for the remainder of the war.

Many writers dwelled on the apparent emancipatory potential of electric appliances for beleaguered housewives. Even as the first restrictions on appliance production were introduced in 1941, a *Toronto Globe and Mail* writer gushed that "modern science and electrical appliances have transformed the kitchen of the average home into a constant source of pride and joy to the thankful housewife, who not so many years ago had to spend weary hours over a cumbersome cookstove and perform many other back-breaking tasks in the course of her daily duties."[134] Obviously, electrical appliances could never quite live up to that, nor to what they promised in advertisements but, then, nothing ever did. Nonetheless, in the early years of the war, advertisers aggressively promoted the alleged time-saving qualities of electrical appliances, and Canadian consumers took advantage of their renewed purchasing power to buy them in unprecedented numbers. During the first two years of the war, hardware and appliance dealers across the country reported record business.[135] Home radio production reached an all-time high of nearly half a million units in 1940, and the production of electric refrigerators, washing machines, irons, and toasters reached its highest volume to date in 1941. A survey conducted by *Hardware and Metal* found most appliance dealers in late 1941 in an optimistic mood and concluded that consumers' increased spending power had more than offset their increased tax burden.[136]

After this surprising and often overlooked boom in appliance production and sales, the combination of the expanding war effort and the difficulty in securing parts and materials from the United States in 1941

Table 5.4

Production of electrical domestic appliances (units), 1939-45

Year	Refrigerators	Stoves and rangettes	Washing machines	Irons	Radios	Toasters	Vacuums
1939	51,534	46,952	92,057	188,346	384,507	163,839	49,669
1940	53,165	44,470	99,562	233,817	485,010	171,015	43,441
1941	64,093	51,311	104,583	271,535	386,372	196,030	44,494
1942	37,792	24,316	52,198	133,786	177,149	131,327	35,034
1943	358	9,867	5,373	60,483	979	7,788	4,163
1944	237	17,798	23,967	113,484	0	6,981	1,899
1945	2,418	31,502	44,809	179,259	50,317	142,044	14,220

NOTE: Unit retail sales of appliances are not available for the war years. However, production figures can be taken as roughly equal to apparent consumption, given restrictions on exports. In 1939, 18.0 percent of refrigerators were exported. In 1940, just 2.3 percent were. The Wartime Prices and Trade Board's Research and Statistics Administration produced estimates of apparent consumption that accord roughly with the figures above. See LAC, RG 64, Wartime Prices and Trade Board, vol. 1460, file A-10-9-4.

SOURCE: *The Electrical Apparatus and Supplies Industry in Canada* (Ottawa: Dominion Bureau of Statistics, 1939-45), various pages.

forced the DMS to issue a succession of orders regulating production. In October 1941, it ordered a reduction in the manufacturing of radios, refrigerators, electric stoves, gas stoves, vacuum cleaners, and electric washing machines to 75 percent of their 1940 output.[137] A subsequent order reduced production to 50 percent.[138] In August 1942 – the halfway point in the war, it should be noted – the production and sale of most electrical appliances were suspended except by permit.[139] The "bare shelves" period that followed is the one that resonates in home front histories, whose natural emphasis is on the sacrifices made by civilians and the uniqueness of wartime life. But the production of many non-electrical appliances (and, curiously, electric irons) remained surprisingly high (see Table 5.4). A 1943 study undertaken by the WPTB's research division concluded that there was an "urgent" and "imperative" need to replenish the nation's supply of appliances in recognition of the fact that housewives were overburdened. The study suggested that the small diversion of resources necessary to produce a few thousand irons, electric washers, ranges, and other appliances would pay disproportionate dividends in labour savings – housewives would have more time for war work.[140] The agencies that produced ads for Westinghouse and General Electric could not have put

Table 5.5

Production of coal, wood, and gas stoves in Canada (units), 1939-45

Year	Coal and wood Cooking stoves	Coal and wood Heating stoves	Gas cooking stoves
1939	89,355	102,125	25,292
1940	111,463	103,520	31,228
1941	123,485	119,476	29,700
1942	96,991	109,899	19,064
1943	98,154	113,276	8,820
1944	93,755	121,284	8,439
1945	97,546	168,850	8,595

SOURCE: *The Electrical Apparatus and Supplies Industry in Canada* (Ottawa: Dominion Bureau of Statistics, 1939-45), various pages.

it better. Accordingly, significant increases in the production of irons, washing machines, and stoves began in early 1944. In fact, in March of that year, the officials considered the supply of electrical stoves sufficient to discontinue the practice of rationing them by permit.[141]

Obviously, some of this production was absorbed by the armed forces, but the majority of output was intended for civilian consumption. In addition, military conversion never completely eliminated the production or sales of certain kinds of consumer durables, as demonstrated by the figures for coal, wood, and gas stoves in Table 5.5.

The falling off in the production for electrical appliances after 1941 was very sharp, but most consumers seem to have understood and appreciated the necessity for the restrictions. One measure of this is the fact that the Women's Regional Advisory Committees received very few complaints regarding the cessation of consumer durable production, especially in comparison to the many they heard about food rationing and the shortages of soft goods. In addition, the drastic cuts to electrical appliance production may have contributed to the levelling off of retail spending in 1943, but they did not reduce it (see also the discussion in the Appendix). In large part, this was because consumers redirected their discretionary spending toward the surprisingly wide range of goods still available – and also to the cost of keeping their aging appliances working. Like auto dealers, hardware and appliance retailers, hard hit by the restrictions, attempted to cope with the loss of sales through appliance repair. With some hesitation, they also began to sell new lines of merchandise, including

Table 5.6

Gross production value of selected household furnishings at current market values ($), 1939-45

	Furniture				
Year	Bedroom	Upholstered living room	Dining room	Lawn and veranda	All
1939	5,300,425	6,082,003	2,147,003	302,515	25,629,270
1940	7,003,809	7,855,516	2,695,755	206,746	32,294,385
1941	9,546,571	10,209,806	3,390,158	236,712	42,776,336
1942	10,622,644	9,744,716	3,708,768	126,461	45,650,224
1943	10,268,197	7,824,354	2,735,592	271,835	47,107,520
1944	11,399,062	8,653,023	2,731,211	238,160	51,296,574
1945	12,595,956	10,630,937	3,066,030	263,227	58,739,829

SOURCES: Dominion Bureau of Statistics, *The Furniture Industry in Canada* (Ottawa: Dominion Bureau of Statistics), 1941, 1945; *Canada Year Book*, 1945, 395; 1946, 403; 1949, 531. Note that the "All furniture" column includes furniture types not listed to the left.

sporting goods, children's toys, and dishware, that would subsequently become staples of post-war hardware stores.[142] One notable arrival on the scene was a host of household items including kitchen tools, bathroom fixtures, and even some home furnishings made of coloured plastic that was cheap, durable, and mostly unrestricted.[143] These new designs were permitted under the rules, as they constituted a net material savings. Children's toys underwent similar changes: wood, paper, and plastic substituted for metal – and an extraordinary range of new war-themed toys hit the market. The Toronto Toy Fair quintupled in size over the course of the war.

Other durable goods such as wooden furniture continued to be produced with very few restrictions on the volume of output. Granted, a 1942 edict from the WPTB reduced the number of lines of furniture to half of what it had been, but the total volume of production continued to grow (see Table 5.6).[144] As the editors of *Canadian Woodworker* wrote, "It is doubtful if fabricators of wood products ever faced a more favourable opportunity to add new lines and extend the market for wood products."[145] Once again, part of the growth in output can be attributed to the need to supply the requirements of the armed forces for base furnishings. However, figures from department stores indicate an after-inflation increase of 24 percent in home furnishings between 1941 and 1945, and furniture stores experienced a very healthy 44 percent after-inflation increase throughout the war.[146]

Only in the category of lawn and veranda furniture – which was more likely to be made of metal – did the production value of furniture decrease. Overall, the adjusted value of household furnishings produced during the war nearly doubled, a fact reflected in the daily department store advertisements in major newspapers. Retail ads for Eaton's, the Hudson's Bay Company, and Simpson's in 1943 and 1944 routinely featured such items as beds, sofas, dining room suites, and even appliances, and consumer magazines such as *Canadian Homes and Gardens* presented a steady stream of articles on home decorating with the newest interior fashions (see Figure 5.2).

Retail jewellers were affected by the shortage of metals but saw their sales grow despite this, the 25 percent "luxury" tax, and the avalanche of anti-consumerist propaganda generated by government agencies and patriotic organizations (on the growth of jewellery store sales, see the Appendix, Table A.2). When the war began, the jewellery business had been fast out of the gate with gifts designed for servicemen (watches, pens, cigarette cases, and personal grooming items being among the most popular) and a whole host of "V for Victory" pins, badges, cufflinks, and the like for patriotic civilians.[147] At their conferences and in their trade papers, jewellers defended their business in the customary manner – by appealing to the urgent cause of maintaining morale. "We must continue to offer attractive articles of adornment, and goodness knows, during wartime, in the interests of public morale, women should be permitted to exercise at least the privilege of buying what jewellery you can offer for sale," commented one writer for *Trader and Canadian Jeweller*. Another, on the specific topic of wartime weddings, wrote that brides "should have as firm a foundation of worldly goods, as lovely an engagement ring, as fine a wedding ring, as beautiful a wedding as in normal times."[148]

Like most other retailers, jewellers seem to have viewed the restrictions on consumer credit, the price ceiling, and the 25 percent luxury tax with equanimity – at least publicly. In the trades, they grumbled that the luxury tax would not reduce consumer spending so much as redirect it, and they shared the concerns expressed by retailers everywhere about the viability of the price ceiling and the possibility that they might have to shoulder the burden of any price increases that did occur.[149] Their own requirements for metals, though small, were critical. There could hardly be a jewellery business without some supply of metals. Costume jewellery

FIGURE 5.2 As this ad from the summer of 1943 demonstrates, "thrifty" wartime planning on the Canadian home front could include ice refrigerators and five-piece dinette sets. | "August at Eaton's College Street," *Toronto Daily Star*, 10 August 1943, 29.

was hit first and hardest by military demands for tin. Then, in December 1942, the WPTB required jewellery manufacturers to reduce their number of lines to just 25 percent, banned a variety of pieces deemed excessively "fancy," and decreed that individual manufacturers of flatware could produce no more than two patterns each.[150] Furthermore, precious metals were banned from a variety of goods, such as lockets, lapel pins, chains, and charms. But like so many retailers, jewellers adjusted to shortages with alacrity. They sold everything they had and, thanks to consumer credit restrictions, increasingly without the long "lay-aways" that had been usual before the war. Many took to selling estate jewellery and antiques, or items fashioned from wood, and the trades were full of articles advising them about how to merchandise all manner of giftware and piece items that they had been unaccustomed to selling in the past. When *Trader and Canadian Jeweller*'s Elton Plant took stock of the situation in December 1943, by which time many of the most severe restrictions on their business had already begun to be lifted, he wrote, "Now as we reach this 5th wartime Christmas it can be seen that much of the worry was not necessary because almost all retail businesses are still being operated successfully. Most of them, in fact, are in as good a position as before the war or better, even with greater taxation and consequently lower self-profits."[151] Over the course of the war, their sales increased by 140 percent.

After victory, the regulations on appliance and automobile manufacturing gradually eased. In June 1945, C.D. Howe authorized the production of ten to twelve thousand new passenger cars. In August, two days after Japan announced its surrender, he lifted all limitations on car production.[152] During the next eighteen months, quotas on appliances were raised or eliminated, permit rationing was suspended, and – over the protests of many consumers but few retailers – the price ceiling was lifted. With patriotic incentives to restrain consumption evaporating and their personal expectations growing, consumers looked forward to replacing their aging cars and appliances. Drivers were especially eager. A comprehensive December 1944 survey undertaken by Maclean-Hunter found that 300,000 Canadians wanted a new car immediately after the war, a further 175,000 wanted one within two years, and nearly three-quarters of a million present car owners wanted tires within a year.[153]

Given gasoline and tire rationing, anyone fortunate enough to have purchased a car in late 1940 or 1941 probably had not driven it more than a few thousand miles before the war's end. On the whole, however, Canada's motor pool was positively geriatric by 1945. In the short term, however, domestic production could not meet anything remotely like the level of demand indicated in the poll. Resuming production required retooling plants and securing the necessary parts and materials, and the automobile industry's reconversion plans were thwarted that fall by the massive United Automobile Autoworkers strike that brought parts manufacturing to a halt in the United States. Total passenger car production in 1945 was a meagre 1,868.[154] In 1946, it clawed its way to 80,000 – slightly below the level reached in 1941.[155]

Before the war, automobiles and appliances had been symbols of prosperity and objects of consumer desire. During the war, as Joy Parr writes, they became "tools and tools alone, allocated only on the basis of the need for goods and services that they would produce."[156] Certainly, this was the utilitarian position that government officials began to take very late in 1941. As we have seen, however, in the world of advertising, and perhaps even in the real world of consumer desire, durables were much more than that: they signified the right of citizens to secure prosperity through consumption; not merely weapons of war, they became a spoil of war. Maclean-Hunter's March 1945 follow-up to its December 1944 poll found Canadians positively ravenous for new homes and a whole slate of mod cons to go with them. It is perhaps inevitable that the social memory of the war tends to dwell upon those aspects of the home front that were unique: regulation, rationing, and shortages. The privations suffered by consumers were not so protracted and often not as severe as is sometimes claimed, however. Many families actually acquired their first cars and electrical appliances during the two-year consumer boom at the beginning of the war. In its last half, the overall picture was much more Spartan indeed, but perhaps not so dire or long lasting as is sometimes believed. For those Canadians who already owned cars and electrical appliances, the biggest challenge in the final half of the war was to keep to them running. For those who did not, nothing changed except their expectations.

6
"The Grim Realities of War, as Pictured by Hollywood"
Consuming Leisure

War is Hell – let's go to the movies!
   – Canadian Moving Picture Digest, *9 September 1939*

To return home after a year's absence is to realize something which is, to say the least, disquieting. In the last three or four weeks I have seen, I frankly admit, only three Canadian cities, Montreal, Ottawa, and Toronto, but what I have seen in those cities is to me as alarming as it is tragic. If I may generalize from these local observations I would say that Canada at the moment is not so much a nation motivated by a full-out war effort, but it is, on the other hand, it would seem, in many ways a nation enjoying the greatest prosperity in its history. These days appear to me to be as gilded and as giddy as those of 1929.
   – *Group Captain Denton Massey, MP for Toronto-Greenwood, to the House of Commons, April 1944*

WITH JOBS APLENTY BUT fewer big ticket items to buy, Canadians naturally looked for other ways to spend their money. The commodification and consumption of leisure was one of the more notable innovations of the modern consumer society but also one of the most contested in wartime. On the one hand, Canadians were entreated at every turn to boost their morale and ease their frayed nerves by indulging themselves in diverting forms of entertainment; on the other, they were ceaselessly admonished for living it up while the boys fought and died overseas. Whatever the case, for millions of civilians and for many servicemen stationed in Canada, drinking, dancing, dining out, domestic tourism, attending spectator sports, and above all, going to the movies became an integral part of their lives.

Dance halls, resorts, restaurants, and movie theatres enjoyed burgeoning business. Even gas rationing failed to stop people from taking their summer vacations. A nationwide 1944 survey conducted by the Wartime Prices and Trade Board (WPTB) found that two-thirds of those surveyed (including three-quarters of middle- and upper-income earners) still took vacations, nearly all of them away from home.[1] On average, restaurants saw their business triple over the course of the war. Before building materials became scarce, many new restaurants opened, and existing ones expanded their facilities to accommodate the growing crowds. In 1942, the Sparks Street Woolworth's in Ottawa installed a fifty-metre lunch counter that was, it claimed, the longest in North America. With seventy-nine pedestals, six cash registers, and two soda fountains, it was built to provide fast service for the throngs of civil servants flowing to and from adjacent government buildings.[2] Some of this could be excused by disapproving moralists: weary shift workers and time-strapped office staff needed to grab quick bites, after all. But domestic tourism, dancing, drinking, and movie-going (the principal subject of this chapter) were different – to the morally disapproving, such things could only undermine the war effort.

Not that the moral disapproval was new. The pursuit of leisure had long been subject to the opprobrium of those who equated luxury and pleasure with vice and moral decay. As we have seen, non-essential consumption began to come under additional censure in 1941 on the grounds that it diverted resources from the war and because it was unseemly for Canadians to be living the high life while so many suffered overseas. Denton Massey's complaint about what he called the "carnival" atmosphere in wartime Canada may have been bluntly stated – he even chastised his fellow parliamentarians for taking the war too lightly – but it was a commonplace sentiment. Plenty of speeches and editorials by government officials and representatives of women's groups, churches, and voluntary organizations fretted that this most moral of wars might coincide with an erosion of moral behaviour at home. Examples abound. Sunday "ski trains" (aimed in particular at American tourists drawn to Canada prior to Pearl Harbor) earned a sharp rebuke from the editors of the *United Church Observer*, who saw this as the first in a series of moves that would eventually abolish the Sabbath, much as "Hitler first stirred up troubles in the border countries ... then annexed and despoiled them."[3] When an October 1944 issue of *Maclean's* published an enthusiastic five-page article on the nightclub scene in Montreal ("night life in Montreal is booming like Big Ben on Armistice Day"), it prompted letters from readers who were incensed that Canadians at home were drinking and dancing while Canadians overseas were fighting for their lives.[4] Even Canada's most beloved spectator sport, professional hockey, became the subject of controversy as governments on both sides of the border debated whether or not the NHL should be permitted to continue, the particular point of contention being that the teams consisted of young men fit for military service.[5] For servicemen from small towns, the big city offered a variety of off-duty temptations that alarmed some of their loved ones back home. Clarence Bourassa of tiny Lafleche, Saskatchewan, serving with the South Saskatchewan Regiment, wrote to his wife from Toronto in late 1940, "Maybe the officers did choose Toronto for its night life. Well, to tell you the truth there certainly is a lot of entertainment for the troupes [sic]: circuses, vaudeville, boxing, wrestling, shows, boating, cruising, etc., etc., all innocent as you see." A short time later, he issued a further and somewhat more dubious reassurance: "Yes there are burlesque shows in town, and I saw one and it's all show and talk. There is nothing to them; in fact, I consider them disgusting, especially these 'stripteases' as they are called. So you can ease your worries about them, because I am quite sure that I wouldn't waste a nickel on one again."[6]

For many Canadians, imbibing was another way to take the edge off the rigours of life. Increased consumer purchasing power, longer working hours, and a forthright sense of entitlement on the part of those serving the war effort led to an explosion in the consumption of beer, both at home and in beer parlours. This in turn aroused a major resurgence in public calls for temperance and prohibition, many of them made by the very women's organizations that were the linchpin of WPTB efforts to maintain the price ceiling. Ever since temperance and prohibition had arisen as a powerful social movement in the late nineteenth century, supporters had argued that alcohol lay at the root of social evils. In their view, drinking led to indolence and poverty, the breakdown of families, and public violence.[7] The First World War had intensified the temperance movement's efforts, with advocates arguing that drunkenness served the interests of the enemy. One by one, provincial legislatures had passed prohibition ordinances, and for a brief period in 1918, Ottawa had deployed its authority under the War Measures Act to ban the manufacture, import, and sale of alcohol. But the federal measures expired almost immediately after the war, and most provincial prohibition regimes had been short-lived as well, replaced in the 1920s with provincial control boards.[8] As historian Craig Heron puts it, in the interwar period, "The new watchword was 'moderation' ... It embraced the proletarian desire for the right to respectable imbibing ... It was an appeal to greater personal freedom for sensible, orderly behavior, under the still watchful eyes of the state."[9] The new provincial liquor outlets, Heron writes, were "coldly austere places, more like banks than retail stores," that usually required buyers to possess an annually renewable permit. One equally important development in the interwar years was the advent of the modern equivalent of the working man's tavern, the provincially regulated beer parlour, where strict rules governed the serving of alcohol and the behaviour of customers. Patrons pushed the rules of conduct to their limit, however, and over increasingly shrill objections from the still powerful advocates of prohibition, women were gradually permitted entry to the parlours when suitably "escorted."[10]

The outbreak of war galvanized flagging temperance supporters. The National Council of Women and its various member organizations began to work with Protestant churches to campaign for new temperance legislation, deploying patriotic arguments nearly identical to those that had been so successful a generation earlier.[11] In a typical column, the editors of the *United Church Observer* expressed their frustration with King's government for its failure to deploy the War Measures Act to stem the growth in the consumption of alcohol. Imbibing, the editors wrote, "is weakening the moral fibre of our youth, interfering with the efficient war effort, and piling up profits for owners and stock holders of breweries and distilleries." Moreover, "Beverage rooms in the towns and cities crowded nightly with young men and women, the daily budget of crimes and violence, accidents, and stories of broken homes, in many of which our soldiers are involved, are tragic evidence of the blighting ravages of intoxicating liquors."[12] The Consumer Branch's Women's Regional Advisory Committees (WRACs), too, heard from many women who complained about the ready availability of beer when necessities such as meat and butter were in short supply. Reducing the production of beer was not about to make butter appear, but some local WRACs passed motions calling for temperance legislation anyway.

Temperate himself, though not abstinent, Prime Minister King was not unsympathetic to these concerns. In September 1942, he met a delegation from the United Church and promised to speak publicly on the need for personal temperance.[13] On 16 December, he gave a long radio address entitled "Temperance and a Total War Effort" in which he called on Canadians to demonstrate "self-denial and self-discipline" in the form of "temperance in the use of alcoholic beverages." King had agonized for weeks, writing and revising the speech, and at times expressed considerable frustration with the process. "I never encountered such complete incapacity to secure information or to grasp a point of view to be presented to the public, as I have on this matter of temperance," he wrote in his diary the week before the broadcast.[14] On the day he completed the speech, he sensed the momentousness of the issue, reflecting that it was not merely political but spiritual as well: "I have never lived a day in which I felt a closer communion with invisible forces of good than I have before today. I am as sure as I am living that I was being helped, and given strength and joy in the preparation of bringing into being, this much needed reform at this time of war."[15]

For a speech so inspired, it was vintage King – overlong, overwritten, dour, and sanctimonious. The "cultivation of temperance in all things" he said, would be like "putting on the whole armour of God" for the trials ahead. The speech also showcased one of King's great political strengths – some might say his foremost political vice – his "sensitivity to the prevailing political winds" as one historian has described it, or his tendency to "do nothing by halves / that can be done by quarters" as the poet F.R. Scott was later to put it.[16] Polls from earlier in the year had revealed surprising support for temperance measures. Nearly half of Ontarians favoured tougher regulation of wine and beer, and two-thirds of Canadians generally approved limits on the consumption of hard liquor. On the other hand, only one in five supported outright prohibition.[17] King also had to consider his Cabinet's position that, in the interests of provincial and labour relations, and especially public opinion in Quebec – where support for temperance was thought to be lowest – sterner measures of the kind taken during the First World War ought to be avoided.[18] Consequently, few of the prime minister's speeches so demonstrated his ability to be simultaneously self-righteous and equivocating:

> At a time when nearly all of our citizens are denying themselves, or are being denied, some of the comforts and enjoyments which, in normal times, have come to be regarded as necessities, to see others spending more money than ever on alcoholic beverages is bound to occasion resentment. It tends to destroy the spirit of mutual aid, and of community cooperation, which are never more needed than at a time of war.[19]

Table 6.1

Apparent consumption of beer, wine, and spirits (imperial gallons), 1939-45

Year	Beer	Wine	Spirits	Total	Per capita consumption*
1939	63,302,752	3,461,867	3,433,644	70,198,263	8.65
1940	66,289,690	4,012,917	3,818,409	74,121,016	9.04
1941	78,629,148	4,812,614	3,714,790	87,156,552	10.49
1942	89,505,475	4,167,243	4,348,440	98,021,158	11.68
1943	97,610,326	4,627,567	4,729,919	106,967,812	12.6
1944	90,709,847	3,593,946	3,443,716	97,747,509	11.36
1945	110,223,815	3,712,456	3,719,918	117,656,189	13.54

* Persons 15 and over.
SOURCES: Dominion Bureau of Statistics, *The Control and Sale of Alcoholic Beverages in Canada to 1946* (Ottawa: Dominion Bureau of Statistics, 1947), 40-41. Per capita statistics, computed by the author, are based on population figures in M.C. Urquhart and K.A.H. Buckley, eds., *Historical Statistics of Canada* (Cambridge: Cambridge University Press, 1965), Series A1.

Such lofty sentiments were greeted with enthusiasm by temperance forces, but then, in typical fashion, King split the difference and announced a series of half measures. He reiterated that the government was already taxing alcohol to the hilt, noted that sugar rationing had taken its toll on domestic wine production, and pointed out that the majority of the country's distillation capacity was already at the disposal of the war effort. Then he announced moderate reductions in the quantities of alcohol that would be made available for public sale (10 percent for beer, 20 for wine, and 30 for spirits) and a prohibition on liquor advertising. Finally, he appealed to the provinces to reduce the operating hours of provincial alcoholic beverage outlets, including taverns, to no more than eight per day.[20]

So the advertising vanished (though not from American magazines sold in Canada), the quantity of booze for sale declined, and the provinces mostly fell into line with King's request to reduce the hours in which people could buy it. Most provinces proceeded to ration beer and wine to stave off hoarding. Once again, however, we find that the official ethos of moderation and restraint ran up against the actuality of consumption. As Table 6.1 shows, per capita consumption of alcoholic beverages increased by nearly 46 percent from 1939 to 1943 and by nearly 60 percent throughout the war as a whole. The reductions in saleable quantities of beverage alcohol that King announced did not affect actual consumption in 1943, presumably because a greater percentage of available stocks was actually bought, and the slight drop in per capita consumption in 1944 nearly disappears altogether if the 400,000 or so young males stationed overseas that year are deducted from the population computations.

The combination of increased demand and decreased supply had more than the usual consequences for consumers. For many, buying liquor at provincial outlets thereafter became an often tedious and nerve-wracking experience, especially at holiday time. "I went down to the Vendors today and I got my Xmas liquor," wrote Edmonton's Kathlyn Fish in 1943 to her husband, stationed overseas. She went on to describe a scene of agitated shoppers and holiday pandemonium:

> I hope I don't have to go back there for awhile, as it was a riot from beginning to end. First you go down and take your place in the lineup, then, at intervals, about 50 or 75 people are admitted. When the officer gives the word, the ones in front leap ahead and you have to leap right after them to keep from being knocked down by the onrushing throng in the rear. When you finally get inside, you line up and wait to give your order. I got in behind a soldier and fairly clung to the belt of his greatcoat or I'd have been elbowed out of line before reaching the desk ... Everyone is very discourteous to everyone else and the clerks are rude to the customers.[21]

Scenes of long lines and frazzled customers at provincial outlets confirmed the fact that the temperance victories of the First World War would not be repeated. The renewed prohibition movement was confronted with changing social mores, declining disapproval of moderate alcohol consumption, and by "wet" forces far better organized and prepared than they had been a generation earlier. Brewers who had been on the defensive during the First World War, hapless in the face of patriotic arguments that cast them as subverting the war effort, now countered with a patriotic barrage of their own. Soldiers, sailors, airmen, and the men and women labouring to manufacture the implements of combat in the nation's factories had earned the right to moderate consumption, they claimed. This time, it was the proponents of prohibition who were portrayed as undermining morale and with it, the war effort. Within a month of King's speech, Canadian Breweries Limited responded with a widely printed institutional ad titled "An Alternative Speech on Temperance," which it proposed was a "more suitable" speech than the one King had actually given. It stressed that Canadians were already temperate drinkers, consuming less alcohol per capita than either Britons or Americans, that the morale of the nation would be grievously harmed by further restrictions, and that the "evil spectacle of prohibition" must not be permitted to return.[22] Tactics such as these were probably predictable and might not have been taken altogether seriously – although the *United Church Observer* mounted several ferocious denunciations of the ad. What did have to be taken seriously was the threat that Cabinet perceived from organized labour. King was informed in early 1943 that unionized workers had begun wearing buttons with such slogans as "No Beer – No Bonds," threatening to withhold Victory Bond purchases if prohibition were renewed.[23] The rather tepid measures that King announced in December 1942 were therefore the furthest that Ottawa went in terms of supporting temperance. By February 1943, Cabinet was already pressing King to reverse the decision about reducing the beer available for sale. He held out until August 1945, but in the meantime, the provincial outlets and beer parlours stayed open, drinking went up, and despite all its efforts and protestations, the renewed prohibition movement fizzled.

AFTER PUBLIC DRINKING, no form of recreation generated so much revenue – or controversy – as the movies. On the surface, movie-going might seem an innocuous activity, but the silver screen had from the very beginning been subject to the closest oversight by the morally disapproving. For years, the motion picture industry had been forced to contend with charges that the movies were impious and even wicked. In light of this, film offers a fruitful case study in the many tensions inherent in Canada's wartime consumer economy. During the war, grave fears about the cinema's potential to undermine public morality merged with the growing tension between demands for sacrifice and the everyday realities of increasingly well-to-do consumers seeking to satisfy their wants and needs. The possibility of patriotic service offered the movie industry the opportunity to defend its reputation and to secure a share of renewed prosperity. And all the while, people flocked to the theatres in record numbers, seeking news, entertainment, and yet another opportunity to serve the war effort through patriotic consumption.

Like so many other retailers, movie theatre owners had sensed, even before the war began, that a great opportunity was at hand. In August 1939, Ray Lewis, the long-time editor of *Canadian Moving Picture Digest*, urged her colleagues in the business to face the prospect of hostilities both stoically and optimistically. "We cannot be worse off than we have been," she reflected. War would, at least, end the "state of uncertainty" and the "bog of business depression" under which the industry had toiled for a decade.[24] Canadian exhibitors had been especially hard hit by the Depression. Revenues from ticket sales had declined by a third in the first half of the 1930s and had not yet recovered.[25] Nationwide, an average of only one seat in four was sold for any given performance in 1939.[26] Although there were more theatres – about twelve hundred, compared to just nine hundred in 1930 – nearly 20 percent of them had annual receipts totalling less than $2,500. On the Prairies, the figure was closer to 40 percent. In 1939, those poorest 163 Prairie theatres grossed an average of just $1,400 each, the equivalent of a paltry seventeen ticket sales per business day. Some of those theatres were just community halls with projection equipment installed, and in some small towns, they operated only on weekends or in the summer, but most Canadian exhibitors remained mired in the Depression. As was the case for so many retailers and service providers, war brought them the prospect of improved business but also unforeseeable perils.[27]

In September 1939, Canadian motion picture exhibitors expressed their intention to place their theatres at the disposal of the war effort. Following Britain's declaration of war, Lewis deployed the language of cinematic criticism to state that Hitler's "unholy show" and "putrid serial thriller" must be "censored right off the map."[28] For those purposes, she wrote, the North American film industry would be ready to counter Nazi propaganda with its vastly more sophisticated and benevolent version. Lewis assumed, correctly as matters would have it, that Hollywood movies would favourably portray the Allied war effort, even if the United States remained neutral; she even speculated that the right kind of films might sway Americans from neutrality to co-belligerency with the Allies. "Watch the war pictures from Hollywood," she wrote. "The Nazis will be the villains. The British and French will be the heroes. How neutral will the people of the United States be with one hundred and twenty-six million of them attending moving theatres and looking and listening to the voice and drama of the screen?"[29]

Paradoxically, Lewis also became a tireless proponent of what I have ventured to call the "escape thesis": the idea, widely held at the time, that civilians on the home front had an urgent psychological requirement for diverting forms of entertainment, one that the movies were particularly well suited to satiate. "Theatres are as shelters from the bombs of news which tear through our brain and break our hearts," she wrote with customary hyperbole in the spring of 1940.[30] Throughout the war, the escape thesis was advanced from every corner of the film industry, a version of the familiar advertising argument that luxury goods were justifiable if they bolstered civilian morale. In the spring of 1942, Franklin Delano Roosevelt defended Hollywood movie making on precisely these grounds.[31] As for Canada's prime minister, his diaries reveal him to be a frequent and frequently enthusiastic moviegoer, positively transported by trifles such as *Lassie Come Home* (a "beautiful film" that he saw three times) and by such forgotten fare as Cecil B. DeMille's *North West Mounted Police* and *Abe Lincoln in Illinois*, the latter of which prompted a lengthy and introspective diary entry on political leadership.[32] Unlike temperance supporters, moralistic enemies of modern cinema found no ally in the prime minister.

Ray Lewis's conviction that the movie industry was ideally positioned to thwart Nazi propaganda reflected a broader belief that film was a uniquely powerful and influential medium. That the movies possessed vast powers of suasion was perhaps the only point of consensus between the industry and its many social critics. The contours of the dispute are familiar even today, having remained essentially the same since the earliest days of motion pictures, and they are themselves derivations of very old arguments about the moral implications of live theatre. Moviemakers and exhibitors assert that film can instruct, entertain, and offer respite to the weary; their detractors charge that the silver screen is awash in sex, violence, and other forms of moral degeneracy that can pervert the minds of the young and naive. The careful observer will note that there is no necessary contradiction between these two points of view, but in the 1930s and '40s, they seemed poles apart. During the Depression, moral campaigners in the United States scored a succession of victories against Hollywood, the impact of which was felt in all countries that screened American movies. Early in the decade, producers were forced to acquiesce to the authority of a powerful regulatory body, the Production Code Administration (PCA), whose mandate was to suppress realistic depictions of sex and violence.[33] In 1938, anti-trust suits against the vertically integrated studios reached the US Supreme Court, and in 1939, members of the US Congress's House Un-American Activities Committee embarked on the first of several witch hunts for communists and other subversives who were thought to lurk in the acting, writing, and directing guilds.[34]

In Canada and western Europe, cultural and economic nationalists voiced fears of their own as they observed, aghast, the vast tide of movies emanating from Hollywood.[35] As early as 1926, Hollywood's dominance of the global motion picture industry had been considered alarming enough to make the agenda at that year's seminal Imperial Conference. In a brief prepared for the conference, delegates were warned that it was "clearly undesirable that so very large a proportion of films shown throughout the Empire should present modes of life and forms of conduct which are not typically British."[36] Here, encapsulated in a sentence, was the essence of the fears felt so acutely by Canadian cultural nationalists; in a slightly modified form, they persist today. In theatre after theatre, from Halifax to Winnipeg to Vancouver, American features rolled day in and day out. Canadian exhibitors, including the Canadian-owned Famous Players chain, were wholly prostrate before Hollywood producers. Every attempt to loosen Hollywood's hegemonic hold over theatre audiences, from early attempts at banning "excessive" displays of the American flag to the introduction of a quota system mandating the production and exhibition of British-made films, failed entirely to dissuade audiences from choosing American movies at the box office.[37]

Moreover, the outbreak of war severely disrupted British and European feature film production, further intensifying Hollywood's grip on Canadian theatres. By 1939, Canada's own motion picture industry, was, in the words of historian Peter Morris, "an unmistakable branch plant of Hollywood." Canadians' very few ventures into feature film making were "scattered" and "uncoordinated" and of "minimal economic or cultural relevance" in Morris's view.[38] "Stillborn," is how historian Ted Magder has described Canada's feature film industry, but by his own account, it is probably more precise to say that it died in its infancy, a "feeble enterprise" that "withered further from government neglect."[39] Granted, the fledgling National Film Board, which hoped to bolster the country's already respectable reputation for documentary filmmaking, seemed better positioned to produce the kind of "benevolent propaganda" that Ray Lewis and others in the industry had called for when war began in 1939. But documentaries did not fill theatres – Hollywood features did. In 1943, 557 of 686 feature films booked in Canadian theatres were American. Just 72 were from Britain.[40] Montreal teenager Mary Peate later recalled how a friend reflected guiltily that war movies made her wish she were an American. As Peate recalled, "a great deal of Canadian chauvinistic pride went untapped" because so few war movies featured Canadian heroes – Laurence Olivier's dreadful turn in *49th Parallel* as a Quebec fur trapper who runs afoul of a shipwrecked U-boat crew notwithstanding.[41] Even the mere mention of Canada in a Hollywood movie, Peate remembered, would send Montreal audiences into frenzied whistling, clapping, and thumping.[42]

The fear that Hollywood's domination was not merely economic but cultural, and the harbinger of a particularly vulgar sort of culture at that, sometimes resulted in American movies being subjected to additional censorship upon arrival in Canada. Provincial censors and regulators sometimes took an even more puritanical view of the cinematic representation of sex and violence than did the American PCA, although their position would soften somewhat during the war. In 1939, for instance, thirteen films that had earned the PCA's always grudgingly bequeathed approval were banned outright by the Manitoba Censor Board. More than a hundred more were edited to remove "objectionable dialogue or action." The banned films, innocuous to the modern eye, included *A Child Is Born*, a tearjerker about nurses in a maternity ward whose subject matter concerning pregnancy and birth was deemed "unsuitable for public entertainment," and *The Phantom Creeps*, a twelve-part serial starring a sadly diminished Bela Lugosi as a mad scientist, considered "too strong for public exhibition."[43] In Quebec, provincial regulations barred children under the age of sixteen from movie theatres. No exceptions were granted for children who were accompanied by an adult. As Quebec theatre owners never tired of observing, the government's professed reason for the ban – that theatres posed a fire safety hazard to children – seemed a mere facade for what was in fact ecclesiastical disapproval of movie content.[44] An initial exemption permitted for Disney's *Snow White* was rescinded when provincial regulators decided that the Wicked Queen would frighten children – which was precisely what she was supposed to do – and no exemption was granted when the equally terrifying tale of the flying elephant Dumbo arrived in theatres in 1942.[45] An impolitic decision in 1944 to grant a special exemption for the Dionne quintuplets to attend a screening of King's beloved *Lassie Come Home* brought mocking and derisive responses from the trade papers, but the Quebec government's policy remained otherwise intact.[46] Quebec's regulations were the most stringent in Canada, but every province kept movie exhibitors on a tight leash. The war initially made provincial regulators more than usually sensitive to anything that might be deemed offensive or that could undermine morale. Many films were banned or removed from circulation in September 1939, including, notably, director Lewis Milestone's adaptation of Erich Maria Remarque's novel *All Quiet on the Western Front*. Already considered a classic and still making the rounds in repertory theatres, the movie was pulled across Canada on the grounds that it constituted pro-German and anti-war propaganda and might prove detrimental to the war effort. The irony that both the film and the novel had already been banned in Nazi Germany was apparently lost on censors.[47]

It was against this backdrop of economic uncertainty and the persistent opprobrium of regulators that Canada's motion picture exhibitors braced themselves for war. Movie-going, they said, would be an instrument of democracy. They were eager to demonstrate their civic worth through patriotic service. As Ray Lewis saw it, the war was nothing less than "civilization's last stand," and the movies were "ammunition" in that epochal struggle.[48] But the extent to which the industry committed itself to supporting the war effort – a commitment that reflected the usual combination of patriotic altruism and economic self-interest – coupled with the nature of the movie-going experience itself, probably precluded the possibility that any night at the pictures could offer the alleged "escape" from troubles in the way that Ray Lewis and so many others claimed. With their late closing hours, large seating capacities, and in the case of many older venues, actual stages, movie theatres were ready-made to serve a variety of patriotic purposes. They offered recruiters and voluntary organizations a large and largely captive audience for their messages. In exchange for their entertainment, audiences were harangued by armed forces recruiters, Victory Bond salespeople, and service club fundraisers seeking donations for aid to the USSR and the Red Cross, to buy milk for British orphans, "smokes" and shaving kits for the boys overseas, and innumerable other patriotic causes. Few other retailers so readily embraced the war effort, and few so indisputably profited from it.

By 1944, the movie theatre business in Canada had rebounded from the Depression to such a degree that Ray Lewis, writing shortly before D-Day, predicted that future exhibitors would look back on the period as the best in the industry's history:

> The war years were good; good for production; good for distribution; good for exhibition; good for our governments which cleaned up in the collection of super super taxes, good for morale, because of world-wide motion picture war services, good for our good-will, because we drew closer to our public, having a kinship in the sufferings which this world-war generated, and good for our relationship with our governments, because we injected showmanship into the government's war effort.[49]

This may have been hyperbole, but it was not wholly without justification. People really did flock to the theatres during the war. Admissions passed

Table 6.2

Motion picture theatres, admissions, and value of receipts, 1939-45

Year	Number of establishments	Value of receipts/ Amusement taxes ($ thousands)	Admissions (thousands)
1939	1,183	33,696	137,899
1940	1,229	37,474	151,599
1941	1,240	40,796	161,678
1942	1,247	57,277 (45,720/11,557)	182,846
1943	1,265	64,645 (51,485/13,160)	204,678
1944	1,298	66,729 (53,173/13,556)	208,167
1945	1,323	69,486 (55,431/14,055)	215,573
Increase (%)	12	35 (adjusted for inflation)	57

NOTE: In 1942, a federal amusement tax of 25 percent was added at point-of-purchase to the cost of admission. Bracketed figures for 1942-45 indicate the value of receipts (including concession stand sales) and the value of amusement taxes.
SOURCE: M.C. Urquhart and K.A.H. Buckley, eds., *Historical Statistics of Canada* (Cambridge: Cambridge University Press, 1965), Series T213-26.

the 200 million mark in 1943, and that year, Famous Players, the nation's largest movie theatre chain, reported that its profits had increased 50 percent since 1939 (see Table 6.2).[50] Impressive as they are, these figures do not include itinerant operators who entertained as many as 1.5 million patrons annually; nor do they account for the thousands of screenings that occurred on armed forces bases and in military hospitals across the country.[51]

In general, however, film attendance ranked rather low on the list of things that attracted Canadian spending money during the Second World War. Although moviegoers did allocate a record $67 million to the pursuit in 1944, this worked out to a little under $6 per person – just over 1 percent of total consumer spending. But this figure understates the actual significant of the pastime. A pre-war study by the Dominion Bureau of Statistics (DBS) had found that the movies accounted for a remarkable 90 percent of the average household's spending on public amusements, compared to just 9 percent for spectator sports and 1 percent for live theatre and music.[52] There is every reason to think that this pattern continued to the war. With admission to most evening shows no more than a quarter, going to the pictures was cheap entertainment even for lower-income Canadians. A nationwide survey by the WPTB found that 80 percent of those polled were moviegoers and that one in four went more than once per week. A third had gone the week before the poll was taken, and another 8 percent had been more than once.[53] Particularly in small towns and midsized cities, where residents lacked the many diversions offered by the big city, movies were an essential part of most people's leisure hours. The DBS pre-war study had found that in Montreal, movies accounted for 62 percent of all entertainment expenditures by the city's 1 million citizens. In Quebec City, population 150,000, they accounted for 92 percent.[54] Similarly precise figures are not available for the war, but some crude indicators suggest a comparable situation across Canada. In Halifax, where seventy thousand civilians rubbed shoulders with tens of thousands of soldiers, sailors, and airmen from at least three armed forces, the nine movie theatres sold 4.5 million tickets in 1944.[55] The seven theatres in London, Ontario, sold a total of nearly 3 million tickets during 1944 – the city had a population of just eighty thousand.[56] Citizens of Regina, population forty thousand, had one of the highest per capita movie-going rates in Canada: the city's theatres sold 2.25 million tickets in 1944 – an average of 55 per person, compared to about 30 in Toronto.[57] In tiny Picton, Ontario, the Edwardian-style Regent Theatre, a converted opera house, could seat eight hundred people, more than a quarter of the population – and it was not the only one in town. Until an airbase, subsequently utilized as a British Commonwealth Air Training Plan (BCATP) school, opened on the outskirts of town in late 1940, the Regent was seldom sold out. After that, the theatre manager usually called in the police to help his ushers manage the crowds on busier nights.

As Table 6.3 demonstrates, theatres in every province benefitted from the public's increased rate of movie-going. (It is equally apparent that the war did not significantly alter the very wide regional discrepancies in the rate of film attendance that predated it.) In 1939, Prince Edward Island's six theatres, for instance, were operating at just one-fifth of their seating capacity, and ticket sales were barely 60 percent of what they had been in 1930. In the countryside of this poorest and least urbanized province, going to the movies was "a rare and golden event," writes island historian Edward MacDonald. "Out there, local dances, community concerts, and amateur theatre still ruled the social universe."[58] During the war, however, the island's theatres experienced a remarkable boom. Box-office receipts had nearly tripled by 1944 – the presence on the island of several BCATP schools, teeming with fliers from a dozen countries, surely helped. In Halifax, theatres also benefitted from the presence of armed forces and then suffered from their withdrawal. In 1950, Halifax theatres reported

Table 6.3

Per capita spending on movie entertainment by year and province ($)

Province	1939	1940	1941	1942	1943	1944	1945	Adjusted increase (%)
PE	1.23	1.26	1.52	2.52	3.35	3.41	3.31	122
SK	1.57	1.76	1.92	2.56	3.31	3.54	3.83	102
QC	2.19	2.30	2.48	3.81	4.21	4.26	4.36	65
NB	1.84	2.21	2.41	3.75	4.53	4.51	4.76	102
MB	3.03	3.23	3.41	4.39	4.81	4.93	5.13	40
AB	2.61	2.80	3.11	4.22	5.27	5.35	5.34	69
NS	2.59	3.27	3.82	5.89	6.68	6.73	6.56	109
ON	4.08	4.63	5.07	6.53	6.97	6.84	7.16	45
BC	4.83	4.98	5.08	7.52	8.29	8.15	8.15	39
Canada	3.03	3.35	3.63	5.01	5.61	5.61	5.77	57

NOTE: Figures from 1942 onward include the federal amusement tax.
SOURCES: Dominion Bureau of Statistics, *Motion Picture Exhibitors in Canada* (Ottawa: Dominion Bureau of Statistics, 1939-50). Population figures from M.C. Urquhart and K.A.H. Buckley, eds., *Historical Statistics of Canada* (Cambridge: Cambridge University Press, 1965), Series A2-14.

well over a million *fewer* admissions than they had in 1944. Per capita spending on movies in Nova Scotia in general declined from $6.73 per person in 1945 to $5.10 in 1948, a loss of 50 percent after adjusting for post-war inflation. Prince Edward Island, too, saw per capita movie expenditures stagnate and lose significant ground against inflation after the war, even while the national trend was one of modest growth in theatre attendance.[59]

What was it like to actually go to the movies at this time? The American entrepreneur Marcus Loew, whose theatre chain operated in both the United States and Canada, boasted in the 1920s that he sold tickets to his theatres rather than to movies.[60] He made the remark in an insouciant mood, no doubt, but he was also acknowledging the fact that the theatre itself was an important aspect of the entertainment experience. In Canada, nearly every small town and nearly every big city neighbourhood had a theatre of some kind, but it was the majestic movie "palaces," ostentatious relics of the late teens and twenties, that remained the most visibly commanding presence in Canada's theatre circuits in 1939. Vancouver's Orpheum, Winnipeg's Metropolitan, Toronto's Pantages and its veritable twin, the Uptown, Sherbrooke's Granada, Moncton's Capitol: they were intended to suggest something of the splendour and sophistication of Europe's great opera houses and had been built, as architectural historian

FIGURE 6.1   Built to suggest the opera houses of the old world, movie palaces such as Montreal's Orpheum Theatre offered on-screen spectacles. | Library and Archives Canada, PA-119689.

Harold Kalman puts it, without "discipline or restraint."[61] Some had been constructed to stage vaudeville but had been converted to screen motion pictures whereas others were purpose-built movie theatres. "Orgies of architectural excess," one theatre historian has called them, and indeed they often were, with their gilt, glass, marble, and mirrors, the grand sweep of their staircases, the vast interior spaces of their domed auditoriums, and their atmospheric affectations (see Figure 6.1).[62] Halifax's Capitol resembled a baronial castle, complete with faux fortress walls and battlements, drawbridge, timber ceiling, and suits of armour in the lobby. Montreal's Empress had been designed in the Egyptian Revival style, intended to evoke an Egyptian palace, situated near the banks of the

Nile.[63] The Granada, in Sherbrooke, Quebec, resembled the courtyard of a picturesque Spanish villa, and it utilized lighting effects to create the illusion of a twilight sky on the ceiling.[64]

Most of the palaces were located in the downtowns of larger cities, but a few, such as Sherbrooke's Granada and Timmins's Palace, were in smaller centres, where they were always the source of authentic if slightly swollen civic pride, proffered as an indication of the town's urbanity and sophistication. Such distinctions were reinforced not only by architecture but also by the kind of courteous, even fawning, service that they offered to patrons. Ivan Ackery, long-time manager of Vancouver's palatial twenty-seven-hundred-seat Orpheum, recalled that his managers wore tuxedos on most nights and that uniformed and white-gloved ushers and usherettes were "very carefully selected to meet and handle the public graciously."[65] One of Ackery's ushers recalled that the Orpheum kept up appearances even through the doldrums of the late Depression. "It's very hard to describe," she wrote, "in this day and age, the graciousness of the staff. It was a world of charm and fascination and fantasy and, really, it was a fairyland ... Ladies and gentlemen came in formal dress, and not only for the big premieres; Saturday nights, especially, were dress nights."[66] In the palaces, pretenses such as these were maintained throughout the Depression and seem to have continued even in the face of wartime pressures toward conservation and thrift, an indication, perhaps, that concerted efforts on behalf of the war effort could conceal a multitude of profligate sins. They might also have provided some genuinely amusing non sequiturs, as formally dressed ushers guided grubby shift workers and badly behaved servicemen to their seats, where the patrons tore open boxes of Cracker Jacks and settled in to watch such middling fare as Abbott and Costello's *Keep 'Em Flying* (1941) and *I Walked with a Zombie* (1943).

Despite their huge boost in revenue, dilapidated theatres were increasingly the norm rather than the exception by 1945. Ontario's chief theatre inspector, O.J. Silverthorne, estimated in September 1944 that at least sixty Ontario theatres, and probably twice that many, required major renovations to be brought up to code.[67] His reports describe rundown exteriors, decrepit interiors, and unsanitary and even non-existent toilet facilities. One Sudbury theatre, he said, posed "a distinct menace to the attending public." Owners and operators shrugged and pointed to the austerity measures imposed by the WPTB and other agencies.[68] Shortages of labour and restrictions on building materials delayed much-needed repairs and renovations to many theatres. In early 1942, the WPTB had also decreed that no new theatres could be built without its approval, and this was seldom forthcoming.[69]

Coping with regulations and inspectors had always been part of a theatre operator's job, but the war imposed a baffling array of new rules and regulations. Theatre operations were immediately affected, often in connection with civil defence. In Ontario, they were required to install emergency lights by 30 September 1939, in order to prevent a repetition of the panics that occurred in Toronto and St. Thomas when the power failed during one of the first screenings of a war newsreel.[70] In Nova Scotia and New Brunswick, the theatres "went dark" in mid-September, their neon and electric light marquees extinguished as an air-raid precaution.[71] Movie theatre blackout regulations varied from place to place. Nearly every city in Canada adopted some sort of blackout precautions and air defence scheme, none of which seemed terribly unreasonable in coastal regions, especially where theatres were concerned. The pulsating marquees were among the brightest landmarks in any city, after all. For the many Canadians who lived far from the coast, however, the precautions often seemed pointless and irritating. They knew that the Germans and Japanese did not have intercontinental bombers and doubted that such cities as Saskatoon and Waterloo would be high on the list of targets even if they did. Even Ontario's notoriously by-the-book theatre inspector O.J. Silverthorne agreed that the theatres did not need additional blackout regulations. They were windowless and marquees were easily extinguished in the event of an emergency.[72] By 1942, at least some operators had had enough of unwarranted blackout and air-raid regulations, and began to distribute among themselves a set of gag precautions. It read, in part,

1) As soon as the bombs start dropping, run like hell.
   a) wear track shoes if possible – if the people in front of you are slow, you won't have any trouble getting over them
2) Take advantage of opportunities afforded you when air raid sirens sound the warning of attack ie)
   a) if in a bakery, grab some pie or cake, etc.
   b) if in a tavern, grab a bottle
   c) if in a movie, grab a blonde

Other "precautions" included the advice to "drink heavily, eat onions, limburger cheese etc. before entering a crowded air raid shelter" – your breath would guarantee you greater personal space and privacy.[73]

As this satire demonstrates, theatre operators might have been willing to demonstrate their commitment to the war effort, but they did not meekly acquiesce to every regulation. Above all, they took exception to the government's categorization of their business as non-essential. With great indignation, they pointed out that they had donated their theatres to patriotic organizations and had launched their own efforts to mobilize moviegoers for the purposes of serving the war effort, and they wondered why officials did not give them greater consideration. Practically every retailer and service provider claimed that his business was essential, but theatre operators felt that their argument was more plausible than others. It was not entirely pretense – their organizational efforts on behalf of the war effort had begun very early. In the spring of 1940, they mounted a coordinated coast-to-coast Victory Bond drive, which they encumbered with the inelegant title "Canadian Moving Picture Industry Win the War Campaign." Commencing on Dominion Day with the sale of Victory Bonds in theatres and culminating in a free show two weeks later to anyone who bought a minimum of two war savings stamps, the campaign involved hundreds of theatres. Assistance arrived from Hollywood, with director Alfred Hitchcock promising top studio talent to promote it. Most of the stars who turned out were Hitchcock's fellow British expatriates. Vivien Leigh, fresh from her triumphant turn as Scarlett O'Hara in *Gone with the Wind*, appeared with her husband, Laurence Olivier, in Toronto. Maureen O'Sullivan, best known for playing Jane to Johnny Weissmuller's Tarzan, appeared alongside actor Ronald Colman in Winnipeg. Sir Cedric Hardwicke, one of the first modern actors to be knighted, appeared in Montreal, and Anna Neagle, a top box-office draw of the era, appeared in Vancouver. By all standards, the campaign was a ringing success. In Ontario, all but 2 of 375 theatres took part; even in Quebec more than half of them participated. For the culminating event, a nationwide free showing on 15 July, Winnipeg's forty theatres were filled to capacity. In tiny Fort Qu'Appelle, Saskatchewan, population 580, where the theatre sat only 200, the manager had to add a late screening for everyone who showed up.[74]

Like-minded campaigns were mounted throughout the war. Hundreds of theatres ran scrap metal drives, presented tickets to people who had bought Victory Bonds, and supported innumerable other patriotic causes. The Palace Theatre in Timmins offered free admission to patrons who brought two or more pounds of waste fat to a show.[75] The more they volunteered to support the war effort, the more theatre operators resented the continued censure of people described by one trade paper as "citizens of mature years who have been reared in the atmosphere of homes governed by the precepts and restrictions of Puritan philosophy."[76] A particular point of contention between operators and their critics of mature years was midnight and Sunday screenings, which became routine to accommodate shift workers and soldiers on leave. "Pity the poor theatre manager," said a writer for *Canadian Film Weekly*, "who wants to put on a Sunday show for the bomb victims, milk for British babies, smokes for the boys overseas or any of a number of worthy causes. Next day, sure as shooting, representatives of religious groups protest loudly that the Lord's Day Act is being violated."[77] Indeed, when the customarily disapproving executive of the IODE passed a motion urging Sunday showings for men and women in uniform, the editors of the *United Church Observer* accused them of having become "the spearhead of subversive movements" threatening the moral fabric of the nation by undermining the solemnity of the Lord's Day.[78] In most cases, civic officials supported Sunday theatre openings, provided that the facilities were simultaneously engaged in patriotic fundraising activities. As Hamilton's exasperated mayor barked to opponents of Sunday screenings, "Hitler doesn't care on what day he parades his soldiers or sends his airplanes over Britain."[79]

NO ONE WAS MORE enthusiastic about the use of movie theatres for patriotic purposes than Ray Lewis, but by 1944, she had begun to wonder if audiences were not being oversaturated with war news, war movies, and wartime fundraising. The movies, after all, were supposed to provide an escape from everyday worries. "Certainly three or four propaganda appeals during an evening is two too much, to do us or the public, or our Government, or our War Effort any good," she wrote.[80] Even John Grierson, director of the National Film Board (NFB), fretted about overdoing it. Given the NFB's own serial monthly newsreel, *The March of Time*, its other documentaries, and the immense number of American and British "shorts" being screened across Canada, Grierson worried that more would be self-defeating.[81] Far from being an avenue of escape, an evening at the movies might actually have furnished an immediate reminder that moviegoers were inescapably in a state of war. In many cities, they would have entered the cinema under a blacked-out marquee, made their way through a lobby plastered with recruitment and Victory Bond posters, watched a succession of newsreels and war-themed documentary shorts, and then settled in for a feature presentation that might very well have been a hyper-violent war movie. Can such patrons really be said to have psychologically escaped from the war? If anything, movie-going was probably the aspect of Canadian consumer culture most visibly altered by the war in its first two years, and the relationship between film attendance and the war simply intensified after American entry. In July 1942, *Canadian Film Weekly* reported that of seventy-six features presently in production in Hollywood, one-third were war movies.[82] When the American trade journal *Film Daily* polled movie critics in 1943 for a list of the year's ten best pictures, all of them had war themes. Of the forty-seven films nominated by the critics, half were war-related.[83] That same year, when the Department of National Defence produced its own list of the films most suitable for distribution to troops overseas, it included no fewer than five war movies: *Corvette K-225*, *Desert Victory*, *Heroic Stalingrad*, *In Which We Serve*, and *Mission to Moscow*.[84]

Even those pictures that were not explicitly about the war seldom offered audiences straightforwardly escapist entertainment. As film historian Robert Sklar has observed, even the comedies of the war years were decidedly darker and more jaded than we might suppose, and moreover, the period gave rise to that genre of gloomy, violent, cynical, and even sinister thrillers that French critics would later dub film noir. Among the early examples of the genre were John Huston's *The Maltese Falcon* (1941), director Fritz Lang's adaptation of Graham Greene's schizophrenic spy thriller *The Ministry of Fear* (1944), and Alfred Hitchcock's most claustrophobic film of all, 1944's *Lifeboat*, in which the captain of a capsized German U-boat is rescued by the survivors of a liner he has just torpedoed. "The hallmark of *film noir*," Sklar writes,

> is its sense of people trapped – trapped in webs of paranoia and fear, unable to tell guilt from innocence, true identity from false. Its villains are attractive and sympathetic, masking greed, misanthropy and violence. Its heroes and heroines are weak, confused, susceptible to false impressions ... In the end, evil is exposed, though often just barely, and the survival of good remains troubled and ambiguous.[85]

Director Billy Wilder's *Double Indemnity* (1944), based on a novella by James M. Cain, takes the motif a step further: middle-class life itself becomes the trap. What motivates the film's conspiring couple to commit murder is not revenge or even financial gain, but the ennui and purposelessness of middle-class consumer life. Amid a deluge of such fare, Marie

Williamson, who had taken in two evacuee children from the United Kingdom, wrote to their mother in the summer of 1942 about her frustrations in finding something appropriate for the children to watch at the movies: "I had hoped Captains of the Clouds or Sergeant York or something similar would be at one of the local houses but it always seems when you want them to go, on a special occasion, every movie in the vicinity is playing 'Lady of the Tropics' or murder films or something equally unsuitable!"[86]

Even the bleakest and most violent of the film noir thrillers did not match the unprecedented levels of cinematic brutality audiences would encounter in many of the era's war movies. According to historian Stephen Prince, wartime filmmakers progressively challenged the authority of the Motion Picture Production Code. In particular, they demanded that the PCA grant them greater latitude in depicting the brutality of war, lest their films seem to diminish the actual sacrifices being made by Allied soldiers overseas.[87] Prior to the war, Prince writes, American filmmakers had considered the human body to be inviolate on screen. Blood and mutilation were forbidden. Actors whose characters were shot or stabbed would "clutch and fall" – throwing their hands over a bloodless, imaginary wound and then pitching forward.[88] In movies such as *Bataan* (1943) and *Pride of the Marines* (1945), however, the PCA permitted depictions of modern warfare with scenes of violence that, in Prince's words, "easily surpass anything that gangster or horror movies had shown to audiences."[89] Even the "clutch and fall" scenes of the era seemed somehow more brutal, with scores of actors falling in the face of chattering machine guns.[90] *Bataan* actually portrayed an American soldier impaled through the neck by a Japanese bayonet; *The Purple Heart* (1944), a dramatization of eight Allied airmen captured after the famous Doolittle Raid, strongly implied acts of torture and depicted the execution of Allied POWs.[91] *Cry "Havoc"* (1943) concluded with perhaps the most infamous scene of any wartime movie. As Montreal's Mary Peate later recalled, "We shrank back in dread during the final scene in 'Cry Havoc' where the nurses emerged one by one from their dugout, with their hands on their heads, knowing they faced rape and probable death at the hands of their captors."[92]

"Every week the war films get longer, louder, and more violent," *Saturday Night*'s always caustic film reviewer, Mary Lowrey Ross, wrote in March 1944, singling out the recent Randolph Scott–Alan Curtis war epic *Gung Ho!*

> There is not one touch of insight or imagination in a film of this sort. When it is over you know no more than you did before how men feel when they go

out to face death and destroy their fellow-creatures. All you have seen are the strictly dehumanized mechanics of killing, which you react to as "entertainment" simply with your nerves. Before it is over even your nerves refuse to respond, so that instead of being excited or exalted or even sickened you are merely bored.[93]

"Fourth class scrub and dirt," is how the members of Winnipeg's school board responded to the new war movies in a complaint to provincial authorities, focusing on one – probably *Bataan* – which featured a gruesome bayoneting. "It is terrible the number of young children that attend these motion pictures and see these scenes," one teacher remarked.[94] A year later, the *Canadian Forum*'s film reviewer made the same observation, noting that the net effect of recent films was to make one aware of the "hundred curious ways in which death may creep up on you."[95] Arguably, that was the whole point, and during the last half of the war, censors in Canada seem to have eased up on the censorship regulations. In 1943 and 1944, just 56 of 1,767 American films (including newsreels and documentaries) exhibited in Ontario movie theatres were cut or edited beforehand.[96] In the specific case of *Bataan*, which ran for more than six months, Ontario censors permitted the infamous bayoneting to remain, although the soldier's scream was cut.[97]

Few of Hollywood's war movies were intended to stand the test of time. Hastily produced, most were not much more than propaganda in the guise of adventure epics – though in fairness this affliction has been suffered by innumerable war movies ever since.[98] As propaganda, what such movies did do was cast the war and its unpredictable dangers into a narrative where ultimate Allied victory was assured, regardless of any temporary setbacks. Even Allied defeats, such as the one depicted in *Bataan*, were presented as Pyrrhic victories for the Axis. Movie reviewers acknowledged the increasingly sanguinary nature of Hollywood's output, but they also believed that war movies served the eminently useful purpose of arousing the public's hatred of the enemy. Referring to the graphic portrayal of the torture and subsequent execution of Allied POWs in *The Purple Heart*, the *Canadian Moving Picture Digest* reviewer wrote, "Any man, woman, or child who can sit through this picture without getting the urge to go all-out in his or her personal war effort is either as yellow as the Japs' skin or a potential Quisling."[99] In any case, the disapproval of the morally indignant did not deter audiences, if the huge increase in ticket sales is anything to go by. In an era of innumerable, rapidly produced, and often (even in the estimation of contemporary critics) vapid melodramas and tiresome comedies, most audiences seem to have yearned for weightier fare. In her wartime memoir, *Sun in Winter,* British expatriate Gunda Lambton recalls crossing the river to Hull, Quebec, where Sunday screenings were legal. The picture was the now forgotten *Music for Millions,* about a soldier's lonely wife. "Sober Ontarians would most likely have approved of the movie we saw in Hull," Lambton reflected, but therein lay the problem. "There's nothing in this film that could not be seen on Sundays, and we were vaguely disappointed," she concluded rather dejectedly.[100] "The public prefers the strife stuff," wrote the editors of *Canadian Film Weekly,* recognizing the disjuncture between the escape thesis and the reality of theatre going: "What does the public want of films, recreation and entertainment or inspiration and information? More exhibitors would say recreation and entertainment. But according to the latest assay of public preferences, the movie patron wants a well-balanced program, one that includes everything. And he or she is not afraid of the grim realities of war, as pictured by Hollywood."[101]

Moviegoers' interest in war films and crime thrillers should not necessarily be construed as evidence that they did not also seek diversion and amusement from the silver screen: the history of the arts gives us ample reason to believe that people find synthetic violence highly entertaining. Still, the success of war movies and film noir suggests that the Canadian consumer-moviegoer sought something more in the experience than a mere distraction from wartime anxieties, or perhaps that the anxieties themselves were not so great as is sometimes supposed. People allegedly seeking a respite from such worries flocked to a succession of films of shocking and unprecedented violence, and were in the process inundated by a barrage of war news and patriotic propaganda.

Film attendance was yet another study in the contrasts and contradictions of wartime consumer culture. The concerns felt by many Canadians about American economic and cultural imperialism, and their fears about the decline of the values of thrift and abstemious morality, far from being subsumed by the war, were often intensified by it. To these charges the film industry's critics added the now familiar argument that movie-going was a wasteful extravagance in wartime. And yet Canadians on the whole went to the pictures in greater and greater numbers, every year of the war. Like so many other retailers of the era, movie exhibitors resented and openly contested accusations that their business agenda was at cross-purposes with the war effort. The industry defended itself from its critics on the grounds that it performed an essential function. When the war ended, theatre operators felt they could point with pride to the efforts they had made on behalf of their country. The movies had aroused patriotic fervour, disseminated war news, and entertained the troops and the public; governments had raked in millions of dollars in amusement tax revenues from ticket sales; and theatres had served as venues for recruiting, Victory Bond drives, and patriotic gatherings of all kinds. As for consumers themselves, they went to the pictures for many reasons, not simply to escape their wartime jitters. As we have seen throughout this study, consumers sought to chart a middle course between restraint and the potential for excess that increased earnings had given them, serving, however imperfectly, their own needs, the needs of the producers and sellers of commodities, and the demands of a nation at war.

Conclusion

The advertisements for skin cream, flattering garments, and other aids to the allure which leads to marriage and a home of one's own have, indeed, flourished unabated through the war years. They will not have to undergo even a difficult transition period before appearing again as the peace-time props of a dying civilization.

– Harriet Roberts Forsey, Canadian Forum, *August 1944*

No one can sell me the idea anymore, after having lived through two world wars that people have become so educated, so civilized, that they are now epicureans and all-wise guys, too choosy, or too clever to be sold anything. After Hitler, I believe that you can sell the people a dead dog.

– Ray Lewis, Canadian Moving Picture Digest,
  2 December 1944

Our self-renewing lords who spell democracy
as private enterprise and public rape
may yet be wrong. That was another war, and we
are haunted by our frustrated fathers and the late
souring of a milksop truce, when Steves, with brains
and hands alone to trade with, and no credit,
were paid in promises, or jailed, or warned off freights
and politics and love, unless they peddled
the latest brightest stones to all who asked for bread.

– Earle Birney, "For Steve," *1944*

EARLE BIRNEY, WHO SERVED with the Canadian Army overseas, wrote these words about a glacial era – the Great Depression – and as Allied victories mounted, he, like many Canadians, became preoccupied with the possibility that it might return. Perhaps no other country had suffered the anguish of the Depression so acutely, and Canadians understood that economic mobilization for war in 1939 had delivered them from it. What would happen when hostilities ceased, the plants closed, and hundreds of thousands of soldiers came home, looking for jobs? As early as the summer of 1942, Cyril James, a respected economist who was the principal of McGill University and chairman of the newly appointed Committee on Reconstruction, gave voice to many Canadians' fears when he told a House of Commons committee, "There will inevitably be a post-war depression, either immediately after the war or after a brief period of prosperity."[1] Gloomy prognostications of this type proliferated during the last half of the war. In the introduction to an early volume on reconstruction, Arthur Lower, then chair of the Department of History at United College, Winnipeg, cautioned readers that "victory will see the job only begun."[2] The rest of the "job" would entail the even more daunting task of maintaining wartime prosperity in a post-war world.

No doubt such warnings seemed eminently plausible to many Canadians as they took into consideration the vast human and economic resources their country was devoting to the global struggle. By D-Day, nearly three-quarters of a million Canadians were serving with the armed forces, and domestic war industries employed a million more.[3] Tens of thousands of others had found work in the expanded administrative ranks of dozens of government departments and the more than twenty Crown corporations created under the auspices of the Department of Munitions and Supply. Although the war resulted in serious labour shortages in several sectors of the civilian economy, to many observers it nonetheless seemed inconceivable that the post-war economy could sustain anything like the full employment of wartime, even if tens of thousands of women returned, willingly or otherwise, to the home. Even as commercial advertisers promised a future of boundless prosperity, polls found many Canadians in a decidedly more pessimistic frame of mind. A December 1943 poll conducted by the Canadian Institute of Public Opinion found that a third of those surveyed expected to lose their jobs after the war. A follow-up, conducted in mid-1944, found 71 percent of respondents believing that a post-war period of high unemployment was unavoidable.[4]

It may be true, as J.L. Granatstein has argued, that Canada went to war in 1939 because Britain did and for few other identifiable reasons. No doubt, but it is also true that Canadians fervently hoped that the war, once won, would stand for something more than that. As we have seen, Canadians grafted their existing social concerns onto the country's war effort, in the hopes that a future amenable to their vision of what their society ought to be like might emerge from the crucible of war. The question of what *kind* of world would result had been asked from the start. In November 1939, A.R. Mosher, president of the Canadian Congress of Labour, reflected that "we all remember the promises which were made by political leaders during the last war. It was to be a 'war to end war' and to 'make the world safe for democracy.' Canada and the other nations were to become 'fit for heroes to live in.' We know that those promises were not kept."

This war, he said, would above all be "a war against economic insecurity," an aim he regarded as fundamentally incompatible with capitalist control of the economy.[5] Other constituencies had their own visions of what the future should entail – obviously, Mosher's view differed from that of a free market ideologue such as John Kirkwood – but nearly all of them alluded to, in at least some fashion, the centrality of the need for future prosperity. Churchill and Roosevelt had themselves acknowledged as much in the Atlantic Charter, a highly symbolic document that the two leaders agreed to (though never formally signed) aboard the cruiser USS *Augusta* in Newfoundland's Placentia Bay during August 1941. The charter had enumerated "improved labour standards, economic advancement, and social security" and "freedom from fear and want" as a common heritage of humankind, paramount rights that the Allies were struggling to realize in the world. But it did not, of course, clarify what these words meant, leaving the door open for nearly every political constituency to uphold them as an endorsement of its particular worldview.

In the last three years of the war, dozens of books and hundreds of articles were published in Canada on these and related issues. Almost invariably, they included cautionary and sometimes bitter reflections on the disillusionment that had followed the failure of so many ambitions held out during the Great War. "The last war came to be called 'the war to end all wars,'" the author of *Canada: The War and After*, published in 1944, wrote in a fairly typical passage. "But while we won the war, the victory turned out to be an empty one."[6] The strangest and most acerbic of all works on the topic of reconstruction was an "economic satire" called

The Permanent War, or, Homo the Sap, by Lorne Morgan, a noted political economist at the University of Toronto. "Never before in the history of man has his economy functioned as it is functioning today," Morgan wrote. "Never before has that economy distributed the purchasing power it is distributing today. Within ten short years, the modern industrial and capitalist world has literally jumped from the depths of its greatest depression to the peak of its greatest prosperity. Why? *Because the world was fortunate enough to blunder into war.*"[7] Morgan's mordant conclusion was that the wartime boom could be sustained only by perpetual war. Irreverently – and rather tastelessly – he proposed that when Germany and Japan were defeated, Canada might declare war on a minor power such as a Latin American country. By contrast, the editors of the *Monetary Times* seemed quite serious in December 1944 when they expressed a slight sense of relief about the German counteroffensive in the Ardennes (then being played out in what became known as the Battle of the Bulge), because in lengthening the war it had at least temporarily postponed the reckoning with "unemployment, and the forebodings of industrial stagnation."[8]

Satire or not, Morgan's work, like dozens of others, underscored a problem of real complexity. What was to sustain the Canadian economy when hostilities ended? This was a question that King's government took seriously, and in Cabinet and inside the ranks of the civil service, planning for a prosperous peace had been in the offing almost from the beginning of the war. By Order-in-Council, a Cabinet committee on Demobilization and Re-Establishment was struck as early as December 1939. In October 1940, a perilous month when the prospect of peace, let alone victory, seemed very far off indeed, Ian Mackenzie, then minister of pensions and national health, took the lead in establishing a broader interdepartmental body to explore the problems of demobilization – converting the economy back to a peacetime footing – and reconstruction, or establishing the basis for long-term national prosperity.[9] In early 1941, he took the additional step of convening the Committee on Reconstruction, to be headed by Cyril James. James's committee drew its members from outside the ranks of government and in turn spawned Leonard Marsh's famous 1943 *Report on Social Security for Canada*. Marsh was inspired, in part, by Sir William Beveridge's 1942 report that had proposed the creation of a comprehensive welfare state in the United Kingdom, and he had himself been a long-time advocate of social reform, having been a member of the League of Social Reconstruction, a left-leaning advocacy group, alongside the likes of Frank

Underhill, Frank R. Scott, and J.S. Woodsworth. His proposal called for nearly $1 billion worth of programs – a dollar figure that, as Desmond Morton put it, "horrified business leaders and their editorial allies."[10]

The frugality of the finance department precluded the possibility of any wholesale adoption of the programs Marsh proposed. Most Canadians never heard about them – a 1944 poll by the Wartime Prices and Trade Board (WPTB) found that 90 percent of those polled could not correctly identify what the Marsh Report was about.[11] Arguably, the report, though of great interest to future historians, had little direct impact. Nonetheless, there was a general agreement inside King's government that some form of social welfare planning was necessary to secure both a smooth transition to peacetime and the electoral fortunes of the Liberal Party.[12] Perhaps the greatest change in the federal government during the war was not the vast and more-or-less permanent expansion of the bureaucracy's size and power, but the intellectual transformation prompted by the realization that macro-economic planning was actually possible. The government could, civil servants discovered, successfully intervene on a massive scale in the market economy. It could regulate wages and prices, it could assume direct control of whole industries and forge working relationships with moderate elements of organized labour, and above all, it could engage in large-scale deficit spending without bringing about immediate economic ruin.[13] From a ministerial perspective, this meant that the principle of "limited liability" could be realized – at least as far as the material well-being of civilians went. Reflecting on the state of the economy in 1944, J.L. Ilsley wrote,

> On the whole, Canadians lived well in 1944, better than I would have thought would be possible during the fifth year of total war. In a world where there is so much misery, we have reason to be thankful. Nor need we be ashamed, for our comparatively comfortable living has not been at the expense of the war effort ... Our standard of living has been maintained by a better utilization of our productive resources.[14]

By the latter part of the war, many Canadians had come to agree that Ottawa had a responsibility to involve itself in matters of economic planning and social welfare for the betterment of the common good. A December 1943 Canadian Institute of Public Opinion poll found that a remarkable 61 percent of those surveyed believed that all utilities should be owned by the government (as opposed to 27 percent who favoured their privatization), and just under 40 percent felt that "workers would be better off if all the industries in Canada were owned and run by the government," an expressly socialist vision that even many members of the Co-operative Commonwealth Federation (CCF) were often reluctant to endorse.[15] The war even convinced some reluctant businesspeople that a carefully managed relationship with the government could be a mutually beneficial one – many of the "Ottawa men" had been drawn from the nation's business elite, after all.[16] But nothing so alarmed the business community as the possibility that the wartime regulatory state might mutate into some form of state socialism. Admittedly, there was little chance of this occurring with the Liberals in power (though the editors of the *Toronto Telegram*, with customary hyperbole, were already accusing King's government of "despotism"), but what if the CCF, with its radical social and economic agenda, won the next federal election?

In late 1944, this possibility could not be dismissed. Over the past two years, a series of dramatic electoral battles had transformed the CCF from a marginal force in Canadian politics to a serious contender at all levels of government. In February 1942, former prime minister Arthur Meighen, once again leader of the Conservatives but without a seat in the House of Commons, was trounced by Joseph Noseworthy, a one-time insurance salesman and history teacher running for the CCF in what was supposed to have been an easy by-election in the riding of York South.[17] The following summer, the CCF was instrumental in driving Mitch Hepburn's Liberals from power in Ontario, forming the official Opposition in a razor-thin loss of just four seats to George Drew's Conservatives. Then, in June 1944, the CCF under Tommy Douglas won a sweeping victory in Saskatchewan, one that heralded the arrival of the first socialist government anywhere in North America. More ominously, from the point of view of the two old parties and many in the business community, polls at the federal level had the CCF running ahead of the Conservatives and in a dead heat with King's Liberals.[18]

"Never has the occasion been riper for a permanent change in the old order," the CCF's national chairman, F.R. Scott, wrote in the autumn of 1944, a sentiment echoed in the party's pre-election manifesto, *Security with Victory*, adopted by the National Convention later that year.[19] *Security with Victory* laid down an ambitious – one might even say grandiloquent – vision for Canada's future. It promised voters a lavish social security state and also the necessary financial stability to purchase "electric refrigerators, radios, houses, and cars," and all the material accoutrements of modern living. The difference was that these goods would be manufactured by publicly owned or strictly regulated businesses whose production would be guided by social need rather than by market forces that the CCF leadership characterized as exploitive and wasteful.[20] "The choice which people make in the coming federal election," the manifesto stated, "will determine whether we shall go forward to a new period of national development and social progress, or return to the poverty, waste, and stagnation of the prewar system."[21]

Historian Alvin Finkel has argued that there was a surprising degree of support within the business community for the welfare measures proposed during the Depression by R.B. Bennett's Conservatives and subsequently during the war by King's Liberals. In this, Finkel sees the hand of a "ruling class" seeking to undercut more radically redistributive proposals by supporting a succession of tepid half measures that would, at least, leave existing power structures intact.[22] Perhaps, but at their conferences and in countless editorials in the business press, business leaders expressed an almost feverish opposition to the adoption of nearly any social security measures – let alone the radical proposals of the CCF. A consistent theme of this study has been that business leaders and their political partners defined consumer choice as a fundamental right, one fully equal in importance to freedom of speech, religion, and the right to vote. Ideologically, this was easy to reconcile with the war aims articulated by Churchill and Roosevelt in such documents as the Atlantic Charter. As the editors of the trade journal *Drug Merchandising* saw it, "Next to winning the war and the peace, our greatest responsibility is to preserve our Canadian way of life which revolves around the system of initiative and enterprise."[23]

In the last two years of the war, many businesses mounted institutional advertising campaigns in defence of consumer capitalism and against proposed social securities measures. As we have already seen, many of them envisioned a high-tech "world of tomorrow" where Canadians would lead lives of comfort and prosperity thanks to the availability of inexpensive consumer goods, obviating the need for any sweeping social and economic reforms whose purpose was creating a socialistic welfare state. "Social security," corporate style, would result from the only thing that, in the advertisers' view, had ever been proven to generate widespread wealth: the unfettered operation of free enterprise in a consumer economy. One notable institutional ad employed the cliché of the misguided friend (see Figure C.1). It depicted an "old-timer" in the Dominion Oilcloth

Conclusion 189

FIGURE C.1 Consumer capitalism's answer to the emerging social welfare state: widespread prosperity secured through mass consumption. | "Social Security? ... Why We've Had It for Years at Dominion Oilcloth!" *National Home Monthly,* September 1944, 27.

cafeteria, explaining to a newcomer, "Social Security? ... Why we've had it for years at Dominion Oilcloth! ... The best unemployment insurance is a job – and work to do." He felt no anxiety for the future either, since "there's going to be plenty of linoleum needed after the war."[24]

In addition, a new advertising cliché emerged in the last year of the war – that of the "fifth freedom." In his 1941 State of the Union Address, F.D.R. envisioned "a world founded upon four essential human freedoms": freedom of speech, freedom of religion, freedom from want, and freedom from fear. To the many detractors of Roosevelt and the New Deal, "freedom from want" smacked of socialism, and the reiteration of the same words in the Atlantic Charter (along with the words "social security") merely reinforced their misgivings. The "fifth freedom" cliché of advertising – the freedom of free enterprise – was therefore the crucially important one. "Four freedoms aren't enough!" cries a character in one 1944 ad,

> Freedom of speech, freedom of worship, freedom from want, and freedom from fear are great stuff – as far as they go. But they may never go very far beyond the stage of bright idealism if they don't make room for the greatest democratic freedom of all – freedom of individual enterprise ... So let's boil it all down to this, the right of free choice ... to choose our opinions, our words, our religion, our homes, our clothes, our books, and breakfast foods, friends, and amusement.[25]

This encapsulated what was and remains the essence of the fiscally conservative argument against a social welfare state. In the last two years of the war, in a succession of editorials in the business press and in speeches to conferences, proponents of this view reiterated that the struggle for freedom now being won against the Axis necessarily included the defence of free enterprise and consumer choice. As social welfare planning turned into concrete reality, and with the CCF no longer a discountable threat, the argument sometimes reached an almost hysterical pitch. Speaking to the Advertising and Sales Executive Club of Montreal, John Martin, ad manager of Massey-Harris, said that Canadians were not fighting a war against totalitarianism only to acquiesce to the regimentation of a planned economy in peacetime:

> It would appear that the ideas we abhor in the policies and practices of our enemies and which we resist with all our might and our very lives are given

free acceptance and put forth as the means to establish a 'New Order' in Canada. What the German armies could not force on the freedom-loving people of Canada would be imposed on us by those who profess to be motivated by the common good.[26]

Similarly, in a 1944 speech to the Canadian Manufacturers' Association, Ronald McEachern, editor of the *Financial Post*, warned, "We stand in serious danger of losing the peace at home. The disease of totalitarianism is widespread in the world. That germ has infected many Canadians."[27] Economic regimentation would stifle free enterprise, and socialized welfare would undermine the qualities of hard work and individual self-reliance that were responsible for Canada's greatness and the defeat of the Axis. In the CCF manifesto, the editors of *Marketing* saw the threat of totalitarian socialism. Social security proposals, they wrote, "should be recognized for what they are: projects for revolutionizing our economic and social system, with the abandonment of all rights to freedom of choice in how we earn what we spend and spend what we earn."[28]

But the predicted CCF victory never materialized. On 4 June 1945, the Ontario wing of the party suffered a crushing defeat in the provincial election, losing twenty-six of its thirty-four seats. In the federal election a week later, the party secured just twenty-eight seats and only 16 percent of the popular vote. Although the Liberals were reduced to 125 seats, and King experienced the indignity of losing his own riding, his government retained its majority.[29] "When the final test came ... in 1945, the result was decisively against socialist experimentation," wrote the editors of the *Monetary Times*, with a palpable sense of relief. "The wisdom of the Canadian people has saved the country from such experimentation. It deserves to be acclaimed as the most important single decision taken by Canadians in 1945."[30] Historians have offered several explanations for the CCF's failure to secure greater electoral success in 1945: the Liberal Party's vast election-campaigning experience, the apprehension of voters, and above all, the Liberals' adoption of several social welfare measures that seem to have pulled the carpet out from under the CCF's own platform. It might also be unwise to discount the cumulative impact of anti-CCF propaganda. The Liberal Party's own reconstruction plans were not as socialistic as its conservative and business community critics sometimes alleged; nor were they the wholesale capitulation to corporate interests that some CCFers accused them of being.[31] The concrete steps taken by the Liberals toward the creation of a national welfare system –

the adoption of unemployment insurance in 1940, the Family Allowance Act of 1944, and various measures referred to as the Veterans Charter – were undoubtedly motivated in part by the desire to undercut the more radical agenda of the CCF. It is also true, however, that in King's government and throughout the civil service, there was a consensus that a federal system of social security could and should operate in tandem with free enterprise, helping to provide the economic stimulus needed to keep the engine of consumer capitalism running.[32]

Accordingly, the WPTB began the process of lifting the price ceiling and other regulations in the summer of 1945, even before Japan had surrendered. By mid-1946, all restrictions on production had ended, and the price ceiling applied only to a handful of goods in short supply. Donald Gordon resigned from the WPTB in March 1947. His successor, K.W. Taylor, had the unglamorous duty of overseeing the final suspension of the few remaining controls. The board effectively shut down by year's end.[33] The Women's Regional Advisory Committees continued to meet throughout 1946, although liaisons complained that it was increasingly difficult to get women involved. Having developed what Magda Fahrni calls "a sense of economic citizenship cultivated over the war years," some soldiered on to form their own peacetime consumer organizations to agitate for quality control and fair prices.[34] Ironically, some of these groups, having been convened by the government in the first place, fell under suspicion during the post-war period by overzealous officials who feared communist infiltration into their ranks. In any case, their efforts at price control came to naught. When the ceiling came off, inflation soared. Between 1946 and 1947, the cost of living increased by nearly 10 percent – more than it had in the preceding five years put together, according to the official figures. But nothing like the depression predicted in 1942 by Cyril James emerged, and the gross national product suffered only the smallest decline in 1946, after which it raced ahead, fuelled by the release of pent-up consumer demand and by exports to a world recovering from war.

If the pessimism about the future voiced by some commentators proved to be unwarranted, it is equally true that the grandiose visions of consumer abundance proffered by others never quite lived up to reality, either. Joy Parr argues that the anticipated boom was to an extent circumscribed by the higher per capita tax burden that Canadians quite willingly accepted in order to underwrite the cost of the fledgling welfare state.[35] Another impediment to any immediate boom was the fact that reconversion took time. Although the Department of Munitions and Supply had lifted most restrictions on production by the end of 1945, shortages of parts and materials meant that the actual output of most consumer durables remained well below expectations. Unit sales of new passenger cars, for example, were slightly lower in 1946 than they had been in 1941, and they were significantly less than the levels of the first two years of the war.[36] In addition, many semi-durables and soft goods remained in short supply, sugar rationing continued until 1947, and meat rationing resumed in September 1945 and continued until April 1947, once again to fill export requirements to the starving continent of Europe. (As a writer for *Food in Canada* put it, "When Allied troops landed in France on D-Day they not only broke the lock of Germany's fortress Europe but also opened the door to new world food problems.")[37] For more than a year after hostilities ended, the WPTB directors continued to urge consumers to be cautious and restrained, reminding them that in the First World War, the worst inflation had followed victory. But though the initial post-war boom might have been born on shaky legs owing to problems of demobilization, inflation, and tax burdens, there can be no doubt that the general trend in consumer sales was up, and that by the end of the decade, record numbers of new homes, cars, and electrical appliances were being built and bought.

IT HAS BEEN MY contention in *A Small Price to Pay* that the Second World War was, in many respects, a period of progress in the development of the modern consumer economy, rather than the time of consumer deprivation that it is usually made out to be. In place of the "penurious patriotism" of social memory, where home front consumers pulled together and sacrificed everything on behalf of the war effort, we find a far more complex and often contradictory relationship between consumers, consumption, and the war effort. Even a cursory examination of the home front reveals an obsessive concern being voiced everywhere with how the conflict would affect consumerism in Canada and, indeed, how consumerism would affect Canada's war effort. By contrast, most histories of the home front, when they have addressed consumption at all, have placed an inordinate emphasis on rationing, shortages, and propaganda urging consumer restraint. Although these were undeniably important aspects of home front life, there were few shortages until late 1941, rationing did not begin until 1942 (and in some cases, it ended before the war did), and in the first two years, calls for increased consumer spending were far more common than calls for restraint. Moreover, even allowing for the possibility of errors in the price indexes compiled by the Dominion Bureau of Statistics, there is every indication that per capita retail sales continued to rise even after the cessation of the production of many consumer durables in late 1941 and early 1942. A surprisingly wide array of goods remained for sale, and advertisers and retailers unapologetically converted wartime anxieties into rationales for buying them. It is perhaps difficult to reconcile the patriotic mythology of self-sacrificing Canadians with the image of department stores, restaurants, and movie theatres jammed to the rafters with people happily spending their dollars, but it is worth reflecting that many people at the time were just as uneasy about the contradiction. As the writer Dave Mullen reflected in 1944,

> Toronto was very gay and ever-so prosperous. I think as far as big business is concerned, the war is practically over. The stores are full of merchandise and people are extravagantly dressed and the money seems everywhere ... And so I sat in Eaton's and wondered how many men felt the last blinding flash between the time my coffee-cup left its saucer and touched my lips and the young woman across from me finished putting on her lipstick.[38]

I have also argued that the history of women on Canada's home front is in need of revision. That history has been inordinately concerned with the movement of women into non-traditional professions such as munitions work and military service. By contrast, I contend that a crucial, and for the most part neglected, aspect of women's lives on the home front is what I have ventured to call "patriotic consumerism." This was a highly malleable concept, but what was unchanging was the understanding that the female consumer's conception of citizenship and civic duty in wartime was closely related to ideas about consumption that were themselves highly contested. The essence of patriotic consumerism was the claim that consumerism, undertaken in a patriotic manner – and, as we have seen, this meant different things at different times – could be part of an attempt to defend the country, the family, and the place of women within it; it need not be at cross-purposes with the war effort, as was sometimes suggested. Given the centrality of the defence of family to the concept of patriotic consumerism, one can argue that it was part of a sexist backlash against the advancement of women into non-traditional roles. However, just as Canada's business leaders did not recognize any necessary contradiction between the maintenance of the nation's consumer economy and the prosecution of the war effort, so too did many Canadian women and the organizations that represented them see no distinction between defending Canada and defending what they regarded as its central institution – the family.

My conclusion that patriotic citizenship became closely related to the politics of wartime consumerism echoes arguments made by some historians regarding the Cold War. These historians have demonstrated how the Cold War era's denunciation of socialism and communism in Canada often centred, as it did in the United States, on the greater prosperity of societies whose material comforts and democratic institutions were held to be predicated upon free enterprise.[39] I have suggested that, though there was no consensus about the meaning of "free enterprise," these sorts of rhetorical devices were employed in Canada throughout the Second World War against the country's Axis foes and later against domestic social reformers. Rather than originating in the Cold War, the effort to equate consumer choice with democratic freedom was transposed, and rather easily, from the Second World War.

A Small Price to Pay has also hinted at certain broader implications concerning the social history of wartime Canada. No consensus is possible in an ethnically and regionally diverse nation of 12 million people, as Canada was at the time. Beneath the veneer of patriotic unanimity and consensus, we find that the whole compass of political, social, cultural, and economic disputes that had always been part of Canadian life continued unabated. In many cases, the arguments actually intensified, for it seemed to everyone who had a stake in them that national survival depended on their satisfactory resolution. It is therefore impossible to make a final conclusion about what consumerism "meant" on the home front. It meant many things to many different people. Some exalted it and embraced it, others resented it and resisted it, and still others sought to temper it or harness its power, but in the end, they all became consumers. In 1945, per capita retail spending in Canada was $380, or about $4,400 adjusted for sixty years' inflation. By the sixtieth anniversary of the war's end, retail sales in Canada had reached nearly $370 billion, the equivalent of just under $12,000 in spending by each Canadian.[40] On average, Canadians living sixty years after victory over the Axis spent nearly three times as much per capita as their wartime counterparts, even after adjusting for inflation. In a century where writers, philosophers, and politicians preoccupied themselves with the ideologies of fascism, communism, and imperialism, consumerism was the ideology whose victory was complete.

Appendix
Guns and Butter:
Consumer Spending, Inflation, and Price Controls

We must face the fact that there are not enough men; there are not enough machines; there are not enough materials to meet both the demands of consumers and the demands of war ... We have no choice but to reduce our consumption of consumer goods. To us, too, has come the choice between guns and butter.

– William Lyon Mackenzie King, October 1941

To Market! To Market! With Money to Spend!

– Advertisement, Marketing, *January 1944*

ONE OF THIS WORK'S core arguments is that a consumer-spending boom coincided with Canada's economic mobilization for war. Abundant evidence attests that Canadians on the home front not so much reduced spending, as they were urged to do beginning in late 1941, as increase it on more readily available goods. As the war progressed, consumers often complained that many goods were hard to come by, but they also said that, on the whole, things had never been better. This fact sits uneasily alongside the patriotic memory of rationing, shortages, and other hardships endured by self-sacrificing citizens waging "total war." This overused phrase is not applicable to the Canadian experience in the Second World War, at least not if it is used in the sense suggested by one scholar of Nazi Germany: "the *complete* orientation of society in its political, economic, and social life to the pursuit of the war effort."[1] For most Canadians, the war involved only comparatively minor material sacrifices along with much greater improvements in their overall standard of living. Undeniably, shortages of consumer durables and occasional seasonal and regional shortages of other commodities decelerated the growth of consumer spending in 1942 and 1943. Moreover, some local shortages, though usually

Table A.1

Consumer spending by category at current market values, 1939-45 ($ millions)

Category	1939	1940	1941	1942	1943	1944	1945	Adjusted increase (%)
Durables	330	381	402	262	177	196	225	-42
Semi-durables	531	669	813	903	916	987	1,102	76
Non-durables	1,717	1,884	2,179	2,435	2,750	2,905	3,225	60
Services	1,394	1,530	1,695	1,866	1,940	2,172	2,420	47
Total expenditure	3,972	4,464	5,089	5,466	5,783	6,260	6,972	49

short-lived, could be quite severe. Nonetheless, wartime economic indicators demonstrate clearly that real consumer spending increased steadily over the course of the war. I contend that what is often described as a post-war consumer boom can be more accurately characterized as a post-Depression boom that began in 1939. In this appendix, I argue for the empirical validity of this claim by examining retail sales, per capita consumer spending, and selected consumption figures for commodities not considered in earlier chapters.

Consumer spending in Canada fell precipitously at the beginning of the Depression in 1929, hit bottom in 1933, and then began a slow recovery in 1934. The general economic recovery proceeded at a comparably sluggish pace. As late as January 1939, unemployment remained in the double digits. Adjusting for Depression-era price deflation (cumulatively negative 17 percent), we find that real retail spending had only just returned to 1929 levels by the outbreak of the Second World War that September. Thereafter, however, consumer expenditure began a remarkable growth, easily exceeding pre-Depression levels by the end of 1940. It continued to rise, albeit at a reduced pace, even after orders suspending or hugely curtailing the production of cars, appliances, and other durables came into effect in late 1941 and early 1942. Table A.1 shows the growth in consumer spending from 1939 to 1945. The final column of the table indicates the percentage change in each category after adjusting for 17.7 percent inflation from 1939 to 1945.

Spending on "services" includes non-essentials such as movie-going, resort vacations, and the like but also in categories including health care and education that do not normally come to mind when one thinks of

Table A.2

Retail sales by category at current market values, 1939-45 ($ millions)

Category	1939	1940	1941	1942	1943	1944	1945	Adjusted increase (%)
Grocery	404	469	567	663	707	768	849	58.01
Alcohol	103	119	145	177	191	217	277	128.49
Meat markets	60	68	83	92	96	102	110	55.76
Other food	120	124	136	155	164	163	179	26.73
General	183	194	215	245	274	298	324	50.42
Department	291	327	378	419	420	460	510	48.90
Variety stores	59	70	85	98	99	104	113	62.72
Auto dealers	294	340	371	217	180	201	240	-30.64
Gas stations	160	189	205	116	89	94	109	-42.12
Men's clothes	60	68	80	96	98	105	115	62.84
Family clothes	51	61	74	88	94	100	111	84.92
Women's clothes	40	55	71	87	94	102	111	135.77
Shoe stores	30	34	44	54	57	62	69	95.41
Hardware	59	65	73	81	85	89	104	49.76
Lumber and building materials	53	66	80	82	84	97	100	60.31
Furniture	46	57	64	66	62	69	79	45.91
Appliances	35	43	46	42	33	31	37	-10.18
Restaurants	69	87	131	158	196	216	232	185.67
Fuel dealers	83	87	99	123	138	131	137	40.24
Drugstores	76	84	101	115	128	138	148	65.45
Jewellery	25	32	38	44	52	60	71	141.29
Tobacco	31	36	43	49	56	59	65	78.15
All other retail	248	260	312	352	393	427	482	65.13
All retail	2,578	2,935	3,441	3,619	3,790	4,093	4,573	50.71

NOTE: It should be noted that there are two very small errors in *Retail Sales* and the *Historical Statistics of Canada* tables that are derived from them. For example, total retail spending for 1939 is listed as 2,578 (million), but the sums add up to 2,580. For 1945, the total is given as 4,573 but is in fact 4,572. I have been unable to determine the source of the original error, however. It may be a simple mistake in addition. On the other hand, perhaps a typographical error occurs in one of the categories for retail sales and thus the sum total as recorded by the Dominion Bureau of Statistics (DBS) and in Historical Statistics of Canada is actually correct. (A few obvious typographical errors do occur in DBS documents.) Since the difference is very small (less than a tenth of a percent), I have left the figures as they appear in the original sources. The DBS based its computation of retail sales on monthly samples of retail spending: by 1945, over seven thousand retailers were included in the sample.

SOURCE: M.C. Urquhart and K.A.H. Buckley, eds., *Historical Statistics of Canada* (Cambridge: Cambridge University Press, 1965).

"consumerism." Therefore, the figures for retail sales by category in Table A.2 may be of greater interest in the context of this study, with the final column once again adjusted for average price increases. As the table reveals, retail sales underwent a remarkable growth throughout the war. Admittedly, the figures are crude. Food prices, for example, increased somewhat faster than the general cost of living.[2] Even if we narrow our focus to non-food items for the years of rationing and shortages, 1942 to 1945, we find that, for instance, department store sales increased a further 18 percent after inflation, women's clothing store sales by 23 percent, men's clothing by about the same, jewellery stores by an extraordinary 56 percent (despite the hefty point-of-purchase luxury tax), and alcoholic beverage outlets by 51 percent, which is particularly noteworthy, given the provincial regulations imposed on the consumption of beer, wine, and spirits. Both during the war and after, it was sometimes claimed that rationing was part of a process of "siphoning off" consumer purchasing power. As we have seen, however, the rationing regime was not especially severe and applied to only a handful of food items and gasoline. The only retailers that saw total sales decline after 1941 were sellers of consumer durables and related businesses: appliance, radio, and auto dealers, filling stations, and the like, and many of them saw recovery begin as early as 1944.

The effect of the diversion of materials and productive capacity for military purposes can also be seen when examining department store sales (see Table A.3). Department stores – and Eaton's in particular – have captured the imagination of Canadian historians but actually accounted for only about 10 percent of overall retail sales in the 1930s and '40s. Nonetheless, given their cultural significance and importance as retail "anchors" in downtown shopping districts, their sales deserve closer scrutiny. Once again we find that the only areas of decline or negligible growth in sales occur in those departments selling consumer durables.

The surprising increase in consumer spending through the whole period of rationing, controls, and shortages, when Canadians ostensibly were forced to choose between guns and butter, can also be seen in Table A.4, which demonstrates real consumer spending per capita in 1939 prices over the course of the war. For the sake of ease, the figures were computed by using the standard method of dividing consumer spending by aggregate population estimates. However, a very good case could be made for basing them on the *resident* population alone, deducting those members of the

Table A.3

Department store sales by selected departments, 1941-45 ($ thousands)

Category	1941	1942	1943	1944	1945	Adjusted increase (%)
Home furnishings	26,953	28,956	22,008	26,294	30,372	5
Appliances and electrical	11,254	11,120	7,823	8,121	9,630	-20
Hardware and kitchen utensils	14,229	16,549	14,954	16,275	19,389	27
Radios, musical instruments	5,024	5,813	4,219	3,315	3,883	-28
Piece goods	27,558	32,116	31,411	36,939	41,177	40
Stationery, books, magazines	6,209	7,322	8,368	9,519	10,730	61
Footwear	27,418	30,198	30,327	33,207	37,541	28
Women's dresses, coats, and suits	37,190	44,709	48,631	54,023	60,177	51
Other women's and children's apparel	89,518	103,549	109,449	119,857	130,235	28
Men's and boys' clothing	43,465	49,995	49,935	54,535	59,233	28
Total, all departments[a]	377,800	421,964	423,618	464,880	516,141	28

a Includes departments not listed above.

NOTE: Note the very slight variance between the figures quoted here and the ones in *Historical Statistics of Canada*. Department-by-department sales figures are unavailable prior to 1941.

SOURCE: Dominion Bureau of Statistics, *Department Store Sales and Stocks: January, 1941, to July, 1948, by Months* (Ottawa: Dominion Bureau of Statistics, 1948).

armed forces overseas – over 325,000 at the peak of deployment in 1944 – or perhaps by deducting the net difference between Canadians overseas and Allied personnel stationed in Canada. One could even compute the figures solely on the basis of the resident *civilian* population, on the grounds that soldiers, sailors, and airmen stationed in Canada were for the most part clothed and fed by the armed forces and were major consumers of leisure services only. Therefore, the figures in Table A.4 should be taken as somewhat conservative estimates of actual spending per head, with the percentage change once again adjusted for wartime inflation.

As I have suggested, historians have sometimes overgeneralized when assessing the impact of the war on the civilian consumer. It will be recalled that some earlier histories argued that wartime shortages and controls

Table A.4

Per capita personal expenditure and retail sales at 1939 prices, 1939-45

Category	1939	1940	1941	1942	1943	1944	1945	Change (%)
Population (thousands)	11,267	11,381	11,507	11,654	11,795	11,946	12,072	7
Retail sales ($ millions)	2,578	2,821	3,127	3,140	3,249	3,494	3,884	51
Retail sales per capita ($)	229	248	272	269	275	292	322	41
Per capita change from previous year (%)	–	8.33	9.62	–0.86	2.25	6.18	10.01	–
Total expenditure ($ millions)	3,972	4,291	4,624	4,742	4,958	5,344	5,922	49
Total expenditure per capita ($)	353	377	402	407	420	447	491	39
Per capita change from previous year (%)	–	7.0	7.0	1.0	3.0	6.0	10.0	–

SOURCE: Retail sales from M.C. Urquhart and K.A.H. Buckley, eds., *Historical Statistics of Canada* (Cambridge: Cambridge University Press, 1965), series T1-24. Total expenditure from F.H. Leacy, ed., *Historical Statistics of Canada*, 2nd ed. (1983), series F76-90; population from series A-1.

prevented consumer purchasing power from rising above Depression-era levels.[3] As Table A.4 indicates, real per capita spending increased significantly throughout the war: by 40 percent in retail sales and 39 percent in total consumer expenditure. On the other hand, the growth in per capita consumer expenditure was admittedly very small in 1942 and 1943. Retail sales actually declined very slightly (by less than 1 percent) in 1942, the first year of coupon rationing and serious shortages of consumer durables, and were a modest 2 percent the following year. However, as suggested above, the effect of reducing the population figures to the approximate *resident* population is significant: subtracting the net difference between Canadian servicemen overseas and Allied servicemen stationed in Canada (about 175,000 in mid-1942 and about 250,000 in mid-1943), for instance, increases the real per capita growth of retail sales in 1942 to just under 1 percent and to over 4 percent in 1943.[4] Again, this is crudely done, but the point is to demonstrate that the choice between "guns or

Table A.5

Personal expenditure on goods and services in 1939 prices, as a percentage of disposable income, 1939-45

Category	1939	1940	1941	1942	1943	1944	1945	Increase (%)
Disposable income ($ millions)	4,207	4,612	5,068	6,002	6,311	6,873	7,096	69
Per capita disposable income ($)	373.39	405.21	440.40	514.97	535.07	575.32	587.78	57
Total personal expenditure ($ millions)	3,972	4,291	4,624	4,742	4,958	5,344	5,922	49
Personal savings ($ millions)	202	288	402	1,233	1,323	1,502	1,148	468
Per capita savings ($)	17.93	25.34	34.92	105.78	112.15	125.77	95.05	530
Expenditure as percentage of disposable income (%)	94	93	91	79	79	78	83	–

SOURCE: Personal disposable income and personal savings from M.C. Urquhart and K.A.H. Buckley, eds., *Historical Statistics of Canada* (Cambridge: Cambridge University Press, 1965), series E-66-78. Converted to 1939 prices by the author.

butter" seldom had to be made on the Canadian home front. Canadians chose both. Rather than reducing retail sales, the combination of shortages, rationing, taxation, and moral exhortations in the form of propaganda seems to have more or less levelled off the expansion of consumer spending for about twenty-four months before it resumed its steady upward climb.

Another remarkable aspect of Canada's wartime consumer economy is that absolute consumer spending remained high, even when consumer spending as a percentage of disposable income fell off sharply in 1942. Despite unprecedented taxes and the wage ceiling, per capita disposable incomes increased by an extraordinary 57 percent between 1939 and 1945, even after adjusting for inflation. In the same period, however, Canadians multiplied their real personal savings by an astonishing five times. For what was perhaps the first and only time in Canadian history, the growth in consumers' incomes outstripped their ability to actually spend their money, as Table A.5 shows.

Several factors coalesced to create this unusual set of circumstances, where Canadians had more money than ever and spent more money than ever, but also saved more than ever. The largest single factor is the extraordinarily rapid growth in incomes brought on by high employment. This enormous increase in purchasing power, coupled with a diminishing supply of goods, is what so deeply alarmed economists and other financial experts in 1941, leading them to endorse price controls and various methods to reduce consumer purchasing power in a bid to divert inflation. Table A.5, however, suggests that Canadians had plenty to spend – and indeed, spent plenty – but not as much as they might have.

Anti-consumer propaganda, too, may have had a chilling effect on spending, but as this book has argued, it is hard to say how far these patriotic appeals influenced Canadians, just as we have no certain means of gauging the impact of the many advertising campaigns that used the war as a rationale for increased spending. The cessation of consumer durable production and temporary and regional shortages of unrestricted and partially restricted goods would have taken their toll, too, even with the diversion of consumer spending to those goods that were still available. Certainly, most retailers of semi- and non-durables reported in their trade papers that their biggest problem was not getting customers but getting enough merchandise to sell. As I have contended, despite the consumer boom, the war years were not smooth sailing for retailers. An analysis of department store inventories, for example, reveals that the quantity of merchandise for sale declined generally and not just in radio and appliance departments. Total inventory values in department stores were $103 million in December 1941, $95 million in December 1942, $89 million in December 1943, and $79 million in December 1944: a decline of about 30 percent after inflation. Durable goods accounted for a large portion of this reduction in the value of inventory, but women's and men's clothing inventories also declined by 20 percent.[5] Clothing provides an interesting case study in the often contradictory nature of the wartime consumer economy. Clothing sales increased, of course, and women's magazines offered non-stop advice on what was both fashionable and patriotic to wear, but shortages of fabric for civilian use forced the Wartime Prices and Trade Board (WPTB) to impose a slate of economies on manufacturers. Consumers simply had fewer styles and colours of suits, dresses, socks, and shoes from which to choose. In early 1942, the Clothing

Administration even specified that henceforth men's socks would be available only in white, black, grey, brown, blue, grey mix, brown mix, blue mix, green, and maroon. A heavy burden, to be sure, but there was a war on, after all.[6]

CANADA'S WARTIME CONSUMER boom stands in marked contrast to the circumstances faced by consumers in the United Kingdom and Germany, and to a surprising degree, in the United States. A persistent myth, sometimes still repeated in military histories, holds that the Nazi leadership, believing that the "blitzkrieg" doctrine would produce a quick victory, favoured civilian over military production until late 1942. Even leaving aside serious doubts about the existence of blitzkrieg as a novel operational doctrine that would have been recognized by German leaders, R.J. Overy and others have confirmed that German consumer expenditure began to decline rapidly and steadily in 1939 as the Nazi regime struggled to mobilize its chaotic and inefficient economy for a long war. Between 1939 and 1943, real consumer expenditure in the Greater German Reich declined by 31 percent, and the next two years saw the progressive obliteration of the German economy by Allied strategic bombing.[7]

In Great Britain, consumer expenditure (in constant 1938 prices) on clothing had fallen by 44 percent by 1943 and on durable household goods by 73 percent by 1944. Overall retail sales in the United Kingdom had diminished by 16 percent by 1943 before starting a slow recovery in 1944. As we have seen, private motoring had virtually ceased to exist in Britain by the middle of the war, and the famously pallid "British Restaurant" replaced the experience of dining out. Whereas in Canada, rationing was designed to promote equitable distribution and force modest reductions in consumption of a few goods, nearly every consumer product was rationed in Britain, and the impositions were often severe – a fact that WPTB administrators never failed to mention when they had the chance. Sugar rationing in the United Kingdom persisted for eight years after the war and meat rationing for nine.[8]

In fairness, there may be little basis for a comparison between the Canadian consumer economy and those of European countries directly under attack. The United States may serve as a more valid basis for comparison, especially given the close integration of the Canadian and American economies. The extraordinary productive achievements of the United States during the Second World War are well known and have been described by some military historians of a deterministic bent as the lynchpin of Allied victory.[9] As was the case in Canada, America's economic mobilization for war was achieved without imposing severe material hardship on consumers. As the economic historian Hugh Rockoff puts it, "the United States could have fought much longer and harder had it proved necessary" – a statement that could apply equally to Canada.[10] One somewhat greater hardship that Americans had to endure, however, was higher inflation. The American equivalent of the WPTB, the Office of Price Administration, was described by R. Warren James in his landmark study of wartime economic cooperation between Canada and the United States as having "quite inadequate authority to control prices" and as being afflicted by "serious and administrative and jurisdictional obstacles."[11] James concludes,

> In Canada, executive powers under the War Measures Act were virtually unlimited with the result that the imposition of rigid price control was a relatively easy step. In the United States, on the other hand, it was necessary to appeal to Congress for legislative authority, the authority being given on the condition that some protection be given to special interests.[12]

According to official figures, wartime inflation in the United States was significantly higher than in Canada (about 22.5 percent between 1941 and 1945 alone), but the growth in real consumer expenditure, approximately 28 percent from 1939 to 1945, was strong enough that the economist John Kenneth Galbraith was later to reflect, "never before had there been so much talk of sacrifice amid so little actual want" – yet another remark that might equally be applied to Canada.[13] More recently, some economists have wondered whether the apparent growth of consumer spending in the United States during the peak years of the war effort might not have been a statistical illusion resulting from underestimates of the actual rate of inflation. I will now turn to a brief discussion of the possibility that this is true for Canada as well.

Granatstein (1995), McInnis (2002), and Keshen (2004) each estimate that inflation in Canada was approximately 18 percent for the first two years of the war and about 2 to 3 percent thereafter, whereas Morton (1998) puts it at 20 percent to the end of 1941 "and less than 10" thereafter.[14] My own calculations, using the annual average of the Consumer Price Index (CPI), indicate a growth of 17.7 percent for the period from 1939 to 1945 as a whole. This corresponds roughly to the figure of 17.95 percent produced by the Bank of Canada's on-line historical cost-of-living calculator,

Table A.6

Monthly cost-of-living index, 1939-45 (1935-39 average = 100)

	1939	1940	1941	1942	1943	1944	1945
January	101.1	103.8	108.3	115.4	117.1	119.0	118.6
February	100.7	103.8	108.2	115.7	116.9	118.9	118.6
March	100.6	104.6	108.2	115.9	117.2	119.0	118.7
April	100.6	104.6	108.6	115.9	117.6	119.1	118.7
May	100.6	104.9	109.4	116.1	118.1	119.2	119.0
June	100.5	104.9	110.5	116.7	118.5	119.0	119.6
July	100.8	105.6	111.9	117.9	118.8	119.0	120.3
August	100.8	105.9	113.7	117.7	119.2	118.9	120.5
September	100.8	106.6	114.7	117.4	119.4	118.8	119.9
October	103.5	107.0	115.5	117.8	119.3	118.6	119.7
November	103.8	107.8	116.3	118.6	119.4	118.9	119.9
December	103.8	108.0	115.8	118.8	119.3	118.5	120.1
Average	101.5	105.6	111.7	117.0	118.4	118.9	119.5

which computes year-to-year inflation by using the price index for the month of November as its basis for comparison.[15] The Consumer Price Index from January 1939 to December 1945 is reproduced in Table A.6.

Using these data, we cannot produce the oft-repeated figure of 18 percent inflation for the first two years of the war. Instead, Table A.6 indicates a more modest overall growth of 13.8 percent for its first twenty-four months. What was noted with despair by contemporary observers, however, was the alarming 6 percent growth in the cost of living that occurred from April to September 1941 alone. From the establishment of the price ceiling in December 1941 until September 1945, however, the official figures indicate that inflation was held to just 3.5 percent. Privately, the WPTB estimated that the price ceiling saved Canadian consumers $1 billion by the end of 1943.[16]

That consumer spending in Canada continued to rise against a backdrop of diminishing availability of certain goods, without visibly rampant inflation, can be seen as indicative of the general success of the board's price controls. There may be grounds for skepticism about the validity of the Dominion Bureau of Statistics (DBS) Cost-of-Living Index, however. Although the DBS's successor, Statistics Canada, holds that the CPI tends to slightly *over*estimate inflation, many contemporary critics of the WPTB believed that the overall cost of living between 1942 and 1945 increased faster than the official figures suggested. This accusation was made most frequently in socialist and labour periodicals, especially when the cost-of-living bonus remained tied to the official inflation figures. In addition, in two unpublished PhD dissertations dating from 1947 and 1981, respectively, E.J. Spence, a former employee of the board, and historian Christopher Waddell (using Spence as the primary source for this claim) argued that the board had insufficient resources to investigate more than a fraction of the complaints it received regarding price ceiling violations. Some inflation in prices, then, may have gone unnoticed by board officials. Even when investigations did occur, Spence and Waddell argue, the board tended to issue warnings rather than press charges against most first-time offenders, which may have done little to deter further transgressions. Furthermore, the authors claim, the board was not unsympathetic to the plight of retailers (though one would not know it from reading the incessant complaints retailers made in their trade papers) and sometimes looked the other way when price infractions occurred.[17]

These claims rest on evidence that is largely anecdotal and must be weighed against those of many retailers who insisted that they complied with the price ceiling, even at the expense of their own profits. We must remember, too, that board investigators often found complaints about price increases to be the result of public misunderstanding. The board frequently permitted small increases that many consumers were unaware of despite the best efforts of the Consumer Branch.

There are, moreover, empirical grounds on which to question the argument that infractions of the price ceiling were commonplace. As indicated in Chapter 1, a nationwide survey of consumers conducted on behalf of the board in 1944 offers remarkable proof that, if such breaches were routine, consumers either did not notice them or were not bothered by them. The survey indicated an extraordinary 92 percent approval for the price ceiling. Furthermore, it found only moderate regional variations (from a low of 85 percent in Quebec, to a high of 97 percent in British Columbia) and surprisingly small variations in support between differing income groups (90 percent approval in low-income groups, 96 percent in high-income groups). Asked if the ceiling had been successful in keeping prices down, 55 percent of respondents stated that it had achieved *unqualified* success, 34 percent that it had been partly successful, and only 7 percent that it had been altogether unsuccessful. Once again, the regional and income-based variations were surprisingly small, with just 11 percent of Quebecers surveyed opining that the ceiling had been unsuccessful versus 4 percent of Ontarians. There was, moreover, remarkably little variation in the poll results among income groups, with just 8 percent of lower-income consumers indicating that the ceiling had failed versus 4 percent in the upper-income group. Another measure of the ceiling's general popularity is the fact that, overall, 73 percent indicated that it ought to be continued after the war ended, with 53 percent favouring its retention until the economy was "back to normal" and 18 percent approving its use indefinitely. The point is to indicate that if systemic or widespread failure of the price ceiling occurred, it either did so in the year after this mid-1944 poll or the failure was not widely perceived by consumers.[18] To this must be added three Canadian Institute of Public Opinion polls (July 1942, November 1943, and July 1945) that showed similarly strong support for the ceiling, its effectiveness, and the desirability of its continuation into the post-war period. One rather telling statistic is that in July 1942, less than a year after the ceiling was put in place, only half of those polled felt that it should be maintained after the war, whereas 77 percent supported its continuation three years later, after Germany was actually defeated.[19]

The second basis for suggesting that inflation was higher than official figures indicate stems from the claim that the quality of many goods declined during the war but without a corresponding reduction in prices. The cost-of-living index would therefore have concealed a de facto form of price inflation: people were paying more for inferior goods. The Consumer Branch's Women's Regional Advisory Committees heard innumerable complaints about the quality of goods, and a survey commissioned by the board in 1945 found that two-thirds of women believed that they had purchased goods whose quality seemed very poor, given the price they had paid. As board officials observed, however, this was a very common peacetime complaint as well.[20] It also became the subject of another Consumer Branch one-act play, *Libel or Label?* which made the rounds of fall fairs in 1944.[21] It is very difficult to evaluate the legitimacy of these claims or to distinguish them from general objections about the quality of goods.[22] The board did employ quality inspectors, but "quality" was often very subjective. In most cases, the board refused to agree that the various economies it imposed on manufacturers (such as the removal of cuffs and watch pockets from men's pants) or the materials substitutions it required constituted a reduction in quality. It insisted that it was rigorously inspecting goods to ensure that their quality was maintained. Moreover, board investigators found that many of the complaints about quality were unfounded, unrelated to the war, or the fault of the consumer herself misusing or abusing the product in question. It seems probable that the quality of some goods did decline because of the war, but in matters concerning quality, as in matters concerning prices, some women deployed the enforcement apparatus of the WPTB to follow up on complaints that had nothing to do with the war.[23]

It is not possible to refute conclusively the validity of Spence's and Waddell's claims, but it bears repeating once more that if widespread and inordinate price increases did occur, they were not detected in any polls on the issue. Strictly for the sake of argument, however, let us assume a worst-case scenario: that the prices reached in 1947, after the price ceiling had been lifted in full, had in fact already been reached in 1945. In this hypothetical situation, wartime inflation would have been approximately 33.5 percent, rather than the 17.7 percent that the official figures indicate. Even under this set of assumptions, in which official inflation figures are doubled for the war as a whole and approximately *quadrupled* for the price control period, we still find total consumer spending increasing 31.5 percent between 1939 and 1945.[24] Once again, this is strictly for the sake of argument – we have no evidence beyond the anecdotal that prices were significantly higher than what the board claimed, and such claims must be weighed against consumer surveys indicating a widespread satisfaction with the price ceiling.

Arguments such as these can have something of a glass-is-half-full, glass-is-half-empty character about them. As Hugh Rockoff observes in regards to the United States, even if higher-than-recorded inflation rates depressed the actual growth in consumer spending, the war years nonetheless "look pretty good compared to the Great Depression."[25] Undoubtedly, many Canadians continued to live in what historian Magda Fahrni has called "rickety" economic circumstances throughout the war. There is also no denying that after 1941, temporary and regional shortages – often brought on by consumers themselves – were quite frequent and that the supply of many kinds of durables was very sparse indeed.[26] As I have demonstrated, however, the overall flow of goods for consumer consumption remained surprisingly large throughout the war, and the circumstances faced by consumers generally were not nearly so spartan as historians sometimes claim. The rest of this study has been an effort to understand the cultural context of consumerism on the Canadian home front. It remains a topic worthy of further investigation.

Notes

Introduction

1 "Go On, Spend It ... What's the Difference?" Advertisement, *Maclean's*, 1 July 1942, 28 (emphasis in original).
2 *Drug Merchandising*, 1 October 1943, 26.
3 C.P. Stacey, "Generals and Generalship before Quebec, 1759-1760," *Canadian Historical Association Report* 38, 1 (1959): 1.
4 Jeffrey Keshen, *Saints, Sinners, and Soldiers: Canada's Second World War* (Vancouver: UBC Press, 2004), 5; Jennifer Anne Stephen, *Pick One Intelligent Girl: Employability, Domesticity and the Gendering of Canada's Welfare State, 1939-1947*, Studies in Gender and History (Toronto: University of Toronto Press, 2007); Serge Marc Durflinger, *Fighting from Home: The Second World War in Verdun, Quebec*, Studies in Canadian Military History (Vancouver: UBC Press, 2006); Stephanie Bangarth, *Voices Raised in Protest: Defending North American Citizens of Japanese Ancestry, 1942-49* (Vancouver: UBC Press, 2008).
5 I acknowledge that the word "consumerism" is somewhat anachronistic when applied to the Second World War, as it was very seldom used at the time. The word never appears in the *Toronto Globe and Mail* during the war, if the digital databases are to be believed. The *Oxford English Dictionary* dates the word to 1944, although in the course of this study, I have seen earlier examples. Initially, it usually referred to activism undertaken for the protection of consumer interests. This work uses the term in the sense employed by Peter Stearns: "Consumerism describes a society in which many people formulate their goals in life partly through acquiring goods that they clearly do not need for subsistence or for traditional display." Peter Stearns, *Consumerism in World History: The Global Transformation of Desire* (London: Routledge, 2001), ix.
6 Here, there are too many works to mention. Important histories of the North American consumer society include T.J. Jackson Lears, *No Place of Grace: Antimodernism and the Transformation of American Culture, 1880-1920* (New York: Pantheon, 1981); Roland Marchand, *Advertising the American Dream: Making Way for Modernity, 1920-1940* (Berkeley: University of California Press, 1985); and William Leach, *Land of Desire: Merchants, Power, and the Rise of a New American Culture* (New York: Vintage, 1993). Stearns's *Consumerism in World History* is a useful overview of the emergence of the *global* consumer society. Histories of Canadian consumerism are fewer, but a number of excellent recent studies have bracketed the war years. These include Donica Belisle's excellent *Retail Nation: Department Stores and the Making of Modern Canada* (Vancouver: UBC Press, 2011); Joy Parr, *Domestic Goods: The Material, the Moral, and the Economic in the Postwar Years* (Toronto: University of Toronto Press, 1999); and Russell T. Johnston, *Selling Themselves: The Emergence of Canadian Advertising* (Toronto: University of Toronto Press, 2001).

7 It has sometimes been argued that, strictly speaking, the consumer is the person who consumes (that is, uses) the product and not necessarily the person who buys it. For example, by the Second World War, advertisers, retailers, and government statisticians had long since discovered that women were the principal buyers for their families, but this does not necessarily mean that they were principal consumers. At times, the distinction between buyer and consumer is useful though admittedly rather obvious. At other times, however, the distinction imposes an altogether too utilitarian conception of what it means to consume. In this perspective, a mother who buys candy for her children is merely a buyer; her children are the consumers. On the other hand, she might also have bought the candy for her own purposes – such as to experience a parent's joy in those very elusive moments when children are content. In this sense, she too is a consumer, having derived utility from food that someone else ate. Presumably, this is the case with a great many purchases made by women who did most of the shopping for their families. I have therefore tended to use the word "consumer" interchangeably with "shopper" and "buyer," except where circumstances necessitated greater precision.
8 See, for example, John Kenneth Galbraith, "The Dependence Effect," in *The Consumer Society Reader*, ed. Juliet B. Schor and Douglas B. Holt (New York: New Press, 2000), 20-25; Lawrence B. Glickman, "Born to Shop?" in *Consumer Society in American History: A Reader*, ed. Lawrence B. Glickman (Ithaca, NY: Cornell University Press, 1999), 1-16; and Gary S. Cross, *An All-Consuming Century: Why Commercialism Won in Modern America* (New York: Columbia University Press, 2000).
9 Michael Bliss, *Northern Enterprise: Five Centuries of Canadian Business* (Toronto: McClelland and Stewart, 1987), 448; J.L. Granatstein, "Canada," in *The Oxford Companion to the Second World War*, ed. I.C.B. Dear and M.R.D. Foot (New York: Oxford University Press, 1995), 183.
10 Ken MacQueen, "Shop until You Drop: The Marching Orders of Consumers Are Clear," *Maclean's*, 15 October 2001, 42.
11 "Carry On," *Maclean's*, 15 October 1939, 15.
12 King explained this policy of "limited liability" to the House of Commons in the first week of September 1939. Canada, *House of Commons Debates*, 8 September 1939), 33-36. For a lengthy analysis, see J.L. Granatstein, *Canada's War: The Politics of the Mackenzie King Government, 1939-1945* (Toronto: University of Toronto Press, 1975), especially Chapter 1.
13 H. Duncan Hall, *North American Supply* (London: H.M. Stationery Office, 1955), 16.
14 Robert Bothwell, "'Who's Paying for Anything These Days?' War Production in Canada, 1939-45," in *Mobilization for Total War: The Canadian, American, and British Experience*, ed. N.F. Dreisziger (Waterloo: Wilfrid Laurier University Press, 1981), 61. The dollar value of British munitions orders in Canada multiplied sixfold between 1940 and 1941, and nearly tripled again by 1944. See R. Warren James, *Wartime Economic Co-operation: A Study of Relations between Canada and the United States* (Toronto: Ryerson Press, 1949), 17.
15 Initially called the War Loan, Canadian war bonds were first issued in February 1940. War Savings Certificates, which had a higher rate of return but limits on the amount Canadians could buy, appeared in May 1940. In 1941, the War Loan was renamed the Victory Bond. Keshen, *Saints, Sinners, and Soldiers*, 32.
16 See C.H. Hebert, "War Savings: How, Why, and When?" *Canadian Banker*, July 1940, 447-45.

17 K.W. Taylor, "Price Control in Canada," *Canadian Banker*, April 1941, 288-303. Taylor worked for the Wartime Prices and Trade Board. For the discussions occurring within the Department of Finance, see David W. Slater and R.B. Bryce, *War Finance and Reconstruction: The Role of Canada's Department of Finance, 1939-1946* (Ottawa: Privately printed, 1995), 129-32.

18 Figures for sales of stoves, refrigerators, and other appliances are from *The Electrical Apparatus and Supplies Industry* (Ottawa: Dominion Bureau of Statistics, 1940-47). Furniture sales are from M.C. Urquhart and K.A.H. Buckley, eds., *Historical Statistics of Canada* (Cambridge: Cambridge University Press, 1965), Series T35-52. "Editorial," *Canadian Automotive Trade*, June 1941, 14.

19 William Lyon Mackenzie King, "Controlling the Cost of Living: The Stabilization of Prices and Wages. Broadcast, CBC, Ottawa, October 18, 1941," in William Lyon Mackenzie King, *Canada and the Fight for Freedom* (Toronto: Macmillan, 1944), 33. The broadcast was widely quoted; see, for example, "Stabilization of Prices and Wages in Canada," *Labour Gazette*, 1941, 1363.

20 Radio and appliance figures are from *The Electrical Apparatus and Supplies Industry*, 1945, 10, 14. Tire production figures are from "Tire Production for Automotive Vehicles, 1939-1944," *Facts and Figures of the Automobile Industry* (Canadian Automobile Chamber of Commerce), 1946, 11.

21 On automobiles and other consumer durables, see Chapter 5. Contemporary observers too numerous to count commented on the significance of the suspension of passenger car production. For example, see P.C. Armstrong, "Wages and Prices," in *Addresses Delivered at the Maritime Conference on Industrial Relations, Saint John, June 25, 1943* (Halifax: Maritime Bureau on Industrial Relations, 1943), 3-4; and Allen May, "Black Market," *Maclean's*, 1 November 1944, 7, 33-36.

22 *Sales and Financing of Motor Vehicles in Canada* (Ottawa: Dominion Bureau of Statistics, 1946), 8.

23 Direct taxes paid by individuals increased from $45.4 million in 1939 to $296.2 million in 1941 and to $698.4 million in 1943. Urquhart and Buckley, *Historical Statistics of Canada*, Series G1-25.

24 Other historians have noted the tendency in consumer societies to equate consumer choice with political freedom. Susan Strasser, for example, has written that "twentieth century rhetoric has conflated democracy with an abundance of consumer goods." Susan Strasser, *Satisfaction Guaranteed: The Making of the American Mass Market* (New York: Pantheon Books, 1989), 288. In my estimation, the express equation of consumerism with political liberty was seldom made in Canada before the Second World War.

25 See, for example, J.L. Granatstein, "Commentary," in *A Country of Limitations: Canada and the World in 1939*, ed. Norman Hillmer et al. (Ottawa: Canadian Committee for the History of the Second World War, 1996), 291.

26 C.P. Stacey, *Arms, Men and Governments: The War Policies of Canada, 1939-1945* (Ottawa: Queen's Printer, 1970), 532-35.

27 Urquhart and Buckley, *Historical Statistics of Canada*, Series T1-24; Stacey, *Arms, Men and Governments*, 532-35.

28 See E.J. Spence, "Wartime Price Control Policy in Canada" (PhD diss., Northwestern University, 1947); and Christopher Waddell, "The Wartime Prices and Trade Board: Price Control in Canada in World War Two" (PhD diss., York University, 1981). In addition, J. de N. Kennedy, *History of the Department of Munitions and Supply: Canada in the Second World War*, 2 vols. (Ottawa: King's Printer, 1950), is cumbersome and

nearly unreadable but an invaluable reference work on the immensely important and powerful DMS.
29 Keith Walden, "Speaking Modern: Language, Culture, and Hegemony in Grocery Window Displays, 1887-1920," *Canadian Historical Review* 70, 3 (1989): 287.
30 See Daniel J. Robinson, *The Measure of Democracy: Polling, Market Research, and Public Life, 1930-1945* (Toronto: University of Toronto Press, 1999).
31 Marchand, *Advertising the American Dream*, xix.
32 Dominion Bureau of Statistics, *Monthly Index of Retail Sales* (Ottawa: Dominion Bureau of Statistics, 1939-45); Urquhart and Buckley, *Historical Statistics of Canada*, Series T1-24. In all cases for the purpose of this study, I tabulated inflation increases personally, using the *Cost of Living Index Numbers for Canada* (Ottawa: Dominion Bureau of Statistics) for the years 1939-45. The cost-of-living index (or consumer price index) is also available as a downloadable data set from Statistics Canada that (as of 2011) uses 2009 as a baseline year. A thorough discussion of wartime consumer spending and differing estimates of the rate of inflation can be found in the Appendix.
33 Urquhart and Buckley, *Historical Statistics of Canada,* Series T213-26.
34 "Meet the Market," *Gift Buyer,* June 1944, 18-19; "Editorial", *Gift Buyer,* October 1945, 6. Attendance grew from 350 buyers to 2,600.
35 "What's Coming Is ... PLENTY!" Advertisement, *Maclean's,* 1 June 1943, 23.
36 Graham Greene, *The End of the Affair* (New York: Penguin, 1951), 7.

Chapter 1: Mrs. Consumer, Patriotic Consumerism, and the Wartime Prices and Trade Board

1 Byrne Hope Sanders, "As an Editor Sees It," *Chatelaine,* September 1940, 60.
2 Cynthia R. Comacchio, *The Infinite Bonds of Family: Domesticity in Canada, 1850-1940* (Toronto: University of Toronto Press, 1999), 150. On this, see also Joyce Boydston, *Home and Work: Housework, Wages, and the Ideology of Labor in the Early Republic* (New York: Oxford University Press, 1990); Lenore Davidoff, *Family Fortunes: Men and Women of the English Middle Class, 1780-1850,* rev. ed. (New York: Routledge, 2002); and, especially, Susan Strasser, *Never Done: A History of American Housework* (New York: Pantheon, 1982), 243-63. For a sociological perspective, see Marjorie L. DeVault, *Feeding the Family: The Social Organization of Caring as Gendered Work* (Chicago: University of Chicago Press, 1991). A discussion also occurs in Sherrie A. Inness's introduction to her edited collection, *Kitchen Culture in America: Popular Representations of Food, Gender, and Race* (Philadelphia: University of Pennsylvania Press, 2001), 1-13.
3 Sanders used this line or some variation of it in several speeches and two *Chatelaine* columns that I examined.
4 *Men's Wear Merchandising,* 1 December 1940, 27.
5 "Purchasing Agent (Just Appointed)," Advertisement, *Marketing,* 16 September 1939, 7.
6 On the emergence of the idea of shopping as a leisure activity, see Erika Rappaport, *Shopping for Pleasure: Women in the Making of London's West End* (Princeton: Princeton University Press, 2000). On the Canadian experience specifically, see also Donica Belisle, *Retail Nation: Department Stores and the Making of Modern Canada* (Vancouver: UBC Press, 2011); and Carol Anderson and Katharine Mallinson, *Lunch with Lady Eaton: Inside the Dining Rooms of a Nation* (Toronto: ECW Press, 2004).
7 Jennifer Scanlon, "Introduction," in *The Gender and Consumer Culture Reader,* ed. Jennifer Scanlon (New York: New York University Press, 2000), 8.

8 Library and Archives Canada (LAC), Wartime Prices and Trade Board (WPTB), RG 64, vol. 1449, file A-10-29-16, Consumer Branch Administration, Address by Byrne Hope Sanders.
9 The Consumer Price Index increased by nearly 80 percent in the five years from December 1915 to December 1920. The Bank of Canada's Inflation Calculator can be found at http://www.bankofcanada.ca/rates/related/inflation-calculator/.
10 On wartime anxieties over women's employment, see Ruth Roach Pierson, "*They're Still Women After All*": *The Second World War and Canadian Womanhood* (Toronto: McClelland and Stewart, 1986), especially pages 129-68.
11 Quoted in National Council of Women, *Yearbook*, 1943, 53.
12 Quoted in Barry Broadfoot, *Six War Years, 1939-1945: Memories of Canadians at Home and Abroad* (Markham: Paperjacks, 1976), 276.
13 Quoted in Richard J. Needham, "Hard Times," *Canadian Spokesman*, April 1941, 54.
14 M.C. Urquhart and K.A.H. Buckley, eds., *Historical Statistics of Canada* (Cambridge: Cambridge University Press, 1965), Series C56-69.
15 Ibid., Series T1-24. The post-inflation growth of retail sales from 1946 to 1948 was a mere 8 percent. See the Appendix for a discussion.
16 "Editorial," *Bookseller and Stationer*, February 1941, 1.
17 The term "phony war" was coined during the war itself to refer to the relative lack of combat after the fall of Poland and the beginning of Germany's offences in the spring of 1940.
18 C.P. Stacey, *Arms, Men and Governments: The War Policies of Canada, 1939-1945* (Ottawa: Queen's Printer, 1970), 6-9. See also J.L. Granatstein, *Conscription in the Second World War, 1939-1945* (Toronto: McGraw-Hill, 1969), 16, 19.
19 Granatstein, *Conscription*, 15-16.
20 Ibid., 19.
21 C.P. Stacey, *Six Years of War: The Army in Canada, Britain, and the Pacific* (Ottawa: Queen's Printer, 1955), 524.
22 Christopher Waddell, "The Wartime Prices and Trade Board: Price Control in Canada in World War Two" (PhD diss., York University, 1981), iv.
23 K.W. Taylor, "Price Control in Canada," *Canadian Banker*, April 1941, 288-303. Several of these orders are discussed in detail in Chapter 5.
24 Department of History, Vancouver Island University, Thompson Archive, *Canadian Letters and Images Project*, http://www.canadianletters.ca/letters.php, Archie Thompson to Donald Fuller, 12 December 1941.
25 William Henry Chamberlin, *Canada: Today and Tomorrow* (Boston: Little and Brown, 1942), 163.
26 Ibid., 134.
27 *National Council of Women Yearbook*, 1940, 29.
28 G.C.D. Stanley, "Buy Victory Now," *Echoes*, December 1940, 6.
29 J.L. Rutledge, "The Fourth Arm of Defense," *Liberty*, 9 November 1940, 3.
30 *Chatelaine*'s subscription figures are from *Lydiatt's Book of Canadian Market and Advertising Data*, 1941, 49. In the 1940s, Lydiatt's was published as an annual insert in *Marketing*.
31 Alice Sharples, "Shopping to Win the War," *Chatelaine*, September 1940, 38 (emphasis in original).
32 Sanders, "As an Editor Sees It," 78.
33 Stanley Alexander Saunders and Eleanor Back, *Come On, Canada!* (Toronto: Ryerson Press, 1941), 36.

34 *The Sword and the Lionheart and Other Wartime Speeches by the Right Honourable Vincent Massey* (London: Hodder and Stoughton, 1943), 64.
35 J.L. Rutledge, "Editorial," *Liberty,* September 1941, 3.
36 Bubbles Schanasi, "September Shopping Spree," *Liberty,* September 1941, 56 (emphasis in original).
37 And *tripled* the year after that! Stacey, *Arms, Men and Governments,* 532.
38 For a detailed examination of the system of priorities established at Hyde Park, see R. Warren James, *Wartime Economic Co-operation: A Study of Relations between Canada and the United* States (Toronto: Ryerson Press, 1949). In addition, see the discussion in Chapter 5 of the present work.
39 LAC, WPTB, RG 64, vol. 1170, file A-10-9-25, Research and Statistics Administration, Price Control, Memorandum by R.W. James re Fiscal Policy and the Price Ceiling.
40 David W. Slater and R.B. Bryce, *War Finance and Reconstruction: The Role of Canada's Department of Finance, 1939-1946* (Ottawa: 1995), 127-28.
41 LAC, National Council of Women, MG 28, vol. 79, file 19, National Council of Women, Resolutions and Correspondence 1940-1941, Hector McKinnon to Beatrice Barber, 21 February 1941.
42 Dominion Bureau of Statistics, *Cost of Living Index Numbers for Canada* (Ottawa: Dominion Bureau of Statistics, 1913-46).
43 Wartime Prices and Trade Board, *Report,* 3 September 1939 to 31 March 1943 (Ottawa: Dominion Bureau of Statistics, 1944), iii, 4-6. See also Slater and Bryce, *War Finance and Reconstruction,* 129-32.
44 Slater and Bryce, *War Finance and Reconstruction,* 129-32.
45 WPTB, *Report,* 1939-43, 18.
46 On securing labour support, see Desmond Morton, *Working People: An Illustrated History of the Canadian Labour Movement,* 4th ed. (Montreal and Kingston: McGill-Queen's University Press, 1998), 174. The text of King's speech appeared in the *Toronto Globe and Mail,* 19 October 1941, 1-2. King discussed the meeting with labour leaders in his diaries, 15 October 1941. *The Diaries of William Lyon Mackenzie King,* LAC, MG 26-J 13, http://www.collectionscanada.gc.ca/databases/king/.
47 J.L. Granatstein, *Canada's War: The Politics of the Mackenzie King Government, 1939-1945* (Toronto: Oxford University Press, 1975), 179. On Gordon's term as WPTB chair, see Joseph Schull, *The Great Scot: A Biography of Donald Gordon* (Montreal and Kingston: McGill-Queen's University Press, 1979). King mentioned his desire to appoint Gordon to the board in his diaries. *The Diaries of William Lyon Mackenzie King,* 14 October 1941. http://www.collectionscanada.gc.ca/databases/king/.
48 "Donald Gordon, Price Boss," *Saturday Night,* 3 January 1942, 7.
49 This story, or variations on it, appeared in many print sources c. 1942-44.
50 LAC, WPTB, RG 64, vol. 1452, Research and Statistics Administration, Consumer Credit. The regulations contributed to a large decrease in the percentage of goods purchased on installment plans between 1941 and 1943. In department stores, the percentage of items bought on installment plans decreased from 15 percent in 1941 to just 8 percent in 1943.
51 The number of pins was mentioned in *Men's Wear Merchandising,* 1 July 1942, 19. The confusion over "conversation" was recounted in *Men's Wear Merchandising,* 1 July 1942, 20.
52 LAC, WPTB, RG 64, vol. 60, Consumer Branch, Speech by Donald Gordon at the Retailers Wartime Conference, 5 April 1943.

53 Peter S. McInnis, *Harnessing Labour Confrontation: Shaping the Postwar Settlement in Canada, 1943-1950* (Toronto: University of Toronto Press, 2002), 33. See also Kenneth C. Cragg, "New Control Measures Announced," *Toronto Globe and Mail*, 6 December 1943, 1-2. A provision was made for revisiting the policy if the cost-of-living increase exceeded 3 percent.
54 Morton, *Working People*, 174.
55 Meg Jacobs, *Pocketbook Politics: Economic Citizenship in Twentieth-Century America* (Princeton: Princeton University Press, 2004), 179-80.
56 K.W. Taylor, "Canadian War-Time Price Controls, 1941-1946," *Canadian Journal of Economics and Political Science* 13, 1 (February 1947): 87.
57 Waddell, "The Wartime Prices and Trade Board," 427. On the mechanics of the price ceiling, see E.J. Spence, "Wartime Price Control Policy in Canada" (PhD diss., Northwestern University, 1947); and, especially, Slater and Bryce, *War Finance and Reconstruction*, 127-63.
58 LAC, WPTB, RG 64, vol. 6, file 145, Donald Gordon speeches, "Radio Address by Donald Gordon," 28 November 1941.
59 "Speech by the Honourable J.L. Ilsley, Minister of Finance, to the National Council of Women, June 17, 1943," National Council of Women, *Yearbook*, 1943, 55.
60 WPTB, Address by Byrne Hope Sanders, March 1942.
61 LAC, WPTB, RG 64, vol. 60, file 1, Consumer Branch, "A Brief Summary of the Origins and Development of the Consumer Branch, WPTB." Proposals for the creation of a consumer relations branch seem to have been in the offing for several months. An undated memo of about fall 1941 noted the need for a "public relations division ... designed to inform the consumer." LAC, WPTB, RG 64, vol. 1464, file A-10-9-37, "Public Relations."
62 LAC, WPTB, RG 64, vol. 1445, file A-10-29-1, Consumer Branch Organization.
63 Like all WPTB directors, Sanders was a salaried employee.
64 WPTB, Address by Byrne Hope Sanders, March 1942.
65 WPTB, Consumer Branch Organization.
66 Ibid.
67 LAC, WPTB, RG 64, vol. 1447, file A-10-29-11, Consumer Branch Conferences, vol. 1. According to the minutes, F.A. McGregor, Enforcement Administrator, claimed that the number of complaints received by the board "went well over 2,000,000" in August 1942 alone. This would seem to be extremely improbable and could be dismissed as a misprint, except for the fact that yet another Consumer Branch document refers to the enforcement agency as receiving "tens of thousands of complaints daily." It may be that "complaints" includes ordinary queries received by WPTB branch offices and the WRACs.
68 *Consumer's News*, 18 June 1942, 12.
69 *Consumer's News*, 25 July 1943, 3.
70 WPTB, "A Brief Summary of the Origins and Development of the Consumer Branch, WPTB," 11.
71 Quoted in Broadfoot, *Six War Years*, 32. The cynicism of so many of Broadfoot's subjects suggests selection bias on his part. Polls and abundant anecdotal evidence from the era suggest far more public support for government measures.
72 WPTB, "A Brief Summary of the Origins and Development of the Consumer Branch, WPTB," 5.
73 Ibid., 9.

74 On rationing in the United Kingdom, see Amy Helen Bell, *London Was Ours: Diaries and Memoirs of the London Blitz* (New York: I.B. Tauris, 2008), 47-80; and Ina Zweiniger-Bargielowska, *Austerity in Britain: Rationing, Controls, and Consumption, 1939-1955* (London: Oxford University Press, 2002), 9-59, 99-150.
75 Waddell, "The Wartime Prices and Trade Board," 429-30.
76 WPTB, *Report*, 1939-43, 33-34; *Report*, 1 January 1944 to 31 December 1944 (Ottawa: Wartime Prices and Trade Board, 1945), 17-19. On the administrative background to the introduction of rationing, see Waddell, "The Wartime Prices and Trade Board," 429-38. The institution of coupon rationing followed several months of unsatisfactory attempts to induce consumers to ration according to the honour system.
77 LAC, WPTB, RG 64, vol. 1447, file A-10-29-11, Eastern Ontario Conference, 18-19 May 1943.
78 The board's ration administration even drew up a detailed scheme for clothes rationing in December 1942 as a contingency in the event of unexpected increases in demand from the armed forces or panicked consumers but never felt the situation required putting it into effect. See LAC, WPTB, RG 64, vol. 83, file A-10-29-84, Consumer Rationing in Canada, Appendix C, Management Committee Minutes, Problems in Connection with Clothing Rationing.
79 "Call Sent for Police as Crowds of Women Raise Clamor for Butter," *Toronto Telegram*, 28 November 1942, 1.
80 "8,000,000 Pounds of Butter Said Held in Cellars," *Toronto Daily Star*, 18 November 1942, 1; "Guarantees Not to Ration Canada Butter," *Toronto Globe and Mail*, 19 November 1942, 3. "Butter Rationing Starts Today," *Toronto Globe and Mail*, 20 December 1942, 1. At several Consumer Branch conferences, Byrne Hope Sanders claimed that agitation from the WRACs through the Consumer Branch had been instrumental in bringing about butter rationing. See also "Premier King Said to Have Ordered Butter Rationing," *Canadian Grocer*, 1 January 1943, 10.
81 "'Action in Nick of Time' 'To Restore Our Sanity' Harassed Merchants Say," *Toronto Telegram*, 22 December 1942, n.p.
82 Mary F. Williamson and Tom Sharp, eds., *Just a Larger Family: Letters of Marie Williamson from the Canadian Home Front, 1940-1944* (Waterloo: Wilfrid Laurier University Press, 2011), 245 (emphasis in original).
83 "Meat Shortage Is Most Acute in Big Cities," *Hamilton Spectator*, 20 January 1943, 1.
84 "Rationing of Meat Plan Said Strong Possibility," *Toronto Globe and Mail*, 5 January 1943, 11.
85 See details on meat rationing in *Consumer's News*, 28 April 1943, 1-4.
86 "Epicures Like Muskrat Meat," *Toronto Globe and Mail*, 26 April 1943, 7.
87 *Consumer's News*, 28 April 1943, 3.
88 Combined Food Board, *Food Consumption Levels in Canada, the United Kingdom, and the United States* (Ottawa: Combined Food Board, 1946), 12.
89 Hedley F. Auld, *Canadian Agriculture and World War II: A History of the Wartime Activities of the Canada Department of Agriculture and Its Wartime Boards and Agencies* (Ottawa: Department of Agriculture, 1953), 112.
90 Urquhart and Buckley, *Historical Statistics of Canada*, Series L233-42.
91 Ibid., Series T1-24.
92 LAC, WPTB, RG 64, vol. 1460, file A-10-9-23, Research and Statistics Administration, Consumer Panels and Surveys.

93 Quoted in "An M.P.'s Warning," *Canada's Weekly*, 5 May 1944, 129. Massey had been serving overseas with the RCAF. A cousin of Vincent Massey, he would leave politics after the war to become an Anglican priest.
94 Jean Bruce, *After the War* (Don Mills: Fitzhenry and Whiteside, 1982), 23.
95 *Consumer's News*, 3 July 1942, 9.
96 LAC, WPTB, RG 64, vol. 1459, file A-10-9-23, Wartime Prices and Trade Board, Research and Statistics Administration, "Consumer Questionnaire Analysis Report No. 1," 2. This report found that the average housewife canned ninety-three pints of fruit, eighteen pounds of jam, jelly, or marmalade, and sixty-one pints of vegetables or pickles, using an average of thirty pounds of sugar in the process: this was more than a year's worth of weekly rations. Vouchers were provided for the release of additional sugar for these purposes.
97 LAC, WPTB, RG 64, vol. 1459, file A-10-9-23, Research and Statistics Administration, "Consumer Questionnaire Analysis Report No. 2," 8.
98 Shirley Orr, quoted in *Fighting for Home and Country: Women Remember World War II*, ed. Janine Roelens-Grant (Guelph: Federated Women's Institutes of Ontario, 2004), 157-58.
99 *Canadian Hotel and Restaurant*, 6 June 1942, 7.
100 LAC, WPTB, RG 64, vol. 1447, file A-10-29-11, Northern Ontario Regional Conferences, Consumer Branch Conferences, vol. 2.
101 F.F. French, "Food Rationing Has Its Problems," *Canadian Business*, December 1944, 58-60, 149.
102 LAC, WPTB, RG 64, vol. 2, file 126, history of the Washington Division of the Wartime Prices and Trade Board.
103 Department of Pensions and National Health, *Annual Report of Nutrition Services* (Ottawa: Department of Pensions and National Health, 1942), 150. Many thanks to Matthew Vanderheide for his assistance in locating this and other sources related to wartime nutrition.
104 LAC, Department of Pensions and National Health (DPNH), RG 29, vol. 928, file 386-3-1, Rationing, November 1941–April 1947.
105 LAC, DPNH, RG 29, vol. 3645, file 381-3-2, "Cooperation with the Wartime Prices and Trade Board."
106 "Potatoes Cause Near Riot," *London Free Press*, 7 July 1945, 1.
107 LAC, WPTB, RG 64, vol. 1447, file A-10-29-8, Consumer Branch Rationing.
108 Quoted in Bill McNeil, *Voices of a War Remembered: An Oral History of Canadians in World War II* (Toronto: Doubleday Canada, 1991), 122.
109 Ibid., 133.
110 For a lengthy examination of rule breaking, see Jeffrey Keshen, *Saints, Sinners, and Soldiers: Canada's Second World War* (Vancouver: UBC Press, 2004). The story of Andy the dog and his owner appeared in *Consumer's News*, 9 October 1942, 6.
111 On the procedural issues related to rationing, see Waddell, "The Wartime Prices and Trade Board"; Slater and Bryce, *War Finance and Reconstruction*, 160; and Yves Tremblay, "La consommation bridée: Contrôle des prix et rationnement durant la Deuxième Guerre mondiale," *Revue d'histoire de l'Amérique française* 58, 4 (2005): 569-607. Meat rationing rules are described in detail in *Consumer's News*, 28 April 1943.
112 LAC, WPTB, RG 64, vol. 60, file 4, history of the Enforcement Branch of the Wartime Prices and Trade Board. On the black market, see Keshen, *Saints, Sinners, and Soldiers*, 94-120.

113 WPTB, *Report*, 1 January 1944 to 31 December 1944, 44.
114 Ella Monckton, *Waiting for Mary* (Ottawa: Consumer Branch, WPTB, 1943), 8. A copy of the play can be found in LAC, WPTB, RG 64, vol. 1446, file A-10-29-7, Consumer Branch Educational Program, vol. 1. A shout out to my History 4292E class, which mounted a production of the play, probably the first since 1945, in 2009.
115 Auld, *Canadian Agriculture and World War II*, 42-43.
116 Urquhart and Buckley, *Historical Statistics of Canada*, Series L83-87.
117 "Carryover of Canadian Grain as at July 21, 1935-1944," *Canada Year Book*, 1945, 210.
118 Urquhart and Buckley, *Historical Statistics of Canada*, Series L233-42. It should be noted that these figures do not include the "victory gardens," planted in back yards across the country, which were undoubtedly a substantial source of produce for many families.
119 The value of food exports to the United Kingdom in 1943 was $230,000,000 versus $211,000,000 for munitions. "Imports and Exports," *Canada Year Book*, 1945, 552.
120 Combined Food Board, *Food Consumption Levels*, 1946, 12. The Combined Food Board was an intergovernmental body established to monitor British, American, and Canadian food supplies.
121 Urquhart and Buckley, *Historical Statistics of Canada*, Series T1-24.
122 *National Council of Women Yearbook*, 1940, 55. The other major aspects of improving public health were, not surprisingly, the campaign against venereal disease (see Keshen, *Saints, Sinners, and Soldiers*, 121-44) and a renewed campaign for prohibition and temperance, which is discussed in Chapter 6.
123 On the Federated Women's Institutes, see Linda Ambrose, *For Home and Country: The Centennial History of the Women's Institutes in Ontario* (Erin, ON: Boston Mills Press, 1996).
124 Edna Guest and Ethel Chapman, *An Experiment in Applied Nutrition for Canadian Communities* (Toronto: West Toronto Printing House, 1944), 14. Guest, a medical doctor, had been vice-president of the Canadian Social Hygiene Council, an expressly eugenicist group. See Angus McLaren, *Our Own Master Race: Eugenics in Canada, 1885-1945* (Toronto: McClelland and Stewart, 1990); and Velma Demerson's memoir of her direct dealings with Guest, *Incorrigible* (Waterloo: Wilfrid University Press, 2004).
125 Guest and Chapman, *An Experiment in Applied Nutrition*, 3.
126 Aleck Samuel Ostry, *Nutrition Policy in Canada, 1870-1939* (Vancouver: UBC Press, 2006), 98-99.
127 E.W. McHenry, "Determination of Nutritional Status," *Canadian Public Health Journal* 32, 5 (May 1941): 231-35; E.W. McHenry, "The Construction and Use of Dietary Standards," *Canadian Public Health Journal* 36, 6 (July 1945): 272.
128 L.B. Pett, "What's Wrong with Canada's Diet?" *National Health Review* 19, 36 (1944): 1-7. See also the original studies, published in the *Canadian Public Health Journal*.
129 L.B. Pett, *Recent Dietary Surveys in Canada* (Ottawa: Department of Pensions and National Health, 1943), 9.
130 Helen P. Ferguson and E.W. McHenry, "A Nutrition Study in East York Township: Repetition of Dietary Studies after Two Years," *Canadian Public Health Journal* 35, 5 (May 1944): 245.
131 Ibid., 246.
132 L.B. Pett and F.W. Hanley, "A Nutrition Survey among School Children in British Columbia and Saskatchewan," *Canadian Medical Association Journal* 56 (February 1947): 188.
133 LAC, WPTB, RG 64, vol. 60, file 1, Consumer Branch, Comments of the WRAC Chairmen.

134 WPTB, Consumer Branch Conferences, vol. 2
135 WPTB, "A Brief Summary of the Origins and Development of the Consumer Branch," 4-5.
136 WPTB, Consumer Branch, Comments of the WRAC Chairmen.
137 WPTB, Consumer Branch Conferences, vol. 2.
138 WPTB, Consumer Branch, Comments of the WRAC Chairmen.
139 WPTB, Consumer Branch Conferences, vol. 2.
140 Quoted in "Must Wage War on Inflation," *Hamilton Spectator*, 19 April 1945, n.p.
141 "'Stick to the End' Women Told in Anti-Inflation Fight," *Toronto Globe and Mail*, 8 May 1946, 13.
142 The Consumer Price Index increased from 115.8 to 119.9 between December 1941 and September 1945. Waddell discusses these claims in "The Wartime Prices and Trade Board," 211-14.
143 Canadian Opinion for the Wartime Prices and Trade Board, "A Nationwide Survey of Canadian Attitudes toward Wartime Ceilings and Rationing," June 1944. WPTB, RG 64, vol. 444, file 10-88, Public Opinion Polls. This poll and others like it are discussed in detail in the Appendix.
144 "Women Urged to Keep Support of Price Controls," *Toronto Globe and Mail*, 7 March 1945, 11.
145 *Canadian Civilian Labour Force Estimates, 1939-1941* (Ottawa: Dominion Bureau of Statistics, 1957). Figures for females employed in war industries are taken from Department of Labour, *Report*, 1946, 89. It is worth stressing once again that all such figures are estimates and should be treated with some skepticism.

Chapter 2: Business as Usual

Credit goes here to Russell Johnston, who coined the word "adworker" in *Selling Themselves*, his excellent history of Canadian advertising, in order to avoid the sexist and imprecise "adman." I have borrowed the term from him. Russell T. Johnston, *Selling Themselves: The Emergence of Canadian Advertising* (Toronto: University of Toronto Press, 2001).

1 Robert F. Legget, "Advertising in Canada," *Queen's Quarterly* 47 (1940): 209.
2 Ibid., 210.
3 Quoted in "Advertising Justified by Its Usefulness," *Marketing*, 10 November 1941, 3.
4 For an early article concerning the financial dependence of periodicals on advertising, see Harold Innis, "The Newspaper in Economic Development," *Journal of Economic History* 2 (December 1942): 1-33.
5 *Maclean's* circulation is from *Lydiatt's Book of Canadian Market and Advertising Data*, 1941; 50. *Maclean's* was Canada's most popular general magazine in terms of subscription sales. However, several daily newspapers and the venerable farm paper the *Family Herald and Weekly Star* surpassed its readership.
6 On advertising not having recovered from the Depression, see "Linage," *Marketing*, 25 January 1941, 6. The article reported that national advertising linage in 1939 remained "one-third shy of the 1929 mark."
7 On this, see, for instance, Carrol A. Lake, "Should Inside Pages Be Sacrificed?" *Canadian Printer and Publisher*, February 1940, 42.
8 Library and Archives Canada, Wartime Prices and Trade Board (WPTB), RG 64, vol. 1460, file A-10-9-23, Research and Statistics Administration, "The Average Man," 15 February 1944, 5. The provincial low was Quebec, at 72 percent. British Columbia was highest at 91 percent. Lower-class people averaged 73 percent, upper class 93 percent.

For newspaper circulation figures in 1940, see *Lydiatt's*, 1941, 24-48, and "A Willing Press," *Canadian Printer and Publisher*, December 1941, 35.
9 "Cost of Advertising in Canada Slightly up since Five Years Ago," *Marketing*, 24 February 1940, 2. Circulation of the seven leading national magazines increased from 671,358 in 1931 to 1,383,450 in 1939.
10 "U.S. Publishers Protest Canada's 'Pulps' Embargo," *Marketing*, 15 February 1941, 3.
11 Circulation of Canadian magazines ca. 1940 is from *Lydiatt's*, 1941, 48-53. Circulation of American magazines is from "Canadian Circulation of American Magazines," *Marketing*, 14 September 1940, 10. *Liberty* was very unusual for publishing a Canadian edition whose content differed substantially from that of its American counterpart.
12 M.C. Urquhart and K.A.H. Buckley, eds., *Historical Statistics of Canada* (Cambridge: Cambridge University Press, 1965), Series A15-19. According to 1931 census definitions, "urban" meant a municipality with a population of a thousand or more. In 1931, 5.6 million Canadians were found to live in urban areas and 4.8 in rural. In 1941, 6.2 million lived in urban areas and 5.2 in rural. This represents a growth of 12 percent for urban areas versus roughly 9 percent for rural areas.
13 Bruce Hutchison, "What Goes On Here?" *Maclean's*, 1 July 1941, 10.
14 Lyon Sharman, "The Rebel," *Canadian Poetry Magazine*, June 1937, 35 (emphasis in original).
15 Dominion Bureau of Statistics, *Eighth Census of Canada, 1941*, vol. 9, *Housing* (Ottawa: Dominion Bureau of Statistics, 1941).
16 Ronald A. McEachern, "Characteristics of the Canadian Market," in *Selling Tomorrow's Production*, ed. E.F. Beach (Montreal: McGill University Press, 1944), 25.
17 "This Is the Farmer's Son," Advertisement, *Marketing*, 18 March 1944, 10.
18 "The War and the Farmer," Advertisement, *Marketing*, 16 September 1939, 3.
19 *Radio Homes in Canada 1941* (CBC Radio Canada, 1944), n.p.
20 Mary Vipond, *Listening In: The First Decade of Canadian Broadcasting, 1922-1932* (Montreal and Kingston: McGill-Queen's University Press, 1992), 284.
21 On the professionalization of the advertising industry, see Johnston, *Selling Themselves*.
22 Walter Kiehn, "Overwhelming Bulk of Advertising in Canada Is Canadian Produced," *Marketing*, 21 October 1944, 10.
23 "Canadian Advertising Volume Higher Than Was Expected," *Marketing*, 4 May 1940, 1. Canadian government expenditures are from Urquhart and Buckley, *Historical Statistics of Canada*, Series G26-44.
24 The number of agencies had declined to forty-one by 1944 (before roaring back to fifty-six firms with sixteen hundred employees in 1945). The size of the advertising workforce was roughly static for most of the war, whereas advertising firms' total billings and gross revenue steadily increased. The number of firms, size, billings, and gross revenue for 1941 and 1945 are from *Advertising Agencies in Canada*, 1950 and 1951 (Ottawa: Dominion Bureau of Statistics, 1951). For 1944, see *Advertising Agencies in Canada*, 1944 (Ottawa: Dominion Bureau of Statistics, 1945).
25 See, for instance, J.H. Simpson, "In Dispraise of Advertising," *Queen's Quarterly* 39 (1932): 326-40.
26 See Roland Marchand, *Advertising the American Dream: Making Way for Modernity, 1920-1940* (Berkeley: University of California Press, 1985), Chapters 1 and 2.
27 See, for instance, Howe Martyn, "In Defence of Advertising," *Dalhousie Review* 13 (1933-34): 336-44.
28 "Canadian Family Living Expenses Show Similarity in Main Items," *Marketing*, 20 May 1939, n.p.

29 The average unemployment rate in 1939 was 13 percent. Urquhart and Buckley, *Historical Statistics of Canada*, Series C47-55.
30 Verna Loveday Harden, "All Valiant Dust," *Canadian Poetry Magazine*, October 1939, 18.
31 See a discussion in Robert Bothwell, Ian Drummond, and John English, *Canada, 1900-1945* (Toronto: University of Toronto Press, 1987), 257-58.
32 "And Then Came a Great Change," Advertisement, *Marketing*, 9 December 1944, 3. In 1954, Yarwood would become a founding member of the influential abstract art collective, Painters Eleven.
33 "And Then Came Advertising," Advertisement, *Marketing*, 25 November 1944, 5.
34 Harold Edward Stephenson and Carlton McNaught, *The Story of Advertising in Canada, a Chronicle of Fifty Years* (Toronto: Ryerson Press, 1940). See Harold Innis's negative review in *Canadian Journal of Economics and Political Science* 7 (1941): 109-12.
35 Samuel B. Stocking, "The Value and Significance of Advertising," *Commerce Journal*, March 1941, 68-69.
36 Harold Innis, "A Note on the Advertising Problem," *Commerce Journal* 3 (April 1943): 65-66.
37 "Phare's Classes Resume," *Marketing*, 18 January 1941, 12.
38 For example, see Frances Hall, "The Education of Consumers," *Public Affairs* 3 (1940): 5-8. Hall succinctly summarizes the theory of "consumer sovereignty" but, it should be noted, dismisses it most contemptuously.
39 Quoted in "Paying Cost of Consumer Education Is a Big Part of Advertising's Job," *Marketing*, 3 February 1940, 3.
40 J.C. Kirkwood, "Non-Advertisers Are Poor Trustees of the Capital They Are Employing," *Marketing*, 5 April 1941, 14.
41 See, for example, "Much Advertising Activity Planned in Spite of Uncertainties for 1940," *Marketing*, 30 December 1939, 1.
42 Philip Spencer, "Does It Sell the Stuff?" *Canadian Forum*, October 1940, 215.
43 See, for instance, "95 Per Cent Advertising Is True," *Marketing*, 4 May 1940, 4. Russell Johnston discusses the origins of the "truth in advertising movement" in Johnston, *Selling Themselves*, 84-87.
44 "Closing Down on False Advertising," *Canadian Printer and Publisher*, July 1939, 32.
45 On this, see Frank W. Fox, *Madison Avenue Goes to War: The Strange Military Career of American Advertising, 1941-1945* (Provo, UT: Brigham Young University Press, 1975). Fox emphasizes, though probably exaggerates, New Deal era efforts to regulate the advertising business in his second chapter.
46 James Cowan, "Public Relations: Penetrating Discussion of Need in Canada to Offset Suspicion in Public Mind toward Business," *Canadian Advertising*, April 1939, 12.
47 E.W. Reynolds, "Advertising Has Grown in Prestige, Winning Fight against Heavy Odds," *Marketing*, 13 April 1940, 43.
48 Cowan, "Public Relations," 12.
49 See, for instance, Martyn, "In Defence of Advertising"; Hall, "The Education of Consumers"; Legget, "Advertising in Canada"; and Stocking, "The Value and Significance of Advertising."
50 Editorial, *Canadian Advertising*, July 1939, 4.
51 Marchand, *Advertising the American Dream*, 7.
52 Quoted in Heather Robertson, *Driving Force: The McLaughlin Family and the Age of the Car* (Toronto: McClelland and Stewart, 1995), 289.
53 J.C. Kirkwood, "Business Is the Blesser of Mankind and Creator of a Finer Social Life," *Marketing*, 23 December 1939, 4.

54 Ibid.
55 "Foreigners Get Very Grotesque Picture from Some of Our Very Modern Copy," *Marketing*, 6 April 1940, 4.
56 "Everybody Knew It but Ellen," Advertisement, *Maclean's*, 15 April 1941, 33.
57 "A Hot-Weather Offender," Advertisement, *Maclean's*, 15 August 1940, 31 (emphasis in original).
58 Marchand, *Advertising the American Dream*, 10.
59 On this, see, for instance, T.J. Jackson Lears, *Fables of Abundance: A Cultural History of Advertising in America* (New York: Basic Books, 1994), Chapter 7, 196-234; Marchand, *Advertising the American Dream*, 1-24; and William Leiss, Stephen Kline, and Sut Jhally, *Social Communication in Advertising: Persons, Products, and Images of Well-Being*, 2nd rev. ed. (Scarborough, ON: Nelson Canada, 1990), 153-55.
60 Leiss, Kline, and Jhally, *Social Communication in Advertising*, 153-55.
61 Marchand, *Advertising the American Dream*, especially 1-24.
62 Johnston, *Selling Themselves*, 268-69.
63 Thornton Purkis, "The Trends in Advertising," *Canadian Advertising*, Second Quarter 1940, 7.
64 "Canadian Advertisers Win Awards in D.M.A.A. 'Fifty Leaders' Contest," *Marketing*, 12 October 1940, 4.
65 Cowan, "Public Relations," 12.
66 According to the Canadian trades, American adworkers showed a keen interest in the war's impact on Canadian advertising. For instance, Ian Macdonald, general manager of the Bureau of Advertising for the Canadian Daily Newspaper Association, gave a talk on this topic for American attendees at the fall 1941 Newspaper Advertising Executives Association in Chicago. See "Canadian Advertising Still Robust," *Marketing*, 25 October 1941, 6. I explore this issue further in Chapter 3.
67 "Business Disruption by War Can Be Held at a Minimum," *Marketing*, 2 September 1939, 1.
68 "We Would Like You to Know: A *Canadian Advertising* Editorial," *Canadian Advertising*, October 1939, 4.
69 Spalding Black, "Advertising Can Help to Win the War," *Saturday Night*, 28 October 1939, 14.
70 "We Would Like You to Know," 4.
71 "1940 Daunts Very Few Advertisers Say Canadian Advertising Agencies," *Marketing*, 30 December 1939, 4.
72 Quoted in "See More Advertising for Home Products," *Marketing*, 3 February 1940, 9.
73 "War Note Sounds in National Copy," *Marketing*, 30 September 1939, 9.
74 "1940 Daunts Very Few Advertisers," 4.
75 "Enlist for the War on Germs," Advertisement, *Maclean's*, 15 April 1941, 28.
76 *Men's Wear Merchandising*, 1 November 1940, 29.
77 "Mentholatum," Advertisement, *Maclean's*, 15 August 1940, 31.
78 "Get Them to Write Often," Advertisement, *Maclean's*, 15 September 1940, 4.
79 "For Your Soldier – For Your Sailor: Ronson," Advertisement, *Maclean's*, 1 November 1941, 63.
80 For a summary of the press reaction to Howe's comments, see "Press Answers 'Sabotage' Charge," *Canadian Printer and Publisher*, March 1941, 41.
81 "The 'Unpatriotic' Press," *Maclean's*, 1 March 1941, 1.
82 B.W. Keightley, "Wartime Advertising Essential," *Canadian Printer and Publisher*, June 1941, 23-24.

83 "Legitimate Wartime Expenditure for Advertising," *Canadian Printer and Publisher,* January 1941, 30.
84 See, for instance, Thornton Purkis, "British Advertising in Wartime," *Canadian Advertising,* Second Quarter 1941, 5-7. Chapter 3 considers the circumstances under which British, American, and other Allied advertisers operated.
85 "Those Who Discontinue Advertising May Wake Up to Find Market Gone," *Marketing,* 5 April 1941, 4. See also "10 Reasons for Continuing Advertising Urged at O.A.A.A. Annual Meeting," *Marketing,* 8 November, 1941, 12; and "How to Advertise When Oversold," *Canadian Advertising,* Third Quarter 1941, 5-9.
86 J.C. Kirkwood, "Buying Less Means Producing Less and Will Curtail Sinews of War," *Marketing,* 1 March 1941, 10.
87 "See and Drive This New Dodge: Built to Last a Long, Long Time!" Advertisement, *Maclean's,* 1 November 1941, 7.
88 "These Spartons Help You 'Do Your Bit' Entertaining the Service Boys," Advertisement, *Maclean's,* 15 September 1941, 46.
89 "Save Now! More Than Ever Before, with Frigidaire," Advertisement, *Maclean's,* 15 March 1941, 7. It is not clear what survey the ad is referring to.
90 "Sacrifice to Buy More War Savings Certificates," Advertisement, *Maclean's,* 15 November 1941, 3.
91 "Thinks Advertising Defenses Are Weak," *Marketing,* 5 June 1941, 12.
92 "Advertising Justified by Its Usefulness," 3.

Chapter 3: Finding a Place for Wartime Advertising

1 S.B. Stocking, "Recent Trends in Consumption," *Canadian Journal of Economics and Political Science* 7, 3 (1941): 371.
2 Quoted in "Seven Sound Reasons for Maintained Advertising in a Seller's Market," *Marketing,* 25 October 1941, 8 (emphasis in original).
3 For predictions on the imminence of rationing, see, for example, "Backstage at Ottawa," *Maclean's,* 15 January 1942, 11, 37.
4 "Many Uncertain Factors Becloud Advertising Outlook for New Year," *Marketing,* 3 January 1942, 2. The poll found that 23.3 percent expected to reduce expenditures versus 11.6 percent who planned increased spending. Of the remainder, 16.6 percent were undecided, and the rest intended to maintain their 1941 expenditures.
5 "Most Agencies Agree Advertising Will Continue as Normal in New Year," *Marketing,* 3 January 1942, 6. The actual content of the article entirely undercuts its optimistic title.
6 "How Wartime Restricts May Affect Advertising," *Canadian Advertising,* First Quarter 1941, 9; "Advertising Expenditure," *Canadian Printer and Publisher,* April 1942, 37; "Many Rumours of Casualties in Advertising Are Unfounded," *Marketing,* 14 March 1942, 3.
7 P.M. Richards, Editorial, *Saturday Night,* 21 March 1942, 30.
8 John C. Kirkwood, "Libraries Discourage Book Sales and Make Bookselling Precarious Calling; Kiddies Born in 1942 Are Lucky," *Marketing,* 31 January 1942, 19.
9 Maurice Brown, "Challenge to Canadian Advertising," *Canadian Printer and Publisher,* December 1942, 24.
10 Editorial, *Canadian Advertising,* Third Quarter 1942, 5.
11 M.C. Urquhart and K.A.H. Buckley, eds., *Historical Statistics of Canada* (Cambridge: Cambridge University Press, 1965), Series E66-78.
12 "Radio Advertising at All-Time High," *Marketing,* 17 January 1942, 10.

13 Quoted in "Marked Growth in Radio Advertising Reported at C.A.B. Annual Convention," *Marketing*, 14 February 1942, 6 (emphasis in original).
14 For 1941 and 1942 military expenditure, see C.P. Stacey, *Arms, Men and Governments: The War Policies of Canada, 1939-1945* (Ottawa: Queen's Printer, 1970), 532. For prewar military expenditures, see Urquhart and Buckley, *Historical Statistics of Canada*, Series G26-44.
15 *Monthly Index of Retail Sales in Canada, 1929-1942* (Ottawa: Dominion Bureau of Statistics, 1943), 4.
16 "Where Will Your Business Stand after the War?" *Canadian Advertising*, First Quarter 1941, 137.
17 Quoted in "Canadian Advertisers Spend Freely Urging People to Avoid Buying," *Marketing*, 31 January 1942, 12.
18 Quoted in "30 Kinds of Wartime Advertising Being Used in Canadian Campaigns," *Marketing*, 25 April 1942, 18.
19 Nonetheless, American adworkers were not unaware that their Canadian counterparts had a two-year lead in wrestling with the difficulties of war. According to a February 1942 editorial in *Marketing*, the American trade paper *Editor and Publisher* had advised US adworkers to study Canadian examples. "Editor and Publisher Surveys Canadian War Advertising," *Marketing*, 28 February 1942, 11. Similarly, a business section editorial in the *Detroit Free Press* (quoted approvingly in *Marketing*) praised the Canadian industry for its example of "splendid patriotism." "Advertising Is Sound Business and Indispensable to Victory," *Marketing*, 18 April 1942, 6.
20 "Objects to Dragging in the War in Advertising Copy," *Canadian Printer and Publisher*, May 1942, 40.
21 For example, "Publishers Foresee Many Advertisers Planning to Run Institutional Copy," *Marketing*, 3 January 1942, 12.
22 "Plan Your Advertising to Help Win the War," *Canadian Advertising*, Third Quarter 1942, 5.
23 See, as examples, Richard P. Dodd, "National Defense and Company Defense," *Canadian Printer and Publisher*, May 1941, 45; Wellington Jeffers, "Declares Advertising Is a Vital Service," *Canadian Printer and Publisher*, November 1942, 32; and Elton Plant, "Don't Break the Buying Habits of Your Customers," *Canadian Advertising*, Fourth Quarter 1942, 7.
24 C.D. Watt, "The War and Advertising," *Canadian Forum*, May 1942, 47.
25 "Advertising and the War," *Canadian Forum*, October 1942, 218.
26 Quoted in J.C. Kirkwood, "'Forget Me Not' Advertising Keeps Consumer True to Absent Product," *Marketing*, 7 November 1942, 10.
27 Dorothy Thompson, "War May Be Lost by United Nations Because of High Standard of Living," reprinted in *Marketing*, 3 October 1942, 6.
28 "Explains Donald Gordon's Statement 'Competitive System Must Go,'" *Bookseller and Stationer*, May 1942, 12.
29 "Advertisers Befogged by Terminology of Wartime Prices and Trade Board," *Marketing*, 14 February 1942, 7.
30 Byrne Hope Sanders, "What the Women of Canada Expect of Advertising Today," *Canadian Advertising*, Third Quarter 1942, 8-13.
31 Quoted in "War Economy: Statement of Advertising Policy by Printing Administrator," *Canadian Printer and Publisher*, October 1942, 31-32.
32 Jeffers, "Declares Advertising Is a Vital Service," 32.
33 "Prime Minister Clarifies Advertising Reference," *Marketing*, 2 January 1943, 1.

34 "Advertising Regulations Clarified," *Canadian Printer and Publisher*, August 1942, 19-20. "Abnormal" was defined as more than 10 percent above the amount spent annually in the period from 1936 to 1939.
35 "Advertising Tax Ruling," *Canadian Advertising*, Third Quarter 1942, 7, 15.
36 Quoted in "Advertising and the War," 218.
37 Quoted in "British Advertising 'Dehydrated' by Smaller Space and Higher Rates," *Marketing*, 14 August 1943, 12.
38 Chas W. Stokes, "Less Than Half of British Agencies Have Survived Ravages of Wartime," *Marketing*, 20 August 1944, 10.
39 "Retail Advertising Drops 50% in Australia," *Marketing*, 25 October 1941, 15.
40 "Advertising in Australia," *Men's Wear Merchandising*, 1 September 1943, 34-35. See also "Australian Advertising in the War as Seen by Sydney Agency Principal," *Marketing*, 2 May 1942, 13.
41 Library and Archives Canada (LAC), Wartime Prices and Trade Board, RG 64, vol. 1443, Consumer Branch Records, "The Place of Advertising in a War Economy," n.d. Given the context, it seems probable that this policy was enacted in May or June of 1942.
42 LAC, WPTB, RG 64, vol. 1443, Consumer Branch Records, John Atkins to R.C. Bertram (Division of Simplified Practice), 27 April 1942.
43 Predictions that the war would end in 1944 became commonplace in 1943. Probably the worst offender of overly optimistic military prognostication was *Maclean's* Douglas Reed, who in 1943 rarely let a column go by without forecasting that the war would end within a year.
44 By contrast, a study in *Canadian Advertising* concluded that linage in Britain's leading eight dailies was halved between July 1940 and December 1941. See *Canadian Advertising*, First Quarter 1942, 16.
45 See Frank W. Fox, *Madison Avenue Goes to War: The Strange Military Career of American Advertising, 1941-1945* (Provo, UT: Brigham Young University Press, 1975), Chapter 4.
46 "To Market! To Market!" *Marketing*, 8 January 1944, 2.

Chapter 4: Advertising to Win the War and Secure the Future

The chapter's second epigraph is from "Buck Up, Bill!" Advertisement, *Maclean's*, 15 February 1943, 41.

1 Carlton McNaught, "Glancing Backward and Ahead at Canadian Advertising," *Canadian Printer and Publisher*, June 1942, 90.
2 Roland Marchand, *Advertising the American Dream: Making Way for Modernity, 1920-1940* (Berkeley: University of California Press, 1985), Chapters 7 and 8.
3 "Nobody Makes a Pass at Me," Advertisement, *Maclean's*, 1 February 1940, 25.
4 "Buck Up, Bill!" 41 (emphasis in original).
5 "Snap Out of It, Sue!" Advertisement, *Maclean's*, 1 March 1943, 15.
6 "I Don't Want to Be an Absentee," Advertisement, *National Home Monthly*, May 1944, 59.
7 "Saboteur!" Advertisement, *Maclean's*, 1 May 1943, 21 (emphasis in original).
8 "So What If There Is a Ceiling on Wages!" Advertisement, *Maclean's*, 15 January 1943, 22.
9 "A Long Time Learning," Advertisement, *Canadian Homes and Gardens*, January-February 1943, 33.
10 "Tonight I Leaned across 10,000 Miles and Kissed You!" Advertisement, *Maclean's*, 15 December 1942, inside back cover.
11 "More Than Ever *This* Year," Advertisement, *Canadian Home Journal*, 2 January 1943, 33 (emphasis in original).

12 "Snapshots Never Meant So Much as Now," Advertisement, *Canadian Home Journal,* December 1941, inside front cover.
13 "Your Hands Now Need Campana's Balm Protection *More Than Ever,*" Advertisement, *Maclean's,* 15 January 1944, 35 (emphasis in original).
14 "In These Times, Good Paint Is More Economical Than Ever," Advertisement, *Canadian Home Journal,* June 1943, 63.
15 "Foods to Keep You Fit Can Taste Delicious, Too," Advertisement, *Canadian Homes and Gardens,* January-February 1943, 39.
16 "Twice as Important ... Now That I'm Working Twice as Hard!" Advertisement, *Maclean's,* 15 February 1944, 24.
17 "Tell It to the Soldier in the Apron," *Chatelaine* Advertisement, *Marketing,* 24 October 1942, 7.
18 "What Is the Most Vital War Work Housewives Can Do?" Advertisement, *Maclean's,* 15 October 1941, 24.
19 "I Man the Home Front," Advertisement, *Maclean's,* 1 September 1942, 37.
20 "Enlist for the War on Germs," Advertisement, *Maclean's,* 15 July 1941, 28.
21 "Old Dutch," *Marketing,* 17 April 1943. Each year, *Marketing* published an unpaginated supplement in which it reprinted advertisements from the previous twelve months.
22 Ruth Roach Pierson, *"They're Still Women After All": The Second World War and Canadian Womanhood* (Toronto: McClelland and Stewart, 1986), 129.
23 See, for example, Diane G. Forestell, "The Necessity of Sacrifice for the Nation at War: Women's Labour Force Participation, 1939-1946," *Histoire Sociale* 22, 44 (1989): 333-47.
24 "A Woman's Place Is Everywhere," Advertisement, *Mayfair,* May 1943, 41-43.
25 Kathy Peiss, "Making Up, Making Over: Cosmetics, Consumer Culture, and Women's Identity," in *The Sex of Things: Gender and Consumption in Historical Perspective,* ed. Victoria de Grazia and Ellen Furlough (Berkeley: University of California Press, 1996), 330. See also Tina Davidson, "A Woman's Right to Charm and Beauty: Maintaining the Feminine Ideal in the Canadian Women's Army Corps," *Atlantis* (Canada) 26, 1 (2001): 45-54; Helen Smith and Pamela Wakewich, "Beauty and the Helldrivers: Representing Women's Work and Identities in a Warplant Newspaper," *Labour* 44 (1999): 71-107; and Heather Molyneaux, "Temporary Heroes 'In the Service of Mars': Women in Uniform, Factories, and the Kitchen during World War II," in *Heroes of Film, Comics and American Culture: Essays on Real and Fictional Defenders of the Home,* ed. Lisa M. DeTora (Jefferson, NC: McFarland, 2009), 96-116.
26 "War, Women, and Lipstick," Advertisement, *Chatelaine,* August 1943, 4.
27 "We Are Still the Weaker Sex," Advertisement, *Chatelaine,* August 1944, inside back cover.
28 "Be Prepared: 'Patriot Red,'" Advertisement, *Chatelaine,* April 1942, 44; "Honor Bright," Advertisement, *National Home Monthly,* September 1944, 46.
29 "Eager to Serve," Advertisement, *Echoes,* Spring 1942, 2.
30 "Me – Enter a Beauty Contest?" Advertisement, *National Home Monthly,* February 1943, 19. Linham was an inspector at Research Enterprises Limited. Judging by the volume of coverage in the *Toronto Daily Star* – nearly a full page in total – this was no small contest. Her prize included a diamond watch and four hundred dollars, about equal to three months' pay. See the *Toronto Daily Star,* 20 July 1942, 3.
31 "Made to Fit the Shapely Feet," Advertisement, *National Home Monthly,* April 1944, 68.
32 "When Rosies Stop Riveting," Advertisement, *Canadian Homes and Gardens,* April 1944, 59.

33 "Pilot without Wings," Advertisement, reprinted in *Marketing*, 17 April 1943, n.p.
34 See, for instance, "'Men of Action' Use Vitalis," Advertisement, *National Home Monthly*, July 1944, 24.
35 "War Spring," Advertisement, *Canadian Homes and Gardens*, May 1944, 41. Permission could not be secured to run this advertisement.
36 "He Drives a Weapon," Advertisement, *Maclean's*, 1 April 1944, 22 (emphasis in original).
37 "My Dad Is *So* a Soldier," Advertisement, *Canadian Homes and Gardens*, March-April 1943, 12 (emphasis in original).
38 "They Call Me a Production Soldier," Advertisement, reprinted in *Marketing*, 17 April 1943, n.p.
39 "Our Job Isn't Done 'Til Victory Is Won," reprinted in *Marketing*, 29 April 1944, n.p.
40 "Miracle Man on the Truck Front," Advertisement, *Maclean's*, 1 March 1944, 8; "Dad, They Ought to Give You a Medal, Too!" Advertisement, *Canadian Automotive Trade*, January 1945, 3.
41 "Perhaps They're Bombing Berlin," Advertisement, reprinted in *Marketing*, 17 April 1943, n.p.
42 "Watch the '43 Fords Go By!" Advertisement, *National Home Monthly*, April 1943, 21.
43 "1943 Models for Victory," Advertisement, *Maclean's*, 15 June 1943, 28-29.
44 "One of Our Aircraft Is Missing," Advertisement, *Maclean's*, 1 March 1943, 24-25.
45 "Survival," Advertisement, *Maclean's*, 15 January 1944, 21.
46 "Surgeons Bless the Sleep That Banishes Pain," Advertisement, *Maclean's*, 1 April 1944, 31.
47 "Swat This Mosquito," Advertisement, *Canadian Homes and Gardens*, August-September 1944, 52.
48 "A Bushel of Trouble for Hitler," Advertisement, *Maclean's*, 15 January 1943, 17.
49 "Coming at You, Schicklgruber!" Wartime propagandists sometimes made sport of the fact that Adolf Hitler's father had changed the family name from Schicklgruber in the 1870s. Advertisement, *Maclean's*, 1 June 1943, 27.
50 "Big Studebaker War Trucks Roll Forward Where Ancient Armies Marched," Advertisement, *Maclean's*, 15 February 1944, 31.
51 "The Engineers Ford a River," Advertisement, *Maclean's*, 15 June 1943, 23.
52 "Crash Action for the Canadian Artillery," Advertisement, *Canadian Homes and Gardens*, May-June 1943, 61.
53 Frank W. Fox, *Madison Avenue Goes to War: The Strange Military Career of American Advertising, 1941-1945* (Provo, UT: Brigham Young University Press, 1975). Canadian adworkers had been producing war-themed advertising longer than their US counterparts, who had paid careful attention to their work in the months before America went to war, a fact noted in trade journals in both countries. Were some of the clichés of wartime institutional advertising Canadian innovations?
54 See, for example, the International Nickel Company ad, "1919: Millions of Tons of Nickel Ore," *Maclean's*, 1 February 1944, 3.
55 "A Profession of Faith," Advertisement, *Maclean's*, 1 May 1943, 3.
56 "We've a War That Must Be Won!" Advertisement, *Maclean's*, 15 November 1941, 18.
57 "Soldiers Like These Advertisements," *Marketing*, 9 September 1944, 8.
58 "Today His Home Is on Wheels," Advertisement, *Mayfair*, 1 September 1944, 51.
59 "Meanwhile, We're Planning Your Dream Kitchen," Advertisement, *Maclean's*, 15 October 1943, 30 (emphasis in original).

60 "Caldwell Towels," Advertisement, *Canadian Home Journal,* July 1945, 23.
61 "Advertising Campaigns Urged to Offset Too Much Dream Product Expectancy," *Marketing,* 19 August 1944, 8.
62 "Today's Victory Bonds Mean Tomorrow's All-Electric Kitchen," Advertisement, *Canadian Homes and Gardens,* May 1944, 63.
63 "Tomorrow's Living Room," Advertisement, *Canadian Home Journal,* June 1945, 79.
64 "Today, the Army Has a New Mule ... *Tomorrow,* the Farmer Will Harness It," Advertisement, *Maclean's,* 15 May 1943, 32.
65 "The Sea Will Give Up Treasure to Men Who Think of Tomorrow," Advertisement, *Maclean's,* 15 November 1944, 53.
66 "What's Coming Is ... PLENTY!" Advertisement, *Maclean's,* 1 June 1943, 23 (emphasis in original).
67 "Buy Victory Bonds and Bring Back the Pleasures of 'Freedom,'" Advertisement, *Marketing,* 8 May 1943, 12.
68 Raymond Williams, "Advertising: The Magic System," in Raymond Williams, *Problems in Materialism and Culture: Selected Essays* (London: Verso, 1980), 170-95.

Chapter 5: Buying and Selling Big Ticket Items

1 Francis Pollock, "Radiator Cap," *Canadian Poetry Magazine,* October 1937, n.p.
2 M.C. Urquhart and K.A.H. Buckley, eds., *Historical Statistics of Canada* (Cambridge: Cambridge University Press, 1965), Series S222-S235. For the purposes of brevity, this chapter will use the word "cars" in place of "passenger cars," as distinct from trucks, commercial vehicles, and motor vehicles manufactured to fill military orders.
3 On the establishment of American automobile subsidiaries in Canada, see Richard White, *Making Cars in Canada: A Brief History of the Canadian Automotive Industry, 1900-1980* (Ottawa: Canadian Science and Technology Museum, 2000). Employment figures for auto manufacturing can be found in *Facts and Figures of the Automobile Industry* (Canadian Automobile Chamber of Commerce), 1933, 5.
4 *Facts and Figures of the Automobile Industry,* 1933, 10. The yearly editions of *Facts and Figures* contain statistics for the previous calendar year. Their figures correspond exactly with those of the annual Dominion Bureau of Statistics report *Sales and Financing of Motor Vehicles in Canada.* I have favoured *Facts and Figures* for ease of availability and use (it provides helpful year-to-year comparisons and international statistics, for instance). However, *Facts and Figures* did not publish between 1942 and 1945. The issue for 1946 makes some attempt to cover those years.
5 Urquhart and Buckley, *Historical Statistics of Canada,* Series S222-S235.
6 *Facts and Figures of the Automobile Industry,* 1933, 16.
7 Urquhart and Buckley, *Historical Statistics of Canada,* Series S222-S235. Motorcycles were not a popular transportation option in Canada, accounting for less than 1 percent of all vehicle registrations in 1940.
8 "Ratio of Canadian Exports to Production" and "Exports of Canadian Automobiles and Parts from Canada, by Principal Countries," *Facts and Figures of the Automobile Industry,* 1940, 9, 29. By far the biggest foreign consumers of Canadian-made automobiles were Australia, New Zealand, and South Africa. By way of comparison, only about 10 percent of American automobiles were exported in the late 1920s.
9 "Retail Sales of New Automobile Vehicles in Canada," *Facts and Figures of the Automobile Industry,* 1940, 15.
10 White, *Making Cars in Canada,* Chapter 5.

11 On the British automobile industry in the 1930s, see Roy Church, *Herbert Austin: The British Motor Car Industry to 1941* (London: Europa, 1979). On Germany, see Bernard Bellon, *Mercedes in Peace and War: German Automobile Workers, 1903-1945* (New York: Columbia University Press, 1990).

12 For Canada's population, see Urquhart and Buckley, *Historical Statistics of Canada*, Series A1. For Germany, France, and the United Kingdom, see Brian R. Mitchell, *International Historical Statistics* (New York: Macmillan, 1992), 4, 8.

13 Among the world's leading automotive producers, the ratio of population to automobile registration was as follows: the United States 4.3:1, Canada 8.0:1, United Kingdom 19.5:1, France 20.0:1, Germany 45.0:1, and Italy 95.0:1. For interest's sake, the figure of Japan, not yet a major producer of automobiles, was 320.0:1. Vehicle registration figures are estimates from *Facts and Figures of the Automobile Industry*, 1940, 10. All population figures are rounded to the nearest million. Population figures for the United States are from *Historical Statistics of the United States: Colonial Times to 1970* (Washington, DC: Bureau of the Census, 1975), Series A29-42. For Canada, see Urquhart and Buckley, *Historical Statistics of Canada*, Series A1. Figures for all other nations are from respective entries in Mitchell, *International Historical Statistics*. The rate of family ownership is from Dominion Bureau of Statistics, *Eighth Census of Canada, 1941*, vol. 9, *Housing* (Ottawa: Dominion Bureau of Statistics, 1941), Table 18.

14 Dominion Bureau of Statistics, *Eighth Census of Canada, 1941*, 9:Table 18.

15 Ibid., 9:164. Given that the 1941 rate of household automobile ownership in Toronto was 50 percent, it is worth noting that as late as 2001, a quarter of Toronto households did not own a car. See *Transportation Tomorrow Survey* (Toronto: University of Toronto: Joint Program in Transportation, 2003), 9.

16 Mary Peate, *Girl in a Sloppy Joe Sweater: Life on the Canadian Home Front during World War Two* (Montreal: Optimum International, 1989), 52.

17 Dominion Bureau of Statistics, *Family Income and Expenditure in Canada, 1937-1938: A Study of Urban Wage-Earner Families, Including Data on Physical Attributes* (Ottawa: Dominion Bureau of Statistics, 1941), 162-63.

18 Adam Tooze, *The Wages of Destruction: The Making and Breaking of the Nazi Economy* (New York: Penguin, 2007), 156.

19 Jonathan Vance, *Building Canada: People and Projects That Shaped the Nation* (Toronto: Penguin, 2006), 41-43.

20 Warren B. Hastings, "The Motor Industry Carries On," *Maclean's*, 15 October 1940, 66.

21 On the social impact of the automobile in Canada, see Heather Robertson, *Driving Force: The McLaughlin Family and the Age of the Car* (Toronto: McClelland and Stewart, 1995); and, especially, Dean Ruffili, "The Car in Canadian Culture: 1898-1983" (PhD diss., University of Western Ontario, 2006). The impact of the automobile in North America more generally is dealt with in David L. Lewis and Laurence Goldstein, eds., *The Automobile and American Culture* (Ann Arbor: University of Michigan Press, 1983). After the war, the authors of the British official history of overseas supply missions even complained about the automobile industry's "undue" domination of Canada's economy. See H. Duncan Hall and C.C. Wrigley, *Studies of Overseas Supply* (London: H.M. Stationery Office, 1956), 48-49.

22 "Exports of Canadian Automobiles," 9. Exports in 1929 were 101,711, compared to 58,723 in 1939. Exports of military vehicles, of course, increased after the war began.

23 In square footage, factory floor space in 1939 was nearly identical to what it had been in 1929, but automobile production that year was 155,426 units as compared to 262,625 in 1929. See *Facts and Figures of the Automobile Industry*, 1940, 6.

24 Passenger car production (as distinct from retail sales) was 108,369 in 1939, 109,911 in 1940, and 96,603 in 1941. Truck production, including trucks built for the armed forces, rose from 47,057 in 1939 to 113,102 in 1940 and to 173,588 in 1941. "Production and Wholesale Value, 1925-1945," *Facts and Figures of the Automobile Industry*, 1946, 5. Unit retail sales figures prior to 1932 are not readily available.
25 On the lack of military orders for Canadian industry in the first months of the war, see Robert Bothwell, "'Who's Paying for Anything These Days?' War Production in Canada, 1939-45," in *Mobilization for Total War: The Canadian, American, and British Experience*, ed. N.F. Dreisziger (Waterloo: Wilfrid Laurier University Press, 1981), 57-70.
26 "Retail Sales of New Automobiles in Canada," *Facts and Figures of the Automobile Industry*, 1940, 15.
27 See White, *Making Cars in Canada*, 66: "Something else not made by the Canadian automotive industry during the war was passenger cars."
28 B.R. Mitchell, *British Historical Statistics* (Cambridge: Cambridge University Press, 1998), 203. This equals a 70 percent decline after accounting for inflation.
29 Ina Zweiniger-Bargielowska, *Austerity in Britain: Rationing, Controls, and Consumption, 1939-1955* (London: Oxford University Press, 2002), 10.
30 United States Strategic Bombing Survey, *The Effects of Strategic Bombing on the German War Economy* (Washington, DC: Government Printing Office, 1945), 281.
31 "Forced Cut Is Looming for Motors," *Toronto Globe and Mail*, 8 March 1941, 20; "Cut U.S. Output of Cars in Half," *Toronto Globe and Mail*, 21 August 1941, 17.
32 R.J. Overy, *Why the Allies Won* (New York: HarperCollins, 1996), 195; "Automobile Plants Turn Their Coats," *Toronto Globe and Mail*, 13 February 1942, 19.
33 "Retail Sales of New Automobiles in Canada by Months," *Facts and Figures of the Automobile Industry*, 1941, 15.
34 In *Saints, Sinners, and Soldiers: Canada's Second World War* (Vancouver: UBC Press, 2004), 95-96, Jeffrey Keshen observes that passenger car sales dropped between June and July 1940, which he attributes to the tax. But this seems unlikely. For one thing, this seasonal dip occurred every year, and overall car sales in the last half of 1940 were only 9 percent lower than in the previous year (32,087 in 1940 versus 35,545 in 1939.) Moreover, unit car sales in the six-month period from November 1940 to April 1941 were actually slightly *higher* than in the equivalent period in 1939 and 1940 (56,200 to 55,869). Finally, some very good individual months in terms of automotive sales lay ahead. In April 1941, for instance, car sales were approximately double what they had been in July 1940.
35 P.M. Richards, "Restrictions Can Do Harm," *Saturday Night*, 28 September 1940, 27.
36 "Dealers Should Speak Up," *Canadian Automotive Trade*, October 1940, 47.
37 Hastings, "The Motor Industry Carries On," 25.
38 Thelma Le Cocq, "Alice in Autoland," *Chatelaine*, November 1940, 58.
39 Canada, *House of Commons Debates* (21 November 1940), 301.
40 "Order in Council Prohibiting Production of New Models of Certain Manufactured Articles and Machine Tools, P.C. 6765, 20 November 1940," *Proclamations and Orders in Council Relating to the War*, vol. 1, (Ottawa: King's Printer, 1941), 152-53. The design freeze did not prohibit various economies such as materials substitution, which was not merely encouraged but in some cases actually mandated owing to shortages of certain metals. See, for instance, "Urge Simplification of Products to Reduce Costs," *Hardware and Metal*, 14 February 1942, 42-43; and "Washing Machines Likely to Show Effect of Wartime Conservation of Metals," *Hardware and Metal*, 16 August 1941, 294.

41 Library and Archives Canada (LAC), WPTB, RG 64, vol. 88, file 102, history of the Motor Vehicles Administration; "Berry Now Supreme Automotive Dictator," *Canadian Automotive Trade*, March 1941, 19. In December, Berry was also appointed administrator of motor vehicles by the WPTB.

42 Order-in-Council P.C. 1121, *Canadian War Orders and Regulations* (Ottawa: Department of Munitions and Supply, 1945), 219-22.

43 In 1941, these rumours were widely discussed in such journals as *Canadian Automotive Trade* and *Canadian Hotel and Restaurant*. The writers usually suggested that they were part of a deliberate sabotage effort, perhaps by German spies or German sympathizers. The government's pamphlets for American tourists, entitled *Canada's War Record*, were issued under the authority of the director of public information and were designed to be kept in a passport book. Their wording varied. A typical example, of 1 August 1941, read, in part, "American tourists can come to Canada and return as easily as in peace time. In Canada, they will enjoy a 10 percent premium on their money and will be able to move about freely." Pamphlet in the author's private collection and also available at Wartime Canada, http://www.wartimecanada.ca.

44 J. de N. Kennedy, *History of the Department of Munitions and Supply: Canada in the Second World War* (Ottawa: King's Printer, 1950), 2:140. See also "First Order Comes from Motor Vehicle Controller," *Canadian Automotive Trade*, April 1941, 19. Note that the DMS records are very skimpy prior to 1944, and few detailed records exist for the critical period of transition from the civilian to war economy.

45 Kennedy, *History of the Department of Munitions and Supply*, 2:140. Berry also forbade the establishment of new automotive manufacturers, apparently in response to the proposal by some US manufacturers to set up new plants in Canada, in order to circumvent the curtailment on imports.

46 *Motor Vehicle Industry in Canada*, 1945 (Ottawa: Dominion Bureau of Statistics, 1946), 5. Monthly totals of passenger car sales can be found in *Facts and Figures of the Automobile Industry until 1941* (which published figures for the calendar year of 1940). *Facts and Figures* suspended publication in 1942 and resumed in 1946.

47 Editorial, *Canadian Automotive Trade*, June 1941, 16. The exact quotation was, "Business in Canada goes on much as usual; there is no outward evidence yet that Canadian manufacturers must make immediate changes."

48 Ford Motor Company of Canada, *Some General Aspects of the Canadian Customs Tariff, the National Economy, and the Automobile Industry in Canada* (Windsor: Ford Motor Company of Canada, 1938), 63.

49 See R. Warren James, *Wartime Economic Co-operation: A Study of Relations between Canada and the United States* (Toronto: Ryerson Press, 1949), especially 67-86, 116-49.

50 "Shortages of Steel to Limit Production of Many Familiar Articles," *Industrial Canada*, December 1942, 43-44.

51 "Ottawa Can Further Restrict or Entirely Prohibit Car Production," *Canadian Automotive Trade*, October 1941, 28.

52 Quoted in "Restrictions on Production of Automobiles Announced," *Industrial Canada*, August 1941, 50.

53 "Gasoline Selling Hours Restricted," *Hardware and Metal*, 19 July 1941, 8.

54 Agnes Macphail, "Gasoline Ban Is Hardship to Farmers," *Toronto Globe and Mail*, 12 August 1941, 13.

55 "New Shortages of Goods Soon," *Toronto Globe and Mail*, 6 December 1941, 2.

56 "Orders Affecting the Use of Rubber Are Announced," *Industrial Canada*, January 1942, 73-74; "The Influence of the War on Manufacturers," *Canada Year Book*, 1942, 357.

57 "Orders Affecting the Use of Rubber Are Announced," 72-76.
58 "Canada Will Bar Auto Production after March 31," *Toronto Globe and Mail*, 2 January 1942, 1-2. See also LAC, Department of Munitions and Supply, RG 28, vol. 244, Wartime Industries Control Board, Motor Vehicle Control, "Department of Munitions and Supply Press Release," 5 January 1942. The *Globe and Mail* article noted that the order came as a surprise. An Order-in-Council, which formalized the suspension and established the specifics, was issued on 2 February. See Order-in-Council MVC 13, *Canadian War Orders and Regulations*, 226-27.
59 Order-in-Council MVC 16, *Canadian War Orders and Regulations*, 229-30. The records of the Motor Vehicle Controller of the Wartime Industries Control Board reveal frustratingly little (which is to say, almost nothing) about the behind-the-scenes decision-making process that went into the ban on new car production. The decision must have been made in the last two weeks of December 1941. No meeting minutes or correspondence regarding it exist from those two weeks, however, and the matter was not discussed in the Cabinet War Committee; minutes of Cabinet itself are not available prior to 1944. My analysis of the decision comes largely from the Motor Vehicle Controller's own unpublished "history" (really, a lengthy report on its wartime operations), which in turn formed the basis of Kennedy's account in his *History of the Department of Munitions and Supply*. See also LAC, WPTB, RG 64, vol. 88, "Record of the Development of the Motor Vehicles and Parts Administration of the Wartime Prices and Trade Board."
60 In 1941, for example, the industry built some 96,600 passenger cars and 189,000 wheeled vehicles for the armed forces; in 1942, it would build 12,000 passenger cars (all of them in the first two months of the year) and 199,000 wheeled vehicles for the armed forces, its peak output for the war. See Kennedy, *History of the Department of Munitions and Supply*, 2:150. Figures are rounded.
61 WPTB, "Record of the Development of the Motor Vehicles and Parts Administration." See also the discussion in Kennedy, *History of the Department of Munitions and Supply*, 2:140-42.
62 "Last Auto, Until the War Is Won, Leaves Oshawa Motors Line," *Toronto Globe and Mail*, 28 February 1942, 9.
63 "Corps Commander Inspects Plants Producing Guns and Ammunition for His Troops," *Toronto Globe and Mail*, 2 March 1942, 15.
64 Quoted in Barry Broadfoot, *Six War Years, 1939-1945: Memories of Canadians at Home and Abroad* (Markham: Paperjacks, 1976), 192.
65 "Wartime Meeting of Federation Encourages Dealers to Hang On," *Canadian Automotive Trade*, August 1942, 11-12.
66 Order-in-Council MVC 13, *Canadian War Orders and Regulations*, 226-27. Pool cars were made available after freely accessible cars on dealer lots were gone.
67 "Dealers and Vehicle Controller Will Distribute Cars through Two Pools," *Canadian Automotive Trade*, April 1942, 63, 67.
68 "Production and Wholesale Value, 1925-1945," *Facts and Figures of the Automobile Industry*, 1946, 5.
69 LAC, DMS, RG 28, vol. 241, Wartime Industries Control Board Motor Vehicle Control, Reserve Passenger Motor Vehicles.
70 Kennedy, *History of the Department of Munitions and Supply*, 2:142-43.
71 Quoted in Broadfoot, *Six War Years*, 193.
72 "Dealers Ready to Fight!" *Canadian Automotive Trade*, April 1942, 39.
73 *Facts and Figures of the Automobile Industry*, 1946, 14. According to the census of industry and manufactures, no detailed census of used car sales was taken during the war years.

A 1937 survey, however, revealed that approximately twice as many used as new cars changed hands that year.
74 "John Public Eyes the Future of the Automotive Market," *Canadian Automotive Trade*, January 1945, 26.
75 Several versions of this poem circulated in the trades. See, for example, *Canadian Hotel and Restaurant*, December 1942, 18.
76 "Garagemen's Ideas," *Canadian Automotive Trade*, June 1942, 29.
77 F.J. Fullerton, "Selling a Car a Day in Wartime," *Canadian Automotive Trade*, August 1943, 21.
78 LAC, DMS, RG 28, vol. 244, file 196-9-8, Wartime Industries Control Board, Labour, "Resolution Adopted Unanimously at the Annual Meeting of the Federation of Automobile Dealers Associations of Canada, Held at the Royal York Hotel, Toronto, Tuesday," 27 October 1942. On the National Selective Service, see Michael Stevenson, *Canada's Greatest Wartime Muddle: National Selective Service and the Mobilization of Human Resources during World War II* (Montreal and Kingston: McGill-Queen's University Press, 2001).
79 LAC, DMS, RG 28, vol. 244, 196-9-8, Munitions and Supply Wartime Industries Control Board, Labour, John Berry, 27 October 1942.
80 "Commercial Failures," *Canada Year Book*, 1945, 626-33.
81 "Average Number of Persons per Motor Vehicle, 1941-1945," *Facts and Figures of the Automobile Industry*, 1946, 16.
82 "Gasoline Shortage Worse Next Spring, Howe Warns," *Toronto Daily Star*, 19 November 1941, 1.
83 A one-dollar "registration fee" was attached to each booklet. "Gasoline Ration Books Needed for Every Car," *Toronto Daily Star*, 13 December 1941, 1.
84 "Quotas Fixed for Gasoline by Categories," *Toronto Globe and Mail*, 30 January 1942, 1. Gasoline rations posed a potentially serious problem for provincial governments. In 1939, automobile registration fees and retail gasoline taxes had accounted for anywhere from a fifth (in the case of British Columbia, Saskatchewan, Manitoba, and Prince Edward Island) to 40 percent (in the case of Ontario) of provincial tax revenues. In a rare gesture of pure magnanimity toward the provinces, Ottawa promised them tens of millions of dollars to offset the loss of gas taxes. See "Ottawa Will Pay 100 Million Dollars to Nine Provinces," *Toronto Globe and Mail*, 16 January 1942, 1.
85 Kennedy, *History of the Department of Munitions and Supply*, 2:164.
86 "Gasoline Cut to Affect 225,000 Drivers," *Toronto Globe and Mail*, 29 September 1942, 1.
87 LAC, WPTB, RG 64, vol. 1464, file A-10-9-43, Research and Statistics Administration, Transportation.
88 Ibid. See also Kennedy, *History of the Department of Munitions and Supply*, 2:274.
89 "Consumption of Gasoline in Canada for Automotive Purposes, 1941-1945," *Facts and Figures of the Automobile Industry*, 1946, 10; Kennedy, *History of the Department of Munitions and Supply*, 2:169.
90 *Facts and Figures of the Automobile Industry*, 1946, 11.
91 Kennedy, *History of the Department of Munitions and Supply*, 2:191.
92 "Penalties for the Destruction of Any Rubber Item," *Canadian Automotive Trade*, June 1942, 59. See also "Tire Conservation Is of Vital Importance to Every Canadian," *Toronto Globe and Mail*, 30 January 1942, 11.
93 Kennedy, *History of the Department of Munitions and Supply*, 2:192.
94 See numerous complaints at LAC, WPTB, RG 64, vol. 1447, A-10-29-11, Consumer Branch Conferences, vol. 1 and vol. 2.

95 "Orders Affecting the Use of Rubber Are Announced," *Industrial Canada,* January 1942, 73-74; "Restrictions Affect Automotive Industry," *Canadian Automotive Trade,* March 1942, 40, 54.

96 "Controller of Supplies Issues Stern Rubber Warning," *Canadian Automotive Trade,* July 1942, 51. The specifics of tire rationing regulations can be found in "Tire Ration Order More Specific and Drastic," *Canadian Automotive Trade,* June 1942, 31-32, 42; and "Controller Sets District Quotas for Tire Rationing," *Canadian Automotive Trade,* September 1942, 57.

97 For the speed limit, see "Speed in Open Country," *Facts and Figures of the Automobile Industry,* 1946, 46; Raymond Souster, "Nada," *Direction,* November 1943, 4.

98 Kennedy, *History of the Department of Munitions and Supply,* 2:169. See also Keshen, *Saints, Sinners, and Soldiers,* 94-120.

99 "Controller Closes Stations for Coupon Infractions," *Canadian Automotive Trade,* November 1942, 50.

100 "Mounties Run Gas Station after Arresting Operators," *Toronto Globe and Mail,* 4 November 1943, 1.

101 "Black Market Crimes," *Toronto Globe and Mail,* 14 April 1943, 6.

102 Wartime Prices and Trade Board, *Report,* 1943-44, 43.

103 "Individuals Can Eliminate Evil Black Market Problem," *Hamilton Spectator,* 22 May 1943, n.p.

104 Harold Don Allen, *Canada: Rationing, a Numismatic Record* (Montreal: Canadian Numismatic Association, 1956), 21.

105 "A National Scandal," *Hamilton Review,* 17 April 1943, n.p.

106 "Use 500,000 Coupons in Cover-Up Racket," *Toronto Daily Star,* 17 November 1943, 1.

107 Keshen, *Saints, Sinners, and Soldiers,* 101.

108 Quoted in Broadfoot, *Six War Years,* 194-95 (emphasis in original).

109 J.V. McAbee, "Gas Black Market a National Scandal," *Toronto Globe and Mail,* 4 April 1944, 6.

110 Joy Oil Company advertisement, *Toronto Globe and Mail,* 30 March 1944, 21. In 1943, it is worth noting, Joy's owners had themselves been fined $800 for selling gasoline without receipt of proper coupons. Cottrelle, a banker, was also the president and part owner of the Toronto Maple Leafs.

111 "Court Dismisses Charge against Joy Oil Head," *Toronto Telegram,* 14 July 1944, 1. See also "Free Speech Prevails," *Toronto Globe and Mail,* 14 July 1944, 6.

112 Wartime Prices and Trade Board, *Report,* 1944, 43-44.

113 "Motorists 'Don't Care a Hang' If Autos Are Commandeered," *Toronto Globe and Mail,* 8 May 1942, 15. The article did not divulge the source of the survey.

114 *Public Opinion Quarterly* 6, 4 (Winter 1942): 655.

115 Mary F. Williamson and Tom Sharp, eds., *Just a Larger Family: Letters of Marie Williamson from the Canadian Home Front, 1940-1944* (Waterloo: Wilfrid Laurier University Press, 2011), 170.

116 Untitled cartoon, *Canadian Automotive Trade,* April 1942, 38.

117 Robert C. Stark, "It Has Come at Last," *Mayfair,* April 1943, 25.

118 Robertson, *Driving Force,* 303.

119 Untitled photograph, *Canadian Automotive Trade,* November 1942, n.p.

120 Kennedy, *History of the Department of Munitions and Supply,* 2:272.

121 Donald F. Davis and Barbara Lorenzkowski, "A Platform for Gender Tensions: Women Working and Riding on Canadian Urban Public Transit in the 1940s," *Canadian Historical Review* 79, 3 (1998): 437.

122 Kennedy, *History of the Department of Munitions and Supply*, 2:272-74.
123 WPTB, Research and Statistics Administration, Transportation.
124 *Canada Year Book*, 1946, 668.
125 "150,000 Bicycles Quota of 1942 for Dominion," *Toronto Globe and Mail*, 26 May 1942, 1.
126 "How Emerson Brothers Adjust Stocks to Wartime Conditions and Needs," *Hardware and Metal*, 15 August 1942, 87; "Used Bicycles Prices Fixed," *Toronto Globe and Mail*, 4 October 1944, 1.
127 "Advocates Bikes-Built-for-Two as Traffic Violations Increase," *Toronto Globe and Mail*, 26 May 1942, 5; "Sale of Gasoline in Canada by Province," *Canada Year Book*, 1945, 680; "Fatal and Non-Fatal Motor Vehicle Accidents, 1939," *Canada Year Book*, 1941, 579.
128 "Convictions for Breaches of Traffic Regulations," *Canada Year Book*, 1948, 284.
129 "Motor-Vehicle Accidents, 1946," *Canada Year Book*, 1948, 713.
130 Robert Bothwell, Ian Drummond, and John English, *Canada, 1900-1945* (Toronto: University of Toronto Press, 1987), 258.
131 Dominion Bureau of Statistics, *Eighth Census of Canada, 1941*, 9: Table 17.
132 See CBC Radio Canada, *Radio Homes in Canada*, 1941, n.p.
133 Vance, *Building Canada*, 210-12.
134 "Model Kitchen Arouses Pride in Housewives" *Toronto Globe and Mail*, 9 May 1941, 9.
135 "Restrictions and 1942 Sales Volume," *Hardware and Metal*, 31 January 1942, 27.
136 "Dealers Extremely Busy," *Hardware and Metal*, 5 July 1941, 11; "All Branches of Hardware Trade Feel Stimulation of Business in 1941," *Hardware and Metal*, 16 August 1941, 1.
137 "Several More Products Named as Supplies – to Be Restricted," *Industrial Canada*, November 1941, 61.
138 "Production of Washing Machines and Refrigerators Reduced Another 15%," *Hardware and Metal*, 3 January 1942, 42; "Electric Toasters, Irons, and Fans Reduced to 50% of Their 1940 Production," *Hardware and Metal*, 17 January 1942, 26.
139 "Markets at a Glance," *Hardware and Metal*, 15 August 1942, 138.
140 LAC, WPTB, RG 64, vol. 1452, file A-10-9-4, Research and Statistics Administration, Civilian Requirements of Consumer Durable Goods.
141 Wartime Prices and Trade Board, *Report*, 1944, 19.
142 "Commence basé sur le 'service' tabli dans un district minier," *Hardware and Metal*, 3 January 1942, 24; "New, Improved and Replacement Lines to Sell during Wartime," *Hardware and Metal*, 15 August 1942, 122.
143 "Plastics in Household Hardware," *Hardware and Metal*, 15 August 1942, 92-94.
144 *Industrial Canada*, July 1942, 239.
145 "Opportunities for Wood," *Canadian Woodworker*, May 1942, 1.
146 See *Department Store Sales and Stocks: January 1941–July 1948* (Ottawa: Dominion Bureau of Statistics, 1948).
147 "Lend a Patriotic Note to Your Displays," *Trader and Canadian Jeweller*, October 1941, 28-29.
148 "Extinction? Does It Face the Jeweller?" *Trader and Canadian Jeweller*, April 1942, 42, 58; "Window Wisdom by the *Observer*," *Trader and Canadian Jeweller*, October 1941, 28-29.
149 For example, Elton M. Plant, "What about '42?" *Trader and Canadian Jeweller*, December 1941, 30.
150 *Trader and Canadian Jeweller*, December 1942, 32.
151 Elton M. Plant, "Tomorrow's Business Depends on the Impression Made Today," *Trader and Canadian Jeweller*, December 1943, 34, 88.

152 Kenneth Wilson, "Can Produce at Least 10,000 Cars This Year," *Financial Post*, 1 June 1945, 1; "Permit Auto Output; Control Distribution," *Toronto Globe and Mail*, 18 August 1945, 1.
153 *Wanted: 762,568 New Cars* (Toronto: Maclean-Hunter, 1944), 5.
154 "Production and Wholesale Value, 1925-1945," *Facts and Figures of the Automobile Industry*, 1946, 5.
155 *Sales and Financing of New Motor Vehicles in Canada*, 1946 (Ottawa: Dominion Bureau of Statistics, 1946), 5.
156 Joy Parr, *Domestic Goods: The Material, the Moral and the Economic in the Postwar Years* (Toronto: University of Toronto Press, 1999), 23.

Chapter 6: "The Grim Realities of War, as Pictured by Hollywood"

1 Library and Archives Canada (LAC), LAC, WPTB, RG 64, vol. 1460, file A-10-9-23, Research and Statistics Administration, "The Average Man," 15 February 1944, 17. The poll found that 78 percent of the upper class, 74 percent of the middle, and 50 percent of the lower took yearly vacations, 83 percent of them in the summer. Just 7 percent of vacationers stayed home.
2 *Soda Fountains in Canada*, 15 November 1942, 33. This trade journal was published as a special insert in *Drug Merchandising*.
3 T.P. Summerhayes, "Is Ski Project First Move towards Sunday Movies and Hockey," *United Church Observer*, 15 February 1941, 8.
4 Jim Coleman, "Night Club," *Maclean's*, 15 October 1944, 12, 58-60.
5 On the NHL in wartime Canada, see J. Andrew Ross, "The Paradox of Conn Smythe: Hockey, Memory, and the Second World War," *Sport History Review* 37 (May 2006): 19-35. Many thanks to Andrew Ross for sharing an advance copy of his dissertation, "Hockey Capital: Commerce, Culture, and the National Hockey League, 1917-1967" (PhD diss., University of Western Ontario, 2008).
6 Rollie Bourassa ed., *One Family's War: The Wartime Letters of Clarence Bourassa, 1940-1944* (Regina: Canadian Plains Research Center Press, 2010), 59, 65.
7 Reginald G. Smart and Alan C. Ogborne, *Northern Spirits: A Social History of Alcohol in Canada* (Toronto: Addiction Research Foundation, 1996), 26.
8 Craig Heron, *Booze: A Distilled History* (Toronto: Between the Lines, 2003), 178-81.
9 Ibid., 269.
10 Ibid., 281-84.
11 Resolutions calling for temperance, if not outright prohibition, were routinely made by Canadian women's organizations throughout the war, as the minutes of the National Council of Women, IODE, and many other groups show. For a typically hostile reaction to temperance forces, see "Beer and the Elections," *Saturday Night*, 18 March 1944, 1. The failure of temperance movements to gain ground in the United States during the Second World War is explored in Jay L. Rubin, "The Wet War: American Liquor Control, 1941-1945," in *Alcohol, Reform and Society: The Liquor Issue in Social Context*, ed. Jack S. Blocker Jr. (Westport: Greenwood Press, 1979), 235-58. Rubin attributes the failure of temperance forces to the greater preparedness of breweries and distilleries to counter them. In Canada, Labatt's mounted institutional advertising campaigns to argue that beer was a temperate drink. See "Brewers Teach True Temperance," *Marketing*, 9 September 1939, 8.
12 "Liquor – Canada's Protected Industry," *United Church Observer*, 15 June 1941, 4.
13 *The Diaries of William Lyon Mackenzie King*, 12 September 1942, LAC, MG 26-J 13, http://www.collectionscanada.gc.ca/databases/king/.

14 Ibid., 11 December 1942. King mentions working on the speech several times in October, November, and early December. He described the day he finished it, 13 December 1942, as "one of the most peaceful and happiest days of my life."
15 Ibid., 13 December 1942.
16 Robert A. Campbell, "'Profit Was Just a Circumstance': The Evolution of Government Liquor Control in British Columbia, 1920-1988," in *Drink in Canada: Historical Essays*, ed. Cheryl Krasnick Warsh (Montreal and Kingston: McGill-Queen's University Press, 1993), 180; F.R. Scott, "W.L.M.K.," in F.R. Scott, *The Eye of the Needle: Satire, Sorties, Sundries* (Montreal: Contact Press, 1957).
17 *Public Opinion Quarterly* 6, 2 (Summer 1942): 310.
18 King had supported a 20 percent reduction in beer sales, but Cabinet had convinced him to stand at 10 percent.
19 William Lyon Mackenzie King, "Temperance and a Total War Effort," in William Lyon Mackenzie King, *Canada and the Fight for Freedom* (Toronto: Macmillan, 1944), 233-34, 236.
20 King, *Canada and the Fight for Freedom*, 240-41.
21 "Kathlyn's Letters," *The Beaver* 81, 5 (2001): 16-17.
22 "An Alternative Speech on Temperance" appeared in Canadian newspapers on 14 January 1943.
23 *Diaries of William Lyon Mackenzie King*, 23 February 1943.
24 Ray Lewis, "Ray Presents," *Canadian Moving Picture Digest*, 28 August 1939, 3.
25 Receipts in 1930 totalled $38.5 million, compared to $33.5 million in 1938 and $34.0 million in 1939. M.C. Urquhart and K.A.H. Buckley, eds., *Historical Statistics of Canada* (Cambridge: Cambridge University Press, 1965), Series T213-26.
26 *Motion Pictures in Canada, 1939* (Ottawa: Dominion Bureau of Statistics, 1940), 3.
27 Ibid., 7, 12.
28 Ray Lewis, "Hitler's Unholy Show," *Canadian Moving Picture Digest*, 2 September 1939, 1.
29 Ray Lewis, "Ray Presents," *Canadian Moving Picture Digest*, 16 September 1939, 4.
30 Ray Lewis, "Ray Presents," *Canadian Moving Picture Digest*, 25 May 1940, 19.
31 Wellington Jeffers, "Canada Curbs Industry," *Canadian Film Weekly*, 17 June 1942, 5.
32 *The Diaries of William Lyon Mackenzie King*, 4 February 1941. Lassie Come Home also inspired a lengthy rumination on the part of the dog-loving prime minister, who in February 1944, wrote after his third viewing that he found it "symbolical of the hound of heaven" and "how the Hindus might well have believed in human spirits." King's diaries contain almost non-stop references to the supernatural; he saw spiritual significance in nearly every terrestrial event, no matter how trivial. That some historians have argued such matters were of no real or lasting importance to him is inexplicable.
33 On the Production Code Administration, see Robert Sklar, *Movie-Made America: A Cultural History of American Movies*, rev. ed. (New York: Vintage Books, 1994), 173-74.
34 Martin Dies, "Is Communism Invading the Movies?" *Liberty*, 24 February 1940, 47-49.
35 On western European responses to Hollywood, see Frank Costigliola, *Awkward Dominion: American Political, Economic, and Cultural Relations with Europe, 1919-1933* (Ithaca, NY: Cornell University Press, 1984). For Canada, see Ted Magder, *Canada's Hollywood: The Canadian State and Feature Films* (Toronto: University of Toronto Press, 1993); and Peter Morris, *Embattled Shadows: A History of Canadian Cinema, 1895-1939* (Montreal and Kingston: McGill-Queen's University Press, 1992).
36 Quoted in Magder, *Canada's Hollywood*, 38-39.

37 Morris, *Embattled Shadows*, 54.
38 Ibid., 239.
39 Magder, *Canada's Hollywood*, 329-30.
40 "Canadian Per Capita Expenditure for Film Entertainment – $5.61," *Canadian Moving Picture Digest*, 26 August 1944, 15.
41 Mary Peate, *Girl in a Sloppy Joe Sweater: Life on the Canadian Home Front during World War Two* (Montreal: Optimum International, 1989), 146. My assessment of Olivier's performance as a French Canadian trapper is subjective, but few viewers will take issue with the matter.
42 Ibid., 145.
43 "Manitoba Censor Board Bans 13 Films in Past Year," *Canadian Moving Picture Digest*, 7 March 1940, 4.
44 In fact, both claims were true. In January 1927, seventy-seven children were killed in a fire that engulfed the Laurier Palace Theatre in Montreal. The fire occurred on a Sunday, and during the funeral masses that followed, a succession of prominent Quebec clergymen took the opportunity to rail against cinema and for the sanctity of the Lord's Day. Quebec children were banned from theatres until the 1960s. See Rene Schmidt, *Canadian Disasters* (Toronto: Scholastic, 2006).
45 "Special Permission for Quebec Juveniles to See 'Wizard of Oz,'" *Canadian Moving Picture Digest*, 7 October 1939, 9; "'Dumbo Denied Quebec Kids,'" *Canadian Film Weekly*, 14 January 1942, 3.
46 "Quints Movie Visit Stirs Quebec Parents," *Canadian Moving Picture Digest*, 5 February 1944, 13.
47 John Whiteclay Chambers, "*All Quiet on the Western Front:* The Antiwar Film and the Image of Modern War," in *World War II: Film and History*, ed. John Whiteclay Chambers and David Culbert (New York: Oxford University Press, 1994), 13-30. Hollywood films were not the only targets of provincial censors. In March 1940, Ontario premier Mitchell Hepburn banned the National Film Board documentary *Canada at War*, citing it as an example of "political propaganda for the federal government" (which it certainly was). See "Premier Hepburn Bans 'Canada at War' in Ontario," *Canadian Moving Picture Digest*, 9 March 1940, 4.
48 Ray Lewis, "Screen Power versus Hitler," *Canadian Moving Picture Digest*, 10 August 1940, 1.
49 Ray Lewis, "Good Morning, God!" *Canadian Moving Picture Digest*, 13 May 1944, 1.
50 "Famous Players Can. Corp. Ltd.," *Saturday Night*, 22 April 1944, 46.
51 "Army Entertainment Big Task: Military Centers Provide No. 2 Dominion Exhibition Circuit," *Canadian Film Weekly*, 25 February 1942, 1. In June 1944, *Canadian Moving Picture Digest* announced that some sixty theatres were to be built in Canadian military hospitals. J.J. Conklin, "Winnipeg News," *Canadian Moving Picture Digest*, 3 June 1944, 9. Military bases received their films through the regular movie exhibitor trade distribution channels. However, they were not subject to government inspection; nor were military projectionists subject to the same licensing as civilian operators.
52 Dominion Bureau of Statistics, *Family Income and Expenditure in Canada, 1937-1938: A Study of Urban Wage-Earner Families, Including Data on Physical Attributes* (Ottawa: Dominion Bureau of Statistics, 1941), 123.
53 WPTB, Research and Statistics Administration, "The Average Man," 12.
54 Inexplicably, a 1947 DBS report, which might have offered a truer reflection of the actual wartime expenditure on movies by various income brackets than these

Depression-era statistics, lumped entertainment and educational expenditures together. The figures are therefore essentially without value, as it is impossible to determine if any given dollar was allocated to a movie or a schoolbook.
55 *Motion Picture Theatres in Canada*, 9-10.
56 Dominion Bureau of Statistics, *Family Income and Expenditure in Canada, 1937-1938*.
57 *Motion Picture Theatres in Canada*, 10.
58 Edward MacDonald, *If You're Stronghearted: Prince Edward Island in the 20th Century* (Charlottetown: PEI Books, 2000), n.p. I am grateful to Ed MacDonald for bringing his chapter on the island at war to my attention.
59 *Motion Picture Theatres, Exhibitors, and Distributors, 1950* (Ottawa: Dominion Bureau of Statistics, 1952), n.p.
60 Harold Kalman, *A Concise History of Canadian Architecture* (Toronto: Oxford University Press 2000), 499.
61 Ibid.
62 John C. Lindsay, *Palaces of the Night: Canada's Grand Theatres* (Toronto: Lynx Images, 1999), 65.
63 Kalman, *A Concise History of Canadian Architecture*, 503.
64 Jonathan Rittenhouse, "'Our Granada': The Granada Theatre, Wellington Street, Sherbrooke, Quebec, Canada, America, the World and Me," *Theatre Research in Canada* 18, 2 (1997): n.p.
65 Ivan Ackery, *Fifty Years on Theatre Row* (Vancouver: Hancock House, 1981), 13, 15.
66 Quoted in ibid., 15.
67 Public Archives of Ontario, Ontario Theatre Regulatory Files, RG 56-14, Theatre Inspector Reports, September 1944.
68 Ibid., 1 October 1943.
69 "Ottawa Defines Board's Power," *Canadian Film Weekly*, 25 February 1942, 1.
70 "Order Emergency Lighting Systems Installed in Ontario Theatres," *Canadian Moving Picture Digest*, 16 September 1939, 3.
71 "Canada at War Seriously Affects Theatres in Maritime Provinces," *Canadian Moving Picture Digest*, 16 September 1939, 4.
72 Theatre Inspector Reports, 6 January 1943.
73 "Air Raid Advice," *Canadian Film Weekly*, 4 March 1942, 5.
74 *Canadian Moving Picture Digest*, 14 July 1940, 1, 3.
75 "Timmins Fats Show," *Canadian Moving Picture Digest*, 14 October 1944, 14.
76 *Trenton Quinte Sun*, quoted in "Midnight Show Ban Called Unfair," *Canadian Film Weekly*, 28 January 1942, 5.
77 "In the Middle," *Canadian Film Weekly*, 4 March 1942, 2.
78 "On Guard," *United Church Observer*, 1 December 1942, 4.
79 Quoted in "Hamilton Whacks Midnite Shows," *Canadian Film Weekly*, 11 February 1942, 1-2.
80 Ray Lewis, "Too Much of a Good Thing!" *Canadian Moving Picture Digest*, 27 May 1944, 1.
81 John Grierson, "The National Film Board and You," *Canadian Film Weekly*, 25 February 1942, 5.
82 "Movie Patrons Are Realistic," *Canadian Film Weekly*, 2 July 1942, 3.
83 Cited in "Critics Select 'Random Harvest' Year's Best," *Canadian Moving Picture Digest*, 22 January 1944, 1.
84 Bill Press, "Toronto and District," *Canadian Moving Picture Digest*, 29 January 1944, 5.

85 Sklar, *Movie-Made America*, 253.
86 Mary F. Williamson and Tom Sharp, eds., *Just a Larger Family: Letters of Marie Williamson from the Canadian Home Front, 1940-1944* (Waterloo: Wilfrid Laurier University Press, 2011), 207.
87 Stephen Prince, *Classical Film Violence: Designing and Regulating Brutality in Hollywood Cinema, 1930-1968* (New Brunswick, NJ: Rutgers University Press, 2003), 164.
88 Ibid., 153-55.
89 Ibid., 164.
90 Ibid.
91 Ibid., 161, 63.
92 Peate, *Girl in a Sloppy Joe Sweater*, 148.
93 Mary Lowrey Ross, "Stepping-up the Violence May Bore the Suffering Populace," *Saturday Night*, 11 March 1944, 30-31.
94 J.J. Conklin, "Winnipeg News," *Canadian Moving Picture Digest*, 3 June 1944, 9.
95 D. Mosdell, "Film Review," *Canadian Forum*, March 1945, 284.
96 "Silverthorn Praises War Effort of Industry," *Canadian Moving Picture Digest*, 20 May 1944, 8.
97 Prince, *Classical Film Violence*, 163. Unfortunately, Prince does not give his source for the claim that Ontario cut only the soldier's scream.
98 There is a large literature on Hollywood's wartime movies. Among the most perceptive are Robert L. McLaughlin and Sally E. Parry, *We'll Always Have the Movies: American Cinema during World War II* (Lexington: University Press of Kentucky, 2006); and Robert Fyne's aptly titled *The Hollywood Propaganda of World War II* (Metuchen, NJ: Scarecrow Press, 1994). Robert Fyne's *Long Ago and Far Away: Hollywood and the Second World War* (Toronto: Scarecrow Press, 2008) is both straightforward and pedantic, and therefore much admired by the present author. Britain's film industry was similarly placed at the disposal of the war effort, to such an extent that a famous scene was excised from Laurence Olivier's Oscar-winning 1944 version of *Henry V*. Hal's murderous threat to the civilian population of the French town of Harfleur was considered unfit for wartime audiences in the United Kingdom. S.P. MacKenzie's *British War Films, 1939-1945* (London: Hambledon and London, 2001) deals with British wartime cinema generally.
99 "'Heart' a Patriotic 'Must,'" *Canadian Moving Picture Digest*, 1 April 1944, 7.
100 Gunda Lambton, *Sun in Winter: A Toronto Wartime Journal, 1942-1945* (Montreal and Kingston: McGill-Queen's University Press, 2003), 234.
101 "Strife Stuff," *Canadian Film Weekly*, 26 August 1942, 2.

Conclusion

1 Quoted in Harry Cassidy, *Social Security and Reconstruction in Canada* (Toronto: Ryerson Press, 1943), 4-5.
2 A.R.M. Lower, "Introduction: The Problems of Reconstruction," in *War and Reconstruction: Some Canadian Issues; Addresses Given at the Canadian Institute on Public Affairs, August 15 to 23, 1942*, ed. A.R.M. Lower and J.F. Parkinson (Toronto: Ryerson Press, 1942), v.
3 C.P. Stacey, *Arms, Men and Governments: The War Policies of Canada, 1939-1945* (Ottawa: Queen's Printer, 1970), 51. For a discussion, see pages 403-12.
4 "Public Opinion Polls," *Public Opinion Quarterly* 8, 1 (Spring 1944): 158-59. The latter found that 68 percent of respondents were confident of keeping their jobs in the

post-war period, whereas 32 percent either thought they would have to find a new one or were unsure. See also the discussion in Kenneth Norrie and Douglas Owram, *A History of the Canadian Economy* (Toronto: Harcourt Brace, 1991), 390-93.

5 A.R. Mosher, "The War-Aims of the Workers," *Canadian Unionist*, November 1939, 152.
6 W.E.C. Harrison, ed., *Canada: The War and After* (Toronto: Ryerson Press, 1944), 58.
7 Lorne Thompson Morgan, *The Permanent War, or, Homo the Sap* (Toronto: Workers' Educational Association, 1944), 15 (emphasis in original).
8 "Prospects for the Year 1945," *Monetary Times Annual*, 1945, 5.
9 "Re-establishment," by contrast, meant finding employment for members of the armed forces who were released from service.
10 Desmond Morton, *Working People: An Illustrated History of the Canadian Labour Movement*, 4th ed. (Montreal and Kingston: McGill-Queen's University Press, 1998), 182.
11 Library and Archives Canada, Wartime Prices and Trade Board (WPTB), RG 64, vol. 1460, file A-10-9-23, Wartime Prices and Trade Board, Research and Statistics Administration, "The Average Man," 15 February 1944, 17.
12 Robert Bothwell, Ian Drummond, and John English, *Canada, 1900-1945* (Toronto: University of Toronto Press, 1987), 390.
13 Norrie and Owram, *A History of the Canadian Economy*, 390-93.
14 J.L. Ilsley, "Tougher Year in Store for Canadians in 1945," *Monetary Times Annual*, 1945, 23.
15 "Public Opinion Polls," 144, 159.
16 See J.L. Granatstein, *The Ottawa Men: The Civil Service Mandarins, 1939-1957* (Toronto: Oxford University Press, 1982), 134-35.
17 Bothwell, Drummond, and English, *Canada, 1900-1945*, 228-29.
18 Ibid., 330.
19 Frank R. Scott, "The Nature of Economic Planning," in Co-operative Commonwealth Federation, *Planning for Freedom: 16 Lectures on the CCF, Its Politics and Program* (Toronto: Ontario CCF, 1944), 6. See also Co-operative Commonwealth Federation, *Security with Victory: CCF Manifesto* (Ottawa: National Office of the CCF, 1944).
20 Walter D. Young, *The Anatomy of a Party: The National CCF, 1932-1961* (Toronto: University of Toronto Press, 1969), 118.
21 Co-operative Commonwealth Federation, *Security with Victory*, 5.
22 Alvin Finkel, "Origins of the Welfare State in Canada," in *The Canadian State: Political Economy and Political Power*, ed. Leo Panitch (Toronto: University of Toronto Press, 1977), 344-70.
23 *Drug Merchandising*, 1 October 1943, 1.
24 "Social Security? We've Had It for Years at Dominion Oilcloth!" Advertisement, *National Home Monthly*, September 1944, 27.
25 Published by the E.B. Eddy Company, this ad ran in many mass-market and trade publications, such as *Marketing*, 15 October 1944, 14; and *Maclean's*, 15 October 1944, 41.
26 "Martin Voices Warning," *Marketing*, 13 November 1943, 10.
27 R.A. McEachern, "The Financial Post's Survey of the Manufacturing Industry," in *Post-War Planning Conference Held at the 73rd Annual General Meeting of the Canadian Manufacturers' Association, Royal York Hotel, Toronto, June 12, 13, and 14 1944*, 27.
28 "Small Scope for Advertising If Beveridge Ideas Adopted," *Marketing*, 2 December 1944, 1.
29 Leo Zakuta, *A Protest Movement Becalmed* (Toronto: University of Toronto Press, 1964), 71.

30 "The Canadian Scene in 1945," *Monetary Times Annual,* 1946, 10.
31 On the King government's plans, see J.L. Granatstein, *Canada's War: The Politics of the Mackenzie King Government, 1939-1945* (Toronto: Oxford University Press, 1975); and Robert Bothwell and William Kilbourn, *C.D. Howe: A Biography* (Toronto: McClelland and Stewart, 1979). On the emergence of the social welfare state in this period, see Alvin Finkel, *Our Lives: Canada after 1945* (Toronto: James Lorimer, 1997). On the cultural aspects of reconstruction, see L.B. Kuffert, *A Great Duty: Canadian Responses to Modern Life and Mass Culture, 1939-1967* (Montreal and Kingston: McGill-Queen's University Press, 2006), 65-103.
32 Norrie and Owram, *A History of the Canadian Economy,* 390-95.
33 Christopher Waddell, "The Wartime Prices and Trade Board: Price Control in Canada in World War Two" (PhD diss., York University, 1981), 719-25.
34 Magda Fahrni, "Counting the Costs of Living: Gender, Citizenship, and a Politics of Prices in 1940s Montreal," *Canadian Historical Review* 83, 4 (December 2002): 483.
35 See Joy Parr, *Domestic Goods: The Material, the Moral and the Economic in the Postwar Years* (Toronto: University of Toronto Press, 1999), Chapter 1.
36 M.C. Urquhart and K.A.H. Buckley, eds., *Historical Statistics of Canada* (Cambridge: Cambridge University Press, 1965), Series T61-66.
37 "Sugar Supplies Present and Post-War," *Food in Canada,* April 1945, 30.
38 Dave Mullen, "Letter from a Young Artist," *Direction,* 1944, n.p.
39 Michael Dawson, "Leisure, Consumption, and the Public Sphere: Postwar Debates over Shopping Regulations in Vancouver and Victoria during the Cold War," in *Creating Postwar Canada: Community, Diversity, and Dissent, 1945-1975,* ed. Magda Fahrni and Robert Rutherdale (Vancouver: UBC Press, 2005), 193-216; Peter S. McInnis, *Harnessing Labour Confrontation: Shaping the Postwar Settlement in Canada, 1943-1950* (Toronto: University of Toronto Press, 2002), 47-86.
40 For 2005 retail sales, see *Retail Sales by Trade Sectors, Canada 2005 and 2006,* http://www.statcan.gc.ca/.

Appendix

Further thanks to Amanda Green for her assistance in preparing a number of Excel worksheets for this appendix. These worksheets can be requested from the author.
1 Eleanor Hancock, *The National Socialist Leadership and Total War, 1941-1945* (New York: St. Martin's Press, 1991), 2 (emphasis added).
2 In the category of grocery store sales, I did not attempt to make an adjustment for the greater increase in food prices, because grocery stores also sold non-food items.
3 One such estimate was made in Michael Bliss, *Northern Enterprise: Five Centuries of Canadian Business* (Toronto: McClelland and Stewart, 1987), 448.
4 Unfortunately, I could not locate figures for the number of non-resident ration cards issued at any given time. Determining the resident population of Canada during the Second World War poses many more challenges than would be worth the effort, especially given the comings and goings of Allied government and military personnel – particularly through the British Commonwealth Air Training Plan, which trained something on the order of sixty thousand pilots and air crew from other countries (mainly the United Kingdom, Australia, and New Zealand). See F.J. Hatch, *The Aerodrome of Democracy: Canada and the British Commonwealth Air Training Plan, 1939-1945* (Ottawa: Directorate of History and Heritage, 1983), 202. At any given time in 1942 and 1943, it is likely that about ten thousand foreign personnel were progressing through the program. Add to this unknown numbers of sailors in ports such as Halifax,

British and American administrators in Ottawa and elsewhere, and the figure may approach something like twenty thousand. And what to do with institutionalized populations, including interred Japanese Canadians? Determining the number of Canadian armed forces personnel out-of-country is easier. C.P. Stacey's figures for the Canadian Army's strength in the European Theatre are 147,519 in June 1942, 242,409 in June 1943, and 270,867 in June 1944. See C.P. Stacey, *Six Years of War: The Army in Canada, Britain, and the Pacific* (Ottawa: Queen's Printer, 1955), 191.

5 See wartime figures in *Department Store Sales and Stocks, January, 1941, to July, 1948, by Months* (Ottawa: Dominion Bureau of Statistics, 1948), 18-32.
6 *Men's Wear Merchandising*, 1 February 1942, 10.
7 On the German economy at war, see the collected essays in R.J. Overy, *War and Economy in the Third Reich* (Oxford: Clarendon Press, 1994); and Adam Tooze, *The Wages of Destruction: The Making and Breaking of the Nazi Economy* (New York: Penguin, 2007). On the blitzkrieg, see, for example, the translation of the German official history, Karl-Heinz Frieser with John T. Greenwood, *The Blitzkrieg Legend: The 1940 Campaign in the West* (Annapolis: Naval Institute Press, 2005).
8 On this, see Ina Zweiniger-Bargielowska, *Austerity in Britain: Rationing, Controls, and Consumption, 1939-1955* (London: Oxford University Press, 2002).
9 For example, Paul Kennedy, *Rise and Fall of the Great Powers: Economic Change and Military Conflict from 1950 to 2000* (New York: Random House, 1987); or for that matter, Winston Churchill, *The Second World War*, vol. 3, *The Grand Alliance* (Boston: Houghton Mifflin, 1950), 606-7. Churchill later recalled that, upon hearing the news of the Japanese attack on Pearl Harbor, he had reflected, "So we had won after all ... All the rest was merely the proper application of overwhelming force."
10 Hugh Rockoff, "The United States: From Ploughshares to Swords," in *The Economics of World War II: Six Great Powers in International Comparison*, ed. Mark Harrison (New York: Cambridge University Press, 1998), 98.
11 R. Warren James, *Wartime Economic Co-operation: A Study of Relations between Canada and the United States* (Toronto: Ryerson Press, 1949), 60, 62.
12 Ibid., 396.
13 Inflation figures are from the United States Department of Labor, Bureau of Labor Statistics, "Consumer Price Index," ftp://ftp.bls.gov/pub/special.requests/cpi/cpiai.txt. For the growth in consumer spending, see Rockoff, "The United States: From Ploughshares to Swords," 90-91. John Kenneth Galbraith is quoted in Studs Terkel, *"The Good War": An Oral History of World War II* (New York: New Press, 1984), 323.
14 J.L. Granatstein, "Canada," in *The Oxford Companion to the Second World War*, ed. I.C.B. Dear and M.R.D. Foot (New York: Oxford University Press, 1995), 183; Peter S. McInnis, *Harnessing Labour Confrontation: Shaping the Postwar Settlement in Canada, 1943-1950* (Toronto: University of Toronto Press, 2002), 32-33; Jeffrey Keshen, *Saints, Sinners, and Soldiers: Canada's Second World War* (Vancouver: UBC Press, 2004); Desmond Morton, *Working People: An Illustrated History of the Canadian Labour Movement*, 4th ed. (Montreal and Kingston: McGill-Queen's University Press, 1998), 174.
15 I rejected the use of November as a benchmark for this study, preferring yearly averages, on the obvious grounds that retail sales occur throughout the year and that inflation can vary dramatically within a year. For example, the CPI for November 1941 is several points higher than the average for that year as a whole.
16 Library and Archives Canada (LAC), Wartime Prices and Trade Board (WPTB), RG 64, vol. 1460, file A-10-9-25, Research and Statistics Administration, Price Control.

17 E.J. Spence, "Wartime Price Control Policy in Canada" (PhD diss., Northwestern University, 1947). See Christopher Waddell's discussion in "The Wartime Prices and Trade Board: Price Control in Canada in World War Two" (PhD diss., York University, 1981), especially 211-314 and 727-49.
18 LAC, WPTB, RG 64, vol. 444, file 10-88, Public Opinion Polls, Canadian Opinion Company, "A Nationwide Survey of Canadian Attitudes toward Wartime Ceilings and Rationing," June 1944, n.p.
19 "Public Opinion Polls," *Public Opinion Quarterly* 8, 1 (Spring 1944): 145; "Gallup and Fortune Polls," *Public Opinion Quarterly* 9, 3 (Autumn 1945): 376.
20 LAC, WPTB, RG 64, vol. 1448, file A-10-20-12, Wartime Prices and Trade Board, Research and Statistics Administration, WPT Panels, Consumer Questionnaire Analysis, Report No. 2. The questionnaire asked consumers if they had "purchased any articles that seemed to you to be of especially poor quality for the price you paid."
21 Harriet Parsons, *Libel or Label?* (Ottawa: Consumer Branch, Wartime Prices and Trade Board, 1943). The play can be found in LAC, WPTB, RG 64, vol. 1446, file A-10-29-7, Consumer Branch Educational Program, vol. 1.
22 WPTB, Consumer Questionnaire Analysis, Report No. 2.
23 LAC, WPTB, RG 64, vol. 1447, file A-10-29-11, Consumer Branch Conferences, vol. 3.
24 Credit for this methodology goes to Harold Vatter, who used a similar version in "The Material Status of the U.S. Civilian Consumer in World War II," in *The Sinews of War: Essays on the Economic History of World War Two,* ed. G.T. Mills and Hugh Rockoff (Ames: Iowa State University Press, 1993), 219-42.
25 Rockoff, "The United States: From Ploughshares to Swords," 98.
26 Magda Fahrni, "Counting the Costs of Living: Gender, Citizenship, and a Politics of Prices in 1940s Montreal," *Canadian Historical Review* 83, 4 (December 2002): 493.

Selected Bibliography

Archival Collections
Library and Archives Canada (LAC)
Canadian Home Economics Association fonds, MG 28
Catholic Women's League of Canada fonds, MG 28
Department of Labour fonds, RG 27
Department of Pensions and National Health fonds, MG 38
Imperial Order Daughters of the Empire fonds, MG 28
National Council of Women of Canada fonds, MG 28
Wartime Industries Control Board fonds, RG 28
Wartime Prices and Trade Board fonds, RG 64

Public Archives of Ontario
Ontario Theatre Regulatory files
Timothy Eaton Company fonds

Periodicals
Bookseller and Stationer
Canada's Weekly
Canadian Advertising
Canadian Automotive Trade
Canadian Banker
Canadian Business
Canadian Film Weekly
Canadian Forum
Canadian Geographic Journal
Canadian Grocer
Canadian Home Journal
Canadian Hotel and Restaurant
Canadian Medical Association Journal
Canadian Moving Picture Digest
Canadian Poetry Magazine
Canadian Printer and Publisher
Canadian Unionist
Canadian Woodworker
Chatelaine
Commerce Journal
Drug Merchandising

Facts and Figures of the Automobile Industry
Food in Canada
Gift Buyer
Hamilton Spectator
Hardware and Metal
Industrial Canada
Liberty
Lydiatt's Book of Canadian Market and Advertising Data
Maclean's
Marketing
Mayfair
Men's Wear Merchandising
Monetary Times Annual
National Council of Women, *Yearbook*
National Home Monthly
Public Opinion Quarterly
Queen's Quarterly
Saturday Night
Soda Fountains in Canada
Toronto Daily Star
Toronto Globe and Mail
Toronto Telegram
Trader and Canadian Jeweller
United Church Observer

Government Publications

Canada Gazette. 1939-45.
Canada Year Book. 1939-48.
Labour Gazette. 1939-45.
National Health Review. 1942.
Canada. *House of Commons Debates*. 1939-45.
CBC Radio Canada. *Radio Homes in Canada*. 1941.
Combined Food Board. *Food Consumption Levels in Canada, the United Kingdom and the United States*. Ottawa: King's Printer, 1944.
Combined Production and Resources Board. *The Impact of the War on Civilian Consumption in the United Kingdom, the United States, and Canada*. Washington, DC: United States Government Printing Office, 1945.
Department of Munitions and Supply. *Canadian War Orders and Regulations*. Ottawa: Department of Munitions and Supply, 1945.
Department of Pensions and National Health. *Annual Report of Nutrition Services*. 1942-45.
–. *Annual Report of the Canadian Council of Nutrition*. 1941-45.
Dominion Bureau of Statistics. *Advertising Agencies*. 1950
–. *Consumer Market Data*. 1941.
–. *The Control and Sale of Alcoholic Beverages in Canada to 1946*.
–. *Cost of Living Index Numbers for Canada, 1913-1946*.
–. *Cost-of-Living Quiz*. 1943.
–. *Department Store Sales and Stocks: January 1941-July 1948*.

–. *Drug Store Sales.* 1939-45.
–. *Eighth Census of Canada, 1941.* 11 vols.
–. *The Electrical Apparatus and Supplies Industry in Canada.* 1940-47.
–. *Monthly Index of Retail Sales.* 1939-45.
–. *Motion Picture Exhibitors in Canada.* 1939-50.
–. *Motor Vehicle Industry in Canada.* 1939-1945. Ottawa: Dominion Bureau of Statistics, 1946.
–. *New Motor Vehicle Sales and Motor Vehicle Financing in Canada.* 1939, 1941, 1946.
–. *Retail Chains.* 1943.
–. *Retail Consumer Credit Annual Summary.* 1941, 1948-50.
–. *Retail Trade.* 1930-61.
–. *Sales and Financing of Motor Vehicles in Canada.* 1939-46.
–. *The Sporting Goods Industry in Canada.* 1944.
–. *The Tobacco Industries in Canada.* 1939-45.
Pett, L.B. *Recent Dietary Surveys in Canada.* Ottawa: Department of Pensions and National Health, 1943.
Proclamations and Orders in Council Relating to the War. Vol. 1. Ottawa: King's Printer, 1941.
Wartime Information Board. *Canada at War.* 1939-45.
Wartime Prices and Trade Board. *Report.* 1939-47.
–. *Consumer's News.* 1941-47.
–. *Food Press Conference.* 8 September 1943.
–. *Price Control in Canada.* December 1941.
–. *Report on Consumer Credit.* 1941-44.

Other Sources

Ackery, Ivan. *Fifty Years on Theatre Row.* Vancouver: Hancock House, 1981.
Allen, Harold Don. *Canada: Rationing, a Numismatic Record.* Montreal: Canadian Numismatic Association, 1956.
Anderson, Carol, and Katharine Mallinson. *Lunch with Lady Eaton: Inside the Dining Rooms of a Nation.* Toronto: ECW Press, 2004.
Auld, Hedley F. *Canadian Agriculture and World War II: A History of the Wartime Activities of the Canada Department of Agriculture and Its Wartime Boards and Agencies.* Ottawa: Department of Agriculture, 1953.
Beach, E.F., ed. *Selling Tomorrow's Production.* Montreal: McGill University Press, 1944.
Bellon, Bernard. *Mercedes in Peace and War: German Automobile Workers, 1903-1945.* New York: Columbia University Press, 1990.
Bliss, Michael. *Northern Enterprise: Five Centuries of Canadian Business.* Toronto: McClelland and Stewart, 1987.
Bothwell, Robert. "'Who's Paying for Anything These Days?' War Production in Canada, 1939-45." In *Mobilization for Total War: The Canadian, American, and British Experience,* ed. N.F. Dreisziger, 57-70. Waterloo: Wilfrid Laurier University Press, 1981.
Bothwell, Robert, and William Kilbourn. *C.D. Howe: A Biography.* Toronto: McClelland and Stewart, 1979.
Bourassa, Rollie, ed. *One Family's War: The Wartime Letters of Clarence Bourassa, 1940-1944.* Regina: Canadian Plains Research Center Press, 2010.
Broad, Graham. "Shopping for Victory." *The Beaver* 85, 2 (April-May 2005): 40-45.
Broadfoot, Barry. *Six War Years, 1939-1945: Memories of Canadians at Home and Abroad.* Markham, ON: Paperjacks, 1976.

Campbell, Robert A. "'Profit Was Just a Circumstance': The Evolution of Government Liquor Control in British Columbia, 1920-1988." In *Drink in Canada: Historical Essays*, ed. Cheryl Krasnick Warsh, 172-92. Montreal and Kingston: McGill-Queen's University Press, 1993.

Canadian Manufacturer's Association. *Post-War Planning Conference Held at the 73rd Annual General Meeting of the Canadian Manufacturers' Association, Royal York Hotel, Toronto, June 12, 13, and 14 1944*. Toronto: Canadian Manufacturers' Association, 1944.

Cassidy, Harry. *Social Security and Reconstruction in Canada*. Toronto: Ryerson Press, 1943.

Chambers, John Whiteclay. "*All Quiet on the Western Front:* The Antiwar Film and the Image of Modern War." In *World War II: Film and History*, ed. John Whiteclay Chambers and David Culbert, 13-30. New York: Oxford University Press, 1994.

Church, Roy. *Herbert Austin: The British Motor Car Industry to 1941*. London: Europa, 1979.

Comacchio, Cynthia R. *The Infinite Bonds of Family: Domesticity in Canada, 1850-1940*. Toronto: University of Toronto Press, 1999.

Co-operative Commonwealth Federation. *Planning for Freedom: 16 Lectures on the CCF, Its Policies and Program*. Toronto: Ontario CCF, 1944.

–. *Security with Victory: CCF Manifesto*. Ottawa: National Office of the CCF, 1944.

Costigliola, Frank. *Awkward Dominion: American Political, Economic, and Cultural Relations with Europe, 1919-1933*. Ithaca, NY: Cornell University Press, 1984.

Dawson, Michael. "Leisure, Consumption, and the Public Sphere: Postwar Debates over Shopping Regulations in Vancouver and Victoria during the Cold War." In *Creating Postwar Canada: Community, Diversity, and Dissent, 1945-1975*, ed. Magda Fahrni and Robert Rutherdale, 193-216. Vancouver: UBC Press, 2005.

De Grazia, Victoria, and Ellen Furlough, eds. *The Sex of Things: Gender and Consumption in Historical Perspective*. Berkeley: University of California Press, 1996.

Durflinger, Serge Marc. *Fighting from Home: The Second World War in Verdun, Quebec*. Studies in Canadian Military History. Vancouver: UBC Press, 2006.

Fahrni, Magda. "Counting the Costs of Living: Gender, Citizenship, and a Politics of Prices in 1940s Montreal." *Canadian Historical Review* 83, 4 (December 2002): 483-504.

Dear, I.C.B, and M.D.R Foot., eds. *The Oxford Companion to the Second World War*. New York: Oxford University Press, 1995.

Fish, Lynn. "Kathlyn's Letters." *The Beaver* 81, 5 (2001): 16-17.

Ford Motor Company of Canada. *Some General Aspects of the Canadian Customs Tariff, the National Economy, and the Automobile Industry in Canada*. Windsor: Ford Motor Company of Canada, 1938.

Fox, Frank W. *Madison Avenue Goes to War: The Strange Military Career of American Advertising, 1941-1945*. Provo, UT: Brigham Young University Press, 1975.

Fyne, Robert. *Long Ago and Far Away: Hollywood and the Second World War*. Lanham, MD: Scarecrow Press, 2008.

Glickman, Lawrence B., ed. *Consumer Society in American History: A Reader*. Ithaca, NY: Cornell University Press, 1999.

Granatstein, J.L. *Canada's War: The Politics of the Mackenzie King Government, 1939-1945*. Toronto: Oxford University Press, 1975.

–. *Conscription in the Second World War, 1939-1945*. Toronto: McGraw-Hill, 1969.

Greene, Graham. *The End of the Affair*. New York: Penguin, 1951.

Guest, Edna, and Ethel Chapman. *An Experiment in Applied Nutrition for Canadian Communities*. Toronto: West Toronto Printing House, 1943.

Hall, H. Duncan. *North American Supply.* London: H.M. Stationery Office, 1955.
Hall, H. Duncan, and C.C. Wrigley. *Studies of Overseas Supply.* London: H.M. Stationery Office, 1956.
Hancock, Eleanor. *The National Socialist Leadership and Total War, 1941-5.* New York: St. Martin's Press, 1991.
Harrison, Mark, ed. *The Economics of World War II: Six Great Powers in International Comparison.* New York: Cambridge University Press, 1998.
Harrison, W.E.C., ed. *Canada: The War and After.* Toronto: Ryerson Press, 1944.
Inness, Sherrie A., ed. *Kitchen Culture in America: Popular Representations of Food, Gender, and Race.* Philadelphia: University of Pennsylvania Press, 2001.
Innis, Harold. "The Newspaper in Economic Development." *Journal of Economic History* 2 (December 1942): 1-33.
Jacobs, Meg. *Pocketbook Politics: Economic Citizenship in Twentieth-Century America.* Princeton, NJ: Princeton University Press, 2004.
James, R. Warren. *Wartime Economic Co-operation: A Study of Relations between Canada and the United States.* Toronto: Ryerson Press, 1949.
Jhally, Sut. *The Codes of Advertising: Fetishism and the Political Economy of Meaning in the Consumer Society.* New York: Routledge, 1990.
Johnston, Russell T. *Selling Themselves: The Emergence of Canadian Advertising.* Toronto: University of Toronto Press, 2001.
Kalman, Harold. *A Concise History of Canadian Architecture.* Toronto: Oxford University Press, 2000.
Kennedy, J. de N. *History of the Department of Munitions and Supply: Canada in the Second World War.* 2 vols. Ottawa: King's Printer, 1950.
Keshen, Jeffrey. *Saints, Sinners, and Soldiers: Canada's Second World War.* Vancouver: UBC Press, 2004.
King, William Lyon Mackenzie. *Canada and the Fight for Freedom.* Toronto: Macmillan, 1944.
Lambton, Gunda. *Sun in Winter: A Toronto Wartime Journal, 1942-1945.* Montreal and Kingston: McGill-Queen's University Press, 2003.
Leach, William. *Land of Desire: Merchants, Power, and the Rise of a New American Culture.* New York: Vintage, 1993.
Lears, T.J. Jackson. *Fables of Abundance: A Cultural History of Advertising in America.* New York: Basic Books, 1994.
Leiss, William, Stephen Kline, and Sut Jhally. *Social Communication in Advertising: Persons, Products, and Images of Well-Being.* 2nd rev. ed. Scarborough, ON: Nelson Canada, 1990.
Lindsay, John C. *Palaces of the Night: Canada's Grand Theatres.* Toronto: Lynx Images, 1999.
Lower, A.R.M., and J.F. Parkinson, eds. *War and Reconstruction: Some Canadian Issues; Addresses Given at the Canadian Institute on Public Affairs, August 15 to 23, 1942.* Toronto: Ryerson Press, 1942.
MacDonald, Edward. *If You're Stronghearted: Prince Edward Island in the 20th Century.* Charlottetown: PEI Books, 2000.
Magder, Ted. *Canada's Hollywood: The Canadian State and Feature Films.* Toronto: University of Toronto Press, 1993.
Marchand, Roland. *Advertising the American Dream: Making Way for Modernity, 1920-1940.* Berkeley: University of California Press, 1985.

Maritime Conference on Industrial Relations. *Addresses Delivered at the Maritime Conference on Industrial Relations, Saint John, June 25, 1943.* Halifax: Maritime Conference on Industrial Relations, 1943.

Massey, Vincent. *The Sword of Lionheart, and Other Wartime Speeches by the Right Honourable Vincent Massey.* London: Hodder and Stoughton, 1943.

McLaughlin, Robert L., and Sally E. Parry. *We'll Always Have the Movies: American Cinema during World War II.* Lexington: University Press of Kentucky, 2006.

McNeil, Bill. *Voices of a War Remembered: An Oral History of Canadians in World War II.* Toronto: Doubleday Canada, 1991.

Mitchell, Brian R. *International Historical Statistics.* New York: Macmillan, 1992.

Morgan, Lorne Thompson. *The Permanent War, or, Homo the Sap.* Toronto: Workers' Educational Association, 1944.

Morris, Peter. *Embattled Shadows: A History of Canadian Cinema, 1895-1939.* Montreal and Kingston: McGill-Queen's University Press, 1992.

Norrie, Kenneth, and Douglas Owram. *A History of the Canadian Economy.* Toronto: Harcourt Brace, 1991.

Ostry, Aleck Samuel. *Nutrition Policy in Canada, 1870-1939.* Vancouver: UBC Press, 2006.

Overy, R.J. *War and Economy in the Third Reich.* Oxford: Clarendon Press, 1994.

Parr, Joy. *Domestic Goods: The Material, the Moral and the Economic in the Postwar Years.* Toronto: University of Toronto Press, 1999.

Peate, Mary. *Girl in a Sloppy Joe Sweater: Life on the Canadian Home Front during World War Two.* Montreal: Optimum International, 1989.

Peiss, Kathy. "Making Up, Making Over: Cosmetics, Consumer Culture, and Women's Identity." In *The Sex of Things: Gender and Consumption in Historical Perspective,* ed. Victoria de Grazia and Ellen Furlough, 311-36. Berkeley: University of California Press, 1996.

Pierson, Ruth Roach. *"They're Still Women after All": The Second World War and Canadian Womanhood.* Toronto: McClelland and Stewart, 1986.

Prince, Stephen. *Classical Film Violence: Designing and Regulating Brutality in Hollywood Cinema, 1930-1968.* New Brunswick, NJ: Rutgers University Press, 2003.

Rittenhouse, Jonathan. "'Our Granada': The Granada Theatre, Wellington Street, Sherbrooke, Quebec, Canada, America, the World and Me." *Theatre Research in Canada* 18, 2 (1997): n.p.

Robertson, Heather. *Driving Force: The McLaughlin Family and the Age of the Car.* Toronto: McClelland and Stewart, 1995.

Robinson, Daniel J. *The Measure of Democracy: Polling, Market Research, and Public Life, 1930-1945.* Toronto: University of Toronto Press, 1999.

Roelens-Grant, Janine, ed. *Fighting for Home and Country: Women Remember World War II.* Guelph: Federated Women's Institutes of Ontario, 2004.

Ross, J. Andrew. "Hockey Capital: Commerce, Culture, and the National Hockey League, 1917-1967." PhD diss., University of Western Ontario, 2008.

–. "The Paradox of Conn Smythe: Hockey, Memory, and the Second World War." *Sport History Review* 37 (May 2006): 19-35.

Rubin, Jay L. "The Wet War: American Liquor Control, 1941-1945." In *Alcohol, Reform and Society: The Liquor Issue in Social Context,* ed. Jack S. Blocker Jr., 235-58. Westport: Greenwood Press, 1979.

Ruffili, Dean. "The Car in Canadian Culture: 1898-1983." PhD diss., University of Western Ontario, 2006.

Saunders, Stanley Alexander, and Eleanor Back. *Come On, Canada!* Toronto: Ryerson Press, 1941.
Scanlon, Jennifer, ed. *The Gender and Consumer Culture Reader.* New York: New York University Press, 2000.
Schull, Joseph. *The Great Scot: A Biography of Donald Gordon.* Montreal and Kingston: McGill-Queen's University Press, 1979.
Schmidt, Rene. *Canadian Disasters.* Toronto: Scholastic, 2006.
Scott, F.R. *The Eye of the Needle: Satire, Sorties, Sundries.* Montreal: Contact Press, 1957.
Sklar, Robert. *Movie-Made America: A Cultural History of American Movies.* Rev. ed. New York: Vintage Books, 1994.
Slater, David W., and R.B. Bryce. *War Finance and Reconstruction: The Role of Canada's Department of Finance, 1939-1946.* Ottawa: D.W. Slater, 1995.
Spence, E.J. "Wartime Price Control Policy in Canada." PhD diss., Northwestern University, 1947.
Stacey, C.P. *Arms, Men and Governments: The War Policies of Canada, 1939-1945.* Ottawa: Queen's Printer, 1970.
–. *Six Years of War: The Army in Canada, Britain, and the Pacific.* Ottawa: Queen's Printer, 1955.
Stephen, Jennifer Anne. *Pick One Intelligent Girl: Employability, Domesticity and the Gendering of Canada's Welfare State, 1939-1947.* Studies in Gender and History. Toronto: University of Toronto Press, 2007.
Stephenson, Harold Edward, and Carlton McNaught. *The Story of Advertising in Canada: A Chronicle of Fifty Years.* Toronto: Ryerson Press, 1940.
Strasser, Susan. *Satisfaction Guaranteed: The Making of the American Mass Market.* New York: Pantheon Books, 1989.
Terkel, Studs. *"The Good War": An Oral History of World War II.* New York: New Press, 1984.
Tooze, Adam. *The Wages of Destruction: The Making and Breaking of the Nazi Economy.* New York: Penguin, 2007.
Tremblay, Yves. "La consommation bridée: Contrôle des prix et rationnement durant la Deuxième Guerre mondiale." *Revue d'histoire de l'Amérique française* 58, 4 (2005): 569-607.
United States Strategic Bombing Survey. *The Effects of Strategic Bombing on the German War Economy.* Washington, DC: Government Printing Office, 1945.
Urquhart, M.C., and K.A.H. Buckley, eds. *Historical Statistics of Canada.* Cambridge: Cambridge University Press, 1965.
Vance, Jonathan. *Building Canada: People and Projects That Shaped the Nation.* Toronto: Penguin, 2006.
Vipond, Mary. *Listening In: The First Decade of Canadian Broadcasting, 1922-1932.* Montreal and Kingston: McGill-Queen's University Press, 1992.
Waddell, Christopher. "The Wartime Prices and Trade Board: Price Control in Canada in World War Two." PhD diss., York University, 1981.
Walden, Keith. "Speaking Modern: Language, Culture, and Hegemony in Grocery Window Displays, 1887-1920." *Canadian Historical Review* 70, 3 (1989): 285-310.
White, Richard. *Making Cars in Canada: A Brief History of the Canadian Automotive Industry, 1900-1980.* Ottawa: Canadian Science and Technology Museum, 2007.
Williams, Raymond. "Advertising: The Magic System." In Raymond Williams, *Problems in Materialism and Culture: Selected Essays,* 170-95. London: Verso, 1980.

Williamson, Mary F., and Tom Sharp, eds. *Just a Larger Family: Letters of Marie Williamson from the Canadian Home Front, 1940-1944*. Waterloo: Wilfrid Laurier University Press, 2011.

Young, Walter D. *The Anatomy of a Party: The National CCF, 1932-1961*. Toronto: University of Toronto Press, 1969.

Zakuta, Leo. *A Protest Movement Becalmed: A Study of Change in the CCF*. Canadian Studies in Sociology. Toronto: University of Toronto Press, 1964.

Zweiniger-Bargielowska, Ina. *Austerity in Britain: Rationing, Controls, and Consumption, 1939-1955*. London: Oxford University Press, 2002.

Index

Note: "(i)" after a page number indicates an illustration; "(t)" after a page number indicates a table. "CCF" stands for Co-operative Commonwealth Federation; "WPTB," for Wartime Prices and Trade Board; "WRAC," for Women's Regional Advisory Committee. Government departments are alphabetized by departmental name (e.g., Munitions and Supply, Department of). The eight photographs in the plate section have been identified by their order; for example, "PL1" refers to "plate no. 1."

Abbott and Costello, 173
Abe Lincoln in Illinois (film), 165
Ackery, Ivan, 173
Adams, John, 113
Advertiser's Weekly (UK), 81
advertising: and championing of progress/modern consumer lifestyle, 50-63; clichés used in, 89-124, 188-90; criticisms of, 58, 59, 78-79, 82, 85; and democratic values/free enterprise, 14, 54-59, 72-73, 78, 81-82, 85, 87, 89, 102-3, 106, 108-14, 122, 124, 188, 190-91; as economic driver, 56-57; vs editorial content, 51; efficacy of, 59; false claims in, 58-59; of "finer things" in life, 59-60, 106, 108, 122; of gifts for service personnel, 66, 67(i), 69, 95-96, 97(i), 99; in magazines/newspapers, 50-52; mundane preoccupations of, 58, 60-61, 87, 90-91, 100-1; and patriotic consumerism, 89; and postwar future, 114-24; as propaganda, 14, 77-78; on radio, 50, 53, 54, 57, 73-74, 89; to rural population, 52-54; as "salesmanship in print," 61-62; ubiquitous nature of, 50-54; and wartime consumer culture, 71-87; wartime regulation of/restrictions on, 79-82; to women, 56, 57-58, 60-61, 62, 85, 89, 99-103. *See also* entries immediately below; clichés, advertising; institutional advertising, *and entry following*
advertising, institutional. *See* institutional advertising, *and entry following*
advertising agencies, 54, 56, 72-73, 88, 222*n*24; American, 54, 62, 76, 112; British, 81; commercial/government work done by, 70; number of, 54, 222*n*24. *See also* adworkers, Canadian; adworkers, US
advertising of early war years (1939-late 1941), 14, 49, 50-70; absence of "war copy" in 64, 65(i), 66; and "business as usual" message, 4-6, 63-70, 72, 233*n*47; and championing of progress/modern consumer lifestyle, 50-63; early war themes in, 66, 67(i); ethics of, 68-69; vs government regulatory measures, 66, 68; linage of, 51, 63, 72; serious tone of, 61-62; uniformed figures in, 66. *See also* consumerism of early war years (1939–late 1941)
advertising of later war years (late 1941-45), 71-124; and ban on alcohol ads, 59, 80, 93, 110, 161-63; and "business as usual" message, 6, 70, 71-72, 76, 87, 99; clichés used in, 89-124, 188-90; contradictory messages of, 2, 7-8, 14,

255

26-27, 74-76; eventual optimism of, 82-87; by government, 73-74; institutional, 77-78, 80, 83, 84-85, 112-13; and life on home front, 69-70; linage of, 72, 81, 83-85, 83(t), 84(t); of luxury goods, 2, 68-69, 95-96, 97(i), 99; and need for sacrifice/reduced spending, 1-2, 7, 74-79; in post-Pearl Harbor era, 71-87; regulation of/restrictions on, 79-82; and suspended auto/consumer durables production, 69, 72-74; for Victory Bonds, 69-70, 76, 78, 95, 95(i), 99, 123(i), 124; for victory/prosperous future, 88-124; war themes in, 69, 119, 122. *See also* adworkers, Canadian; adworkers, US; clichés, advertising; consumerism of later war years (late 1941-45); institutional advertising, *and entry following*

adworkers, Canadian, 11, 14, 50-70, 88; and "adworker" term, 221; agencies of, 54, 56, 70, 72-73, 88, 222*n*24; and American counterparts, 62-63, 76, 112-13, 224*n*66, 226*n*19, 229*n*53; and Canadian identity, 112-13; as champions of progress/modern consumer lifestyle, 50-63; as consumers, 12; and free enterprise, 14, 55, 57-59, 72-73, 78, 85, 87, 106, 108, 122, 124; and institutional advertising, 77-78; and need for sacrifice/reduced spending, 76-79; and promise of prosperous future, 114-24; and wartime gender roles, 99-106

adworkers, US, 62-63, 76; and ad agencies, 54, 62, 76, 112; and "American dream/way of life," 112-13; clichés used by, 89-90, 112-13, 229*n*53; as following Canadian examples, 224*n*66, 226*n*19, 229*n*53; restrictions on, 81

Agricultural Press Association (APA), 53

Agriculture, Department of, 37-38

alcohol advertising, ban on, 59, 80, 161; and industry ads, 93, 94(i), 110, 119, 120(i), 162-63, 238*n*11

alcohol sale/consumption, control of, 158-63, 165, 199, 238*n*11, 239*n*18; and ban on ads, 59, 80, 161; industry's counterattack on, 93, 94(i), 162-63,

238*n*11; King's speech on, 159-61, 162; labour's campaign against, 163; by provinces, 7, 35, 159, 161, 162; and retail sales, 162, 198(t), 199; and shopping pandemonium, 162; as unsuccessful policy, 161(t), 161-63, 199; War Measures Act and, 158, 159; WRACs and, 159

All Quiet on the Western Front (film), 167-68

American Caterpillar Diesel, ad for, 110-11

Anaconda American Brass, ads for, 93, 105-6, 107(i)

Andy (dog with ration card), 41, 219*n*10

appliances, 1, 6, 51, 90, 147-51, 152; advertising of, 13, 70, 73, 108, 115, 116(i), 153(i); and female emancipation, 61, 148; household ownership of, 147-48, 148(t); as "pleasures of freedom," 123(i), 124; production of, 6, 148-50, 149(t), 150(t); of promised postwar future, 115-16, 116(i); repair of, 150; retail sales of, 72, 148-49, 150, 193, 198(t), 199, 200(t), 203; suspended production of, 72, 134-35, 154, 197; as symbols of prosperity, 155. *See also* consumer durables, *and entry following*; *specific appliances*

As a Matter of Fact (WPTB Consumer Branch radio program), 34

Atkins, John, 80, 82

Atlantic Charter, 184, 188, 190

automobile dealers/dealerships, 129, 131, 133-34, 136-39; closure of, 139; government support of, 136-37; and loss of mechanics to military, 139; regulations/paperwork faced by, 138; repairs done by, 138-39, 150; and reserve pool of cars, 6, 136-37; retail sales by, 134, 198(t), 199; used cars sold by, 137-38, 139

automobiles, 6, 125-47; advertising of, 59, 65(i), 69, 72, 127, 131-32, 134; as desirable consumer objects, 51, 61, 127, 129, 131, 154-55; economic influence of, 128-29; export of, 126, 129, 230*n*8; futuristic, 117(i); maintenance needs of, 139; ownership of, 53, 127-28, 128(t),

138, 139-40, 144, 147, 154, 231*n*15; retail sales of, 126-27, 128(t), 129-31, 132-33, 134, 137, 155, 193, 232*n*34; and road/highway construction, 128; tax on, 131, 132-33. *See also entries below;* trucks, *and entry following*
automobiles, suspended production of: pl.6, 6, 14-15, 72, 82, 135-40, 154, 234*n*59; auto dealers and, 136-39; end of, 154; gas stations/garages and, 136, 139; gasoline rationing and, 140-46, 154; metal/rubber shortages and, 133, 134-35, 141; as preceded by curtailment policies, 132-34; and reserve pool of cars, 6, 136-37; tire shortages and, 140-42, 144, 146-47; US-Canadian economic agreement and, 133, 135-36; US war situation and, 134-35. *See also* gasoline rationing; tires, *and entry following*
automotive industry, 126-27; as dependent on US investment/materials, 126-27, 130, 132-36; government regulation of, 132-40; importance of, 128-29, 131; institutional advertising by, 108-14; and military production, 108, 109(i), 110, 129, 132, 133-34, 135-36, 137; overseas, 127-28, 130. *See also specific companies*
Axis powers, 19, 28, 77, 89; ad industry and, 54-59, 85, 87, 99, 106, 108-14, 122, 190-91, 195; as depicted in films, 179; occupation by, 99. *See also* Germany, Nazi; Hitler, Adolf; Japanese, as Pacific War enemies; Pearl Harbor, Japanese attack on

Bangarth, Stephanie: *Voices Raised in Protest*, 2
Bank of Canada, 5, 28, 205-6
Bannerman, Glen, 73-74
Bataan (film), 178, 179
Battle of Britain, 5, 24, 64
Battle of Mons (First World War), 70
Battle of the Bulge, 185
beer, 35, 93; government controls on, 158-63, 199, 239*n*18; increased consumption of, 158, 161(t), 161-62, 163; labour's campaign for, 163; vs meat/butter, 159; rationing of, 35, 93, 161. *See also entries below*
beer industry/breweries: anti-temperance ads by, 93, 94(i), 162-63, 238*n*11; postwar future advertising by, 118(i)
beer parlours, 158, 159, 163
Bennett, R.B., 22, 52, 128, 188
Berry, John (motor vehicle controller), 6, 132, 133, 135, 136-37, 139, 233*n*45
Beveridge, Sir William, 185
bicycles, use of, 146-47
big ticket items. *See* automobiles, *and entry following;* consumer durables, *and entry following*
Birney, Earle: "For Steve," 182, 183
Blachford Shoes, ads for, 103
Black, Spalding, 63
black market activity, 35; in gasoline/tires, 42, 142-43, 144, 147; in meat, 37, 41; Washington office set up to monitor, 39-40
Bliss, Michael, 3
"blue books," for price-ceiling monitoring, 33, 47
Bolster, Bob, 41
Bon Ami household cleaner, ad for, 99
bonds. *See* Victory Bonds, *and entry following;* War Savings Certificates
Bookseller and Stationer, 22
Bothwell, Robert, 5
Bourassa, Clarence, 158
Bradette, Joseph, 80
Britain. *See* United Kingdom
British Commonwealth Air Training Plan (BCATP), 170, 244*n*4
Broadfoot, Barry: *Six War Years,* 21, 137, 217*n*71
Brown, Maurice, 73
Bryson's Drug Store (Montreal), pl.8
burlesque shows, 158
buses, 126, 128; and gasoline rationing, 140, 146; increased use of, 146; retail sales of, 129
Bush, Jack: Ford ad illustrations by, 109(i), 112
"business as usual" message: during early war years, 4-6, 63-70, 72, 233*n*47;

as evolving with advertising, 71-87, 99; after Pearl Harbor, 6, 70, 71-72, 76
Business Week, 76
butter rationing, 7, 35, 36-37; anonymous poet on, 16; vs available beer, 159; consumer demand for, 36-37; enforcement of, 41; and hoarding, 36, 42; King on, 6, 196; medical exemptions from, 40; promised end to, 119, 121(i), 123(i); WRACs and, 36, 218*n*80
"buy British"/"buy Canadian" campaigns, of early war years, 5, 7, 24-25, 26, 31, 49

Cain, James M.: *Double Indemnity*, 177
Campana's Italian Balm, ad for, 96, 98(i)
Campbell, Wallace, 112
Canada at War (NFB documentary), 240*n*47
Canadian Advertising, 58-59, 62, 63, 73, 76, 77, 81, 84, 227*n*44; Sanders article in, 79-80
Canadian Association of Advertisers, 73
Canadian Association of Broadcasters, 73
Canadian Automotive Trade, 6, 131, 133, 137, 139, 233*n*43, 233*n*47
Canadian Breweries Limited: "An Alternative Speech on Temperance," 162-63
Canadian Broadcasting Corporation. *See* CBC Radio
Canadian Club, 5
Canadian Congress of Labour, 184
Canadian Council on Nutrition, 45
Canadian Countryman, 53
Canadian Dietary Standard, 45
Canadian Film Weekly, 176, 177, 180
Canadian Forum, 58, 59, 71, 78, 182; Victory Bonds poster in, 95(i); on wartime movies, 179
Canadian General Electric: ads for, 106, 116
Canadian Geographical Journal, 125
Canadian Home Journal: Pepsi-Cola ad in, 98(i); "To Market!" ad for, 85, 86(i), 196
Canadian Homes and Gardens, 51; Anaconda ad in, 105-6, 107(i); GM "Mosquito" ad in, 110, 111(i); home-decorating articles in, 152; Labatt's ad in, 93, 94(i); White Label Ale ad in, 118(i)
Canadian Industries Limited, 62, 63
Canadian Institute of Public Opinion, 12, 183, 186-87, 208
Canadian Journal of Economics and Political Science, 71
Canadian Manufacturers' Association, 191
Canadian Moving Picture Digest, 156, 163, 179, 182. *See also* Lewis, Ray
Canadian Pacific Railway, ad for, 113
Canadian Printer and Publisher, 50, 51, 58, 88
Canadian Women's Army Corps, members of (CWACs): in cosmetics ads, 103
Canadian Woodworker, 151
capitalism. *See* free enterprise
Capitol Theatre (Halifax), 172
Capitol Theatre (Moncton, NB), 171
Capitol Theatre (Ottawa), PL7
Cartier, George-Étienne, 113
Catholic Women's League, 19
CBC Radio: Gordon's speech on, 30-31; King's speeches on, 6, 28, 159-61; Massey's speech on, 26; nutritional announcement on, 44; WPTB Consumer Branch programs on, 34. *See also* radio
Chamberlin, William Henry, 23-24
Chatelaine, 24; early wartime advertising in, 51; four-page auto buying guide in, 131; "Purchasing Agent" ad for, 17, 18(i), 100; Sanders as editor of, 16-17, 25, 31, 32, 64, 79; "shopping to win the war" issue of, 5, 24-25; Tangee Cosmetics ads in, 102-3, 104(i); on women as "soldiers in aprons," 100
A Child Is Born (film), 167
Chrysler Corporation of Canada, 127
Churchill, Winston, 20, 113, 114, 245*n*9; and Atlantic Charter, 184, 188
civilian men/farmers, as soldiers (advertising cliché), 103-6; in Anaconda ad, 105-6, 107(i); in Canadian General Electric ad, 106; in Green Giant ad, 105; in International Harvester ads, 105,

106; in life insurance ad, 103-4; in Ontario Farm Service Force ad, 105; in Perfect Circle Piston Rings ad, 106; in Vitalis ad, 104
civilians, 10-12; patriotic consumerism of, 100, 103-6; wartime contributions of, 99-100, 103-6, 107(i), 108
clichés, advertising, 89-124; civilian men/farmers as soldiers, 103-6, 107(i); clenched fist, 93; direct addresses to enemy, 110-11, 111(i); "fifth freedom," 122-24, 190; free enterprise, 106, 108-14, 122-24, 188-90; "misguided friend," 90-95, 99, 108, 124, 188-90; "now more than ever," 95-99; promise of "tomorrow," 114-19, 120(i), 121(i); in US ads, 89-90, 112-13, 229*n*53; women as soldiers, 97, 99-101, 102(i), 103. *See also* free enterprise; *specific advertising clichés*
clothing: restrictions on, 29, 203-4; shortages of, 36, 218*n*78
Clothing Administration (WPTB), 203-4
coal-burning stoves, 150, 150(t)
Cockfield, Brown (ad agency), 73, 112
coffee rationing, 7, 35, 38, 41, 93; elimination of, 38; and hoarding, 42; promised end to, 119, 121(i), 123(i)
Colgate, ads for, 60, 102(i)
Colman, Ronald, 175
Combined Food Board, 37, 43, 220*m*120
Commerce Journal (University of Toronto), 57
Committee on Demobilization and Re-establishment, 185
Committee on Reconstruction, 183, 185; and Marsh Report, 185-86
Committee on Special Rations, 40
consumer boom, wartime, PL8, 12-13, 193-95, 196-209; as compared to experiences elsewhere, 204-5; despite shortages, 83, 196-97, 199, 200-1, 202, 203-4, 206, 209; and inflation, 205-9; and myth of "penurious patriotism," 2, 3-4, 12-14, 20-21, 26-27, 130, 149, 155, 193-94, 196, 209. *See also entry below*; consumer culture, of wartime Canada; inflation; "penurious patriotism," myth of

consumer boom, wartime, statistics on: consumer spending, 197(t), 197, 199, 203; consumer spending as percentage of disposable income, 202(t), 202-3; department store inventories, 203-4; department store sales, 199, 200(t); monthly cost-of-living index, 205-6, 206(t); per capita consumer spending/retail sales, 199-202, 201(t); and resident population, 199-200; retail sales by category, 198(t), 199. *See also* retail sales
Consumer Branch (WPTB), PL4, 32-43, 47-49; CBC Radio programs of, 34; *Consumer's News* bulletin of, 1, 34, 41-42; and coupon rationing, 34-43; as liaison between WPTB and WRACs, 12, 32, 33, 36, 39, 46, 47, 48, 192; origins of, 32, 217*n*61; and price-ceiling enforcement, 30-31, 33-34, 46-48, 207, 217*n*67; propaganda plays by, 42-43, 208; Sanders as director of, PL4, 16, 19-20, 32-33, 46, 47-48, 49, 100; surveys by, 12, 207-9; volunteer force of, 32-33; and WPTB regulations, 33-34; WRACs in, 32-49, 159. *See also* price ceiling; Sanders, Byrne Hope; Women's Regional Advisory Committees
consumer credit, restrictions on, 6, 29, 152, 153-54, 216*n*50
consumer culture, of wartime Canada, 1-15, 193-95; adworkers and, 50-70; American influence on, 8-9; automobiles/big ticket items in, 14-15, 125-55; and concept of "consumerism," 2-3, 8-12, 211*n*5; as consumer boom, PL8, 12-13, 193-95, 196-209; early "business as usual" approach to, 4-6, 63-70, 72, 233*n*47; as economic driver, 9-10, 56-57; film industry and, 15, 156-57, 163-81; importance of studying, 8-10; leisure and, 15, 156-81; and myth of "penurious patriotism," 2, 3-4, 12-14, 20-21, 26-27, 130, 149, 155, 193-94, 196-97, 209; as patriotic, 4, 7-8, 12-13, 16-49, 89, 100-6, 194-97; place of advertising in, 71-87; temperance movement and, 158-63; and victory/prosperous future, 14, 15, 88-124; women and, PL3, 14, 16-49,

212n7. *See also specific topics;* consumerism, *and entries following*
consumer durables, 6, 147-52, 154-55; advertising of, 13, 70, 73, 108, 153(i); ban on design changes in, 23, 132, 151, 232n40; continued production of, 150, 150(t), 151-52; curtailed production of, 133-34; furniture as, 151(t), 151-52, 153(i); household ownership of, 147-48, 148(t); jewellery compared to, 152-54; as "pleasures of freedom," 123(i), 124; of promised postwar future, 115-16, 116(i); as rarely advertised on radio, 73; retail sales of, 7, 14-15, 150, 150(t), 193, 197(t), 199; retailers' adaptation to restrictions on, 150-52; suspended production of, 6, 7, 14-15, 69, 72-74, 83, 149-52, 193-94, 196, 201, 203; wood and, 150, 150(t), 151-52, 154. *See also entry below;* appliances; automobiles; *specific appliances*
consumer durables, suspended production of, 6, 7, 14-15, 69, 72-74, 83, 149-52, 193-94, 196, 197, 201, 203; consumer support for, 150-51; end of, 154; metal shortages and, 134-35, 150-52
Consumer Price Index (CPI), 205-6, 206(t)
Consumer's News (WPTB Consumer Branch), 1, 34, 41-42
consumerism, 2-3; competing views of, 8; and definition of "consumer," 212n7; as ideology, 193-95; propriety of, 8; study of, 8-12; as term, 211n5
consumerism, patriotic. *See* patriotic consumerism
consumerism of early war years (1939–late 1941), 14, 50-70; and "business as usual," 4-6, 63-70, 72, 233n47; and "buy British"/"buy Canadian" campaigns, 5, 7, 24-25, 26, 31, 49; and "phony war," 4-5, 22, 31, 64, 66, 215n17. *See also* advertising of early war years (1939–late 1941)
consumerism of later war years (late 1941-45), 6-8, 14-15, 71-124; appliances/consumer durables and, 6, 147-52, 154-55; automobiles and, 6, 14-15, 72, 125-47; and "business as usual" message, 6, 70, 71-72, 76, 87, 99; and consumer credit restrictions, 6, 29, 152, 153-54, 216n50; contradictory messages of, 2, 7-8, 14, 26-27, 74-76, 194; and control of alcohol sale/consumption, 7, 93, 158-63; and coupon rationing, 7, 34-43; criticism of, 78-79; and need for sacrifice/reduced spending, 1-2, 7, 74-79; and security of war, 21-22, 184-85; and wage/price controls, 6, 27-31. *See also* advertising of later war years (late 1941-45)
Co-operative Commonwealth Federation (CCF), 59, 82, 131-32; election victories of, 187; as equated with totalitarianism, 190-91; manifesto of, 187-88, 191
Corvette K-225 (film), 177
cosmetics, 2, 9; ads for, 101-3, 104(i); wartime branding of, 103
Cost-of-Living Index (DBS), 206-7
Cottrelle, George, 144, 236n110
coupon rationing, PL2, 7, 21, 34-43, 49, 193; and black-market activity, 35, 37, 39-40, 41, 42, 142-43, 144, 147; cards for, 34, 41, 219n110, 244n4; consumer support for, 13, 35-37, 43; and coupon trading, 39, 41, 42; enforcement of, 39, 41-42; and equitable distribution, 35, 36-37; and failed honour system, 218n76; and food production/availability, 43-44; and hoarding, 35, 36, 39, 42-43, 161; as inevitable sequel to price ceiling, 35, 71-72; as not affecting retail sales, 13, 83, 99, 193-94, 199, 201-2; and nutrition, 40, 44-46; promised end to, 119, 121(i), 123(i); and reduced consumption of scarce goods, 35; requests for exemption from, 39, 40; and shortages, 35-37, 40-41, 42, 43, 45, 46; in UK, 35, 38, 204; violations of, 35-36, 41-42, 43; Washington office set up to monitor, 39-40; WRACs and, 36-37, 39, 40, 218n80. *See also specific food and consumer items*
Criminal Code, 58
Cry "Havoc" (film), 178
Curtis, Alan, 178
Cutex nail polish, 103

D-Day, 168, 183, 193
Dalhousie Review, 59
DeMille, Cecil B., 165
democracy/political freedom: advertising and, 14, 54-59, 78, 81-82, 85, 87, 89, 102-3, 106, 108-14, 122-24, 188, 190-91; consumerism/consumer choice and, 7-8, 81-82, 102-3, 122-4, 188, 190-91, 193-95, 213*n*24; inflation vs, 29; socialism/social welfare as threat to, 185-92, 195. *See also* free enterprise
department stores, PL3, 194; amenities of, 19; decreasing inventories at, 203-4; furniture sales at, 151-52, 153(i); installment plans at, 216*n*50; and sales by department, 199, 200(t); and suspended appliance production, 14-15, 72
departments, government. *See entries for names of specific departments*
Depression. *See* Great Depression
Desert Victory (film), 177
DeSoto Motor Car Company: ad for, 65(i); Canadian closure of, 127
Dieppe Raid, 78
Dionne quintuplets, 167; as Colgate "soldiers," 102(i)
Disney, Walt, 167
disposable incomes, rise in, 30, 73; spending as percentage of, 202(t), 202-3
Division of Simplified Practice (WPTB), 81
Dominion Bureau of Statistics (DBS), 10, 48; on alcohol consumption, 161(t); on auto ownership, 127; and Cost-of-Living Index, 206-7; on department store sales, 200(t); on durable commodities ownership, 148(t); on movie-going, 169-71, 171(t), 240*n*54; price indexes of, 194; on production of electrical appliances, 149(t); on production of stoves, 150(t); on production value of household furnishings, 151(t); on retail sales, 198(t)
Dominion Income Tax Department, 68
Dominion Oilcloth and Linoleum Company, ads for, 115, 188, 189(i), 190
Dominion Rubber Company, ad for, 110
Donnell, Effie, 41

Doolittle Raid (US air raid on Japan), 178
Double Indemnity (film), 177
Douglas, Tommy, 187
Drew, George, 187
Drug Merchandising, 188
Durflinger, Serge: *Fighting from Home*, 2

East York Township (Toronto), dietary study in, 45
Eastman, Morgan, 80-81
Eaton's department store, PL3, 72, 194, 199; ad for big ticket items from, 152, 153(i)
E.B. Eddy Company, ad for, 190, 243*n*25
Echoes (IODE magazine), 24
Elliott, T.R., 125
Empress Theatre (Montreal), 172

Fahrni, Magda, 192, 209
Family Allowance Act, 192
Family Herald and Weekly Star, 53, 221*n*5
Famous Players movie theatre chain, 166, 169
Farm Service Force (Ontario), 105
Farmer's Advocate, 53
farmers/farm families, 52-54; and gasoline pump closures, 134; and meat/butter rationing, 41; newspapers of, 53, 221*n*5; and postwar prosperity, 117, 119; and price ceiling, 33, 47; and rural electrification, 53, 147-48; as shown in ads, 105, 113, 117, 119; and suspended auto production, 139; as untapped advertising market, 53-54; wartime contributions of, 105, 136
Fathers of Confederation, 113-14
Federated Women's Institutes, 5, 19, 39, 44, 49
Federation of Automobile Dealers Associations, 139
"fifth freedom" (advertising cliché), 122-24, 190; in E.B. Eddy ad, 190; in Rapid Grip and Batten ad, 123(i), 124
film industry. *See* motion picture industry
film noir, 177-78, 180
Finance, Department of, 27-28, 33
Financial Post: on free enterprise, 191; Howe and, 68; on urbanization, 53

Findlay stoves, ad for, 108
Finkel, Alvin, 188
First World War, 7, 23, 55, 72, 126; advertising of, 63, 76-77, 89; consumer panic of, 63; disillusionment following, 14, 184; inflation of/following, 4-5, 8, 20, 22, 29, 42-43, 193; poetry of, 70; profiteering during, 77, 108; temperance movement/measures of, 158-59, 160, 162; veterans of, 21, 106
Fish, Kathlyn, 162
food: canning/gardening efforts and, 39, 219*n*96, 220*n*118; as exported to UK/Europe, 16, 43, 193; and nutrition, 40, 44-46, 49, 90-91, 96-97, 100; production/availability of, 43-44; rationing of, 34-43. *See also* coupon rationing; *specific food items rationed*
Ford, Henry, 59
Ford Motor Company of Canada, 127; ads for, 108, 109(i), 112
Forsey, Harriet Roberts, 182
49th Parallel (film), 166
Foster, Lillian, 50
Fox, Frank W.: *Madison Avenue Goes to War*, 84, 112, 223*n*45
France: D-Day landing in, 168, 183, 193; fall of, 5, 12, 22, 27, 130-31, 132
Frankfurt School, 58
Franklin, Benjamin, 113
free enterprise: ad industry's championing of, 14, 54-59, 72-73, 78, 85, 87, 106, 108-14, 122, 124, 188, 190-91; black market activity as, 142-43; as ensuring Allied victory, 106-12; as justification for war, 7-8, 71-87; New Deal as threat to, 58-59, 190; socialism/social welfare as threat to, 185-92, 195; and stigma of profiteering, 64, 74, 76, 77, 108; as term preferred to "capitalism," 106. *See also* democracy/political freedom
Frigidaire, ads for, 70
furniture/home decorating items, 51, 151(t), 151-52, 153(i); retail sales of, 198(t)
future, postwar, 183-95; advertising geared toward, 114-24; appliances of, 115-16, 116(i); and consumer prosperity, 14, 15, 88-124; and defence of free enterprise, 59, 88, 106, 108-14, 122, 124, 185-92, 195; inflation and, 48, 192; polls on, 154-55, 183, 186-87, 208; and rise of socialism, 187-88, 190-91; and social welfare state, 59, 88, 183-92, 195; WPTB concerns over, 192, 193. *See also* social security, *and entries following*

Galbraith, John Kenneth, 205
Garrett, Paul, 71
gas stations/garages, 129; and gasoline rationing, 140, 142-44, 146, 236*n*110; retail sales at, 198(t), 199; and suspended auto production, 136, 139
gas stoves, 148(t), 149, 150, 150(t)
gasoline conservation campaign, 134
gasoline rationing, 7, 47, 125, 135, 140-46, 154, 199; and bicycle use, 146-47; and black market activity, 42, 142-43, 144, 147; and decline in driving/traffic offences, 146-47; editorial cartoons/humour on, 144-45, 145(i), 146; gas stations and, 140, 142-44, 146, 236*n*110; and industry fraud allegations, 143-44; promised end to, 123(i); provincial governments and, 235*n*84; and public transit use, 146; taxis and, 140, 141; travelling salesmen and, 80; violations of, 42, 142-44, 146, 236*n*110
gasoline taxes, 128, 235*n*84
General Electric, 149. *See also* Canadian General Electric
General Motors Corporation, 59, 71, 113
General Motors of Canada, 101, 127, 146; patriotic ads of, 113-14; "Victory Is Our Business" slogan of, 108, 110, 111(i); "woman's place" ad of, 101
General Steel Wares, ad for, 115, 116(i)
Germany, Nazi: ad industry's war on, 85, 87, 106, 108-12; Allied victories against (1943-44), 82-83, 114, 193, 204; auto production/ownership in, 127-28, 130; and Battle of Britain, 5, 24, 64; and Battle of the Bulge, 185; and concept of "total war," 196; defeat of, 185, 208; deprivation in, 79; economic measures

taken by, 30, 204; film/movie theatre industry and, 167-68, 174, 177; and invasion of Soviet Union, 6, 22, 133; leaflet raids over, 63; and need for sacrifice/reduced spending in war on, 59, 79; offensives of (spring 1940), 5, 22, 215*n*17; and pre-war Weimar inflation, 8, 29; surrender of, 119. *See also* Hitler, Adolf

Globe and Mail: on appliances as emancipatory, 148; butter rationing poem in, 16; and gasoline rationing, 142-44; Joy Oil ad in, 143-44; Macphail's defence of farmers in, 134; Thompson column in, 78

Gone with the Wind (film), 175

Gooderham and Worts, ad for, 110

Goodyear Tires, ad for, 117(i)

Gordon, Donald, pl.1, 1, 79; character/reputation of, 28-29; resignation of, 192; and wage/price controls, 28-31, 47-48; on women as wartime consumers, 30-31, 32, 48, 49, 100; and WPTB Consumer Branch, 32, 47-48; and WPTB Simplified Practice Division, 81-82. *See also* Wartime Prices and Trade Board (WPTB)

Granada Theatre (Sherbrooke, QC), 171, 173

Granatstein, J.L., 3, 9, 184, 205

Great Depression, 3, 5, 15, 34; advertising and, 72-73, 77; auto industry and, 126-27, 129-30; consumer boom/prosperity after, 12-13, 21-22, 63, 68-69, 164, 193-95, 196-209; deflationary effect of, 27; and economic stimulus of war, 4, 21, 72-73; feared return of, 115-16, 183, 192; film industry and, 163-64, 165, 168; and increased urbanization, 52; "modern conveniences" of, 56, 147; movie theatres and, 163-64, 173; newspaper/magazine readership during, 51-52; poetry on, 182-83; radio boom during, 54; recollections of, 21, 34; rural electrification during, 147; Saskatchewan's recovery from, 43; Trans-Canada Highway as project of, 128; unemployment of, 21, 30, 55, 197; welfare policies of, 188, 190; women as household managers during, 17, 32

Great War. *See* First World War

Green Giant, ad for, 105

Greene, Graham: *The End of the Affair*, 15; *The Ministry of Fear*, 177

Grierson, John, 176

grocery stores: and food rationing/shortages, 36, 37-38, 40-41; wartime boom of, 43-44; retail sales at, 198(t); window displays of, 11

Gruen watches, ad for, 95-96, 97(i)

Guest, Edna, 44, 220*n*124

Gung Ho! (film), 178-79

Harden, Verna Loveday: "All Valiant Dust," 55

Hardware and Metal, 148

Hardwicke, Sir Cedric, 175

Heinz (H.J.) Company, ad for, 96-97

Helena Rubinstein cosmetics, ad for, 103

Hepburn, Mitchell, 187, 240*n*47

Heroic Stalingrad (film), 177

Heron, Craig, 159

Hitchcock, Alfred, 175, 177

Hitler, Adolf, 28, 29, 157, 182, 229*n*49; advertising/propaganda war against, 1-2, 7, 42-43, 88, 91-93, 110-11, 122; direct addresses to, 110-11; movies and war against, 164, 176; as shown in ads/propaganda, 1-2, 7, 74, 75(i). *See also* Germany, Nazi

hoarding: early discouragement of, 23; and inflation, 42-43; vs rationing, 35, 36, 39, 42-43, 161; as "sabotage," 42, 91, 92(i), 93

hockey, 158

Hong Kong, Battle of, 78

"Horse laugh" editorial cartoon (*Sudbury Star*), 144-45, 145(i)

horse and buggy, as alternative to automobile, 146

House of Representatives, US: Un-American Activities Committee of, 165

The Household Counsellor (WPTB Consumer Branch radio program), 34

Howe, C.D., 135, 140, 154; and *Financial Post*, 68

Hudson's Bay Company, 72, 152

Huston, John, 177
Hutchison, Bruce, 52
Hyde Park Declaration, 27, 133, 136

I Walked with a Zombie (film), 173
Ilsley, J.L., 20, 31, 186
Imperial Conference (1926), 165-66
Imperial Order Daughters of the Empire (IODE), 5, 44, 48, 49, 176
imported goods: ads for, 2; and big ticket items, 133, 141; and "buy British" campaign, 5, 7, 24-25, 26, 31, 49; and price ceiling, 29; rationing of, 35, 41
In Which We Serve (film), 177
income tax, 68, 93
inflation, 205-9; ads/propaganda designed to combat, 1-2, 7, 74, 75(i); cost-of-living figures and, 206-9; of/following First World War, 4-5, 20, 22, 193; food prices and, 44, 48; hoarding and, 42-43; and need for sacrifice/reduced spending, 1-2, 7, 74, 75(i), 77, 78; postwar, 48, 192; in pre-war Germany/Austria, 8, 29, 42-43; prices adjusted for, 21-22, 151-52, 171, 195, 196-205; retail sales and, 1-2, 13, 21-22, 66, 68, 74; in US, 205; wage/price controls and, 6, 27-28, 66, 192; women enlisted in war on, 19-20, 30-43; WPTB and war on, 19-20, 22-23, 27-31, 47-48, 72, 77, 99, 206-7
Innis, Harold, 57, 62
institutional advertising, 77-78, 83-85; by automotive industry, 108-14; Canadian and American, 112-13; on civilians as soldiers, 99-100, 105-6, 108; and direct addresses to enemy, 110-11, 111(i); and free enterprise message, 78, 106, 108-14, 188-90; historical allusions in, 112-13; *Maclean's* linage of, 84, 84(t); "misguided friends" in, 93-95, 108, 188-90; and postwar prosperity, 103, 114-19; vs temperance, 93, 94(i), 162-63, 238*n*11; WPTB's defence of, 80. *See also* clichés, advertising; free enterprise
institutional advertising, examples of: American Caterpillar Diesel, 110-11; Anaconda, 93, 105-6, 107(i); Canadian Breweries, 162-63; Canadian General Electric, 116; Canadian Pacific Railway, 113; Dominion Oilcloth, 115, 188, 189(i), 190; Dominion Rubber, 110; E.B. Eddy Co., 190, 243*n*25; Findlay stoves, 106; Ford, 108, 109(i), 112; General Motors, 108, 110, 111(i), 113-14; General Steel Wares, 115, 116(i); Gooderham and Worts, 110; Goodyear, 117(i); International Nickel, 113, 117, 119; Labatt's, 93, 94(i), 238*n*11; Northern Electric, 117; Rapid Grip and Batten, 123(i), 124; Sanforized, 119, 121(i); Seagram's, 110, 119, 120(i); Standard Sanitary, 103; Studebaker, 112; White Label Ale, 118(i)
International Harvester, ads for, 105, 106
International Nickel, ads for, 113, 117, 119
irons, 148, 149; production of, 149(t), 150

James, Cyril, 183, 185, 192
James, R. Warren, 205
Japanese, as Pacific War enemies, 178, 185; and attack on Pearl Harbor, 5, 31, 70, 130, 134, 142, 157, 245*n*9; deprivation of, 79; and impact on auto manufacturing, 130, 134-35, 142; as shown in movies, 178, 179; surrender of, 48, 154, 192
Jefferson, Thomas, 113
jewellery, 2, 13; industry magazine of, 1, 152, 154; luxury tax on, 152, 199; metal shortages and, 152-54; retail sales of, 152-54, 198(t), 199; as wartime gift, 95-96, 97(i), 152
Joy Oil Company, 143-44, 236*n*10

Kalman, Harold, 171-72
Keep 'Em Flying (film), 173
Keightley, B.W., 62
Kellogg's All-Bran, ads for, 88, 90-91
Keshen, Jeffrey: *Saints, Sinners, and Soldiers*, 2, 205
Kilbourn, F.B., 133
King, William Lyon Mackenzie: anti-inflation regulations/policies of, 6, 22-23, 28, 66, 68; on "choice between guns and butter," 6, 196, 199; and

conscription, 79; and control of alcohol sale/consumption, 80, 159-63, 239*n*14, 239*n*18; and Gordon, 28; in institutional ads, 113; on "limited liability" war, 4-5, 22, 63, 64, 66, 212*m*12; loss of seat by, 191; as moviegoer, 165, 167, 239*n*32; Scott's satirical poem on, 160; and social welfare state, 185-92; spiritualism of, 239*n*32; and wage/price controls, 28; and war expenditures, 9; and WPTB, 22-23
Kipling, Rudyard: "For All We Have and Are," 70
Kirkwood, John, 58, 59-60, 66, 68, 69, 70, 71, 73, 82, 184
Kodak, ad for, 96
Kotex sanitary napkins, ad for, 91

Labatt's, ads by, 93; and arguments against temperance, 93, 94(i), 238*m*11
Labour, Department of, 48
labour, organized: on cost-of-living figures, 48, 206-7; and possible prohibition, 160, 162, 163; and postwar society/social welfare state, 183-92; and US auto workers' strike, 154; and wage/price controls, 27-28, 30, 31, 93. *See also* social welfare state; socialism
Ladies' Home Journal, 52
Lake, Carrol A., 51
Lambton, Gunda: *Sun in Winter*, 180
Lang, Fritz, 177
Lassie Come Home (film): as favourite of King, 165, 167, 239*n*32
Laurier Palace Theatre (Montreal), fire at, 240*n*44
League of Social Reconstruction, 185-86
Legget, Robert, 50, 54, 89
Leigh, Vivien, 175
leisure activities, 15, 156-81; alcohol consumption, 158-63; film industry/movie-going, 156-57, 163-81; morality/propriety of, 156, 157-58; at nightclubs, 157-58; at restaurants, 156, 157; vacations, 2, 64, 156-57, 197, 238*m*1. *See also* alcohol sale/consumption, control of; film industry; movie theatres; movies
Lend-Lease (US war supply program), 27, 130; enactment of, 133

Lewis, Ray, 163-64, 168, 182; on "benevolent propaganda," 164, 166; and "escape thesis," 164-65, 168; on film as weapon against Nazism, 164, 165, 168; on war propaganda overkill, 176
Liberty, Canadian edition of, 24, 26, 52, 222*m*11
life insurance ads: on civilian men's efforts, 103-4; on women as soldiers, 100
Life Savers, comic-strip ads for, 66
Lifeboat (film), 177
Lifebuoy Soap, ad for, 60
"limited liability": of early war years, 4-5, 22, 64, 66; and later macro-economics, 186
Lincoln, Abraham, 113, 165
Linham, Dorothy, 103, 104(i), 228*n*30
liquor control boards, provincial, 7, 35, 161; austerity of, 159; shopping pandemonium at, 162
Loew, Marcus, 171
Lord's Day Act, 176
Louis Philippe lipstick, 103
Lower, Arthur, 183
Lugosi, Bela, 167
luxury goods: advertising of, 2, 68-69, 95-96, 97(i), 99; consumption of, 71; justification for, 68-69, 99, 165. *See also* jewellery
luxury tax, on jewellery, 152, 199
Lysol, ads for, 60, 97, 99; and "war on germs," 66, 101

MacDonald, Edward, 170
Macdonald, John A., 113
Mackenzie, Hugh, 29
Mackenzie, Ian, 185
Maclean, John Bayne, 68
Maclean Publishing Company (later Maclean-Hunter), 68, 138
Maclean-Hunter Publishing Company: polls by, 154-55
Maclean's, 4, 51, 52, 68, 221*n*5, 227*n*43; advertising linage in (1939-45), 72, 83-85, 83(t), 84(t); on auto industry's importance, 129, 131; automotive ads in, 72; and contempt of Howe, 68; and early absence of "war copy," 64, 65(i);

early war-themed ads in, 66, 67(i); Hitler ad in, 1-2, 7, 74, 75(i); on Montreal nightclub scene, 157-58

Maclean's, ads in (specific): American Caterpillar Diesel, 110-11; Campana's Balm, 98(i); Colgate toothpaste, 102(i); DeSoto ("Enjoy life!"), 65(i); Goodyear tires, 117(i); Gruen watches, 97(i); Mentholatum balm, 66; Modess, 102(i); Parker Pens, 66, 67(i); Sanforized washable fabrics, 92(i), 121(i); Seagram's, 120(i); War Savings Stamps (Hitler), 1-2, 7, 74, 75(i)

Macphail, Agnes, 134

MacQueen, Ken, 4, 7

magazines, 9, 50, 51-52, 53; and calls for sacrifice/reduced spending, 14, 25; Canadian and American, 24, 52, 63, 161; fashion advice in, 24-25, 203; and gasoline rationing/tire shortages, 42, 144-45; home-decorating articles in, 51, 152; sales of, 200(t); on women as household managers, 17, 19, 31-32, 41, 44. *See also entry below; specific magazines*

magazines, advertising in, 13, 50-51, 54, 60, 64, 89; alcohol, 161; automotive, 72, 131-32; contradictory messages of, 14; vs editorial content, 51; by government, 74, 84; and government's hard line on restraint, 1-2, 7, 74, 75(i), 76; institutional, 83-85, 112-14; spending on, 54; war-themed, 64, 119, 122; wartime linage of, 72, 82-85, 83-84(t); on women's roles, 17, 19

Magder, Ted, 166

The Maltese Falcon (film), 177

Manion, Robert, 22

Manitoba Censor Board, 167

The March of Time (NFB serial newsreel), 176

Marchand, Roland: *Advertising the American Dream*, 12, 54-55, 61-62, 89, 93

Marketing, 63, 81, 84, 88; Kirkwood's articles in, 58, 59-60, 66, 68, 69, 71, 73, 82, 184; Lydiatt's information in, 215n30; Spanish tourist story in, 60, 61; surveys by, 66, 72; and threat of socialism, 191; and war-themed advertising, 64, 76

Marketing, ads in (specific): for *Canadian Home Journal*, 85, 86(i), 196; for *Chatelaine*, 17, 18(i), 100; for Victory Bonds, 123(i), 124

Marsh, Leonard: *Report on Social Security for Canada*, 185-86

Martin, John, 190-91

Massey, Denton, 38, 156, 157, 219n93

Massey, Vincent, 26

Massey-Harris Company, 190

Mayfair, 51, 145

McCall's, 52

McEachern, Ronald A., 53, 191

McGee, Thomas D'Arcy, 113

McInnis, Peter S., 205

McKim Limited (ad agency), 56

McLaughlin, R. Samuel, 146

McNaught, Carlton, 88; as co-author of advertising history, 56

McNaughton, Andrew, 136

meat rationing, PL2, 7, 13, 35, 37-38, 193; vs available beer, 159; of beef and pork only, 37; and black market activity, 37, 39, 41; brief suspension of, 38; consumer demand for, 37; enforcement of, 41-42; and hoarding, 42; and nutrition, 45; and per-person allotment, 37-38; in postwar UK, 204; requests for exemption from, 39, 40; violations of, 41-42; WRACs and, 37

Meighen, Arthur, 187

men, as shown in ads: as civilians serving in war effort, 103-6, 107(i)

Mentholatum ointment, ad for, 66

metal shortages, effect of: on automobiles, 133, 134-35, 141; on consumer durables, 134-35, 150-52; on jewellery, 152-54

Metropolitan Life Insurance Company, ad for, 100

Milestone, Lewis, 167

The Ministry of Fear (film), 177

"misguided friend" (advertising cliché), 90-95, 99, 108, 124, 188-90; in Anaconda ad, 93; in Dominion Oilcloth ad, 188, 189(i), 190; in Kellogg's All-Bran ad, 88, 90-91; in Kotex ad, 91; in Labatt's anti-temperance ad, 93, 94(i); Sanforized's grandmother as, 91,

92(i), 93; and Victory Bonds ad, 95, 95(i)
Mission to Moscow (film), 177
modern conveniences ("mod cons"), 53, 56, 155. *See also* appliances; consumer durables
Modess sanitary napkins, ad for, 100-1, 102(i)
Monckton, Ella: *Waiting for Mary* (play), 42-43
Monetary Times Annual, 185, 191
Montreal Advertising and Sales Club, 63
Morgan, Lorne: *The Permanent War, or, Homo the Sap*, 184-85
Morris, Peter, 166
Morton, Desmond, 30, 186, 205
Mosher, A.R., 184
Mosquito, de Havilland (bomber), 110, 111(i)
motion picture industry, 15, 156-57, 163-81; Hollywood's domination of, 9, 164-68, 177; production code of, 165, 167, 178; and war movies, 176-80. *See also* movie theatres; movies; *specific movies and film industry individuals*
Motion Picture Production Code, 178; administration of, 165, 167, 178
Motor Vehicle Controller, Office of (MVC), 6, 132-33, 139; and possible seizure of civilian vehicles, 132, 233*n*43; and suspended auto production, 136-37, 234*n*59
movie theatres, 13, 157, 163-64, 168-76; blackouts imposed on, 174, 176; Depression-era losses of, 164; midnight/Sunday screenings at, 176, 180, 240*n*44; as "palaces," PL7, 171-73, 172(i); as performance venues, 168, 170; poor condition of, 173-74; and pride in war effort, 175-76, 180-81; Quebec ban on children in, 167, 240*n*44; Victory Bond promotion/wartime fundraising in, 168, 175, 176, 181; and wartime attendance/receipts, 168-71, 169(t), 171(t), 180; wartime regulations governing, 174-75; WPTB and, 173-74
movies, 156-57, 163-81; amusement taxes on, 169(t); banning of, 167-68, 240*n*47; censorship of, 167-68, 179; and depictions of war, 176-80; as escapism, 156, 164-65, 168, 176-77, 180, 181; film noir, 177-78, 180; Hollywood's domination of, 9, 164-68, 177; King's love of, 165, 167, 239*n*32; midnight/Sunday screenings of, 176, 180, 240*n*44; morality of, 157, 163, 165-66, 167, 176; pre-war attendance at, 169, 170; reviews of, 178-79; as screened for military personnel, 169, 170-71, 176, 240*n*51; US production code for, 165, 167, 178; wartime attendance at, 168-71, 180; as weapon against Nazism, 164, 165, 168. *See also* motion picture industry; *specific movies and film industry individuals*
Mullen, Dave, 194
Munitions and Supply, Department of (DMS), 10, 68; and consumer durables, 132, 193; Crown corporations of, 183; and gasoline rationing, 42, 135. *See also* Howe, C.D.
Music for Millions (film), 180

Nabob Coffee, ad for, 64
National Association of Industrial Advertisers, 70
National Council of Women, 19, 24, 27, 49; Ilsley's speech to, 20, 31; and nutrition, 44; and temperance, 159
National Defence, Department of, 9, 177
National Film Board (NFB), 166; *Canada at War*, 240*n*47; *The March of Time* newsreel, 176
National Hockey League (NHL), 158
National Home Monthly, 44, 52; ads in, 104(i), 109(i), 116(i), 189(i)
National Revenue, Department of, 80
National War Finance Committee: Hitler ad run by, 1, 7, 74, 75(i)
Nazism, 85; rise of, 8, 29. *See also* Germany, Nazi; Hitler, Adolf
Neagle, Anna, 175
Needham, Richard J., 21
New Deal, 30; as threat to free enterprise, 58-59, 190, 223*n*45
newspapers, 1, 51-52, 53, 57; Australian, 81; and calls for sacrifice/reduced spending, 14, 25; and curtailed auto production, 131; and gasoline

rationing/tire shortages, 42, 142-45, 145(i); importance of advertising to, 51, 57, 82; and informed citizens, 57; and women's wartime role, 20, 41, 44. *See also entry below; specific newspapers*

newspapers, advertising in, 13, 50-51, 89; by ad industry, 56; to attract American tourists, 23; contradictory messages of, 14; by department stores, 152, 153(i); double-page, 80; vs editorial content, 51; and free press, 57, 82; on gasoline black market, 143-44; by government, 74; importance of, 51, 57, 82; spending on, 54; war-themed, 64, 119, 122

Nicholson, A.M., 131-32

North West Mounted Police (film), 165

Northern Electric, ad for, 117

Noseworthy, Joseph, 187

"now more than ever" (advertising cliché), 95-99; in Bon Ami ad, 99; in Campana's Balm ad, 96, 98(i); in Gruen ad, 95-96, 97(i); in Heinz ad, 96-97; in Kodak ad, 96; in Lysol ad, 97, 99; in Pepsi-Cola ad, 96, 98(i); in Pratt and Lambert ad, 96

nutrition, 40, 44-46, 49; of Canadian families/students, 45-46; as promoted/referred to in ads, 90-91, 96-97, 100; standards/guidelines for, 44-45; as women's responsibility, 44, 100

Nutrition Services Division (Department of Pensions and National Health), 40, 44-46

Office of Price Administration (US counterpart to WPTB), 30, 205

Old Dutch household cleanser, ad for, 101

Olivier, Laurence, 166, 175, 242*n*98

Oneida silverware, ad for, 114-15

Orpheum (Vancouver movie theatre), 171, 173

Orpheum Theatre (Montreal), 172(i)

O'Sullivan, Maureen, 175

"Ottawa men," 28, 187

Overy, R.J., 204

Packard Motor Car Company, 127

Palace Theatre (Timmins, ON), 173, 175

Palmolive, ad for, 103, 104(i)

Pantages Theatre (Toronto), 171

Parker Pens, ad for, 66, 67(i)

Parr, Joy: *Domestic Goods*, 3, 155, 192

Parsons, Harriet: *Libel or Label?* (play), 208

patriotic consumerism, 4, 7-8, 12-13, 89, 196-97; ad industry and, 89; and "buy British"/"buy Canadian" campaigns, 5, 7, 24-25, 26, 31, 49; of civilians, 100, 103-6; and early encouragement of spending, 5-6, 7, 20-21, 24-25; evolution of, 20-21, 25, 96; and later calls for sacrifice/reduced spending, 1-2, 6-7, 25-49, 59, 74-79; movie-going as, 156-57, 163-81; and threat of inflation, 27-31; women's importance to, 14, 17, 19-21, 24-49, 89, 100, 101-3, 194-95. *See also* civilians; women, as consumers/household managers

Pearl Harbor, Japanese attack on, 5, 31, 70, 157, 245*n*9; and impact on auto manufacturing, 130, 134-35, 142

Peate, Mary, 127, 166, 178

Peiss, Kathy, 101

Pensions and National Health, Department of, 185; Nutrition Services Division of, 40, 44-45

"penurious patriotism," myth of, 2, 3-4, 7, 155, 193-94, 209; and auto sales, 130; and consumer spending, 12-14, 20-21, 26-27, 193-94, 196-97; and suspended appliance production, 149

Pepsi-Cola, ad for, 96, 98(i)

Perfect Circle Piston Rings, ad for, 106

Pett, Lionel, 40, 44

The Phantom Creeps (film), 167

"phony war" (before May/June 1940), 4-5, 22, 64, 66, 215*n*17; as ended at Pearl Harbor, 31

Pierson, Ruth Roach, 101

Plant, Elton M., 154

plays, propaganda, put on by WPTB Consumer Branch: *Libel or Label?* (Parsons), 208; *Waiting for Mary* (Monckton), 42-43

poetry: on automobile, 125-26; on butter rationing, 16; on Great Depression, 182-83; on King, 160; on modernity,

55; on pastoral life, 52-53, 59; in patriotic General Motors ad, 113-14; on regulations/paperwork faced by automobile dealers, 138; on tire-saving speed limit, 142; in Victory Bond ad, 70
Pollock, Francis: "Radiator Cap," 125-26
polls and surveys, 12, 217*n*71; of ad industry, 72; of appliance dealers, 148; on automobile ownership, 138, 144, 154; on nutrition, 44-46; on postwar consumer wants, 154-55; on postwar economy/welfare state, 183, 186-87, 208; on price ceiling, 30, 48, 207-8, 209; on public ownership, 186-87; on rationing, 13, 36; on temperance, 160; as undocumented, 70, 144, 225*n*89, 236*n*113; by WPTB/Consumer Branch, 12, 207-9. *See also* Wartime Prices and Trade Board, polls/surveys by
postwar society. *See* future, postwar; social security, *and entries following*
Pratt and Lambert paint, ad for, 96
preserves: home canning of, 39, 219*n*96; rationing of, 35; shortages of, 40
price ceiling, 28-31, 35, 46-49, 70, 73; ad copy as reflecting, 76, 78, 93; consumer support for, 30, 48, 207-8, 209; enforcement of, 30-31, 33-34, 46-48, 207, 217*n*67; estimated savings achieved by, 206; how it worked, 29-30; and inevitability of rationing, 35, 71-72; infractions of, 33-34, 46-47, 207, 217*n*67; jewellers and, 152; lifting of, 154, 192, 209; postwar support for, 192, 208; rules/regulations of, 30, 33-34; retailers and, 152, 154; as unique experiment, 30; women/women's organizations and, 16, 30-31, 33-34, 44, 46-49, 158; WPTB and, 28-29, 33, 47, 207. *See also* Consumer Branch (WPTB); Women's Regional Advisory Committees
Pride of the Marines (film), 178
Prince, Stephen, 178
Production Code Administration (PCA; US film industry regulatory body), 165, 167, 178
profiteering, 64, 74, 76, 77, 108
prohibition, 7, 80, 93, 143, 158-59, 160, 162-63, 238*n*11

propaganda: advertising as, 14, 77-78; aimed at women, 20, 89; anti-CCF, 191-92; anti-consumerist, 1-2, 7, 12, 74, 75(i), 152, 203; and defence of free enterprise, 106, 108-14, 122-24; featuring Hitler, 1-2, 7, 74, 75(i), 110-11; film/movie theatre industries and, 164-68, 176-81, 240*n*47, 242*n*98; military metaphors in, 19-20, 99-106; Nazi, 164, 165-66; on need for sacrifice/reduced spending, 3, 25, 74-78, 83, 99, 193, 202, 203; of WPTB/Consumer Branch, PL5, 34, 42-43, 208
Purkis, Thornton, 62
The Purple Heart (film), 178, 179

Quebec, 22, 34, 147; auto ownership in, 127, 128(t); movie theatres/moviegoing in, 167, 170, 171-73, 172(i), 175, 180, 240*n*44; and price ceiling, 207-8; radio ownership in, 147; and rationing, 13, 41; temperance support in, 160; WRAC liaisons in, 46
Queen's Quarterly, 50, 59

radio: advertising on, 50, 53, 54, 57, 73-74, 89; American programs on, 9, 63; butter-rationing announcement on, 36; government addresses on, 6, 26, 28, 30-31, 159-61; government advertising on, 73-74; nutritional announcement on, 44; patriotic consumerism message on, 7, 20, 49; WPTB Consumer Branch programs on, 34
radios, 9, 54; household ownership of, 21, 53, 54, 56, 147, 148(t); of postwar future, 123(i), 187; retail/department store sales of, 199, 200(t), 203; wartime production of, 14, 72, 149, 149(t)
rationing. *See* coupon rationing; *specific food and consumer items*
Recommended Daily Allowances (RDAs), 45
Reed, Douglas, 227*n*43
refrigerators: ads for, 13, 70, 153(i); household ownership of, 53, 56, 147, 148(t); ice, 13, 153(i); of postwar future, 123(i), 187; wartime production of, 6, 14, 72, 125, 135, 136, 148-49, 149(t)

Regent Theatre (Picton, ON), 170
Remarque, Erich Maria: *All Quiet on the Western Front*, 167-68
repair work, as done by retailers, 138-39, 150
Research and Statistics Administration (WPTB), 38, 51, 149(t)
resident population: and consumer statistics, 199-201, 244*n*4
restaurants, 11, 13, 24, 194; coffee/tea rations at, 38; opening/expansion of, 157; retail sales at, 198(t); sugar rations at, 39; in UK, 204
retail sales: of alcohol, 162, 198(t), 199; of automobiles/motor vehicles, 126-27, 128(t), 129-31, 132-33, 134, 137, 155, 193, 232*n*34; as belying myth of "penurious patriotism," 2, 3-4, 12-14, 20-21, 26-27, 130, 149, 155, 193-94, 196, 209; by category, 198(t), 199; of consumer durables, 7, 14-15, 150, 150(t), 193, 197(t), 199; as exceeding war expenditures, 9-10; and inflation, 1-2, 13, 21-22, 66, 68, 74; as not affected by rationing, 13, 83, 99, 193-94, 199, 201-2; per capita, 193-94, 199-202, 201(t); and post-Depression consumer boom, PL8, 12-13, 193-95, 196-209; as suggesting advertiser-consumer harmony, 89-90, 99; WPTB regulations and, 29. *See also specific products*; consumer boom, wartime, *and entry following*
retailers, PL8; and consumer habits, 11-12; decreasing inventories of, 2, 203-4, 209; in era of rationing/production cuts, 2, 7-8, 14-15, 20-21; and post-Depression prosperity, 21-22, 63, 68-69, 164; and price ceiling, 152, 154; repair work done by, 138-39, 150; Toronto gift show for, 13; WPTB regulation/monitoring of, 10, 13, 23, 28-29, 33, 47, 207
retailers (specific types). *See* automobile dealers/dealerships; department stores; gas stations/garages; grocery stores; jewellery; liquor control boards, provincial; movie theatres
Reynolds, E.W., 57-58

Richards, P.M., 72
Rockoff, Hugh, 205, 209
Ronson lighters, ads for, 66
Roosevelt, Eleanor, 79
Roosevelt, Franklin D., 113, 165; and Atlantic Charter, 184, 188, 190; "four freedoms" of, 190; New Deal of, 30, 58-59, 190, 223*n*45
"Rosie the Riveter" figure, 17; in ads, 96, 98(i), 103, 104(i)
Ross, Mary Lowrey, 178-79
rural electrification, 53, 147-48
rural population, 52-54. *See also* farmers/farm families
Rutledge, J.L., 24, 26

Sanders, Byrne Hope: as *Chatelaine* editor, 16-17, 25, 31, 32, 64, 79; defence of advertising by, 79-80; as director of WPTB Consumer Branch, PL4, 16, 19-20, 32-33, 46, 47-48, 49, 100, 217*n*63; Gordon's hiring of, 32; on patriotic advertising, 64; and wartime advice for women, 16-17, 19-20, 25, 32. *See also* Consumer Branch (WPTB)
Sandwell, B.K., 51, 70
Sanforized washable fabrics, ads for: "Saboteur," 91, 92(i), 93; "What's coming," 119, 121(i)
Saturday Evening Post, 52
Saturday Night, 51, 72, 131; film review in, 178-79; on Gordon, 28
Saunders, Stanley, and Eleanor Back: *Come On, Canada!*, 25
Scott, F.R., 160, 186, 187
Scott, Randolph, 178
Seagram's, ads for, 110, 119, 120(i)
Second World War, events/important sites of: Allied victories, 82, 114; Bataan, 178, 179; Battle of Britain, 5, 24, 64; Battle of the Bulge, 185; D-Day, 168, 183, 193; Dieppe Raid, 78; fall of France, 5, 12, 22, 27, 130-31, 132; Hong Kong, 78; Pearl Harbor, 5, 31, 70, 157, 245*n*9; Soviet Union, 6, 22, 133; Stalingrad, 82, 114, 177. *See also* Germany, Nazi; Japanese, as Pacific War enemies; "phony war" (before May/June 1940)

Security with Victory (CCF manifesto), 187-88, 191
September 11, terrorist attacks of, 4
"serve by saving" slogan, of government, 2, 69-70, 74, 96
service stations. *See* gas stations/garages
Sharman, Lyon: "The Rebel," 52-53, 59
Sharples, Alice, 24-25
shortages: 3, 7, 13, 14-15, 39, 46, 69, 193; ad industry and, 21, 76, 106; of auto parts/materials, 132-33, 140; of fruit, 45; local/temporary, 7, 35, 36, 40-41, 43, 209; of metal (automobiles), 133, 134-35, 141; of metal (consumer durables/jewellery), 134-35, 150-54; as not affecting consumer boom, 83, 196-97, 199, 200-1, 202, 203-4, 206, 209; and panic buying/hoarding, 7, 35-37, 42, 63, 91-93; rationing and, 35-37, 40-41, 42, 43, 45, 46; of rubber, 135, 141; of tires, 140-42, 144, 145(i), 146-47; in UK/Australia, 81
Silverthorne, O.J., 173, 174
Simpson's department store, 72, 152
Sklar, Robert, 177
Sloan, Alfred P., 59
Snow White (animated film), 167
social security, 14, 29, 114; in Atlantic Charter, 184, 190; in CCF manifesto, 187-88, 191; Dominion Oilcloth ad on, 188, 189(i), 190; Marsh Report on, 185-86; as threat to free enterprise, 59, 88, 185-92, 195. *See also entries below*
social welfare state, 183-92; ad industry view of, 57, 122, 124, 190-91; Canadians' opinions on, 186-87; and Depression-era measures, 188, 190; and early reconstruction concerns, 183-86; and economic recovery, 192-93; Liberals and, 186-88, 191-92; Marsh Report on, 185-86; social programs of, 191-92; and strength of socialist parties, 187-88, 190-91; as threat to free enterprise, 59, 88, 122, 124, 185-92, 195
socialism, 187-88; electoral successes of, 187; as equated with totalitarianism, 190-91. *See also* Co-operative Commonwealth Federation

Souster, Raymond: "Nada," 142
Soviet Union: Allied victories in, 82, 114, 177; German invasion of, 6, 22, 133
Sparton radio-phonograph, ad for, 69-70
Spence, E.J., 207, 209
Spencer, Philip, 58
Stacey, C.P., 2, 9
Stalingrad, Allied victory in, 82, 114, 177
Standard Sanitary and Dominion Radiator, ad for, 103
Star Weekly, 56
Stark, Robert, 145-46
Statistics Canada, 206. *See also* Dominion Bureau of Statistics
Steeplechase Cigarettes, ad for, 64
Stephen, Jennifer: *Pick One Intelligent Girl*, 2
Stephenson, H.E., and Carlton McNaught: *The Story of Advertising in Canada*, 56
Stocking, Samuel, 57, 70, 71
stoves, 9, 53, 148; ads for, 108; household ownership of, 53, 56, 148(t); and war effort, 108; wartime production of, 6, 14, 72, 136, 149-50, 149(t), 150(t)
stoves, by type: coal/wood, 150, 150(t); electric, 53, 136, 148(t), 149(t), 149, 150; gas, 148(t), 149, 150, 150(t)
Studebaker of Canada: ad for, 112; closure of, 127
sugar rationing, 7, 13, 16, 34-35, 193; and coupon trading, 39, 41; enforcement of, 41; and hoarding, 39, 42; and home canning, 39, 219*n*96; hostility/resistance toward, 38-39; in postwar UK, 204; promised end to, 123(i); requests for exemption from, 40; restaurants and, 39; soft drink/candy industry and, 39; wine production and, 161
Sunday: as day of rest from consumerism, 157, 176, 240*n*44; gasoline pump closures on, 134; movie screenings on, 176, 180, 240*n*44
surveys. *See* polls and surveys; Wartime Prices and Trade Board, polls/surveys by

Taggart, J.G., 36
Tangee Cosmetics, ads for, 102-3, 104(i)
taxes, 12, 202; on amusements (movies), 169(t); on automobiles, 131, 132-33; on excess profits, 68, 80; on gasoline, 128, 235n84; income, 68, 93; on jewellery, 152, 199; personal, 7, 213n23
Taylor, K.W., 30, 192
tea rationing, 7, 35, 38, 93; and coupon trading, 41; elimination of, 38; and hoarding, 42; promised end to, 119, 121(i), 123(i)
telephones, 56; household ownership of, 148(t)
temperance movement, 7, 158-63, 165, 238n11; Canadian Breweries ad and, 162-63; Labatt's ads and, 93, 94(i), 238n11; WRACs and, 159
Thompson, Archie, 23
Thompson, Dorothy, 78-79
Time, 79
tires: and ban on spares, 135; hoarding of, 136; postwar availability of, 110, 123(i), 147, 154; speed limits as imposed to save, 142; on used cars, 137
tires, new: black market in, 42, 142; consumers as discouraged from buying, 4, 76; reduced production/rationing of, 141-42; shortage of, 140-42, 144, 145(i), 146-47
toasters, 56; wartime production of, 6, 72, 135, 148, 149(t)
"tomorrow," promise of (advertising cliché), 114-19; in Canadian General Electric ad, 116; as futuristic, 115, 117(i), 118(i), 119, 120(i); in General Steel Wares ad, 115, 116(i); in Goodyear ad, 117(i); in Northern Electric ad, 117; in Oneida ad, 114-15; in Sanforized ad, 119, 121(i); in Seagram's ad, 119, 120(i); in White Label Ale ad, 118(i)
Tooze, Adam, 128
Toronto Advertising and Sales Club, 17
Toronto Daily Star, 125, 228n30; *Star Weekly* supplement to, 56
Toronto Telegram, 50; on butter rationing, 36; as pro-free enterprise, 82, 187
Toronto Toy Fair, 151

"total war," 1, 130-31, 186; as not experienced by Canadians, 25, 89, 196-97; sacrifices necessary in, 25, 78-79, 159-60, 196
tourists, American: ad campaign to attract, 23; and "buy British" campaign, 25; and gasoline rationing, 140; and possible car seizures, 132, 233n43; Sunday "ski trains" for, 157
Towers, G.F., 5
toys, 13, 23, 26; metal, 135; non-metal, 151
Trader and Canadian Jeweller, 1, 152, 154
trucks, 6, 106, 126, 128, 136, 139; commercial, 140; production of, 129, 135; retail sales of, 129(t), 137. *See also entry below*
trucks, military, 129; as diverted to civilian sector, 137; Ford, 108, 109(i), 112; Studebaker, 112

Underhill, Frank, 185-86
unemployment: of Depression, 21, 30, 55, 197; as ended by war, 21, 30, 66, 185; as postwar fear, 183
unemployment insurance, 190, 192
United Automobile Workers strike, in US, 154
United Church Observer, 157, 159, 163, 176
United Kingdom: advertising in, 64, 68, 81; auto production in, 126, 127, 130; battles of, 5, 24, 25, 64, 78, 176; Beveridge Report in, 185; and "buy British" campaign, 5, 7, 24-25, 26, 31, 49; Canada as ally of, 8-9, 12, 22, 23, 184; civilian motoring in, 130, 204; coupon rationing in, 35, 38, 204; declaration of war by, 23, 164; democratic values of, 78, 106; economic measures taken by, 30; evacuees/expatriates of, 36-37, 177-78, 180; film industry/stars of, 165-66, 175, 176, 242n98; food exports to, 16, 37, 43; and milk-for-orphans campaign, 168, 176; munitions/material supplies to, 5, 22, 26, 27, 133, 212n14; and "phony war," 66; and pilot training program,

170, 244*n*4; wartime experience/economy in, 5, 25-26, 34-35, 38, 78, 204
United Nations, 79, 106
United States: advertising in, 12, 54-55, 61-63, 76, 81, 89-90, 93, 112-13; auto workers' strike in, 154; coupon rationing in, 35; cultural influence of, 8-9; film industry domination by, 9, 164-68, 177; film production code of, 165, 167, 178; and financial/economic cooperation with Canada, 27, 133, 136, 205; Lend-Lease program of, 27, 130, 133; magazines of, 24, 52, 63, 161; New Deal in, 30, 58-59, 190, 223*n*45; and Pearl Harbor attack, 5, 31, 70, 130, 134-35, 142, 157, 245*n*9; price administration office of, 30, 205; radio programs of, 9, 63; and suspended auto production, 126-27, 130, 132-40; tourists from, 23, 25, 132, 140, 157, 233*n*43; wartime experience/economy in, 204-5. *See also* adworkers, US; Roosevelt, Franklin D.
United States Supreme Court, 165
Uptown Theatre (Toronto), 171
urbanization, 52-53, 222*n*12
used cars, 137-38, 139

vacuum cleaners, 53, 72; household ownership of, 148(t); wartime production of, 149, 149(t)
Veterans Charter, 192
Victory Bonds, 3, 4, 31, 68; business support of, 85, 106; consumer spending vs, 78; labour's anti-prohibition campaign against, 163; movie theatre promotion for, 168, 175, 176, 181; "serve by saving" slogan of, 69-70; as War Loan, 5, 212*n*15
Victory Bonds, ads for, 69-70, 76, 78; civilians and soldiers in, 99; "iron sacrifice," 70; "Pleasures of freedom," 123(i), 124; "Strange things go into tanks," 95, 95(i)
Victory recipes, 41, 44
Vipond, Mary, 64
Vitalis, ad for, 104

vitamin deficiencies, of Canadian families/students, 45

Waddell, Christopher, 23, 30, 207, 209
wage and price controls, 27-31, 47-48, 186, 206-9; consumer support for, 48; vs inflation, 6, 27-28, 66, 192; labour and, 27-28, 30, 31, 93; as unique experiment, 30. *See also* price ceiling; wage ceiling
wage ceiling, 30, 93, 202
Walden, Keith, 11
war bonds, 212*n*15
war expenditures: as exceeded by newspaper/magazine sales, 54; as exceeded by retail sales, 9-10; increases in, 27, 74
War Loan (later Victory Bonds), 5, 212*n*15. *See also* Victory Bonds
War Measures Act, 158, 159, 205
war movies, 176-80. *See also* motion picture industry; movies
War Savings Certificates, 5, 28, 70, 212*n*15; "iron sacrifice" ad for, 70
War Savings Stamps, 13; Hitler ad for, 1, 7, 74, 75(i); movie promotion for, 175
Wartime Industries Control Board, 6, 234*nn*58-59
Wartime Prices and Trade Board (WPTB): advertising policy/regulations of, 79-82; and clothing choice restrictions, 203-4; and coupon rationing, 34-43, 204; establishment of, 23; and furniture restrictions, 151; on gasoline-rationing violations, 144; Gordon appointed to head, 28-29; Gordon's resignation from, 192; histories of, 10; and jewellery manufacturers, 153-54; lifting of controls under, 15, 154, 192, 209; and movie theatres, 173-74; and need for sacrifice/reduced spending, pl.5, 74, 77, 79-80, 99; as permitting small price increases, 33, 47, 207; polls on, 34; polls/surveys by, 12, 207-9; postwar concerns of, 193; sweeping regulations of, 29, 30-31, 33-34; US counterpart to, 30, 205; and used car sales, 137-38; and wage/price controls,

27-31, 35, 47-48, 71-72, 158, 186, 206-9; and war on inflation, 19-20, 22-23, 27-31, 47-48, 72, 77, 99, 206-7; and women as consumers, 14, 16-17, 19-20, 32-43, 47-49, 89, 100. *See also* Consumer Branch (WPTB); coupon rationing; Gordon, Donald; price ceiling; Sanders, Byrne Hope; *see also entry below*

Wartime Prices and Trade Board, polls/surveys by, 12, 207-9; on appliances, 149-50; on Marsh Report, 186; on movie-going, 169-70; on newspaper readership, 51; on price ceiling, 30, 48, 207-8, 209; on quality of goods, 208-9, 246n20; on rationing, 36, 38; on vacations, 157, 238n1; on WPTB itself, 34

washing machines, 53, 76; wartime production of, 6, 125, 148, 149(t), 149-50

Washington, George, 113

Watt, C.D., 78

Weimar Republic: inflation in, and rise of Nazism, 8, 29

Weissmuller, Johnny, 175

White, Christine, 35, 36

White Label Ale, ad for, 118(i)

Wilder, Billy, 177

Williams, Raymond, 124

Williamson, Marie, 36-37, 144, 177-78

window displays, 11, 23; advertising as, 58

women, as consumers/household managers, PL3, 14, 16-49, 212n7; advertising and, 56, 57-58, 60-61, 62, 85, 89, 99-103; appliances as boon to, 61, 148; and early encouragement of spending by, 5-6, 7, 20-21, 24-25; Gordon on, 30-31, 32, 48, 49, 100; later calls for sacrifice/reduced spending by, 1-2, 6-7, 25-49, 59, 79; and nutrition, 40, 44-46, 49, 100; and patriotic consumerism, 14, 17, 19-21, 24-49, 89, 100, 101-3, 194-95; and "purchasing agent" role, 17, 18(i), 19-20, 85, 86(i), 100; and rationing, 34-43, 49; and war on inflation, 19-20, 30-43; wartime contributions of, 17, 19-20, 100-1, 102(i); and WPTB Consumer Branch, 32-43, 47-49

women, in military/industrial roles: gender anxieties over, 17, 20, 101-3, 114; as shown in ads, 91, 96, 98(i), 101-3, 104(i); vs "traditional" roles, 97, 99, 100-1, 102(i), 114-15; vs women as patriotic consumers, 17, 20, 49, 194-95

women, as shown in ads: femininity of, 96, 98(i), 101-3, 104(i); in military/industrial roles, 91, 96, 98(i), 101-3, 104(i); monthly "worries" of, 91, 100-1, 102(i); as "purchasing agents," 17, 18(i), 19-20, 85, 86(i), 100; as soldiers on home front, 97, 99-101, 102(i), 103

women as soldiers (advertising cliché), 97, 99-103; in Blachford Shoes ads, 103; in Colgate ad, 102(i); in General Motors ad, 101; in Helena Rubinstein ad, 103; in Lysol ad, 66, 101; in Metropolitan Life ad, 100; in Modess ad, 100-1, 102(i); in Old Dutch ad, 101; in Palmolive ad, 103, 104(i); in Standard Sanitary ad, 103; in Tangee Cosmetics ads, 102-3, 104(i)

Women's Advertising Club of Toronto, 50, 64

Women's Canadian Club, 48

women's organizations, 5; as advocates of consumerism, 14, 19-20, 89; and nutrition, 44-46; and temperance movement, 7, 158, 159. *See also entry below; specific women's organizations*

Women's Regional Advisory Committees (WRACs), 32-49, 159; airing of grievances at, 46-47; Consumer Branch liaisons to, 12, 32, 33, 36, 39, 46, 47, 48, 192; and coupon rationing, 36-37, 39, 40, 218n80; postwar meetings of, 192; price ceiling monitoring by, 30-31, 33-34, 46-48, 217n67; and quality of wartime goods, 141, 208-9; "snooping women" of, 47; and suspended consumer durables production, 150; and temperance movement, 159; tensions within, 46. *See also* Consumer Branch (WPTB); price ceiling

wood, items/consumer durables made of, 151-52, 154
wood-burning stoves, 150, 150(t)
Woodsworth, J.S., 186
Woolworth's department store (Sparks Street, Ottawa): lunch counter at, 157

Yarwood, Walter, 56, 223*n*32
Young Women's Christian Association (YWCA), 44

STUDIES IN CANADIAN MILITARY HISTORY

John Griffith Armstrong, *The Halifax Explosion and the Royal Canadian Navy: Inquiry and Intrigue*

Andrew Richter, *Avoiding Armageddon: Canadian Military Strategy and Nuclear Weapons, 1950-63*

William Johnston, *A War of Patrols: Canadian Army Operations in Korea*

Julian Gwyn, *Frigates and Foremasts: The North American Squadron in Nova Scotia Waters, 1745-1815*

Jeffrey A. Keshen, *Saints, Sinners, and Soldiers: Canada's Second World War*

Desmond Morton, *Fight or Pay: Soldiers' Families in the Great War*

Douglas E. Delaney, *The Soldiers' General: Bert Hoffmeister at War*

Michael Whitby, ed., *Commanding Canadians: The Second World War Diaries of A.F.C. Layard*

Martin Auger, *Prisoners of the Home Front: German POWs and "Enemy Aliens" in Southern Quebec, 1940-46*

Tim Cook, *Clio's Warriors: Canadian Historians and the Writing of the World Wars*

Serge Marc Durflinger, *Fighting from Home: The Second World War in Verdun, Quebec*

Richard O. Mayne, *Betrayed: Scandal, Politics, and Canadian Naval Leadership*

P. Whitney Lackenbauer, *Battle Grounds: The Canadian Military and Aboriginal Lands*

Cynthia Toman, *An Officer and a Lady: Canadian Military Nursing and the Second World War*

Michael Petrou, *Renegades: Canadians in the Spanish Civil War*

Amy J. Shaw, *Crisis of Conscience: Conscientious Objection in Canada during the First World War*

Serge Marc Durflinger, *Veterans with a Vision: Canada's War Blinded in Peace and War*

James G. Fergusson, *Canada and Ballistic Missile Defence, 1954-2009: Déjà Vu All Over Again*

Benjamin Isitt, *From Victoria to Vladivostok: Canada's Siberian Expedition, 1917-19*

James Wood, *Militia Myths: Ideas of the Canadian Citizen Soldier, 1896-1921*

Timothy Balzer, *The Information Front: The Canadian Army and News Management during the Second World War*

Andrew Godefroy, *Defence and Discovery: Canada's Military Space Program, 1945-74*

Douglas E. Delaney, *Corps Commanders: Five British and Canadian Generals at War, 1939-45*

Timothy Wilford, *Canada's Road to the Pacific War: Intelligence, Strategy, and the Far East Crisis*

Randall Wakelam, *Cold War Fighters: Canadian Aircraft Procurement, 1945-54*

Andrew Burtch, *Give Me Shelter: The Failure of Canada's Cold War Civil Defence*

Wendy Cuthbertson, *Labour Goes to War: The CIO and the Construction of a New Social Order, 1939-45*

P. Whitney Lackenbauer, *The Canadian Rangers: A Living History*

Teresa Iacobelli, *Death or Deliverance: Canadian Courts Martial in the Great War*

Peter Kasurak, *A National Force: The Evolution of Canada's Army, 1950-2000*

Isabel Campbell, *Unlikely Diplomats: The Canadian Brigade in Germany, 1951-64*

Printed and bound in Canada by Friesens

Set in News Gothic, Galliard, and New Baskerville by Artegraphica Design Co. Ltd.

Copy editor: Deborah Kerr

Proofreader and indexer: Cheryl Lemmens